# THE FARTHEST CORNER

# THE FARTHEST CORNER

## *New Zealand — A Twice Discovered Land*

CAROL MORTON JOHNSTON

AND

HARRY MORTON

*After a lapse of nearly four months, without seeing aught
but the heavens above us and the wide waste of waters
all around us, the ship, like a thing of life and of more
than moral sagacity, glided with perfect precision,
and without hesitation or mistake,
into its destined place at the farthest corner of the earth.*

– Rev. Thomas Burns, *Philip Laing*, Otago Harbour, 15 April 1848

University of Hawaii Press
Honolulu, Hawaii

First published by Century Hutchinson New Zealand Limited
© MJM Writers 1988
Published in the United States of America by
University of Hawaii Press
2840 Kolowalu Street
Honolulu, Hawaii 96822

Printed in Hong Kong

Library of Congress Cataloguing-in-Publication Data

Johnston, Carol Morton 1945-
    The farthest corner.

    Bibliography: p.
    Includes index
    1. New Zealand — Discovery and exploration
2. Maoris. 3. Navigation — New Zealand. I. Morton,
Harry, 1925-    II. Title.
DU410.J64 1988      993.101      88-17227
ISBN 0-8248-1213-1

# Contents

# *Preface*

Many individuals and organisations have contributed to the creation of this book. The librarians of the Blenheim Public Library have treated us with kindness and consideration in spite of so many requests for assistance and advice about books. Once more we owe much to the efficiency of the New Zealand Libraries Interloan Service, and a special debt to Canterbury University Library, specifically Shirley Shea and Max Broadbent. The Hocken Library at the University of Otago, long-suffering throughout the creation of several books, again provided valuable items and illustrations, with the invaluable help of David McDonald and Annette Facer. The National Library of New Zealand and the Alexander Turnbull Library, with the kindness and efficiency we have learned to expect of them, have been most helpful in the midst of the turmoil of moving into new quarters.

John Dunmore, Paul Bradwell, Jim McLees, Mrs A. E. Woodhouse, Barry Brailsford, Frances Porter, Guy Mannering, Shaughan Anderson, the Canterbury and Otago Museums and the Mitchell Library of the State Library of New South Wales have kindly helped with particular problems of illustrations. The Soviet Embassy in Wellington, in the person of Vladimir Ivanov, was most helpful with the Russian pictures.

Sheila Natusch allowed us to use material she had gathered to write her fine books about the southern islands and waters of New Zealand. We are especially grateful for her permission to use typescript she had worked so hard to prepare.

Doreen Park and Terry McGrail read the manuscript and gave constructive and useful suggestions. Terry's help, particularly in the resources and surveying chapters, but also with diagrams and maps was most appreciated. Our association with Century Hutchinson, in the person of David Ling, has been as pleasurable as useful.

Our main thanks for assistance in the writing of this book are to each other and to Peggy Morton and Dorothy McGrail. It has been a family team effort, each specialising, as Carol did in the pre-European chapters, yet all participating in every part of the book and each contributing to decisions.

# Introduction

Exploration and discovery are different, even though each seeks new knowledge about geography. Exploration is a process, as research is, and the words are almost synonyms. Discovery is a result; useful, interesting or exciting results win rewards. Exploration is slogging work; discovery may follow, sometimes inadvertently. But discovery must be reported so that benefits, along with triumph and fame, may follow in their turn.

To "discover" is to "uncover" new knowledge for the uses of mankind. Columbus did "discover" the Americas. Knowledge about America locked unsung in Viking sagas or unread in Irish monastic chronicles left the world unaffected. It was Columbus who "uncovered" America, to and for the world. Discovery may be accidental, if the "discovered" is not what was sought. But the accident must be proclaimed to the world for it to be discovery; to drift accidentally onto a shore and then die there is not discovering an island. The new information must become part of the world's store of information on charts and maps. For the true position of land is of vital consequence to sailing ships especially, for they had no engines to reverse. Discovery involves publication to the world and charting and mapping in such a way that other people can use it. Polynesians reported their discoveries and successful routes to their own world, where it became part of the Polynesian knowledge of Pacific navigation which so impressed Cook and other early European explorers.

Local guides or pilots do not invalidate discovery. Indian guides did not invalidate Sir Alexander McKenzie's discovery of the route through the Rocky Mountains. The Indians had no way of extensively using such a route, which turned out to be extremely important to the use and exploitation of British Columbia. In other words local guides, although useful, are not always particularly important. They have no conception of the purposes for which the exploration is being done, nor any real conception of the purpose of publicity. They do not "uncover" areas. Using resources locally is not at all the same thing as revealing resources to the world.

After about 1100 A.D. Chinese and European exploration did not result in major migrations, like that of the Angles and Saxons to Britain or the Mongols to China. (One might almost count the Anglo-Saxon settling of Australia and New Zealand, as well as most of North America, as such a migration). But in the Pacific some early exploration and discovery resulted in the settling of islands by groups of Polynesians, and occasionally Melanesians, fleeing war or famine. Sometimes they left their native lands with little knowledge of where their exile would be or what contact with "home" could be maintained. This is exploration perhaps, but it did not always result in discovery. First, of course, because some groups simply did not arrive anywhere but perished at sea. Second, because some groups, immediately or over a period of time, lost contact – except in legend – with the land of their origins. They were discoverers if those at home knew they were there and knew the way, and had the sailing directions to find them, even if continuous contact lapsed. The Maori discovery of New Zealand was a discovery; the finding of Pitcairn Island by the Bounty mutineers was not.

The closest European parallel to these events is the settlement of Iceland and of Greenland, which led to the legendary but undoubtedly real early contacts with America. Such voyages, whether in the vast Pacific or the much more manageable North Atlantic, display human endeavour, skill and fortitude. Not all of them are truly exploration, much less discovery. The discoverer has removed the cover of ignorance. Discoveries which faded from the ken of man, just as those the world never heard of at all, are fair game for rediscovery. Those who rediscover something of which the memory has been eroded by time are as entitled to credit as the original discoverer, if indeed the delving of antiquarians or scientists has uncovered the original discovery at all.

The five great European maritime powers played parts in the exploration of the Pacific; only Portugal was not involved in the exploration of New Zealand. Each great power had its own reason for Pacific exploration: Spain to guard the Americas for Spain; Portugal to find new routes for commerce and bases to protect old routes; France and Holland to find new nations to trade with; Britain at first to war on Spain. Commerce later became the chief motivation of the British, but by then times had changed and they sent scientists and missionaries as well as merchants. The French reason for Pacific exploration was mainly pride; a great power would not be left out. Underlying minor commercial motivation lay a fierce obsession to re-find mysterious Gonneville Land which the Frenchman Gonneville discovered in the earliest part of the 16th century.

Motives for exploration varied. The period, the nationality and the man concerned each made some difference. Commercial gain was always important, often dominant, and by no means confined to Europeans. The simple desire to know also played its part, particularly after the development of European science in the late 17th century. National glory was tangentially involved, for searching for new routes and new lands was usually based on a perceived need to increase and protect commerce already supporting the nation's eminence. Glory's price was not only danger, sweat and blood, but as with most of man's desires, was bought with coin as well.

Of whatever nationality or motive, few of the sailors had realised, before experiencing it, the immensity of the Pacific. Three centuries passed before that immensity was really measured and appreciated. And none of the explorers, any more than the bookmen at home, had comprehended how different the nations and peoples of the Pacific were: China, with tens of millions even in the 16th century; Japan, a closed world fearing and disdaining the one outside; the Americas' almost infinitely varied Indian cultures; Polynesia's thousand-island world, magical to Europeans because battered and bleeding Europe wished to believe in primal innocence and virtue. These worlds became known, one by one and gradually.

By Tasman's time much exploration was simply to fill the maps, although a few gaps still yawned. Filling these unknown spaces meant discovery, exploration and certainly accurate observation, but over such distances that adjustment to the way maps were made was also implied, a story in itself. Maps should not be based on speculation, although all too many were. But accurate knowledge required people to go around the earth, observe the relationship of the stars above it, find its treasures and products, see its capes and islands, test its foods and its cultures.

Much of Europe's effort was directed to discovering a great southern continent which some mapmakers and other geographers thought would be there to balance the world. They knew roughly how much land there was in the northern hemisphere, and certainly after the discovery of America, with the bulk of those two continents north of the equator, it seemed quite absurd in mechanical terms for the world to spin properly with so little land in the southern hemisphere. There must be another continent, and it might be profitable, and would be interesting, to find it. Most of the seeking was done by the agents of the European trading nations, the great chartered companies.

Practicable routes were what was needed. Japan was not discovered by the West, for they knew it was there. It was a practical and safe way by sea that navigators looked for. When they found good routes they protected them. National commercial companies tried to keep routes secret, to safeguard the rewards of commerce, even while the goods they brought home proclaimed the new discovery. But in the multi-national world of sailing ships secrets never lasted long, and successful monopolies of trade really depended on raw naval power, not secrecy. Proclaimed commercial and imperial monopolies over whole continents and oceans, implying secrecy, non-cooperation and violence, gradually gave way to more enlightened attitudes. Nations began to find peaceful but effective ways of fostering national interests, and came to see that new knowledge could mean more safety for all seamen. Hard secrecy of the early days of exploration gradually gave way to accepting all sailors' right to the increased safety scientific knowledge provided. Enough dangers threatened at sea without unnecessary geographical ignorance. Franz Jacobszoon Visscher, a skilled Dutch navigator, pilot and hydrographer, had learned enough to write about navigation, and was interested in exploration. Among several of his venturesome suggestions was a scheme "to discover the southern portion of the world all round the globe, and find out what it consists of – whether land, sea, or icebergs...."

Visscher was discussing the essence of exploration. When a new land – or new sea – is found then its harbours, peoples and resources must be examined, assessed and explained. This gives rise to different and daunting problems. The exploration of New Zealand by land is much more complex than the brief encounters of the first few ships from overseas, or even from Polynesia. Ships cruised from harbour to harbour, their men explored briefly the minds and ways of the people, charted the local waters, and then departed. When Maori or Europeans settled it was different. The resources around, and at a distance, became important. Both groups settled at several locations at slightly different times, and lived in different ways based on different resources. Although sea routes were sufficient for communication and some trade they were not sufficient to find and develop resources or to move inland new resources, especially relatively later ones such as sheep, to such grazing as exploration revealed. Most resources in New Zealand found, and find, their way to the sea rather quickly. But profit was – and is – a different matter; ways to get products to sale cheaply had to be discovered and developed.

On land the routes from resource production to product point of sale had to be charted. And this law of commerce – or of life – applied to Maori greenstone or dried shark as much as to European whale oil or sheeps' wool. This was not at all simple. It was not enough to know that there was good land or excellent greenstone in some distant location. Was there access to and from it which would make production profitable? If it were a mine, how would you get the miners in and support them? How would you get the gold out? Answers in the form of good routes, had to be found to all these questions. Many, perhaps most, explorers were employed by government institutions to find resources which could be developed to support the functions and services of government. Otago, Nelson, Canterbury, Wellington, Hawke's Bay and Auckland needed money, and preferably from a production base other than land. Minerals were easier to tax than crops; miners less likely to be around to vote than farmers.

It was the same with the coastline; both the landmarks and the sea-bottom along its coasts had to be learned and published. Coastal sailors had to be able to recognise the points, the capes, the hills, and the harbour mouths of the land, yet be aware of shoals and reefs as well. So good charting of all New Zealand waters had to be carried out. Again this is recognition that the danger in sailing is near shore. A sound ship is safest out at sea.

After the initial discovery the exploration of New Zealand is divided into two parts: the charting of its waters for safe communication around and between the islands, and the exploration of land routes. Land routes were at first not too important, except for moving livestock. Railways certainly had not yet reached New Zealand, although as we will see one early New Zealand explorer, d'Urville, was killed in a French railway accident. Roads even in highly developed countries could not yet match the Roman roads, and New Zealand had none. In England, the eastern United States, France and Germany most goods travelled by water, even hundreds of miles from the sea. To a surprising extent they still do. But no one would ever need to survey routes for long canals in New Zealand because the sea is everywhere close. Yet also it is almost everywhere a hilly, even mountainous country, as Tasman and Cook had noted. Viable land routes would be the key to winning control of the resources of New Zealand. An inaccessible resource is little better than no resource.

Different groups of people explored for different reasons. The Maori needed routes for trade in food or greenstone, for ways to fisheries or fern or berries, for offensive or defensive strategy. Missionaries were interested in communication itself; with the Maori, between the Maori tribes, and between their own establishments. They needed harbours, pathways and knowledge of the best river routes. These groups did much of the early exploring. Settlers came later, requiring the same knowledge of food sources and fertile land as had the Maori, but in addition yet-to-be-found overland trails with special qualities, width and grazing, for moving sheep inland from ports or from one province to another. Settlers were building a modern economy, based on distant exchange. They needed good harbours from which to send out their wool or lumber and take in their European cloth, machines and luxuries. The provincial system, with its several governments, created the need – or perhaps merely articulated it – for substantial public resources. These could come only from swift, successful private development of resources. So while there was some overlap between the needs of different groups their key motivations were somewhat different. Stealing slaves or saving souls is different motivation from finding routes and making sound title possible so that individuals could commence production of a modern world's goods for a modern world's rewards.

The first explorers left no records, and traces of their lives and travels are still being found and interpreted. Later explorers left written records, often slanted to their own ends. Missionaries, settlers, surveyors, sheepmen, prospectors, mountaineers: there are dozens of land explorers in New Zealand history, who wrote volumes of reports, journals, diaries, letters and books. Even reading all available first-hand material is a daunting task and to condense it into one volume wellnigh impossible. Hence to write of exploration implies selection, which in turn implies criteria. Ours are the assessed importance of the exploration to New Zealand as a whole, the quality and intrinsic interest of the information available, and geographical location. There ought to be a geographical balance, where it does not erase interest.

The main explorers of New Zealand that we deal with will be people who were not only adventuresome and efficient but also literary. Someone who writes full and excellent reports is more likely to go down in history than someone who may well have displayed physical and moral daring yet could not or did not record it properly. For example, d'Urville's writing created his fame as much as did his accomplishments as navigator and commander. Yet exploration which was really important must be sorted from that which was merely well recorded. In this book both the men and the events selected are samples which illustrate a particular problem or a particular type of explorer. Some were men whose work, by choice, was exploring; others were men such as surveyors, who could not do their work without exploring. Our sample explorers may seem to be emphasised, but they are examples, picked for various reasons with no suggestion of paramountcy intended.

If they were to be successful, explorers had to have certain characteristics. Almost without saying they had to be physically tough, strong and healthy. Tenacity might seem to go naturally with those physical characteristics, but it does not. Tenacity is a mental attitude. Great explorers, single-mindedly tenacious to the point of obsession, set out "to seek, to find, to strive and not to yield." But few went alone, and, if they were to be leaders not loners, they had to possess the "power of command", which is difficult to define though not to recognise.

Even such relatively rare qualities were not enough. They would take an expedition to its objective, but there the leader had to become an observer, perceptive and analytical, if exploration were to accurately increase the world's knowledge. The observer, in turn, had to become reporter, had to describe in such fashion that the world would be interested and would understand. The ideal explorer had to be outdoorsman, leader, analyst and publicist in one, with the last by no means the least. Many explorers were never tested in responsible command. Of those we write about, which are indeed only a sample, Cook, Marsden, and Heaphy perhaps combine the qualities most fully. Some, for example Brunner, Dieffenbach, Douglas or Thomson, exceeded them in individual qualities, but not in the total. That is no matter. There was success and honour enough to go around.

CHAPTER ONE

# To the Distant Horizon

Discovery is a side effect of exploration. Although you can systematically explore unknown regions in order to discover new lands or new resources, for gain or for adventure, the actual discovery is always accidental, for you cannot discover what you know is there any more than you can search for something you do not know exists. Nonetheless there is a very wide area between which encompasses searching for things that may exist and discovering things that appear en route. Exploration involves travel into unfamiliar or unknown territory and investigation of whatever is found there. Discovery implies being first to find, or at least first to inform the rest of the world of the find. Exploration does not necessarily mean discovery, but there can be no discovery without exploration.

In discussing the discovery of New Zealand, we are really talking about exploration: first the exploration of the Pacific by the remote ancestors of the Maori, creeping from the Asian mainland on to the islands offshore then in leaps and bounds across the vast ocean to the eastern islands of Polynesia, and from there across thousands of kilometres of empty ocean to the remote outposts to the north, east, and south-west; next the exploration of this south-western outpost to discover its resources and to make use of them, in the process changing its discoverers from Polynesian immigrants to New Zealand Maori; and finally the re-exploration of both the Pacific and New Zealand by the Europeans, part of the 18th century expansion which changed forever man's view of the world, creating for the first time a fairly definite picture of the world as a whole.

The questions of discovery are who, when, where, why, and how. In the case of European exploration all these questions are usually easily answered. Answers become more difficult when we consider the first discoverers and settlers of New Zealand, for they left no written records, and the oral traditions which take the place of written history are tribal and often contradictory, although they help immensely in any attempt to recreate the early history of the land. Only the first and last questions can be answered with any real certainty, although with the help of Maori tradition and various experts we can make good guesses at most of the rest.

New Zealand was discovered by Polynesians, the ancestors of the Maori Tasman and Cook found when they reached New Zealand. There were no earlier inhabitants, no pre-Maori race, and New Zealand had been inhabited for only some eight or nine hundred years before European explorers arrived. This short occupation period was no doubt caused by isolation and relative smallness; Australia had been inhabited for some fifty thousand years.

In any discussion of culture and daily life in New Zealand this extremely short length of time must be remembered. In less than a thousand years the Maori, totally isolated for much of that time, had evolved a culture which impressed the Europeans who first saw it. Tasman was so awed he did not even land. Cook was not so easily daunted, and he had the advantage, through an odd circumstance, of an interpreter. The military art of fortification had developed from scratch in a few hundred years to a point which impressed Cook, who just ten years earlier had gazed up at the formidable fortress of Quebec. At a New Zealand pa he commented, "The Situation is such that the best Engineer in Europe could not have choose'd a better for a small number of men to defend themselves against a greater, it is strong by nature and made more so by Art."

There is no point attempting to compare the Maori with other great stone-age cultures, although the many similarities with those in North, Central and South America led Thor Heyerdahl to theorise that the Polynesians originally arrived from the east not the west, an intriguing idea given some force by the existence throughout East Polynesia of the South American sweet potato or kumara, but not supported by orthodox opinion. The various stone-based cultures in the Americas had millions of people and tens of thousands of years to develop. The Polynesians had neither the time nor the population, although in New Zealand they discovered an island large enough to develop the population and resources to become a great civilisation. Time was not on their side. The rest of the world intervened.

New Zealand's first inhabitants were Polynesian settlers who came from the tropical islands far to the north-east; they came in one, or, almost certainly, several large sailing canoes, bringing with them the language of eastern Polynesia, the language still spoken by their direct descendants, the Maori. It is not known how many canoes came to New Zealand, but it is almost certain that all that did came from the same area in East Polynesia, in spite of the fact that New Zealand is far to the west, and geographically closer to Tonga than to the islands of East Polynesia.

Modern computer models show that one canoe-load of immigrants would have been sufficient to produce the population that was in New Zealand when the first Europeans arrived. Where one canoe could go others could follow; it seems more likely, and in accord with Maori traditions, that there were intermittent arrivals over many years or even centuries. The fact that neither the pig nor the chicken were introduced into New Zealand suggests, however, that only a few groups arrived. Pigs managed the long trip to Hawaii and chickens arrived safely on Easter Island. Only the Polynesian dog and the small Polynesian rat, both probably brought as part of the food supply, reached New Zealand and survived long enough to be established.

Archaeological evidence makes it almost certain there were no new arrivals after about 1200 A.D., 150 years before the date often given for the so-called Great Fleet, the main wave of Polynesian migration to New Zealand.

Speculation about the origins of the Polynesian and New Zealand Maori peoples began with the first European explorers. Writing in 1770 Joseph Banks, scientist with Captain Cook's first Pacific expedition, remarked, "From the similarity of customs, the still greater of Traditions and the almost identical sameness of Language between these people and those of the Islands in the South Sea, there remains little doubt that they came originaly from the same source: but where that Source is future experience may teach us, at Present I

SETTLING THE PACIFIC

It is likely Java Man discovered the Pacific thousands of years before Balboa, and although the vast distances and small land masses would make eastward progress slow, all of Oceania, including the outlying island groups like Hawaii and New Zealand, was settled by about 1000 A.D., before the Norman Conquest of Britain. About 1500 B.C., during Britain's Bronze Age, the Fijian islands were settled by the ancestors of modern Polynesians.

From Fiji, the nearby islands of Tonga and Samoa were quickly settled. The proto-Polynesians inhabiting this fringe area between Melanesia and West Polynesia lived by fishing and growing tropical plants like taro, yam and breadfruit, and they sailed large double-hulled canoes. They also made decorated pottery, known as Lapita Ware, which the later Polynesians did not. However the changes to a Polynesian culture and language took place here, while Britain entered the Iron Age. Fiji, Tonga, and Samoa remained in contact with each other into historical times and Fijians share some physical and cultural characteristics with West Polynesians.

The physical and cultural uniformity of the Polynesian peoples suggest some common centre very early on, probably Samoa, in the millennium after 1000 B.C., while the Celts were invading Britain. In Samoa, the narrow range of basaltic rock required a new approach to tool making and a diverse kit of stone adzes resulted. In the first few centuries A.D., as Fiji developed new pottery forms, pottery styles and types became simpler and then disappeared from the now West Polynesian islands of Tonga and Samoa. The disappearance of pottery from the West Polynesian islands where it had formerly been made is another of the intriguing riddles yet to be solved.

From Samoa, downwind occupation of other island groups would lead to better canoes and bolder seafarers and a foothold in the east, probably the Marquesas, about 300 A.D. The population would soon have spread to the Societies and the Cooks. Changes in culture and language formed a distinctive East Polynesian group. The new arrivals in East Polynesia soon developed local forms of fishing gear, adzes and ornaments which clearly distanced them from their West Polynesian origins, and suggest little further contact with the western groups. In Britain, the Romans had come and gone and King Arthur was attempting to repel the Angle and Saxon invaders from across the North Sea.

In the next few hundred years Hawaii to the north and Easter Island far to the east would have been settled, while Britain was "a fearsome chaos of warring tribes and kingdoms... public and private war the rule rather than the exception." Finally, far to the south and back toward the west, the Polynesians discovered New Zealand, somewhere between 750 and 1100 A.D., probably in the 9th century, while Viking raiders in their longships were harassing Britain.

The Maori traditions tell us their ancestors left the homeland, Hawaiki, for New Zealand. Some writers believe this to be Ra'iatea, near Tahiti, as its old name was Havai'i. It is quite possible the name became more generalised, meaning just East Polynesia, or even simply an island paradise, like the Arthurian Avalon.

can say no more than that I firmly believe that it is to the Westward and by no means to the East."

After many years of study by experts in the fields of archaeology, physical anthropology, comparative linguistics, and ethnology, the orthodox opinion remains much the same as Banks's. The evidence points to a western origin for the Polynesian peoples, probably ultimately and very remotely an Asiatic one. Legends from various Polynesian islands speak of a homeland in a hot country far to the west, whence the earliest voyages set out, ever heading toward the rising sun.

Traditional evidence for the spread of the Polynesians from far in the west to the easternmost islands of the Pacific confirms the archaeological discoveries. New Zealand artefacts such as fishhooks, adzes and ornaments are definitely East Polynesian, in many cases adapted to the new stones and materials, such as moa bone, found in New Zealand.

They also show that New Zealand had been isolated from the rest of Polynesia for some considerable time, the adzes, for example, being of a more archaic type than those in Tahiti, but similar to those in other outlying or marginal islands such as Hawaii, Pitcairn, the Marquesas and the northern Cooks. Cook noted the isolation in 1774: "many of them [Polynesian islands] at this time have no other knowledge of each other than what is recorded in antiquated tradition and have by length of time become as it were different Nations each having adopted some peculiar custom or habit &c$^a$ never the less a carefull observer will soon see the Affinity each has to the other...." The most likely homeland for the settlers of New Zealand are the Societies, the Cooks and the Marquesas, possibly all three.

The Polynesian islands form a rough triangle, as noted by King, some 6500 km in height from Hawaii to New Zealand and a similar distance across from

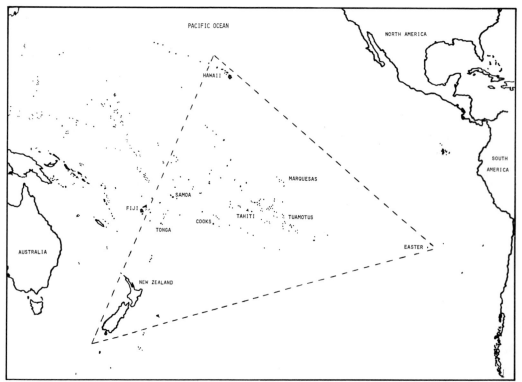

Polynesian triangle. The Polynesians settled not just the numerous islands of central Polynesia but the outlying islands to the north, east and south-west. There can be no doubting the ship-building skills and seamanship of such voyagers.

Tonga and Samoa to its eastern outpost in Easter Island. On Easter Island in 1774 Cook noted, "They are certainly of the same race of People as the New Zealanders and the other islanders, the affinity of the Language, Colour and some of thier customs all tend to prove it... no one will doubt but that they have had the same Origin, it is extraordinary that the same Nation should have spread themselves over all the isles in this Vast Ocean from New Zealand to this Island which is almost a fourth part of the circumference of the Globe...."

There can be no doubting the skill and courage of the early Polynesian explorers. From one tiny tropical island to another they sailed, settling in to grow root and tree crops to supplement the fish from the ocean highway at their door. Why they moved on is guesswork. As population grew the food resources may have been stretched, quarrels may have arisen, losers may have been banished or fled. Given the Polynesian character, some may have sailed for sheer adventure. They were used to the ocean, and knew it to be full of islands. They expected islands to appear, whatever direction they sailed. The great empty ocean stretching south from Rarotonga must have been a shock. The huge islands they finally found were startling too, with the temperate climate, the giant trees, the strange plants and birds. New Zealand prehistory begins with the arrival of these first settlers, and settlers they were, for they had with them not just women but dogs, tropical plant roots and cuttings, and various other necessities.

The historian studies written records. Prehistory involves the study of languages, customs, physical appearance, oral traditions, art and material culture, and the artefacts and discoveries of archaeology. All are open to conflicting interpretation, argument, and new finds. In New Zealand in particular the work done in the last twenty-five years has changed many of the ideas about our earliest settlers. Unfortunately not much of this work appears to have filtered through to the general public, many of whom still hold the idea that the first settlers were of non-Polynesian stock and were driven out or slaughtered by the new wave of settlers, the ancestors of the modern Maori. This so-called Moriori race never existed in New Zealand, and the Chatham Islands Moriori were an isolated group of Polynesians closely related to the New Zealand Maori.

The Chathams may have been settled from New Zealand soon after the first arrivals, or may have been settled, as New Zealand was, direct from East Polynesia. Chatham Islands Moriori and New Zealand Maori were each unaware the other existed until the 18th century. Maori tradition does not mention either the Moriori or the Chatham Islands, and there is no doubt that even if the Chatham Islands Polynesian settlers landed first in New Zealand the two cultures had been isolated for many hundreds of years when the Chathams were rediscovered by Europeans in 1791. One artefact that the two island groups alone share is barbed bone points, attached to wooden shafts, which were used for spearing birds, usually pigeon. Either the earliest settlers in New Zealand invented a new way of catching a relatively scarce protein source and took it to the Chathams, or both areas developed the same method due to the similar environment. Both also used a harpoon in the earliest days, although harpoons have been found in the Marquesas too.

Elsdon Best, a renowned ethnologist whose books on the Maori are still basic references, on flimsy evidence concluded that the original inhabitants of New Zealand were of Melanesian origin, "a dark-skinned folk of inferior culture and non-Polynesian features" called Mouriuri or Maruiwi. They were defeated by the precursors of the fleet and fled to the Chathams. The obviously Polynesian characteristics of the Chatham Islanders were ignored, yet a renowned anthropologist remarks that the Moriori are "the most Polynesian of Polynesians." Best's theory was disproved almost immediately, but it somehow caught the popular imagination and was still being taught in some schools less than a decade ago.

Archaeology deals with the small details of everyday life, the fishhooks and post holes. From these details it attempts to describe the life of a society, and define the changes in culture. What it cannot do is deal with individuals as people, as opposed to skull types, although it is surprising how much information about a person is available from the study of bones and teeth in burial sites. Archaeology can never answer "Who discovered New Zealand?" other than generally; that is, Eastern Polynesians.

To get a name, such as Kupe, we must turn to tradition, and while the answers tradition gives us may not be historically correct, they are the best we are going to find. Oral history and mythology deal with the deeds of individuals, individuals who become larger than life because of their importance to their tribe or race. Each becomes a symbol, a focus of pride, so that whether they personally could have done all the things the stories say they did is not really important any more, provided no one then tries to use the stories as cold hard historical fact. In our own cultures Kupe, King Arthur, Robin Hood, and Toi all fall into this category. Fitted into and around these heroes are the events and other individuals, both friends and enemies, that are important to the tribe.

When a takeover or amalgamation occurs, the traditions of the stronger prevail, sometimes incorporating aspects of the other into new traditions. Facts which do not fit are discarded. Defeated heroes are ignored. The commonly accepted traditions, like languages, belong to winners not losers. Once collected, the traditions became formalised; once written down, they became static. What we read as Maori traditions are those particular traditions that were current when the ethnologists started work on collecting and editing.

Archaeology is supplemented by the oral traditions which provide information about individuals and events which may or may not be historically accurate but which provide insights into the way the Maori viewed the world. These insights belonged to the Maori from whom the tales were collected, not necessarily to earlier members of the same tribe or to even contemporary people from other areas. Oral history is very specifically regional, and the different tribal accounts do not mesh very well. They are not meant to.

Early collectors were not content to merely record them but tried to improve them, editing to make them more coherent. Like standardised Maori, standardised traditions do not accurately represent the whole Maori population. Also, by the time a lot of the collecting work was done the Maori had had a century of contact with Europeans and all sorts of opportunities to embellish and extend the legends to encompass the new knowledge about the Pacific and the world beyond New Zealand brought by the sealers, whalers, missionaries and settlers. The Maori were very adaptable, and eager to accept both superior

## THE   POLYNESIAN   LANGUAGES

The close relationship of the Polynesian languages was obvious to early observers, in spite of the systematic shift in the consonants (waka [canoe], vaka, va'a, wa'a). Lieutenant King of the *Resolution* in 1778 recognised not just the similarity but the inference: "that the Language which is spoke at these Isles [Hawaii], at New Zealand, at Easter Island & the Society & Friendly Isles is the same is clear... not differing more than Provincial dialects of the same Nation.... It cannot but strike the immagination, the immense space thro which this Nation has spread; the extent of its limits exceed all Europe, & is nearly equal to Africa, stretching in breadth from A'toui [Kauai] to New Zealand... & in length from Easter Isld to the Friendly Isles, [Tonga]... all the Isles in the intermediate space are by their affinity or sameness in Speech to be reckond as forming one people...." In spite of the fact that New Zealand had been isolated from the rest of Polynesia for over 500 years when Cook arrived, he did not hesitate to group its ferocious and energetic inhabitants with the gentler peoples of the South Seas, and postulate that "the common ancestors of both were natives of the same country."

Language was a key factor; Cook found it "an [a]greeable surprise" that the Maori understood his Tahitian interpreter "perfectly". "These people", wrote Cook, "speake the same Language as the people of the South Sea Islands we had before Viseted, tho distant from them many hundred Leagues and of whom they have not the least knowlidge or of any other people whatever." Both Cook and Banks made a study of the different dialects of the Polynesian language, including long lists of words in the journals: "nothing is so great a proff of they all having had one Source as their Language which differs but in a very few words the one from the other...."

Linguistic studies put Maori in an East Polynesian grouping with the languages of the Cook Islands, Tahiti, Marquesas, Easter Island and Hawaii. It is possibly the least altered form of the original Polynesian language, again due to isolation. In Mangareva, in the Gambier group, some 1200 kilometres east of Tahiti, also a possible centre of distribution for Eastern Polynesia, Te Rangi Hiroa (Sir Peter Buck) noted in 1934 that "Much of the dialect is very like Maori - much more so than Rarotongan or Tahitian." Again isolation had preserved original forms. In the same manner the distinctive Maori double spiral, used both in carving and in painting, may be an older form preserved by isolation from the newer rectilinear art forms developed after the migration in central Polynesia, although some evidence appears to suggest that the spiral is a truly indigenous art form, developing in tandem with the Maori, as opposed to Polynesian, culture of New Zealand. Similarities to the art of the Mayans are tantalising.

knowledge and tools and turn them to their own use. The almost immediate adoption of whaleboats, as well as of iron tools and guns, was not a rejection of their own culture but the reaction of a highly intelligent and a highly practical people.

The same problem exists with the early historical accounts of the Maori. While of immense value, especially the earliest accounts – those, for example, of Tasman and Cook in the 17th and 18th centuries – it must be remembered that they were seeing isolated examples at one time of year, and that there were communication problems.

And these very early contacts were already changing Maori society so that later accounts, even those of the early 19th century, are no longer describing a society "as it was" before the influence of the European changed things forever. Metal tools, gained from trade with the discovery ships, changed the type and amount of decoration on everyday objects almost immediately. Pigs and potatoes, also introduced by the earliest ships, changed the economies and the lifestyles of several tribes, and the introduction of the musket changed the balance of power and altered patterns of warfare, and defence, very rapidly.

Maori traditional tales tell not only of the discovery and exploration of New Zealand but its creation. The North Island was fished out of the sea by the demigod Maui, who appears in many Polynesian legends. His great fish was hacked about by his brothers, and mountains formed. Perhaps the most interesting thing about Maui's fish is that the early Maori could visualise, without maps, the shape of the Island by sailing around its coasts. Wellington Harbour is the fish's mouth, Cape Reinga forms its tail, and Cape Egmont and East Cape its fins.

The South Island, its shape more regular than the North Island, in some legends was Maui's canoe the *Mahunui*, and Stewart Island its anchor. Maui sighted the back of his big fish while sailing up the Kaikoura coast, and fished it up from a hillside. He returned to Hawaiki but the canoe was sent back and placed on, or became, the South Island. Another South Island legend also sees the island as a canoe, but an even earlier one. After Raki the Sky Father wedded Papa the Earth Mother, four of Raki's sons by a previous union came down to earth to explore. After sailing around Hawaiki they proceeded south in their immense canoe, but on their attempt to return to the Sky Father their canoe turned to stone and sank on its side, with one flank exposed high above the waves, forming the South Island's West Coast. The prow, with its curved fretwork, shattered into pieces and formed the bays and islands of the Marlborough Sounds. The voyagers clambered on to the high flank and were turned to stone. They sit tall above the canoe, the tallest Aoraki (in standardised Maori, Aorangi) or Mount Cook.

Kupe is usually considered to be the first Polynesian to visit New Zealand. Simmons' study of the traditions suggests there may have been as many as three Kupes, all of whom were possibly born in New Zealand, and that he or they lived in the early 14th century. Nonetheless the legends of Kupe and his companion Ngahue may be used to illustrate the sort of voyages which occurred in the early days of discovery and exploration.

Many details are of interest – the reasons given for the voyage, the description of the canoes, the fact that he and Ngahue were accompanied by their wives and daughters, the landfall made by sighting clouds (and thus the Maori name for the North Island, and now the whole country, Aotearoa, long white cloud), the immediate exploration of the coastline and harbours of the new land, the leaving of anchor stones as proof of discovery, the return home to Hawaiki with news of a huge land with food for all in its forests, streams and seas, and sailing directions to take others there. In one legend Kupe met the *Aotea* canoe on his way home and told Turi how to reach Taranaki. This would make Kupe contemporary with the fleet. Generally Kupe is held to be some three hundred years earlier, and only the sailing directions were passed down.

Ngahue had discovered greenstone at Arahura on the West Coast of the South Island, and had also killed a moa and preserved its flesh in a calabash which he took back to Hawaiki. The samples of greenstone and moa attracted much attention back home, and stories of giant birds and plentiful seafood, as well as miraculous stones, may have provided enough reason for others to follow Kupe's directions. The sailing directions vary in different legends, but give a course using the setting sun or moon, and Venus, on a particular day of a particular month. What is certain is that at least some Polynesians made their way safely to New Zealand, either because of, or in spite of, Kupe's directions.

New Zealand, or Aotearoa, was discovered by Polynesians from one or more of the East Polynesian island groups of Tahiti (Society Islands), the Marquesas, or Rarotonga (Cook Islands). It is not known whether the early explorers returned home, but tradition says they did, and although the long north-east voyage would have been difficult, there is little doubt it was possible.

The difficulties of the long sea voyage to New Zealand, and, given the currents and winds, the even longer one back to East Polynesia, make it possible the discoverers and first settlers were one and the same canoe load. If so, New Zealand was discovered by a group who had planned to colonise the island, even if they did not know their exact destination. Neither adventurers nor fishermen blown off course carry women, dogs, and the variety of cultivated plants which were established in New Zealand.

Captain Peter Dillon of the *Research* did say in the 1820s that Polynesians were aware of the possibility of being swept out to sea by storms and tended to carry women and animals with them, and although it is doubtful this was general practice, possibly the plants which needed careful tending on a voyage, as opposed to roots and seeds, provide the best evidence of planned migration. We will never know which individual discovered the new land, and although Ngapuhi legends tell us it was Kupe there is no real evidence he ever existed. Someone from East Polynesia discovered New Zealand, and Kupe is as good a name for him as any.

*When* the first canoes arrived in New Zealand cannot be answered definitely. The date often given for Kupe is 925 A.D., delightfully precise but untenable. The archaeological answer, based on the dating of Marquesan sites which provide artefacts which correspond to the earliest in New Zealand, is somewhere between 600 and 1300 A.D. This is narrowed down by radiocarbon dating in New Zealand sites to the period about A.D. 800-1100, with a possibility of some incomers until about 1200. The old orthodox chronology based on a somewhat suspect concatenation of tribal genealogies and traditions (Kupe 925-50 A.D., Toi 1150 A.D., the Fleet 1350 A.D.) is not correct, but according to Simmons does not represent authentic Maori tradition.

If the Fleet retains its date then it most probably represents the dispersal of the tribes throughout New Zealand, and Hawaiki is probably in Northland. There is some evidence to support this view in that some of the Fleet traditions include native plants and birds in their cargo, and the sacred adze of the *Tokomaru* canoe, rediscovered in 1921, is made of argillite from the South Island of New Zealand.

Just as Hawaiki is a name from the earliest voyages across the Pacific, so the names of the canoes may have been passed down from the canoes which did make the deep-sea voyage to New Zealand. If the Fleet refers to a migration from Polynesia over a period of some hundred or so years then the date needs to be adjusted to fit the evidence of archaeology. This does not mean that the traditions need to be changed or disregarded, as assigning dates to events is a Pakeha not a Maori convention, and Maori history only times events in relation to each other or in relation to the time of a certain ancestor. It is enough that Kupe arrived first, and the Fleet later on.

Simmons' work on *The Great New Zealand Myth* shows that the great canoes of the main tribes were not contemporary, and that the Fleet canoes were not the equivalent of the *Mayflower* or the ships of the New Zealand Company. As Duff so felicitously remarked, the Fleet was a concept, not a convoy.

Any answer to *where* the voyagers landed must be based on tradition or on assumptions made from the known sites of the earliest period. Several of the Fleet canoes speak of specific landing points, but it is possible these were much later arrivals, possibly from within New Zealand. Kupe is said to have made landfall in the far north, and then explored down the east coast of the North Island. This would be the obvious landfall area from Rarotonga, and presumably most of the canoes which reached New Zealand from Polynesia stopped in the Cooks en route. Rarotongan tradition shares the names of many canoes with the Maori traditions, canoes which stayed in Ngatangia lagoon on their way south. Tradition in the Tuamotus names *Tainui*, which sailed away for unknown lands; *Tainui* turns up in New Zealand tradition, and with the same captain.

There is no doubt that Polynesians sailed to New Zealand. The question of *why* they came is one of the more controversial ones, as it presupposes an answer to the question of whether the voyages were planned or were so-called drift voyages. It must be emphasised that drift voyages do not imply a canoe helplessly drifting around the Pacific and finally being cast up on a strange shore, except in the most extreme conditions. It suggests a non-purposeful voyage, a canoe setting out from one island to go to another, or to go fishing, and then being driven out to sea by a storm and lost.

Many early Pacific explorers found evidence of drift or accidental voyages. Peter Dillon of the *Research* in the 1820s met survivors of a drift voyage who had been drifting at sea for five months. Even on the huge double canoes, however, unless the steering oars were broken or lost, the crew would have at least some control and be able to steer for land when and if it appeared on the horizon. Then arises the question of whether the navigator, if one were aboard, would be able to orientate himself from the heavens and set a homeward course. It is this ability that the drift voyage proponents doubt, and probably a more useful term is one-way voyages.

The one-way voyage theory does not stop at unplanned voyages but considers many may have been made purposefully, to escape hunger or war, or personal enemies, or just to seek adventure. A study of the traditions gives many valuable clues. In one version of the Kupe legends Kupe fell in love with his cousin's wife so drowned his cousin, then had to leave home to escape the vengeance of relatives. He had also offended a chief who sent a giant octopus to harass him, and in chasing it Kupe discovered Maui's fish or New Zealand's North Island.

Nuku-Tawhiti, Kupe's nephew or grandson, left the Homeland to escape food shortages brought about by overpopulation and intertribal fighting.

Generations later Whatonga, after winning a canoe race on the lagoon in Hawaiki, was swept through the reef and out to sea by a sudden squall. His grandfather Toi set off to find him, and returning home to discover his grandfather gone, Whatonga in turn set off after Toi. Eventually they were reunited in New Zealand. Their men married tangata whenua, people of the land, descendants of earlier arrivals, and soon the population grew and fighting began in the new land, with insults to be avenged and retaliatory raids to be mounted.

Back in Hawaiki things were getting worse, and the fighting over land and food resources led to the coming of the Fleet, seven or more great migration canoes. The term "fleet" is misleading as it is very doubtful that the canoes left together, much less arrived together. Even if two or more of the ancestral tribal canoes left at the same time, keeping together on the long voyage would have been very difficult. Cook's ships lost each other several times. It is more likely the migration was spread over many years. *Te Arawa* left for complicated reasons involving the theft of fruit in revenge for an injustice, which led to fighting and feuds. Tama-te-kapua gathered his trusted relatives and followers and decided to leave for Aotearoa. He not only abducted *Tainui*'s tohunga but sent Ruaro back for an adze made from Ngahue's greenstone (or in some versions a comb) and sailed off without him, but with his wife. Here again we see island quarrels taken to the new land, as Ruaro followed in another canoe and took his revenge in New Zealand. *Tainui* sailed when Hotu-roa was forced to flee angry relatives after he killed a boy who laughed at his canoe-construction skills.

*Takitimu*, the most sacred of the Fleet canoes, led by a descendant of Maui, Tamatea-ariki-nui, is said to have left because of the cannibalism caused by hunger. The canoe's tohunga was to have been the next victim, but used his powers to find enough shellfish and birds to feed the tribe until the canoe was ready to leave. As a sacred canoe, they could not carry cooked food, and had to rely on dried fish, which was in short supply. In times of hunger the canoe would not be well provisioned in any case and the sea voyage must have been very hard. They did at least have fresh water which they towed overboard in seaweed bags to keep cool.

The reasons for migration given in the Fleet traditions are those of all races and all times. The search for traditional homelands and for adventure are motives those who know of Odysseus and Beowulf can easily understand. Some groups were allowed, or forced, to leave after defeat in war just as in Europe defeated garrisons were allowed to march away disarmed. Some left to search for earlier voyagers, as Toi and Whatonga did. Later in the same ocean Captain Peter Dillon searched for the survivors of the La Pérouse expedition. No doubt many Polynesians left to find a better life elsewhere just as immigrants from France, England, and Scotland left for Quebec, Australia, and New Zealand hundreds of years later.

The question of *how* the Polynesians got to New Zealand at least has a fairly definite answer. Polynesians sailed to New Zealand, and to Hawaii, Easter Island,

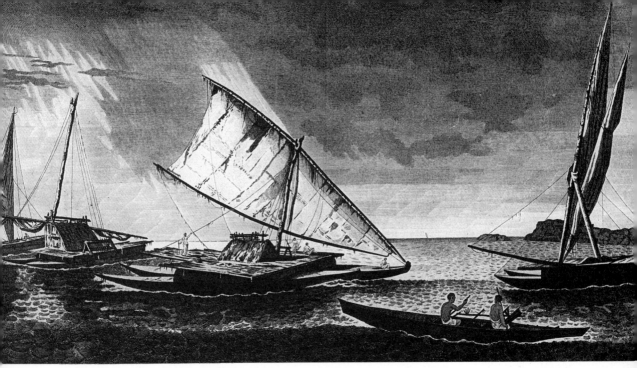

Polynesian double canoes as seen near Tonga by William Hodges, artist on Cook's 1773 voyage. The size of these sailing craft meant they were suitable for long voyages; "canoe" is really a misnomer. Many early European explorers remarked the seaworthiness of the vessels and the seamanship of the Polynesians. *(Hocken Library, Dunedin)*

and the Marquesas in the two types of Polynesian seagoing craft, the single canoe with outrigger and the double canoe, using traditional methods of navigation and seamanship. Of the two the double canoe – two dugout canoes side by side with a gap of up to two and a half metres between them, fastened together with poles stretching right across both canoes and generally extending out even further, and a deck built on the crossbeams on which sat a roofed shelter as well as the mast or masts for the lateen or lugged sail or sails – is the more probable choice for a planned settlement voyage, as some of these canoes were very large as well as seaworthy.

"Canoe" is really a misnomer for these large vessels; they were not, and could not be, paddled, but were sailing craft with steering oars. To sail to New Zealand even from the closest Polynesian island required food and water (carried in gourds or seaweed bags) for the whole group for at least several weeks, as well as animals (and fodder), cuttings and seeds, roots for planting, fishing gear, baskets, mats, tools, weapons, and all the other immediate necessities for life in a new land, as well as tribal gods who had been asked to reside in small sculptures during the trip to the new land.

The double canoe was found in many parts of the Pacific by the early European explorers, although it was not as endemic as some form of single outrigger. It seems a fairly safe assumption that both types were around in basically the same forms when the eastern Polynesians began the final surge to the outposts of their world – Hawaii in the north, Easter Island far to the east, and New Zealand in the south.

When the Europeans arrived some eight hundred years later the canoes on these far-flung islands were still obviously related to each other, and of basically the same designs, with only minor differences – sail type being the most obvious to the casual observer. Materials differed, naturally, and the type of

12

lashings, as well as the way the holes were drilled to tie the topstrakes to the top of the hull, but almost all of the craft, from very small to very large, fitted into the two broad definitions. Only in New Zealand had a major departure occurred, as the vast trees and the inland waterways, as well as the need for exploration, led to the use of a single canoe without outrigger.

The outrigger is found as far west as Ceylon and as far east as Easter Island, and Cook thought the double canoes had as wide a spread, being found "throughout the whole extent of the Pacific Ocean". In 1767 Wallis met both types in Tahiti: "Two of them were generally lashed together.... If they were single they had an outrigger on one side.... With these vessels they sail far beyond the sight of land...." Two years later Cook noted that, "In order to prevent them from overseting when in the water all those that go single both great and small have what is call'd outriggers which are peices of wood fasten'd to the gunel and project out on one side about 6, 8 or 10 feet according to the size of the boat; at the ends is fastened in a parallel direction to the Canoe a long log of wood... this lays in the water & balanceth the boat... those that go double that is two together, which is very common, have no need of any.... Two Canoes are placed in a parallel direction to each other about three or four feet asunder securing them together by small logs of wood laid aCross and lashed to each of their gunels, thus the one boat supports the other and are not in the least danger of over seting...."

Again in Tahiti on his second voyage Cook saw "170 Sail of Smaller double Canoes, all with a little house upon them and rigg'd with Masts and sails.... In these 330 Canoes I judged there were no less than 7760 Men...." Forster added that the war canoes were fifty to ninety feet long, and that the crossbeams projected out beyond the hulls, making a platform "from twelve to twenty-four feet" wide and "fifty, sixty, or seventy feet in length."

As the first Europeans found outriggers and double canoes in all of Polynesia, including the outposts Hawaii and Easter Island, we would expect to find them in New Zealand too. For an idea of the canoes in which Polynesians arrived in New Zealand, we depend on descriptions by the earliest visitors, as well as on Maori traditions.

Most of the fleet canoes were double canoes with deckhouses, although *Tainui* was said to be a large outrigger canoe with a smaller canoe in place of the more usual solid outrigger. *Aotea* was apparently an outrigger canoe, and *Takitimu* was said to be single-hulled, almost certainly with an outrigger for deep-sea voyaging.

In New Zealand in 1642 Tasman writes only of double canoes: "Two long narrow prows side by side, over which a number of planks or other seats were placed... with these vessels they could make considerable speed." He does not mention the outrigger canoe, which, due to the availability of huge trees and thus broad hulls, may have been scarce by this time. Of the Maori canoe, a single canoe without outrigger, he says nothing, unless one remark, "high and pointed in front, manned with seventeen Natives", refers to a single canoe.

We must remember that Tasman did not see much of New Zealand and that after that first encounter with the "prow of villains" generally kept well clear. Cook, 127 years later, was not impressed with Tasman's idea of discovery. "We fell in with the East Coast of New Zeland a very small part of the west coast of

A. *Our Ships at anchor in Diemens road.* B. *Small ftroas belonging to the King of the Country.* C. *Veffells or ftroas joined together* with Coco Nuts &c. F. *The Kings residence.* G. *The ftlace where our Boats lay when they went to Water.* H. *The ftlace where they came to* People kept Guard. K. *The Kings Belay in an inclosure where He received Our ftople* L. *The King & His Nobilitys washing ftlace.* M. *Th* ftanding, & their Cloathing. O. *The Bay where the King lives & His Galley lyes to which Tasman gave the Name of Marias Bay*

Tasman sketched these Tongan craft in 1643. The tongiaki or double canoe, a specialised long-distance deep-sea ship, had hulls of equal length to support the decking. On the right is a tafa'anga or outriggered bonita fishing boat – the bonita rod is to the rear. Similar craft existed throughout Polynesia. Reports note that the fishing boats were sometimes carried to deep-sea fishing grounds on board the larger ship – the "mother ship" carrying crews and supplies as well as providing shelter and a cooking fire. *(Hocken Library, Dunedin)*

which was first discoverd [by] Tasman in 1642, but he never once set foot upon it". Cook remedied this defect, circumnavigating both islands of the "hilly Mountainous Country, but rich and firtile, especially the nothern parts, where it is also well Inhabited", meeting its "brave warlike people with sentiments voide of treachery."

In New Zealand Cook found both single canoes with outriggers and double canoes, especially in the south. Neither were common, as in November Cook remarked, "a large double Canoe full of People came off to us, this was the first double Canoe we had seen in this Country." Banks adds an interesting qualification: "A large double canoe, or rather two canoes lashed together at a distance of about a foot...." In 1773 Furneaux noted that "sometimes they fasten two together with rafters, which we call a double canoe...", and the same year Forster saw a double canoe which "was about fifty feet long, and seemed to be new; both the high stern and the head were very curiously carved with fretwork and spiral lines...." It seems likely that two single war canoes had been joined temporarily, and that most of the Maori double canoes were two open canoes with a deck between rather than the decked-over doubles of Polynesia.

Tasman's 1642 encounter with the Maori. The double canoe does not resemble later forms, and is probably not correct. The top strake and covering battens are clear, however, and the Maori hairstyle is similar to later drawings. Early artists and writers have left a confused picture of Polynesian watercraft and caution is necessary. *(Mitchell Library, State Library of New South Wales)*

Even in 1769 double canoes were rare in the north, although they were used for some years in the rough seas around Otago and Southland. The huge trees available in New Zealand no doubt helped to make them unnecessary, and both double and outriggered canoes would be a nuisance on rivers and creeks, although it is interesting to note that on the Arnold River in the greenstone country of the South Island's West Coast the Maori moved upriver in single canoes but descended in a simplified form of double canoe made by lashing the canoes together in pairs. For occasional sea voyaging two large single canoes could be lashed together.

During Te Rauparaha's invasion of the south in the 1830s, Taiaroa is said to have sailed from Otakau to Banks Peninsula in a fleet of twenty-nine canoes "mainly composed of vessels specially adapted for ocean voyaging, formed by lashing two ordinary war-canoes together, and further strengthening them with a deck." By the 1830s they had virtually disappeared further north. Polack said that, "Canoes are very rarely lashed together... and no platforms are made to surmount them, as is practised by the natives of the islands of Oceanica."

In his report on his first voyage, Cook noted about canoes that "some of the small ones we have seen with out-riggers, but this is not common." Both double and outrigger canoes appear to have lasted longer in the south than in the north. Dr Anderson, the *Resolution*'s surgeon on both the second and third voyages, appended an account of the Queen Charlotte Sound to Cook's third voyage report. "Their boats are well built.... Some are fifty feet long and so broad as to be able to sail without an outrigger, but the smaller sort commonly have one and they often fasten two together by rafters, which we then call a double Canoe." The examples seen by Tasman and Cook suggest that both single canoes with outriggers and double canoes were brought to New Zealand by the earliest explorers, and that the Polynesian-type vessels were used, decreasingly, for something under a thousand years.

In New Zealand, alone in Polynesia, the early European explorers found single outriggerless canoes. Tasman did not describe the single Maori canoe, yet by Cook's time they were everywhere. It is possible that an increase in warfare after about 1350, as well as the proliferation of the superb woodworking tools in greenstone, brought about a revival in the old arts of boatbuilding, adapted to the huge trees, new woods and other materials found in New Zealand. As population increased more inland exploration was necessary to find new resources and additional arable land. Much inland exploration in early New Zealand would be done by canoe.

Tasman only saw parts of the west coast, where settlement was sparse, and the seas rough. It is possible any revival in boat building had not yet reached that far, and never reached the more isolated parts. A small dugout canoe or even a raft is all that is necessary for inland fishing; Cook in 1773 noted that the Dusky Sound natives had no canoes but "two or three logs of wood tied together serves the same purpose... and were indeed sufficient for the Navigation of the River, on the Banks of which they lived...." But transporting war parties is another matter. Canoes need to be not only bigger, but better. And bigger and better canoes meant longer voyages on more dangerous waters and no doubt led to a more rapid exploration and expansion inland, especially in the North Island.

Not just small dugouts but huge war canoes, capable of carrying one hundred men, the indigenous Maori canoe impressed even seamen like Cook. "The People shew great ingenuity and good workmanship in the building and framing their Boats or Canoes. The[y] are long and narrow and shaped very much like a New England Whale boat. Their large Canoes are I beleive built wholy for war and will carry from 40 to 80 or 100 men with their arms, &c. I shall give the demensions of one which I measured that lay a shore at *Tolaga*. Length 68 1/2 feet, breadth 5 feet, and depth 3 1/2 feet. The bottom sharp inclining to a wedge and was made of three pieces hollow'd out to about 2 inches or an inch and a half thick and well fastn'd together with strong plating; each side consisted of one plank only which was 63 feet long and 10 or 12 Inches broad and about an inch and a quarter thick and these were well fited and lash'd to the bottom part; there were a number of Thwarts laid across and lashed to each gunel as a strengthening to the boat. The head or[n]ament projected 5 or 6 feet without the body of the Boat and was 4 1/2 feet high; the stern or[n]ament was 14 feet high, about 2 feet broad and about an 1 1/2 Inch thick, it was fix'd upon the Stern of the Canoe like the Stern post of a Ship upon her keel. The or[n]aments of both head and stern and the two side boards were of carved work and in my opinion neither ill-designd nor executed.... In their War Canoes they generaly have a quantity of birds feathers hung in strings and tied about the head and stern as an additional Or[n]ament. They are as various in the heads of their canoes as we are in those of our shipping but what is most

## MAORI WAR CANOES

The construction of a Maori war canoe meant at least two years of hard work for many people. The elaborately carved stern and stem pieces took even longer and were sometimes completed by the next generation of carvers. The finished canoe, carved, painted, inlaid, decorated with feathers, was a work of art created by hard physical labour, sheer perseverance, and much skill and ingenuity; it was also a seaworthy craft, capable of carrying a hundred men in rough waters. In 1820 Cruise remarked: "We have observed other war-canoes cross the Bay of Islands in perfect safety when it was thought imprudent to lower the ship's boats." Probably in high winds the actual lowering of the boats was more worrying than their seaworthiness once afloat, but many early seamen thought highly of the canoe's capabilities.

The felling of a tree two metres or more in diameter with stone tools and fire took many days. Totara and kauri were the preferred woods, the trees often chosen and marked years earlier. Severing the head of the felled tree would again take four or more days, using fire and stone adzes. Once the canoe makers were left with a huge log, 15 to 20 or even more metres long, and well over two metres thick, they could begin hollowing out, using hot coals to char the hard wood and adzes to chip it away. This long and laborious process was interrupted by the labour of hauling the rough hull out of the forest to river bank, lake shore or sea coast before completing the dubbing and smoothing process. Also from the forest came the two topstrakes, planks arduously dubbed down from logs longer than the hull, about thirty-five centimetres high and five centimetres thick.

Once the hull was smooth inside and out and the gunwale flat, and the topstrakes shaped and flat, many matching holes had to be pierced with chisel or stone-tipped cord drill through both strake and hull, and the strake bent to fit the curve of the hull; then strake and hull could be caulked and lashed together with battens, also shaped, fitted on both sides of the join during the lashing process. This was the strength of the canoe; all else depended on the lashings, which did the job that bolts, rivets, spikes, nails, braces and stays did on the ships of nations with iron. The cords were made of plaited flax fibre. Durable heartwood was split for the thwarts and dressed to fit the curves, after which flooring was added.

Once the practical aspects were dealt with the artistic work could begin, although carving would have been carried on while the other work was in progress. The elaborate carved figurehead with its filigree spirals was a triumph of effort and art, and sometimes handed on to a new canoe; the stern piece, also with pierced spirals and curved ribs for strength, standing perhaps two metres high, was also greatly prized. Both were lashed to the hull and ends of the topstrakes. Canoes were usually painted red with black battens. Topstrakes were carved or painted with designs, and a painted pattern often appeared on the forward hull. The carved figurehead and stern post were usually black. Red colour was a mixture of burnt ochre and shark oil, and black was made by painting with a mixture of oil with soot or charcoal, or by charring the green battens. On special occasions bunches of white feathers were tucked under the lashings to contrast with the dark battens, and long strings or streamers of feathers festooned stem and stern, hanging down almost to the water.

common is an od design'd figure of a man with as ugly a face as can be conceved, a very large tongue sticking out of his mouth and large white eys made of the Shells of sea ears. There paddle[s] are small light and neatly made, they hardly ever make use of sails...."

These were the waka taua, the war canoes. Generally they were kept for expeditions, coastal voyaging, and special occasions. For sea fishing, smaller less ornamented canoes were used, and inland small simple dugout hulls without topstrakes were employed for many purposes. With the giant trees in New Zealand even the war canoe hulls were often made from a single log; if the tree was not long enough an extra piece or haumi could be added at one or occasionally both ends. Haumi and hull were shaped to form a tongue-and-slot join and lashed together. Canoes of the Polynesian islands, where the trees are generally smaller, were often made in parts. The Tahitian canoes that Cook saw had hulls made of three or four pieces and sides built up with planks. (In New Zealand the built-up sides gave way to a single topstrake.) In Easter Island Forster saw the ultimate patchwork canoe: "Their canoe was another curiosity, being patched up of many pieces, each of which was not more than four or five inches wide, and two or three feet long."

Maori tradition mentions that some of the Polynesian canoes which sailed to New Zealand had three haumi or hull pieces and several topstrakes. This is consistent with the canoes Cook saw in the islands. Tradition also suggests that at least one of the migration canoes was a single outrigger rather than a double canoe. There is no reason to doubt this. The canoes coming to New Zealand need not have been especially large, and it is probable that larger canoes were built in New Zealand than ever sailed there. Canoes, especially doubles, of eighteen metres or so in length would be large enough for a colonising venture.

Estimations of the navigational skills and seamanship of the early Polynesians vary widely. Some saw the Polynesians ranging at will in large, swift, seaworthy sailing canoes over the vastness of the Pacific; others insisted that long voyages, more than say 500 kilometres, must have been one-way voyages with no return possible, due to the inability of the canoes to sail to windward and the insuperable difficulties of navigating without instruments.

The question of the navigational skills of the Polynesians is wrapped up in the question of return voyages, not discovery. Navigation involves plotting a route and directing the craft to a known destination. It implies that someone has already found the destination and returned home with information on bearings and distance. Discovery of an unknown land is fortuitous or accidental, and navigational ability assists only if the discovery group wishes to return home again.

There is no doubt that the difficulties in sailing and in navigating without instruments in a huge ocean looking for tiny islands were many and extreme. Only the highly skilled seaman and the highly trained navigator could succeed, and no doubt a large number of canoes disappeared without trace. Ben Finney, initiator of the *Hokule'a* experiment (constructing a traditional double canoe of modern materials and sailing using Polynesian navigational techniques over traditional routes), notes that "the hazards, the inevitable disasters, and the loss of life cannot be minimized. Many voyages undertaken in thoroughly equipped and manned sailing canoes must have come to grief when canoes broke apart or foundered in heavy seas, or when voyagers died of hunger, thirst or exposure before land could be found. An even higher mortality rate must have occurred among hastily mounted voyages, such as when a group was forced to flee from famine or following defeat in war. If, for example, we assume that 10

Maori waka taua or war canoe, as seen by Cook in 1769. New Zealand's huge trees and inland waterways meant the Pacific double canoes and outriggers gave way to single canoes. Some were said to carry over 100 warriors, sometimes three or four abreast, so the paddlers could be spelled. Different editions of Cook's journals used various artists to copy the original drawings, and the canoe detail varies widely. *(Hocken Library, Dunedin)*

canoes with 25 persons each were lost every year, and then multiply the product by the last 2000 years of Polynesian voyaging, we obtain an estimate of a half-million lost souls. And this estimate could be conservative."

Other trial voyages have proven that both canoes and techniques were more than adequate for sustained voyages. David Lewis, doctor, small boat sailor and author, used modern catamarans to approximate the double canoe while studying traditional navigation. In January 1986 the *Hawaiki Nui*, a double canoe built to traditional designs of traditional materials such as pandanas, bamboo, and coconut fibre, arrived in New Zealand after sailing from Tahiti in just over two months.

Cook in 1769 did not doubt that seamanship, navigation and canoes were adequate for voyaging: "they manage them very dexterusly and I beleive perform long and distant Voyages in them, otherwise they could not have the knowledge of the Islands in these seas they seem to have... these people sail in those seas from Island to Island for several hundred Leagues, the Sun serving them for a compass by day and the Moon and Stars by night. When this comes to be prov'd we Shall be no longer at a loss to know how the Islands lying in those Seas came to be people'd...." Much has been made of this statement, some writers suggesting that Cook was somehow remiss in not acquiring more detailed knowledge of the navigational techniques. Cook was particularly interested in navigation, and had he seen anything ridiculous in Polynesian assertions, no doubt would have said so. It must be remembered that Cook too navigated by using the sun in the day and the moon and stars at night – albeit he had instruments to help him – and would not be as surprised by such a notion as modern writers appear to be.

Cook always had an open mind, and on his third voyage another settlement theory occurred to him. On Atiu he and his interpreter found a group of Tahitians who had been blown south and west by a gale when on a journey from Tahiti to Ra'iatea. This incident, he wrote, "very well accounts for the manner the inhabited islands in this Sea have been at first peopled."

The spread of many food plants across the Pacific suggests, however, that many of the voyages were deliberate colonising ventures. Some would grow from seeds or roots taken as food supplies, but others would have had to be purposefully taken and carefully tended en route. In 1934 Te Rangi Hiroa wrote that "Both the breadfruit and the banana were brought here [Mangareva], and both these plants have to be brought in living plant forms as they have no seeds.... One can understand them bringing coconut and taro, which could form part of their sea provisions.... But the bringing of young breadfruit trees and green banana shoots shows that there was the deliberate intention of settling, and not the haphazard spirit of adventure in at least some of the voyages." It seems most likely that a combination of planned and involuntary voyages carried settlers to Polynesia and, finally, to New Zealand.

In most of the Pacific, the gaps between islands are relatively short stretches of less than 500 kilometres, so by hopping from one island to another long sea crossings could often be avoided. Most of the recorded two-way routes in Polynesia were between islands less than 500 kilometres apart, although some more or less regular routes of about 800 kilometres were noted by the early European explorers. (Lewis notes that "the word 'regular' in the context of prehistoric Pacific voyaging does not exclude dallying ashore for indefinite periods, taking advantage of seasonal winds, etc.")

The exceptions were the long stretches of empty sea between the main area of eastern Polynesia and the outlying islands of Hawaii, Easter Island, and New Zealand. Hawaii is some 3500 kilometres from the Marquesas, Easter Island 2500 kilometres from the Gambier group, and New Zealand 3800 kilometres from the Societies and about 2700 from the Cooks. Yet because Polynesians usually sailed only shorter, yet still impressive, distances does not mean they were incapable of longer ones.

It had taken Cook five weeks to get to Atiu from New Zealand and he was still 1000 kilometres from Tahiti. Both wind and current were from the east, so rather than fight against them he sailed to Tonga. This illustrates one of the problems of sail, and one of the solutions. If the winds were against you, you either went somewhere else first or waited where you were until they shifted. Polynesian voyagers were often to be found temporarily settled on an island, waiting for the winds to shift (patience was a necessary virtue in the days of sail).

Cook's problems show the difficulties the discoverers of New Zealand would have had in returning to the Cooks or Tahiti. Certainly the return voyage would be more difficult than the Rarotonga-New Zealand leg, with favourable winds and currents, and a very large target. In spite of the winds and currents from the east, computer simulations of drift voyages show almost no possibility of such voyages between Eastern Polynesia and the three outliers, Hawaii, Easter Island, and New Zealand, leading us back to the idea that the discovery voyagers must have returned and given sailing directions for later settlement ventures.

## VEGETABLE IMMIGRANTS

One canoe sailed for entirely different reasons. Two brothers visited New Zealand and at a feast with Toi's descendants were given manuka fronds, fern root (bracken rhizomes) and berries. Horrified, they offered their hosts a sample of kumara, a sort of sweet potato and native of South America, and were immediately asked to return to Hawaiki and bring back a canoe load of this more palatable and convenient food (fern root had to be grubbed up, cleaned, pounded, soaked, beaten, picked over for fibre and then cooked). A canoe was built of totara and the brothers returned to Hawaiki. The tubers were brought back in another canoe, *Mataatua*.

*Horouta* also brought kumara; many canoes claim the honour of first importation. South Island traditions include the canoe *Arai-te-uru*, which was sent to Hawaiki to obtain kumara about the time of the fleet canoes, but which was unfortunately wrecked on its return off the Moeraki coast, its kumara, eel baskets and water calabashes preserved in the round boulders found on the beach.

*Mahuhu* sailed after a quarrel over plantation management, bringing several varieties of kumara as well as hue, yam, and hoia or taro. Many canoes also carried coconut and the precious aute, or paper mulberry, but neither acclimatised in New Zealand's more vigorous climate, although Cook was shown a few precious aute plants, protected for the hundreds of years since they were brought to New Zealand, "This plant must be very scarce among them as the Cloth made from it is only worn in small peices by way of ornaments at their ears and even this we have seen but very seldom."

The Polynesians did manage to establish, at least in the northern parts of the country, a gourd, a yam, a species of taro, a type of puha (an edible thistle), and the kumara. Tradition also tells us that early arrivals brought the karaka, whose berries are poisonous when raw but edible when cooked, and at least one species of ti or cabbage tree, a sort of palm with an edible root, actually a member of the lily family. *Aotea* is said to have brought the karaka, the kiore or Polynesian rat, and the pukeko or swamp hen.

Both karaka and pukeko are found in the Kermadec Islands, which could have formed a stopping place on the voyage from Rarotonga to New Zealand. The pukeko is sometimes blown to the Kermadecs, according to authorities, so could have been gathered there and returned in the *Aotea*. *Takitimu* and *Tainui* also brought karaka, probably in the form of seeds, as well as kumara, gourds and aute. Until these crops were established, and in the less hospitable parts of the country, the diet was confined to fish, shellfish, birds, berries and fern root, along with the introduced mammals, the Polynesian rat and dog.

It is possible though that the voyagers were aiming at a land which they knew was there because of the migration path of the long-tailed cuckoo. Not knowing how far away the island was would seem of small consequence to Polynesians; what they could not have guessed was that New Zealand lay some 2700 kilometres beyond Rarotonga, much further than any of the distances they had covered before.

Navigation problems begin as soon as the craft is out of sight of land. The navigator must be able to continue on the right path to the destination, in spite of the wind and ocean currents which push the craft sideways as it runs forward through the water. The first problem is one of maintaining a course or heading, the second is dealing with the factors that displace the craft from its course: current, leeway and gales.

Throughout most of the Pacific the heading is kept by reference to horizon or guiding stars, stars low in the sky, having just risen or being just about to set. During the night a succession of stars may be followed. If there is no star right over the destination then one to the side or astern may be used, or you can steer by keeping the guiding star not to the front but, say, over the port bow. If the sky is partially obscured other stars may be used by calculating the appropriate angle.

Andia y Varela, in Tahiti in 1774, was impressed by this method: "When the night is a clear one they steer by the stars... not only do they note by them the bearings on which the several islands with which they are in touch lie, but also the harbours in them, so that they make straight for the entrance by following the rhumb of the particular star that rises or sets over it; and they hit it off with as much precision as the most expert navigator of civilised nations could achieve."

Memorising hundreds of star positions and the bearings of many islands was a formidable task and one for a specialist. The navigator held a special position in island societies, and his knowledge was passed on through the generations. Banks in 1769 was impressed by the Tahitian grasp of astronomy: they knew "a very large part [of the stars] by their Names and the clever ones among them will tell in what part of the heavens they are to be seen in any month when they are above the horizon; they also know the time of their annual appearing and disappearing to a great nicety, far greater than would be easily believed by an European astronomer."

The procedure of estimating distance covered and direction travelled, taking account of leeway and current set, and then calculating position and new course, is termed dead reckoning. Its accuracy depends on the knowledge and experience of the navigator. Andrew Sharp, whose books attempted to demolish, and certainly dented, the idea that the Polynesians roamed the Pacific at will, remarked "that when errors or failures in dead reckoning occurred, the voyagers were powerless to detect or correct them." The star courses, he added, gave "no clue to longitudinal displacement...." The same is true of sun rise and set courses, as the distance is so great that the true course and the false courses, which would take the canoe to the east or west of the destination, were parallel. "These limitations" said Sharp, "apply to the traditional course from Tahiti to New Zealand, 'a little to the left of the setting sun'."

A modern sailor, David Lewis, sailed the course from the Cooks to New Zealand without instruments, by following "the normal Pacific voyaging practice of aiming a little to the eastward of our destination to be sure of arriving up-current." New Zealand provides a good target, being both long and high. The proof of the navigating is in the arriving, which Lewis did.

Even if the navigator's dead reckoning has been accurate, the problems still remain of knowing when to stop going south or north and turn east or west along the correct latitude, and which of these directions to take to reach the destination. To some extent the problem is solved if the voyagers can find a clue to the whereabouts of their destination in visible objects, such as cloud

Early European explorers were amazed to encounter huge sailing canoes far from land. In 1616 the Schouten and Le Maire expedition encountered this craft north of Tonga, out of sight of land. Many European officers considered these so-called canoes to be as fast, manoeuvrable, and seaworthy as their own vessels. *(Alexander Turnbull Library, Wellington)*

formations over land, sea birds, floating debris or wave patterns. Such clues "expand" the target, probably in a rough circle about fifty kilometres around a low-lying target.

Te Rangi Hiroa, approaching Marutea (Lord Hood's Island), observed sea birds and wrote: "Our captain told us that the Tuamotuan skippers when in doubt lay to and waited till about 4 p.m. for the homing birds to show them the direction to land.... Little doubt exists in my mind that the early Polynesian navigators made use of the direction of the flight of the birds to give them additional information as to the direction of the islands." Again both knowledge and experience are needed to make use of such clues. Birds, for example, do not all return to land in the evening, so identification of species and knowledge of their habits is needed. A large flock of birds at sea may indicate a shoal of fish rather than an island. Flotsam only indicates the direction of land if you know the direction of wind and currents. A collection of tenuous and transitory data must be collated and analysed.

Judging when to stop and look for the destination, that is, to find the right latitude, was another of the secret arts known only to the navigators. It involved the finding of the overhead or zenith star for the destination, the star that sat on top of the island. Zenith stars are not steering stars, but are used to determine latitude by deciding when they are directly overhead. Finding an island's zenith star tells you you are in the same latitude as the island. It provides no help in determining whether, or by how much, you are east or west of the island. The margin of error, as Sharp points out, is "the width of the Pacific

Ocean." Theoretically that is so, but practically you ought to be much closer than that.

Celestial observations do not help, so the only way to be sure of ending up on a known side of the destination is to steer a course that will be sure to take you to that side. Standard practice was to steer a course that would make landfall to windward and up-current on a known side, usually eastward, of the destination. When the zenith star was directly overhead, the destination would be nearby, hopefully less than eighty kilometres to the west. This method depends on accurate dead reckoning. In sailing his catamaran to New Zealand, Lewis "turned and headed toward land beneath our zenith star." After sailing 2700 kilometres from Rarotonga, the landfall was forty-two kilometres out.

Navigation without instruments is a dead reckoning system, depending on knowledge acquired by long experience. It had its limitations and no doubt its many failures. What has to be remembered is that sailing in small craft was and is a hazardous business anywhere. One hundred and fifty years ago about one thousand ships a year were wrecked on the coasts of Britain. The sinkings, broken masts, and capsizes of modern yachts in round-the-world races show that danger is a property of the ocean, not the craft.

Not all Polynesians were good navigators or even good seamen. Fishermen blown off course or young adventurers would be less likely to have a skilled navigator on board than would a deliberately mounted exploration or settlement voyage. Archaeological evidence suggests that relatively few canoes reached New Zealand, and probably fewer still returned safely to Polynesia. Nonetheless only one canoe with a trained navigator needs to have done the trip for sailing directions to have survived. And where one could go others could follow. Polynesians do not regard the sea as unfriendly. Familiarity breeds not contempt but confidence, and confidence combined with skill may take a voyager a long way.

New Zealand, Aotearoa, then, was discovered by East Polynesians in the ninth or tenth centuries A.D. Sailing in large double canoes, following traditional sailing directions or just heading south, and using traditional skills to navigate and sail their ships, they probably made landfall on the east coast of the North Island.

The crew of that very first canoe found a land large beyond their wildest dreams, much larger than all the other Polynesian islands put together, and the coastline and vast inland hills must have seemed to go on forever. Neither tradition nor memory could have prepared them for it – more than three thousand years had passed since their remote ancestors had set off from a land mass as big. It was colder than their tropical islands, too, as they had sailed far to the south of any other Polynesian island. The snow-capped uninhabitable mountains in the distance looked made for gods, and the huge forests which loomed everywhere were bound to contain many spirits, if not human enemies. It must have been overwhelming and not a little frightening. Even so, after weeks on the endless ocean, with little food and short water rations, any landfall must have seemed a gift from the gods.

CHAPTER TWO

# *Under Alien Skies*

Although exploration must come before discovery, it generally follows as well. Not many daring enough to explore and find can leave their discovery without learning as much as possible about it. This search is usually more useful than the mere fact of discovery, as the ascendancy of Cook, as opposed to Tasman, in the history and geography of New Zealand shows. Another facet of both discovery and exploration is the subsequent effort to make the facts of both known to peers or to general public and so increase knowledge. A lone survivor who lands on a deserted island and dies there with no one knowing of his fate or of his island is neither discoverer nor explorer, for he adds nothing to anyone's knowledge other than his own. Polynesians however can be satisfied that they both discovered and explored New Zealand long before either Tasman or Cook, even if their voyages were one-way, as Cook found both geographical awareness and communication networks which meant the spread of information throughout their known world.

Exploration is carried out for various reasons: a love of adventure, even of danger; curiosity or a search for knowledge, either specific or general; sometimes, like discovery, because a traveller became lost and had to explore whether he wanted to or not; a search for a new home, or a new harbour; and usually most importantly, a search for new or more plentiful resources – first those necessary for survival and then for wealth.

For the Polynesians first landing in New Zealand, like and yet unlike their island homes, exploration was an absolute necessity. The new arrivals had to discover and assess the food resources, explore the coastal area and decide on sites for settlement, find workable stone deposits and learn new techniques for working them, investigate the local woods and their uses. Landmarks had to be given names, myths had to be adapted to explain this new land and its origin. Eventually trade routes and exchange systems had to be worked out to gain access to resources not available in the area. None of this happened overnight.

First priorities for the weary and probably hungry people who staggered from the canoes after weeks at sea would be food and shelter. Fortunately the coasts of this huge and unknown land provided some resources which would be familiar to them. Others would be miraculous, the huge birds, similar to the house fowls of Polynesia which were called moa, but grown to marvellous dimensions.

The immigrants' response to the new environment was slow but sure, and remained static only for so long as was necessary to find the new resources and learn how to use them. At this point, the Polynesian culture of the newcomers began its gradual development into Maori culture, a slow process of change which took place over the whole country.

Moa reconstructed from a skeleton by Augustus Hamilton, then registrar of Otago University. He persuaded Te Rangi Hiroa (Peter Buck), left, fellow medical student Wi Repa and missionary Koroneho Hemi Papakakura to pose in Maori costume for this 1899 photograph. *(Hocken Library, Dunedin)*

As Polynesians, no doubt the pioneers turned first to the resources of the sea, which had always supplied food, and doubtless too explored the coasts before they wondered about the interior. The main areas of settlement in the South Island were the North Otago coast and the Catlins coast, usually at river mouths, and the edge of the inland basins in Central and North Otago. The west

## FOOD FROM THE SEA

Kai moana, seafood, has always been a favourite part of the Polynesian diet. In New Zealand, rights to traditional shellfishing and fishing grounds were enshrined in the Treaty of Waitangi, although they are only now beginning to be recognised. The first settlers made use of the plentiful food supplies offered by the ocean.

Shellfish were an important food source right from the beginning, important because the various species were available year round and could be gathered by women and children. They were dried for winter use. Sea birds were taken too, albatross and mollymawk, gull and shag, and little blue penguin. Banks reported later that the 18th-century diet included "Birds, especially sea fowl as penguins albatrosses &c." A lot of shellfish or shags are needed to provide the sustenance of one moa or seal.

The largest protein source were the seals, mainly fur seals, but with the occasional elephant seal or sea-lion, or even leopard seal. From the Catlins south the coastal settlers depended on seals with moa contributing a smaller proportion of meat in the diet. Sealing was reliable, as the mammals were there regardless of season, and the breeding colonies were permanent. It was also easy, too easy, as the Europeans were to find as they plundered and destroyed the resource. The early Maori seem to have exercised some caution and only taken young seals, culling in a seasonal fashion usually between December and June.

Fishing of course is another obvious resource and was important right from the start, although when the moa began to grow scarce it became a mainstay for the coastal settlers. Early artefacts show attempts to copy Polynesian fish hooks in available materials, then adaptations to types more appropriate to local fishing. Pearl shell shanks were copied in stone, bone and shell.

In the south, barracouta was the main target, taken by trolling specially crafted lure hooks of stone and moa bone behind a canoe. Red cod was the other important species, taken on moa bone rotating bait hooks. Developments in fish hook manufacture began in the South Island, not in the north. Similarities of some types to those found in Hawaii and Easter Island may be due to a common origin somewhere in Polynesia or to the common effect of new materials, the use of bone rather than shell in these outlying islands. From North Cape to the Bay of Plenty, and near Nelson, snapper was the main catch. In Cook Strait, labrids, tarakihi and red cod predominated.

All sites show many species, and huge catches, which must have been preserved for later consumption. The three seasonal camps at Purakanui Inlet in the 14th century took an estimated quarter million fish, mainly barracouta and red cod. Fish were cooked and hung from poles or racks to dry. Banks saw "vast heaps of Dryd fish" in 1769, and probably techniques had not changed very much over the centuries.

coast was not generally used, due in part to the lack of moa in the denser forests and in part to the inaccessibility of much of the coast to canoes, given the particularly rough seas. The route from Rarotonga would also mean landfalls on the east coast, with difficult access through the main mountain ranges to the west.

Most sites were bounded in front by the river, on one side by an estuary, swamp or lagoon, and on the other by the sea. While some early investigators considered this position to have been chosen so the moa could be driven into a trap, it seems to be a very useful location for people who lived on shellfish, fish and fowl, providing not only food but water, wood, and canoe access to both coast and interior. And one would hardly expect a Polynesian to live by choice out of sight of the sea.

The North Island moa-hunters also chose sites on the coast, many on the coastal sand dunes, where river mouths formed a defensive position and provided a food source. No doubt the settlers attempted to grow breadfruit, sugar cane, banana, coconut, and pandanus, important in the islands, and possibly struggled for years to establish crops which finally died out altogether. Nonetheless, some island plants did grow; kumara in particular was established and then grown widely, once the techniques of storage through the winter were refined. Some areas were only marginal for tropical crops, but exploration and experiment discovered new food resources.

The first settlers would soon have investigated the resources of the huge forests which grew almost everywhere. Birds were an obvious source of food, both the coastal sea birds and the many smaller forest birds who woke the dawn with their chorus. Birds provided not just scarce protein food, but bones for fine tools and feathers for ornamenting hair, ears, clothing, weapons and canoes.

Bird spears, snares, nooses, sticks and traps were used in fowling, as well as dogs (for the flightless species which in New Zealand filled the niches normally occupied by grazing and browsing animals). All birds were taken, from the giant moa to the small fantail and toutouwai or New Zealand robin. Many small

The earliest settlers lived along the shores and travelled inland to hunt and gather food and stone. By the early 19th century, when d'Urville anchored in Tasman Bay, many substantial settlements were inland, and only seasonal or temporary villages remained at shore sites. Note the high storage or drying platform, and the medium-sized deep-sea fishing canoes or waka tete. *(Hocken Library, Dunedin)*

birds were easily captured. Much later von Haast enjoyed the company of the robins at his 1860 camps: "I have seen one of them sit on my hand with which I held my paper when sketching ...." At the other end of the scale ways were soon found to catch the giant moa which browsed the forest verges, as such a protein source could not be ignored.

The 18th-century Maori was adept at using all available resources, and most of them seem to have been exploited from the early days of settlement. As well as birds, the forest provided edible berries, roots, leaves, pollen, and even trunks of trees and shrubs, as well as fungi and occasionally grubs and beetles.

Many forest tree fruits were used which would not usually be considered "berries" – white pine or kahikatea, black pine or matai, red pine or rimu, totara, tawa, hinau and karaka berries were all utilised. Those leaves that were edible were usually steamed and eaten as greens. In marshy areas, pollen from the raupo or bulrush was made into bread and bulrush roots could also be used.

Although early European explorers often use "baked" when referring to food preparation, the Maori oven was a steaming process, and many of the forest foods needed long slow cooking to make them even remotely palatable, and sometimes to make them safe. Karaka and tawa berry kernels needed prolonged steaming. Karaka berries are poisonous unless properly prepared and cooked. Another problem fruit was from the tutu shrub. These, properly squeezed, provided juice in which seaweed or fern root could be steeped; however the seeds in these berries are also poisonous, as Polack found. In spring the foliage is poisonous as well – it was tutu that was suspected of having killed Captain Cook's goats. Hinau berries, pounded into a meal, mixed with water and kneaded, steamed in an earth oven or umu for twelve hours, and stored underwater for up to two years, added to food supplies, especially in inland areas.

Of all the resources in this new land, the moa (and later the precious green stone called pounamu) was of major importance to these first settlers, so much so that they are generally called moa-hunters in spite of the fact that the importance of moa hunting varied greatly from place to place. This new land had a variety of climate and environment unknown in the Polynesian homelands, a diversity which was much greater than the climate differences which made horticulture easier in the north and fishing more important in the south.

Regional differences meant cultural differences, and in spite of contact through trade (obsidian from Mayor Island far to the north is found in all early sites right down to Stewart Island), and displacement of people due to marriage, war, feuds and exploration, the country developed different cultural regions, through mainly geographical factors such as geology, botany and climate.

While the earliest settlers probably remained on the coast for a time, they soon started to explore inland, possibly following the moa. Inland exploration appears to have occurred fairly quickly and thoroughly, as most of the major resources useful to the moa-hunters were used in earliest times. Later refinements and developments in food preservation and storage, stone working and flax working were based on early discoveries and experiments.

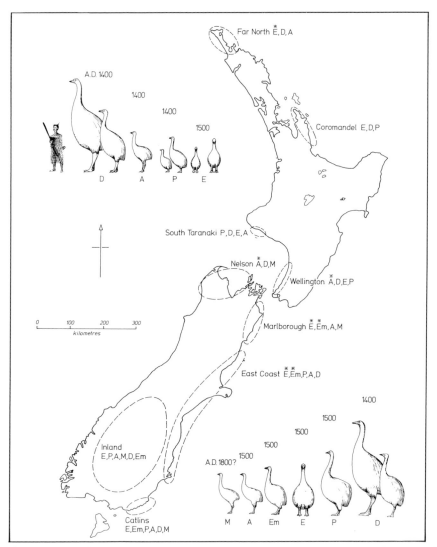

The major moa-hunting regions in New Zealand, and the various genera of moa, with their probable dates of extinction. The asterisks indicate the predominant species in particular regions. M, *Megalapteryx;* A, *Anomalopteryx;* Em, *Emeus;* E, *Euryapteryx;* P, *Pachyornis;* D, *Dinornis.* From *The Prehistory of New Zealand. (Janet Davidson and Longman Paul)*

The inland sites were more specialised, lacking the seals and sea food which added to the diet of the coasters. Butchery sites inland are huge, showing the scale of the operations, especially remembering the total population of southern New Zealand in the 13th century was something in the order of three thousand. Rows of ovens were needed to cook the huge legs. Most of the rest of the meat was discarded, as flightless birds have no breast meat. Stone-working areas are usually nearby, to make the various knives and cleavers used to dismember the birds.

Small knives were needed for skinning, as the skins were saved and used. Quartzite blades and stone knives are restricted to early South Island sites, and the techniques were probably developed there for moa processing. Such sites were not settlement sites but seasonal camps, the hunters covering the surrounding hills and returning with legs or whole carcasses. Overnight hunting trips meant camping out, often in the rock shelters of the river gorges.

By about 1200 A.D. the East Polynesian pioneers had thoroughly explored most of the country, had discovered all the resources they needed, and had adapted or invented ways to use them – food, stone, preservation and storage techniques, trade and communication routes.

In 1769 Cook noted real differences between North Island Maori and the smaller more scattered southern groups. Polynesian crops would not grow in the south, other than in a few small coastal areas, but again exploration and adaptation had discovered adequate substitutes. The southern moa-hunters were hunter-gatherers, and the population's slow growth rate in the south reflected this society. Seasonal resources were gathered and preserved, and the diet was high in protein.

The settlers soon found that their traditional crops would not grow in the south, and some not in the north either. It is widely accepted that horticulture was introduced later in the south by northern immigrants, but it seems more likely the earliest settlers at least attempted to grow the plants they had brought with them, and probably succeeded in a few sheltered areas. Later on, kumara, generally thought of as a northern crop, was cultivated in Canterbury and grown extensively in the extreme north of the South Island.

This horticultural food base was replaced by hunting – birds, including sea birds, seals, and especially the moa. Life in most parts of the country was generally at subsistence level. From middens it has been established that the first New Zealanders ate pretty well everything they could catch, and bones of tuatara, seal, dog, rat, some thirty species of bird, including at least six or seven species of moa, the extinct swan and eagle, a giant rail, weka, and kaka, and many fish varieties have been found, as well as shells from many species of shellfish.

Most areas had no cultivated food source although recent work in parts of the North Island suggests at least some groups practised horticulture very early on. The only domesticated animal was the Polynesian dog, which had come with them, a bonus in a protein-poor country, and any pigs or chickens brought from Polynesia must have died on the way or been eaten before they could become established.

It is likely the early settlers tried at first to live life in this huge land the way they had done on their islands, where food grew and was harvested all year round. But in New Zealand there were definite seasons, with winter a time of want which had to be provided for.

Only a few resources were available all year and right from the beginning preservation of food resources was essential, not just in the colder areas but in the horticultural areas to the north. New horticultural techniques had to be learned before kumara could be grown successfully even in the far north, digging the tubers up before the first frosts; storage techniques had to be developed to keep the tubers through the winter. Various storage pits and storehouses, as well as drying racks and platforms were seen in 1769, and must have existed in some form quite early on, or the kumara would not have survived.

31

Fern root, fish and shellfish were fairly easily dried for future use, but birds required new methods. Preserving meat in fat in kelp bags meant it could be kept for a year or more; it could also be used as gifts in the reciprocal giving which developed into trade. Eels were preserved in fat in kelp bladders and birds were boned, cooked in bark with red-hot stones, and preserved in their own fat in rimu bags. Brunner said, "I have tasted birds kept two years in this manner, and found them very good."

## WHEN MOAS STRODE THE LAND

There were at least eight species of moa in southern New Zealand, the largest much taller than and twice the weight of a heavy man. At first it was assumed that the moa browsed on open grasslands but geographical research and study of the gizzard contents preserved among the moa bones in swamps have proved that they were inhabitants of shrubland and forest, and browsed on twigs and leaves. Much of the southern region was forested well into man's time. Even in Central Otago the lower hill slopes were forested, and there were large moa hunting sites in areas which are still clad with the remains of once extensive forests such as the Catlins.

It is doubtful that the fires which wiped out much of the forest were set to trap moa, as while this might be feasible in tussock country, where moas were once thought to browse, it would be an obvious problem in forested areas. It is also now known that the moa were likely competent swimmers, so the idea of the river mouth sites being traps for catching moas seems unlikely, although it is possible they were driven into water and clubbed from canoes.

It seems more likely they were trapped in some way, possibly in pits, or snared, as the Maori were doing with great success in historical time to wekas and other birds. It is also possible that the Polynesian dogs brought to New Zealand in the canoes were bred for hunting, as the skulls suggest a more powerful jaw and neck muscles than were usual in Polynesia. They could have been used to find and distract the quarry, just as pig dogs are today.

In whatever way moa were caught, caught they were, and in huge numbers. Up to half a million moas were killed and eaten in early southern New Zealand. Moa-hunter camps of several acres are covered in bones of birds which were killed and eaten or killed and butchered for preservation. For several hundred years they formed the main diet of people in what are now South Canterbury and Otago, and were important in the diet of Southlanders as well.

The earliest settlers roamed the interior looking for moa and various stones, as well as hunting along the coast. The huge butchery at the mouth of the Waitaki River had hundreds of moa ovens but few houses, suggesting it too was a seasonal base, probably for cooking and preserving moa brought down the river on canoes or mokihi, the flax or reed rafts. The hunters made short trips up river into the forested areas of north Otago for the summer "round-up", staying overnight in rock shelters, the more artistic whiling away time by drawing on the smooth white walls with charcoal or red ochre brought along especially for the purpose. Most of the drawings in the South Island were made in moa-hunter times, as the bones of bush-dwelling birds found in the shelters suggest the surrounding country was still forested. The shelters are not moa hunter sites but more likely single night shelters for storm-bound hunters or travellers.

Elsdon Best noted: "Comestibles so preserved are termed huahua and so huahua manu denotes birds preserved in fat, and huahua kiore the native rat so preserved, while huahua tangata denotes human flesh so cooked and potted for future use. This latter food-supply was highly appreciated, and raiding parties were wont to rely on it to a considerable extent when in enemy country ...." Although there is no doubt human flesh formed part of the diet of the 18th-century Maori, it was almost certainly a small, probably a very small, proportion.

Evidence for cannibalism is not restricted to later sites, and the practice was possibly introduced by the first settlers, as it existed in other parts of Polynesia. It was probably more common in later times, when warfare expanded, and in the south rather than the north. Banks wrote that "They however as universally agree that they eat none but the bodies of those of their Enimies who are killed in War, all others are buried."

Preservation of bush birds and the delicacy muttonbirds (sooty shearwaters) began very early and although there is evidence of trade the main development of large-scale muttonbirding is probably post-Pakeha, as whaleboats meant muttonbirds from the offshore islands in the far south were caught and preserved in the autumn for exchange as far north as Taranaki. Eels too appear to have formed an important part of later diets rather than earlier, though some bones have been found in early sites.

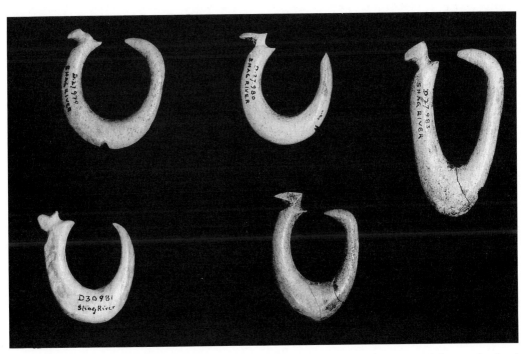

Unbarbed one-piece bait-hooks in moa bone from Shag River on the east coast of the South Island. This type of fish hook is found in early sites, and was probably an adaptation in bone of pearl shell prototypes from East Polynesia. The circular hook responded to movement of fish or line, rotating the hook to force it further into the jaw of the fish. This early innovation meant set lines could be used. *(Otago Museum, Dunedin)*

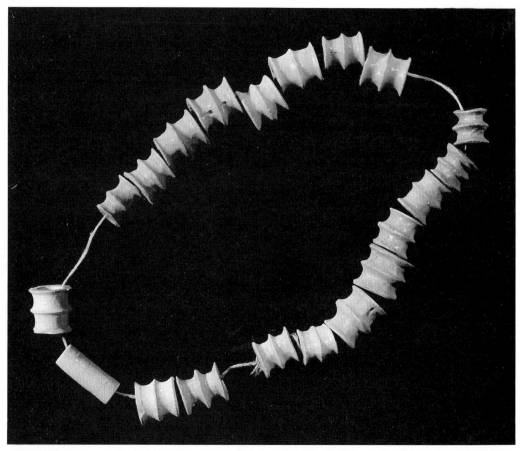

Moa-hunter bone "reel" necklace from Curio Bay, Southland. Necklaces of reels and/or whale teeth (real or carved) were early ornament forms, a fashion brought from East Polynesia, which later gave way to pendants. Most reels were of moa bone, but human bone, dog bone, fossil shell, ivory, stone and the bones of an extinct swan were all used. *(Otago Museum, Dunedin)*

Preservation meant seasonal resources could be gathered when most plentiful and most nutritious: "The natives here preserve the birds they catch during the winter months, when they are in excellent condition ...." Forster, on Cook's second voyage, noted, "they have prudence enough to provide in the proper season stores of all kinds; when they catch more fish than they can eat, they carefully dry, and lay them up; their women go frequently up the hills, which are covered to an immense extent with fern, and dig up the roots, which they likewise dry, and preserve as a food .... We saw great quantities of these provisions in their huts, and frequently found them employed in preparing both fish and fern-roots for the bad season."

After the initial exploration and learning period, life in the south carried on for four hundred years or so and then the resources on which this life was based, the moa and the seal, began to grow scarce. The larger species of both were rare by the 14th century. Evidence from site deposits show fewer birds, of fewer species. The native swan, flightless goose, eagle, goshawk, coot, crow, and a duck were all extinct or very rare, but the moa-hunters could have lived without them. It was the decline and disappearance of the moa which led to vast changes in their way of life.

It is possible the moa was on the way to extinction before man arrived in New Zealand, and the moa-hunters only accelerated the process. Hunting was no doubt a major cause of the decline, as the birds were probably not as abundant as it appeared. Moa appear to have been slow breeders, with only one or two eggs per clutch, and the eggs were hunted as assiduously as the birds. The eggs were not only food but containers. Empty moa shells with a carefully drilled hole in one end have been found at early sites, possibly used for storing water.

But hunting was not the only problem. By this time the forests had begun to retreat. When the first Polynesian settlers arrived almost all of southern New Zealand below 1000-1200 metres was forested, except the dry basins in Central Otago and the Mackenzie country. In the 15th century temperatures dropped slightly, but even a small change would be enough to affect marginal horticultural areas and possibly to influence regeneration rates in the forests. However, the main destructive mechanism appears to have been fire.

Natural fires had occurred before the Polynesians arrived, usually caused by lightning, and lignites may have burned for some time, but evidence now shows that most of the burning occurred between the 13th and 16th centuries, well into the moa-hunter period. Tradition blames the Waitaha, who were possibly trying to create more shrubby fringe areas for moa. Yet there was plenty of burning in the north too, although there the faster regeneration rate made it less obvious. Hawke's Bay pollen studies suggest human fires were having a detectable effect soon after 900 A.D., and by the 1840s much of central Hawke's Bay had been cleared.

Deliberate clearance for kumara and for bracken fern nibbled away at the northern forests, and in the south no doubt much forest was burned for the same reason before it was clear traditional crops would not grow. Clearing areas around the settlements would also encourage the fern, whose edible roots were important.

However archaeologists and historians, in trying to find sensible reasons for such happenings, sometimes forget they are dealing with people, with human quirks. Fire has always fascinated humans, and as prehistorian Janet Davidson points out, the sheer delight of a big burn-off may have been reason enough. The reverent approach to the forest often attributed to all Maori was not as highly developed in these horticultural areas. Much of our knowledge of this attitude comes from Elsdon Best who lived with the Tuhoe in the Urewera country, a non-horticultural area. The forest was all-important here, and rituals and tapu protected it and thus the resources. Whether purposeful or accidental, there is no doubt much of the forest was burnt off during the moa-hunter occupation, and that this contributed to the eventual extinction of the moa.

As numbers dwindled the inland hunting areas were abandoned and attention and foraging were concentrated on the coast. The percentage of food provided by fishing jumped dramatically, supplemented by coastal birds, and especially fern root and ti or cabbage tree stem and taproot. Only specialist camps were set up in the interior, some still for moa-hunting, others at quarries, and one at Dart Bridge for ti cooking and greenstone working.

Interior of an 18th century fortified village, deserted for some time when de Sainson drew it in 1827. The sleeping-houses are rectangular, thatched, and low, with a small opening ("scarce equal to a European dog kennel and resembling one in the door at least", wrote Cook), both to preserve warmth and prevent wind damage. The round-roofed version (like the top of a covered wagon, thought Nicholas in 1814) is possibly of Polynesian ancestry. Excavations of 12th century settlements suggest house designs had changed little. The high racks were for drying or storing food and the triangular buildings in the background are the roofs of kumara storage pits. *(Hocken Library, Dunedin)*

In the north too, the pattern of life was changing. One Lake Taupo site, occupied probably during the 14th century, shows three species of moa were hunted, as well as forest birds, and shows too a steady decline in bird species, probably reflecting destruction of surrounding forest. Even coastal areas suffered as coastal forest dwindled and hunting trips had to be made further inland. In some parts of the North Island, fish and shellfish appear to have totally replaced birds as protein food. Settlement patterns suggest a winter base where provisions were stored and a summer camp or camps where seasonal resources were gathered.

From about the end of the 15th century the wear on teeth caused by constant chewing of fibrous and gritty foods shows a marked increase, although there are regional and chronological variations. The early prehistoric period shows slight wear on teeth, especially the incisors, suggesting a diet including a considerable amount of meat. As both moa and seal diminished, the diet grew less varied, and included more shellfish, which are gritty, especially when dried, and fern root, which demanded considerable chewing even after beating, as it was tough and fibrous – both wore the teeth down rapidly. This extreme wear was widespread throughout the country, including the kumara-growing areas of the north.

Where horticulture could not replace the dwindling resources, sites were eventually abandoned. In favourable areas, horticulture started early and developed rapidly, possibly in part due to the arrivals of new immigrants. New arrivals did not create a new culture but accelerated the rate of change, as well as the rate of population increase. Soon tribal warfare was ending one era and creating the lifestyle Cook found in 1769. Later sites include greenstone ornaments, and show that dogs. seals, and men were the mammals eaten. Human bone was used for fish hook points and other small artefacts. By the late 18th century the population had grown to about 125,000, concentrated on coasts of the northern half of the North Island. This society, based on horticulture, dwindling sources of meat and on fishing required extensive exploration to find the best land, and the best sources of seals and fish. As exploration proceeded the network of trails grew, and warriors used them as well as hunters, farmers or traders.

As resources became scarce, trade increased in importance. The exchange of goods had existed from the earliest period, as is known from the types of stone found in early camps, and in the late period centred on muttonbirds and greenstone. South came obsidian, preserved eels, and, especially pre-19th century, kits of kumara. A wide variety of food items were exchanged, between coast and inland groups as well as north and south – preserved fish, birds, rats, seaweed, fern root, berries and kumara. Shells, feathers, shark oil, moa bones and oven stones also travelled long distances.

Goods were carried by canoe or on foot over mainly coastal trails, with the exception of the pounamu trails over the Alps, and usually only into the next district, so that the system involved many reciprocal exchanges on its way north. Routes included both east and west coasts, as well as cross-country via waterways and alpine passes. Whaleboats eventually replaced both the coastal trails and canoes.

Warfare does not seem to have disrupted the exchange of goods; the distribution of greenstone throughout the North Island went on through the height of pa warfare. The archaeological evidence of communication networks is usually limited to stone, but Cook noted how word quickly spread: "They were no sooner on board than they asked for nails, but when nails were given them they asked Tupia what they were which was plain that they had never seen any before .... [This] proves that their connections must extend as far North as Cape Kidnapper ...." In various parts of New Zealand on his second voyage Cook found complete strangers asking for Tupaia, whose name was "known over great part of New Zealand ... as familiar to those who never saw him as to those who did."

The first explorers were interested in food, water and stone. Stone was one of the most important resources, and very soon after arrival the first settlers would have been exploring to find the deposits of stone needed to make the tools which created shelter, canoes and crops. Most of the important stone resources had been discovered by the 12th century, and possibly earlier. The 12th-century site at Palliser Bay had obsidian from the Coromandel Peninsula and Mayor Island, argillite, schist, talc and serpentine from across Cook Strait, limestone and greywacke from further north, nephrite from Arahura, and silcrete from Central Otago. The geographical knowledge of the early settlers was extensive and so was their trading network.

Most of the stone tools were created by flaking, that is, striking the core with a hammerstone and flaking bits off in a controlled fashion to produce the desired shape. Knives were usually made of quartzite, and adzes of basalts and argillites. A wide variety of adzes were made in the early days, probably related to ship-building, some for dubbing out and some for planing planks, others for a variety of woodwork skills. In a large country with many resources the sea became less important, and canoes useful for inland waterways were all that was needed. As the canoes grew smaller and simpler the various adze types were no longer required and were simply not made any more.

Exploration took the early settlers further afield and new stone deposits were found. The new stones and new stone-working techniques were as likely to

## A   N E W   C U L T U R E   D E V E L O P S

The rise of pa warfare and the decline in moa hunting took place over the same period. It did not happen because, as is sometimes said, the newly mobile tribes of the north went south and destroyed the moa-hunter society, but because after hundreds of years spent adapting Polynesian skills to the new and harsher environment the culture had changed. The Maori had explored most of the resources their new land had to offer; had developed horticulture, along with storage methods for the produce, especially but not exclusively in the north; and had established communication routes by which ideas as well as objects could be traded. The societies were ready to expand their population, their territory, their ideas.

As population grew rapidly, the environment began to suffer, and the old settlement areas could not feed the larger numbers. In the north, where both population and population growth were highest, people moved into the unsettled hinterland, and, as competition for land grew, began to defend their holdings; competition increased and with it a sense of tribal identity, bolstered by an increase in the importance of ritual and beliefs about tapu. In the south, the Maori oversaw the decline and the extinction of the moa, as well as several other hunted species of bird. The southern Maori remained more mobile than the northern, living in smaller groups, and had probably explored more of their territory than had the more settled tribes to the north. Nomads though they were, they did not wander aimlessly but searched out seasonal food supplies and made use of their limited resources.

The pa fortifications of the north never developed in the south, partly because in the south there were no kumara plantations to protect, partly because the small groups could not do the necessary work, partly because in a large area with a very small population it is easier to retreat than to defend. Even in later days the warfare pattern in the south tended more toward mobile raiding than siege warfare, although some fortifications were built, generally more rudimentary than their northern counterparts. Their introduction, and that of some weapons and ornaments, was due to the invasions of northerners; most "classic" artefacts and culture had evolved in the south just as in the north.

There is growing evidence that the earliest settlers practised horticulture, especially in the more favourable areas, and therefore horticulture was not part of the later so-called classic Maori culture but as one would expect was brought from the islands with the first canoes. Even today new excavations are apparently suggesting much earlier dates for pa building than generally assumed, another example of the more gradual development of the Maori culture. The division of New Zealand prehistory into "archaic" and "classic" periods is an oversimplification of a gradual process of change and development which took place over the whole country, although change was no doubt more rapid in the north where the larger population and better climate for horticulture meant time and energy for the development of new ideas.

affect development as the function of the completed tool. Regional variations in techniques soon appeared, complicated by the early exchange of stone resources throughout the country. Basalt from the Coromandel Peninsula and argillites from Nelson and Southland quarries were widely distributed.

Softer stones could be sawed, filed and drilled and were used for fish lures and ornaments. Ornaments of various sorts were used in New Zealand from earliest times. Many early types were possibly replaced by greenstone ornaments, almost all manufactured in the South Island. Tattooing, widespread by 1769, was probably introduced by the first settlers; bone needles used for tattooing occur in early sites. The moa-hunters used bone for small artefacts which had traditionally been made of teeth or shell, but at first they retained the traditional shapes and designs. As exploration proceeded, the greater variety of stone led to a wider range of both tools and ornaments.

Many stones would be tested by the early Maori to see if they could be worked and if they would be strong enough or hold an edge. It is not certain how long it was before the first settlers had time and energy enough to explore right round to the west coast. The explorers who found greenstone on the beaches had discovered a stone unequalled for toughness and which could be sharpened. From the beaches they moved to the rivers that had carried the stone seawards, looking for the source.

These explorers had come by canoe in early times, when the sea-going canoes were still used. The very early settlers who stayed on the west coast worked greenstone, and a trade soon developed which left these greenstones in Maori camps from north of Auckland to Stewart Island. Obsidian, a glassy volcanic rock, was also distributed all over the country, and apparently much earlier, as flakes are common in the earliest camps, where greenstone of either type is rare.

Obsidian came from several sources, but the major supply was from Mayor Island in the Bay of Plenty, on the east coast of the North Island. Mayor Island obsidian is found in almost all sites, including the south of the South Island. Obsidian artefacts are of particular interest to archaeologists as their age can be determined by their curious property of absorbing water at given rates from freshly exposed surfaces. Tools of obsidian were used throughout the prehistoric period but such use died out during the 19th century.

The most valued commodity from the south was of course pounamu – greenstone, nephrite or jade. This useful and beautiful stone was unique to New Zealand in Polynesia, and contributed to some of the divergences from traditional forms of tools and ornaments. It was a gift of the gods, and had spiritual as well as material value, bringing not just wealth but mana to the tribe.

The first settlers must have brought Polynesian rituals and beliefs with them, as well as the concepts of tapu (restricted or forbidden), noa (ordinary, not tapu), and mana (prestige, power, honour), as these concepts existed in the 18th century and were still remarkably similar to those in other Polynesian islands, at least to the casual observer. Cook wrote in 1770 that "They have the same notions of the Creation of the World Mankind &c[a] as the People of the South Sea Islands have …."

No doubt ideas and rituals developed over the centuries, and it is dangerous to assume that the beliefs collected by Europeans in the 19th and early 20th centuries existed in the ninth. Excavations have shown that attitudes to death and burial changed over the centuries, but that some rituals associated with tapu were well established by about 1500, and as they are similar to practices in other parts of Polynesia presumably arrived with the earliest canoes. Ritual is less important to a small struggling group in a large land, and probably developed and increased along with the population. At least some tapu restrictions were essentially laws to conserve and protect resources.

The importance of nephrite to the Maori is translated in the traditional tales by assigning it a supernatural origin, and having it discovered by one of the first Polynesians to discover and explore New Zealand. Ngahue took his greenstone back to Hawaiki, where it was made into two adzes, hei tiki (pendants in the form of a stylised human figure), and ear ornaments. The mention of hei tiki shows the addition of later culture to a legend of the earliest times.

Almost certainly the earliest uses of greenstone were as cutting tools, not ornaments, but offcuts of the beautiful stone were possibly used as neck and ear pendants in very early times. Greenstone pendants dating to about 1500 were found at Shag Point on the South Island's east coast, where a large amount of greenstone finishing was done. The relative scarcity of greenstone artefacts in excavations probably reflects not so much the rarity as the value. Greenstone was highly valued for tools due to its extreme hardness and the subsequent difficulty of manufacture. Because it was greatly prized, and thus scarce, and also because it is extremely beautiful and long-lasting, it was used for ornaments which became family or tribal heirlooms.

Greenstone weapons too were treasured. Brunner noted that "the natives attach a great value to their greenstone meris, or battleaxes of former times, so

Moa butchery knives and cleavers from  Shag River Otago, c.12th century. These blades are of silcrete or quartzite, and were "struck" from a large core and then shaped by flaking. Such tools were made only in the southern South Island, and are found in the earliest sites. *(Otago Museum, Dunedin)*

much so, that they are buried with their owners. After remaining in the ground some five or six years they are dug up, and given to the nearest relative of the deceased. The natives have also safe hiding places for them, in order that, if surprised and conquered, as in former times, their enemies may not find them among their spoil."

In the North Island a greenstone cult developed, as the scarcity of the stone enhanced its intrinsic qualities. Someone thought of carving the stone into the tiki of wood carving, and the hei tiki spread throughout the island, probably reaching the south with the Ngai Tahu in the first few years of the 17th century. Although early European explorers described hei tiki in various parts of the country, they were relatively rare until overseas explorers and traders took an interest; then many greenstone adzes, made redundant by the European axes, were reworked into hei tiki for sale to Europeans; the Maori were never slow to see an economic possibility.

Among the interesting results of the trade in greenstone was the development in the iron-hard stone of fine chisels for carving wood, and the resulting increasing complexity of the wood carvings. The intricate ornamentation of even everyday objects like fish hooks in the Maori era was in part related to improved tools and probably to increased time for non-essential tasks due to a larger population and a more settled and organised way of life. The adzes made from Ngahue's precious stone shaped some of the fleet canoes, and were brought back to New Zealand with the fleet. Some greenstone adzes and ornaments have been found in Polynesia, but there is no reason to believe they were taken there by prehistoric voyagers. More likely Maori seamen on the whaling ships took them as trade goods.

Moa-hunter tanged adzes (Waimate, Shag Valley). The earliest adzes were usually tanged to make it easier to lash the completed adze to its handle, and either rectangular in cross-section, with a broad straight cutting edge, or triangular in section (hog-backed) with a narrow blade. The broad straight blades were best for adzing planks, and the hog-backed adzes useful for working in confined spaces, as when hollowing out a canoe hull. (*Otago Museum, Dunedin*)

Two beautiful pounamu (greenstone) hei matau, pendants in the shape of fishhooks, from the far south and the east coast of the South Island. They were a predominantly southern form of ornament. Now thought to represent the fishhook with which Maui fished up the North Island, they were probably in their early days an attempt to render in the treasured stone the familiar shape of the early southern one-piece bait-hook. Southern tradition says they were worn as a fishing amulet. *(Otago Museum, Dunedin)*

Nephrite is found only in the South Island. The Arahura River was the main source for the Maori and the source named in ancient traditions. Its tributaries also contain large boulders but probably only occasional expeditions were made to the more inaccessible areas. The second great source in the early days was the Wakatipu field, which the Maori were exploiting by about 1500. Both sources were well known.

In 1793 Tukitahua, a Maori chief from the extreme north who had been captured and taken to Norfolk Island to show prisoners how to work flax (unfortunately for the British the chief knew little of women's work), drew a map to show Governor King where he should be returned. Although he had never been to the south he appears to have had some knowledge of greenstone sources as a western river, probably the Arahura, has "Pounammao" beside it,

and further south a lake "where Stone for Hatchets are got" (probably Wakatipu).

In 1844 Edward Shortland, sometime Protector of Aborigines in New Zealand, wrote that "Huruhuru's leisure in the evenings was employed by giving me information about the interior of this part of the island, with which he was well acquainted. He drew, with a pencil, the outline of four lakes, by his account situated nine days' journey inland of us and only two from the west coast .... One of these, named Wakatipua, is celebrated for the 'pounamu' found." Charles Heaphy noted in 1846 that even "the natives from Arahura make excursions to obtain a peculiar kind of greenstone from near Wakatipu". Captain Cook too had noted this field but its existence later came into question until it was rediscovered in the 1930s.

The Routeburn River was an important source of pounamu although it is only semi-nephrite. Semi-nephrite was also reported on D'Urville Island. From Anita Bay in Milford Sound comes the beautiful tangiwai greenstone, actually softer bowenite, more easily worked into intricate hei tiki and ornaments.

Local historian Herries Beattie recorded that Maori from Murihiku (Southland) went by canoe around the south-west of the island or overland from Lake Te Anau to Anita Bay for takiwai, the southern dialect form of tangiwai. One such trip ended in tragedy in the 1820s when sealers shot chief Hupokeka and his party. Apparently the sealers were unable to distinguish the Southland Maori from a Westland tribe, with whom there had been trouble.

Captain Cook was impressed with the green "talc", and in 1770 noted the trade in greenstone which was well established by this time. "Notwithstanding the divided and jealous state in which they live, traveling strangers who come with no ill design are well received and entertained during their stay, which is expected to be no longer than the business they come upon can be transacted. Thus it is that a trade for Poenammoo, or green talc is carried on throughout the whole Northern island ...." Greenstone was not used as money, but was a trade good in its own right, and was the basis of a quite complicated exchange system, generally involving foodstuffs.

Most of the conflict that arose in the greenstone areas was caused by a desire to control the lucrative greenstone sources, trails and trade. Even in the age of iron Te Rauparaha tried to take over the greenstone trade by invading and defeating the Poutini Ngai Tahu in the 1830s. The Taranaki invaders amalgamated with the Poutini tribes and began to work nephrite on a grand scale.

Although the first Maori almost certainly came by sea, by the 1840s there were "no canoes large enough to proceed to sea" and travel was either along the coast or through the mountains. Surveyor Charles Heaphy noted that he had reached "the veritable greenstone country" and that "fragments of greenstone – odd knobs, and rejected cross-grained pieces – were lying about the houses, and down towards the beach, in a way that would have made a ngapuhe crazy ...." (The Ngapuhi were a Northland tribe.)

Early traditions tell of sea voyages down to the west coast for greenstone, and in the early days of its discovery this was probably the usual method. The great seagoing canoes were still in use and could face even the west coast waters. The arduous voyage would only add to its value. There has been some speculation that the climatic changes may have caused the downturn in sea voyaging, as a general increase in storminess would affect coastal transport and offshore fishing and eventually canoe building. As building decreased, skills were lost, and by the time the weather had improved again there would have been no seagoing canoes or builders available.

Archaeological evidence suggests the earliest coasters used greenstone, worked by hammering and flaking. Techniques improved in time and as new tribes moved into the area. With a larger population land trails were discovered and new trade routes set up which avoided the dangerous seas of the west coast. The routes either followed the coast, as Heaphy had done, although carrying huge loads of heavy stone up and down the cliff ladders must have been a problem, or went inland over the alpine passes to Canterbury and Otago.

In at least one fortunate instance the route followed the inland connecting river systems almost direct from the coast to Nelson. A piece of partially worked greenstone was unearthed at the junction of the Buller and the Inangahua, along with ovens and middens. Either a piece had been taken on a

A GREENSTONE AGE

The extreme hardness of the greenstone meant it made superb tools but also made it very difficult to work. No doubt many techniques were tried over the years until a successful method was devised. In the 1840s Heaphy explored the Poutini coast and saw greenstone being worked by traditional methods. "The 'Ara Hura' natives lay in a large stock of thin pieces of sharp quartzose slate, with the edge of which, worked saw fashion, and with plenty of water, they contrive to cut a furrow in the stone, first on one side and then on the other, until the piece may be broken at the thin place. The fragments that come off are again sawn by children and women into ear pendants. With pretty constant work – that is, when not talking, eating, doing nothing and sleeping – a man will get a slab into a rough triangular shape and about an inch and a half thick in a month, and with the aid of some blocks of sharp sandy gritted limestone will work down the faces and edges of it into proper shape in six weeks or more …. A native will get up at night to have a polish at a favourite meri, or take one down to the beach and work away by the surf. A piece of greenstone and some slate will be carried when travelling, and at every halt a rub will be taken at it."

Some greenstone factories show that in places greenstone was worked using flaking and hammer-dressing techniques, rather than cutting. Hammering out the rough blank quickly meant grinding and polishing could begin much sooner. Hammering was faster but riskier, as the stone could shatter or break in the wrong place, and more was wasted. On the West Coast where supply was not a problem this more brutal approach was acceptable.

Early sites in both islands yielded greenstone adzes or chisels; while greenstone tools were apparently common in the south, to the northerners they were a luxury item, to be treasured and passed on, which may in small part account for their rarity in excavations. Shortland felt that a greenstone mere was "as great a treasure as any of the most precious stones are to us. It is thought worthy to be distinguished by a name, as was King Arthur's sword, and is handed down, as heirloom, from father to son." It is likely that in the 18th century every able-bodied male in the South Island owned at least one greenstone adze, and that additional adzes were being produced for trade to the north.

Recent research has suggested some adzes were made in the slightly softer and more easily worked semi-nephrites and then heat treated to harden them. When Heaphy reached the coast cutting was the preferred technique, with the groove kept wet and sand added for abrasion. The most difficult part of the mere was the thong hole in the handle, which was drilled with flint-tipped rotary drills. Adzes, chisels and gouges for woodwork needed different shapes but the same technique. Once shaped they were superb cutting tools. The advent and proliferation of greenstone tools was one reason for the increase in carved decoration, as well as the development of the high timber palisades of the pa. Precision-cut greenstone was a major technological advance.

food-gathering expedition to be worked at in the evenings, as Heaphy had suggested, or it was being worked en route to Nelson for trade to the north. In 1857 Leonard Harper, exploring routes from the east across the mountains to the west coast, noted that the Maori bartered greenstone for supplies, such as blankets, by taking the stone north to Nelson.

Greenstone went north to Cook Strait and then across the water to become a commodity in the complicated trade patterns of the more heavily populated and more organised North Island tribes. Coastal products such as dried fish and seaweed were exchanged for forest harvests of berries and preserved rats and birds. In the north the large river systems formed the main routes, and obsidian and greenstone, worked and unworked, became part of the network.

Greenstone pieces, worked or unworked, were also taken across the Alps to the east coasters. In his travels about the interior the Maori had eventually discovered the high alpine passes which connect the west coast with the central plains of the island. All the major passes were used by the Maori – Lindis, Haast, Mackinnon, Whitcombe, Mathias, Browning's (one of the main invasion routes as well as a greenstone trail), Arthur's, Harper and Lewis. The high passes could only be undertaken in summer, and even then special clothing was needed. No doubt sudden snowstorms caused tragedies. The mountains are no easy road, even with woollen clothes and sleeping bags; flax cloaks and sandals must have offered meagre protection at times.

Several European travellers described the clothing worn on the high trails. Roberts, a surveyor, noted the sandals "made of plaited flax, or of ti [*Cordyline australis*], or of mountain grass. The time they lasted depended on the materials used, the care taken in manufacture, and the nature of the country traversed. The number of pairs of sandals they carried varied – some took five, some twelve, some twenty. Wherever they stopped they made more, using whatever material was handiest. The best ones were made of dry ti leaves, and if double, would last for five or six days on fair ground. In swampy country they would last for three or four days. Mountain flax on stones would not hold out for more than half a day." In 1844 Huruhuru made Edward Shortland a pair of the double-soled sandals: "They no doubt owed their invention to the necessity of protecting the feet from the snow ...."

In the high passes Roberts said they "also wore socks or leggings made of different materials ... plaited ...." Heaphy considered the flax work of the Poutini Maori the finest in the country. The finely woven flax could look like linen, and was used for a variety of clothing worn under the thatch-like rain capes. Weka and dog skins made garments, and possibly the moa skin was used too in earlier times. All these materials were time-consuming to produce so it is not surprising that the Maori adopted European garments with alacrity. Thick plaited ropes, immensely strong, would also be an essential item on alpine trips.

Apart from extra clothing the alpine passes would require better shelter at night than coastal trips. On the Waitaki River section of one route, natural caves or rock shelters were used for more than wall surfaces for drawings. However in the passes warm and waterproof shelters would need to be constructed every travelling day, and in spite of practice and expertise such jobs took time.

Captain Cook saw Maori shelter-building in Queen Charlotte Sound in 1777: "It is curious to see with what facility they build these little temporary habitations: I have seen above twenty of them errected on a spot of ground that not an hour before was covered with shrubs & plants. They generally bring some part of the Materials with them, the rest they find on the spot." Brailsford, a modern writer on the trails, suggests it is possible the Maori carried key building staves with them on the alpine passes, using them as walking sticks, river crossing poles, and the basis for shelters without having to cut new poles with stone adzes each night.

Eighteenth century Maori drawn by Parkinson, artist with Cook in 1769. The greenstone kuru (straight ear pendant) was an ornament form dating back to about 1500 but the origins of the whale tooth pendant (rei puta) can be traced back to East Polynesia; the addition of eyes to this rei puta may be a Maori feature. Rei puta were worn by the moa-hunters, often in combination with reels and it is possible that the treasured Sperm whale tooth had been worn by moa-hunting ancestors. *(Hocken Library, Dunedin)*

Fire for warmth and light was necessary and the Maori could produce fire quickly with a fire plough of wood which was rubbed along a groove in another piece of wood until enough heat was produced to set fluffy beaten flax fibre alight. Torches of bark and flax with fat-saturated grass or of a special fungus were used for light. Fire, or at least smoke, also helped drive off the dreaded sandfly.

The time spent in performing all the essential tasks – hunting and gathering food, building shelter, gathering wood and making fire and preparing and cooking food, making new sandals – added hours to the daily task of mere walking, so that only five or six hours a day, and only in reasonable weather, could actually be spent travelling. The average daily distance covered seems to have been about seventeen kilometres; European explorers often did not do as well. War parties could move at least three times as fast as family groups.

The heavy loads of finished artefacts, unworked slabs (generally about twenty centimetres across, cut to make them manageable), and food were placed in flax kawe or packs, "two long flat bands of plaited flax, the ends of which, dressed and narrowed down, were connected or joined together with a flat band about ten inches [25 cm] in length. In packing the load, the kawe was laid flat on the ground and the load placed parallel with the broad band; the four long ends were then brought together and tied, leaving room for a man's arms to pass through the straps … carrying the load like a knapsack." Engineer Dobson also noted "Very heavy loads, up to 200 lbs [90 kg], were carried in this fashion."

Surveyor Roberts considered the parties were small, usually only five or six, and included men, women, and children. "The chief would carry nothing more than his weapons. His mat and food would be carried by slaves. Each free man carried his weapons, a load of food, and generally two or three mats. The women carried loads." Most accounts suggest that slaves or women carried most of the heavy trade goods, but slavery appears to have been a relatively late addition to Maori life, only expanding when the introduction of potatoes and the demand for flax in return for muskets and powder created a new need for a large labour force, just as war with those same muskets, and the new infectious diseases, were depleting the population. In the early days it is assumed most captives would be killed, if not eaten, and the heavy loads would be carried by all able-bodied members of the group.

Generally the trails involved as much canoe travel as possible, this being not just easier, in spite of portages, but faster. In 1847 Brunner and his party took six weeks to walk from Inangahua Junction to the coast down the Kawatiri (Buller) River. A Maori canoe party made the trip in six hours. Not using water craft was a mistake which cost dog Rover his life. Rochfort in 1859 surveyed the Buller by canoe, building scaffolding to haul the canoe over the precipitous gorge banks, and covered in three weeks the area that Brunner had faced for thirteen.

Where land trails were needed they followed river valleys or proceeded along the ridges of high land. Generally the land trails led from one waterway to the next, the greenstone trails of the south island generally go up river, across the Alps through one of several passes, then down the river systems to the West Coast.

MAORI EXPLORERS

New Zealand's earliest explorers were a hardy people, who travelled widely in search of food and the other resources necessary for life in their new homeland. We know from the foods they ate and the tools they used how extensively they journeyed; skeletal studies tell us they travelled often by canoe and also by land, carrying heavy loads.

They were a robust, tall, muscular people, but the life expectancy was only thirty-one or thirty-two, about the same as the rest of the world at the time. Cook saw many elderly Maori, still healthy, but studies suggest these elders were about thirty-five or forty years of age. Then as now the life expectancy was slightly higher for women, who had an average of three or four children and could expect to lose at least one in infancy. There was little variation in average height throughout New Zealand, so diet appears to have been at least adequate in all areas of the country, with no signs of seasonal deprivation.

More interestingly perhaps, fractures and dislocations, even in the period when warfare was endemic, are uncommon, although arthritis was widespread. The fractures which have been found were adequately set. Pneumonia was probably the major cause of death. There is little evidence of heart disease or cancer, due not to the unrefined diet (smoked eels and crayfish are high in cholesterol) but due to the early deaths. In spite of all the contributory factors, heart disease and cancer are diseases of a society which lives longer, not less healthily.

Severe bone degeneration of the neck and backbone caused by paddling canoes regularly and carrying heavy loads for considerable distances was common in both men and women, and there is evidence that women frequently paddled canoes, especially in early times. Several early visitors remarked on the "peculiar grace" of female paddlers.

Women also did their share or, according to Europeans, more than their share of heavy carrying. In the early days every able-bodied person would be needed to help in transporting seasonal harvests to the base settlements. Although violent deaths did occur, as one would expect, probably due to family feuds or personal quarrels, most of the deaths appear to be related to the very active and physically difficult outdoor life. About a thousand years later Cook wrote: "The Inhabitants of this Country are a strong well made active people, rather above the common size ...." Although average heights have increased dramatically in Europe over the last two centuries, Cook himself was almost six feet tall [183 cm], and Lieutenant Roux of Marion du Fresne's 1772 voyage noted that "These islanders are generally of tall stature, well proportioned .... Some, who appeared to be tallest amongst them, and whom we measured, were all over six feet in height ...."

Suits of armour from medieval Europe suggest the average male height then was about 160 centimetres, and two centuries ago in Cook's time was only 163 centimetres or so. Cook was a tall man. Complicated procedures suggest that the average height of the male prehistoric moa-hunters was five feet eight inches [173 centimetres], tall by any standard of the times except perhaps the 15th-century Tongans, who stood just under five feet ten inches [178 centimetres]. In New Zealand only the moa were taller.

The mountain lakes were essential sources of food en route. Lake Moana [Brunner] was famous for its eels, and in season ducks, freshwater mussels, and birds such as pigeon and weka were taken and preserved from bases on the

Refuge Islands on the lake. Greenstone flakes there suggest work on adze or mere was carried out in the evenings or when the weather was bad.

Forest trails were fairly easily blazed and established, by snapping new growth along the sides. Bracken fern country was more difficult as the fern's rapid growth quickly reclaimed paths. Swampy areas had to be built up, using bracken or manuka, high gullies bridged with poles or vine swing bridges, cliffs made passable with hanging vines, rope ladders, steps or pegs to provide hand- and footholds.

Bridges were rare, although G.F. Angas saw "a native bridge of tea-tree boughs swung by flax from the opposite trees ... which rocked like a cradle over the abyss." In 1854 Major J.L. Richardson crossed a stream on a bridge which "consisted of four poles, each 2 1/4 inches in diameter, placed in contact, vertically, one above the other, spanning a stream twenty feet wide and apparently of drowning depth, the only assistance in this extraordinary calesthenic exercise being a loose piece of supple-jack suspended across it, a few feet higher." Generally the Maori, and no doubt his ancestors, preferred to swim or tread water and let the current carry him across, if a canoe were not available. Swift rivers were crossed using breast poles (tuwhana) or by building a float or a larger mokihi or raft of flax stalks.

All the landmarks and geographical features along the trail were named and the names memorised in order to provide route "maps" for future use. In 1848 his guide drew a memory map of the Waitaki river for W. B. D. Mantell, later Commissioner of Crown lands for Otago, which included all the tributaries on both sides, as well as caves, settlements and camping or resting spots, right up to the three source lakes, "Ohou", Pukaki, and "Takapo". Heaphy noted that his guide, Kehu, could describe the trail for the day ahead, and estimate how long sections would take. In memorising the details of many trails both the early explorers and the later Maori guides were emulating the feats of their ancestors who had memorised the star courses and other navigational information in Polynesia.

In 1846 Surveyors Heaphy and Brunner followed the coastal trail from Pakawau at the top of the South Island down to the greenstone country around the Grey River. They were the first Pakehas to do so, although by this time ship-borne Europeans were fairly common along the coast, especially in the sealing grounds of the south. Along the way they met several parties of Maori, many on their way to Nelson for Christian baptism. Some had never seen a Pakeha before. It was clear that this arduous coastal trail (it took Heaphy's party nearly two months to cover the 300-odd kilometres) was still in common use in the 1840s.

Heaphy and Brunner had a Maori guide and used Maori methods both to follow the trail and to survive. After several days of bad weather and days spent climbing up and down precipitous cliffs they decided they would have to do as Maori travellers did and live off the land. Some travellers carried dried fish or whitebait, some prepared fern root, and in later days, a few potatoes, but basically lived on fish and game caught on the way, supplemented by the steamed stem of tree-fern or mamaku.

Missionary William Colenso, one of the early North Island explorers and one of the foremost botanical explorers, considered the "sago-like pith of the stem

## VEGETABLE FOODS

Edible roots, no doubt found only after much trial and error, replaced the Polynesian root crops. The preferred root was that of the aruhe or bracken fern (*Pteridium aquilinum*), which did not grow in forest shade but grew rapidly on burnt-over areas. This rhizome was to become a staple food over most of the country. Fern root had to be dug, scraped, dried, roasted on an open fire, scraped, pounded, formed into a cake, and reheated. According to some early writers it was sometimes "baked" or steamed in an umu, but roasting was more usual.

The result caused various reactions. Forster, Cook's scientist, called it "that wretched article of New Zealand diet … insipid sticks" broiled and then beaten. Anderson, on the third voyage, was less scathing: "they beat [it] with a stick till it becomes pretty soft, when they chew it sufficiently and spit out the hard fibrous part, the other having a sweetish mealy taste not at all disagreeable." Nicholas, travelling with Marsden in 1815 thought it had a "pleasant sweetish taste" but H. Aubrey, visiting Taranaki in 1841, said that "A very good imitation might be made with a rotten stick, especially if slightly pounded, to which it bears a striking resemblance, both in taste and smell."

The bracken fern grew strongly and where fern was allowed to reach its full development nothing else could grow, so by the time Charles Darwin and the *Beagle* reached New Zealand in 1835 he could say fern "covers the whole country." New Zealand, he added, "is favoured by one great natural advantage; namely, that the inhabitants can never perish from famine. The whole country abounds with fern; and the roots of this plant, if not very palatable, yet contain much nutriment. A native can always subsist on these, and on the shell-fish, which are abundant on all parts of the sea-coast."

The other main root crop was that of the ti or cordyline, the cabbage tree; there are several species of ti, and at least one may have been introduced from Polynesia and cultivated in New Zealand. Ti rapidly became a staple food, especially in the south, and remained so well into the 19th century, as witness many early European explorers. New Zealanders did not eat the "cabbage" but the root and stem, which needed prolonged cooking, at least twenty-four hours.

Hundreds or even thousands of ovens made for cooking the huge stems and roots to extract the sweetness dotted the land. The trees were cut down about October, and the outer trunk chipped away with stone adzes. After drying, the bundles were taken to the nearest wood supply, and huge trenches were dug and filled with wood then stones, and the wood burnt. When the stones were hot and the wood gone, earth covered the stones, then green vegetation, then the bundles of stem or the huge roots, then more vegetation, more earth, and all was left to steam for at least twenty-four hours. The stem was then pounded, stacked, covered, and finally transported back to the villages about December. The roots were prepared the same way. On the West Coast of the South Island in the 1840s Brunner ate both ti stem and roots, "generally from three to four feet [one metre] in length, of a conical shape, with an immense number of fibrous roots attached to it …. It requires an immense oven …."

In 1846 Brunner noted: "Collected a quantity of roots of the ti, or cabbage-tree, which we placed in a humu [umu], or native oven, for the night. The natives prepare a very palatable dish of the ti and fern root. They extract the sweet particles of the former by beating and washing it in a proper quantity of water, and when about the consistency of honey they soak in the liquid some layers of well-beaten and cooked fern-root, which, when properly moistened, is eaten, and has a similar relish to gingerbread."

of the large black tree-fern ... very good and nourishing eating." Seventy years earlier J.R. Forster, also a botanist and with Cook in 1773, had also quite enjoyed mamaku, although he apparently believed it was the root he was eating, when only the upper part of the stem was used: "a species of fern-tree, which they called *mamaghoo* ... full of a tender pulp or pith, which when cut exudes a reddish juice of a gelatinous nature, nearly related to sago. This is so much the less singular, as the real sago tree is a species of fern. The good nutritive root [sic] of the mamaghoo must not, however, be confounded with that wretched article of New Zealand diet, the common fern-root .... The mamaghoo ... is tolerably good eating, and the only fault seems to be that it is not plentiful enough for a constant supply." For travellers, the main drawback was the time involved in the cooking.

This became the basis of the Heaphy diet, although it was neither easy to prepare nor particularly appetising: "The Mamaku requiring to remain steaming for twelve hours, we did not open the oven until breakfast time this morning, when we were grieviously disappointed in our fare, and learnt that twelve hours more would be necessary for the vegetable to cool and consolidate ere it would be palatable. Mamaku, when mixed with wine, sugar, and spice in a tart, might be mistaken for baked apple ... the illusion was not perfect." The time necessary to trap game and prepare food en route, as well as that necessary to build nightly shelters, added greatly to the duration of journeys. Exploration was a long slow process.

They crossed the Karamea on a mokihi made of bundles of flax stalk tied together in the shape (and size) of a canoe or boat filled with flax. "Our raft ... was 22 feet in length by 5 in breadth [6.8 x 1.5 m], and could be carried by the four of us. With our weight upon it of some 700 lbs [310 kg], it floated with its upper surface about an inch above the water."

At the Mokihinui River they could not find enough flax to build another mokihi so had to find a ford and use the other great river crossing technique perfected by the Maori and taught today in bushcraft. "Here, joining our several sticks together in place of a pole, and holding them horizontally before us, we entered the river together abreast, going at once into the deep part of the stream, where the water was breast high, with a current setting seaward that we could barely, with the greatest effort, hold up against."

Another surveyor, Arthur Dobson, added more detail: "The Maoris would take a strong light pole, long enough for all the party to hold in front of them. The strongest and heaviest man took the top end (up stream), and another strong man the lower end, the weaker men and women and children held on between them. The whole party then entered the water, keeping end on to the current." Charles Kettle, surveyor, noted in 1842 that "This is an excellent method of crossing a rapid river: those that are not as strong as the rest have a good support, and all act with a combined force against the stream." Heaphy's party crossed other rivers on old canoes found on the banks.

Other obstacles were solved by the earlier Maori: "The sea washing against the cliffs of Homahu point, we were obliged to take to the bush, and after walking through it upon the summit of the cliffs for about a mile, descended again by a native-made ladder and a steep track to the beach ...." A few days later they climbed down a steep cliff using supplejack in place of rope, tied to a tree and dangling down to the beach. Rata vine was sometimes used for the same purpose.

At Te Miko (Perpendicular Point) the cliff barred the way, but again the early Maori travellers had solved the problem. "There are now two stages of ladders, made of short pieces of the ropy rata, lashed together with flax, with steps at irregular distance, the whole very shaky and rotten .... Our baggage and the dog had to be hoisted up by a flax rope." Poor Rover. He was eaten by a starving expedition the following year.

Later Julius Haast descended the Te Miko ladders, one of his party, "who had already felt giddy at the former cliffs", refusing to try this cliff, "not merely perpendicular but in some places overhangs ... As the second and longest ladder is lashed to a tree which grows in a crevice in the rocks, rendering it necessary to lean over in order to reach the ladder, it was here that I experienced the greatest difficulty in getting him down ...." In spite of these aids and the guide, who was taking them over a well-used trail, it was slow going. The Maori travellers and traders were used to stopping for various reasons, weather probably the main culprit, and put the enforced rests to good use.

Maori travelled in single file, as did all travellers who wished to establish a path without damaging the surroundings more than necessary. Although the Maori knew their own trails well, and had covered much of the interior of the island, as well as the coasts, the later Europeans had to do an immense amount of exploring for new trails which were suitable for their own uses. A trail adequate for a group of traders on foot, or even a war party, may not be suitable for a man on horseback or with a flock of sheep, much less a horse and wagon. The early European explorers were always on the lookout for useful trails. On crossing into the Inangahua River, Brunner noted "the bush is open, and free of roots, and the inclination very slight. A communication from river to river, even for a cart, might be made by simply clearing away the underbrush."

There is little doubt both moa-hunter and Maori had explored the whole of the country adequately for their own purposes. The resources they needed had been found and used. The inland waterways had been supplemented with land trails where necessary, for cartage of food, stone, and trade goods, or for swift travel in time of war. The early Europeans recognised and made good use of the knowledge of the Maori, generally employing Maori guides to lead them around the country.

But the ways of the Pakeha were passing strange, and the canoe routes and land trails which had served the Maori for centuries were not suitable for the Pakeha's large boats and wagons. As a result most of the country was re-explored by Europeans for their own purposes, often renaming the geographical features in the process. Cook began this process in his exploration and charting of the coastline. Over the next one hundred and fifty years other Europeans explored the whole country, even the high mountains which the Maori had tended to leave to the gods. Only sometimes did the newcomers recognise that they were following in the footsteps of New Zealand's first, and much earlier, explorers.

CHAPTER THREE

# New Land, Hardy Landsmen

The first European to see New Zealand was a sailor from the Netherlands. He called his news to his captain as a lookout should, and in 1642 Abel Tasman, commander of a Dutch exploring expedition, saw, distant and awe-inspiring, the high peaks of the Southern Alps. His next impression, on closer acquaintance, was the fierceness of west coast surf. It was truly a rugged land and this he recognised. But he was strong and rugged too. Tasman's sighting of the mountains began a centuries-long association of New Zealand, named after a Dutch province, and Tasman, leader of the expedition which rediscovered it. Descendants of the original discoverers were soon to see the Dutch ship from the shore.

New Zealand has been reasonably generous in its naming of parks, playgrounds, hotels and mountains after the Dutch navigator, in this exceeded only by Tasmania, discovered on that same voyage of exploration for the Dutch East India Company. That great trading enterprise, like its English counterpart, had been founded on the commerce of the Indies. It had constantly to increase revenue to cope with perpetually increasing costs of trade and administration: to find, not new worlds for conquest but new worlds for commerce. By the 1640s, in hope of increasing trade, the Dutch wished to fill out great blank spaces in the map south and east of their route to the East Indies. But great exploration voyages do not spring from nothing. Whoever suggested a special expedition to the south and east engendered Abel Tasman's discovery of New Zealand. All we know is that it must have been someone in the Dutch East India Company high enough or persuasive enough to influence its decisions. Probably it was the Governor-General himself, Anthony van Diemen.

Apart from the question of who made the decision, we know the source of the inspiration. It came from Franz Jacobszoon Visscher, a skilled navigator, pilot and hydrographer learned enough to write about navigation, a sailor who had done much but who thought even more, and consequently was interested in exploration. Among several of his venturesome suggestions was a scheme "to discover the southern portion of the world all round the globe, and find out what it consists of – whether land, sea, or icebergs ...." For all the great Dutch Company knew to the contrary in 1642 there might be vast productive lands south and east of Australia with exotic products for profitable trade. So in spite of Visscher's comments about icebergs, the Governor-General did not ponder long. Van Diemen was ambitious and decisive, both for himself and the Company. Like so many great executives he probably did not make much distinction between the two entities.

Under his direction, the Council decided to send an expedition to find the Southland, under the command of Abel Tasman, with Visscher himself as chief pilot. Tasman's voyage would be the European type of exploration and expansion. The Maori had spread across the Pacific but in each case had broken off from their homeland, become independent upon leaving and remained so upon landing. It was like the swarming of the Angles and Saxons to Britain. The Europeans on the other hand, Spanish, Portuguese, English and French, were looking for new lands, new products, new peoples to add to the prosperity and power of the homeland and remain under its control, doing by sea what Russia, the United States and China had room to do by land. It was to be the mid-20th century before this process which had created so many great powers finally and completely dismantled itself, as far as the sea powers were concerned.

Abel Tasman was forty-one years old and known to be an excellent seaman and strong commander. But to Company gentlemen he was the classic "ranker": rough, readier to punch than pardon, and rampaging when in drink. Lacking the intellect of Visscher or Cook, he offers us no insights about race or creed or geography. Apparently he spurned introspection; certainly we get no sign of that either. That is natural enough; he was a doer not a thinker. In 1642 in frail wooden ships, especially in one sailing south of Australia, there was plenty to do, plenty to worry about, and little profit for most men in thinking too much too long.

The orders given Tasman meant, in the result, the circumnavigation of Australia. Already Dutch ships had many times encountered western Australia – a few of them literally. Ships beating north-eastward after rounding the Cape of Good Hope often were blown south of their route to Batavia, and occasionally saw, or ran into, a great sandy coast. But Tasman's new voyage was to go even further south – much further – and to follow Australia as far south as it went and then to swing east. For all that anyone knew for certain there could be a route home to Europe that way. As indeed there was. Two centuries later the great west winds took the windjammer wheat and wool clippers east across the South Pacific past New Zealand and Cape Horn, far more quickly home than ships sailing westward.

## THE  GREAT  SOUTHLAND

16th and 17th century geographers found many reasons to believe in high-latitude southern land masses. Some clues went all the way back to the Ptolemy's 2nd century B.C. *Geographia*, published with maps in 1477. On one map a "Terra Incognita" drew attention southwards, where continents also appeared on Portuguese maps. One such map in 1531 had on it the name Terra Australis, southern land. The fine Dutch navigator, Visscher, also probably knew the map by Scottish-descended John Rotz (Ross), one of several maps of the known and conjectured world, published in Dieppe in the 1530s and 1540s. The maps appear to be based on relatively accurate astronomical data, with hints on Rotz's map of the entire New Zealand archipelago, and the east coast of Australia. If Iberian sailors had sighted the East Cape of New Zealand they would probably have envisaged it as these maps showed it, as part of a great southern continent.

Such charted information, if it was information and not conjecture, could only have reached Dieppe from Spanish or Portuguese sources. Thus a century before Tasman's voyage there appear to have been clues to the existence of New Zealand. But it had not been revealed to the world, nor discovered in any real sense.

This may or may not be an actual likeness of Tasman. But it is said to be, and it is what he ought to have looked like. *(Alexander Turnbull Library, Wellington)*

The Dutch surmised from northern experience that at best Tasman's ships would encounter temperate climates, and at worst cold and dangerous ones. But even if there were hardships and hazards the expedition was expected to persevere. Tenacity was no novelty to the commander, nor to Dutch sailors. As a sailor and later an officer, Tasman had worked his way up in the Dutch trade to the East Indies and played his part in putting down piracy around the East Indian islands. Responsibility, tediums, hardships and hazards did not daunt him. Nor would exploration be new, for by 1639 he had already, as commander of the ship *Gracht*, been on a precursory voyage around Korea and Japan, and in two subsequent voyages gained valuable experience exploring waters unknown to Europeans. Tasman's ability and familiarity with the waters of the general area won him a post as a temporary member of the council of Dutch officials in Japan. The one-time working sailor had earned high command, for he could handle men. Besides, he had many qualities of an explorer. He wished to know, was willing to question, was wont to dare, and dared to act.

The Dutch East India Company ordered Tasman "to sail to, accordingly to discover, the partly known and still unreached South and Eastern-land ...." The purpose was "to seek out any important lands, or at least convenient passages to known rich places, and to use these at a more convenient time, for the improvement, and increase of the Compy's general welfare." His blueprinted route was as ambitious as his orders were hopeful: several thousand miles from Java to Mauritius, then south to latitude 52, east to the longitude of New Guinea and the "Islands of Salomon" or even further. This was a major voyage based solely on hope. The Dutch Company knew what Spain and Portugal had gained from discovery: "what inestimable riches, profitable tradings, useful exchanges, fine dominions, great might and powers ...." But here was no certainty of rich southern and eastern lands. In fact, there *were* no rich southern lands until European immigrants created the wealth. Great commercial enterprises, then as now, were almost as used to loss as to gain. Even so, the reality of Tasman's discoveries, once recognised, must have been deeply disappointing.

On his voyage Tasman was to sail to Mauritius for food, firewood and fresh water. He was to wait there until the sun on its way south should pass the Equator, the beginning of the southern spring. The Company knew the far south was like the far north; "at night is not without fear, and also is subjected to many storms with hail, snow and cold etc." So delay meant danger and Tasman was told there would be only "3 to 3 1/2 months time to get this discovering now complete ... of large rivers, inlets, rocks, shoals, sands, banks, and depths together with circumstances of the inhabitants, what goods occur there and can be exchanged for others ...." After passing south of Australia sailing eastward, if this were possible, Tasman was to go north to New Guinea. The plan was to sail to "100, 150 to 200 miles farther East" and then sail back up to the Indonesian Islands with the south-east trade wind, returning to Batavia through the Indonesian Archipelago. Of the ships of the 1640s – and the men – they were demanding much.

The Company was very proud of their well-built ships and in its instructions called Tasman's pair "the ship *Heemskerck* and the flute the *Zeehaen*, the first manned with 60 and the other with 50 of the ablest seafaring people here in the roadstead ... duly provided with all useful necessaries, as well as diverse trade goods and minerals for trial in the visited lands, under the command of the Hon. Abel Janssen Tasman who ... is very keen on this discovering ... [and] Pilot Major Frans Visscher, together with the skippers ... both of whom were proved fully experienced navigators ...." Suitable and well supplied, well crewed and commanded, the ships performed well.

The sailors who manned Tasman's two ships were the usual 17th century lot, most in the east involuntarily, given impetus by the crimp or press gang, and probably still in debt for their sea clothes. The crews were almost certainly international, as were most in those early days, for crimps shanghaied men of any nation from any pub for any ship. In the 17th century, apart from a sailor's skills, anything in common in the fo'c'sle was more likely to be religion than allegiance. Dutch crews would be predominantly Calvinist; any Catholics would pray quietly. It was a rough and ready century, war more likely than peace wherever you were, hardships certain and early death probable.

Officers were strict and underofficers simply extra-hard sailors. Dutchmen were tough and strong, and foreign sailors had to meet their standards. Alternatives were grim, for punishment was hard too. If mutiny were contemplated, shipmates knew the Company's arm was lengthened and strengthened by the fabled wealth of the East Indies. Yet Dutch crews had it somewhat easier than others in those early days because Dutch ships reached the borders of the Pacific from the west, coming with the favourable westerly winds. Spanish and English ships usually reached it from the east, having to fight those very westerlies for weeks or months to pass Cape Horn, crews suffering from exposure and many dying of scurvy.

The *Heemskerck* was made Tasman's flagship and Visscher, as pilot major, sailed with him. All higher officers were familiar with the orders and instructions. They had been asked for – and had given – their advice and assistance in drawing them up. In case of unforeseen difficulties the instructions

Tasman's *Heemskerck* and *Zeehaen*, which reached the west coast of New Zealand in 1642. Although not an actual portrayal of the Dutch vessels a very creditable attempt has been made to show the different characteristics of the war-yacht and flute. *(Alexander Turnbull Library, Wellington)*

provided the explorers with the choice of exploring only the southern Australian coast. But the Company hoped for more. If found, a passage from the Indian Ocean to the South Sea (the Pacific) would mean a route to Chile without the disadvantages and dangers of sailing west round Cape Horn. The instructions made clear that much of the reasoning was theoretical; that the many attractive and fruitful lands north of the equator in cold, temperate and hot zones, must have equivalents below the equator. A reasonable assumption, this unfortunately was only partially true, for by far the most land on earth is in the northern hemisphere.

Timing of the voyage (for example, exactly how long the ships should stay at Mauritius) and all other instructions were thorough and detailed. There was no doubt about what Tasman was to do nor what was expected of him. Instructions to Tasman also named the seven members of the expedition's council, and in case of his death, a line of succession. As in most voyages of the period, the commander could alter the instructions if necessary; the Company recognised that circumstance could force sudden decision. But alterations always had to be made with the advice of the council, basically the pilots and commanders of both ships.

One particularly important task was emphasised. Tasman and his pilots were to do a great deal of charting. The orders were specific: "all lands, islands, points, bights, inlets, bays, rivers, shoals, banks, sands, rivers, rocks and reefs &c which [you] will meet with, and pass, you must chart thoroughly, and describe, and also the form and appearance, duly draw, to which end a draughtsman has been provided for you ...." Tasman was instructed to use his judgment about this too: "further attentively observing and noting, what expert navigators ought to observe, and can be useful in future to the navigating of the discovered lands." Another requirement was to describe the weather carefully. Except in most unusual circumstance, the weather today means simply that a plane or ferry goes on time or does not. In the 17th century, to tiny ships in unknown waters, by definition exploring ships, weather could mean success or failure, life or death. Learning climates, as explorers did, meant more sensible provisioning, hence less debilitating hardship; it meant fewer risks, more success.

The Company also gave thought to events if new land were discovered, and gave precise guidance about relations with inhabitants if encountered. The instructions differed somewhat depending on whether the inhabitants appeared to be civilised or not. The Company thought they had good reason for discrimination. "It has been found by experience, no barbarous people are to be trusted, because they usually think, that the people who appear so exceedingly strange and unexpected, come only to take over their lands which (because of carelessness and easy trust) has caused many a treacherous murder in the discovery of America." Tasman and his men were warned to be exceedingly careful in the presence of natives, advice which should have been more carefully followed.

But the Company did not mean its men to be aggressive. Tasman was advised to put up with a great deal from native people: "small affronts of thievery ... [you] shall let pass unmarked, in order not to cause any enmity towards us by punishing them but ... attract them to us so that [you] may the better find out ... whether anything useful is to be got or done there." This seems more mercenary than humanitarian. Even so the Company, wishing to avoid trouble, was willing to appease. And, knowing that much of the trouble in new lands came from the behaviour of the European crews, the Company instructed Tasman that he and his captains were to see that "all insolence and hostility of the crew towards the discovered peoples, [you] will carefully prevent, and take care no harm is done to them in their houses, gardens, craft, property or women &ca. Likewise no inhabitants brought away from their land against their will ...." The Dutch intended to be peaceable and to be seen as such.

The instructions ended by saying that if lands were desirable they were to be taken over in the name of "the High and Mighty Lords States General as Sovereign of the united provinces ...." Tasman was told exactly how to do it. "Uninhabited lands, or which have no lord can be secured by the setting up of a stone as a memorial, or planting of our prince flag, for true possession, since such lands rightly belong to the finder and taker. But in populated lands, or which have undoubtedly lords, the consent of the people or king shall be necessary in the taking of occupation and possession, which is to be fittingly achieved by amicable influence ... placing of a prince-flag in memory of their voluntary submission, or subjection ...."

Today we know much about Tasman's voyage because by immense good fortune the journal, which Tasman ordered to be kept, still exists. It contains drawings of landforms, the shapes of high hills and mountains to be used as landmarks, regular reports of the prevailing winds, and the courses sailed by the ship. Carefully prepared drawings display peoples encountered, for example

Maori in double canoes in New Zealand's Golden Bay. There is an occasional word left out, sometimes a transliteration of words in a sentence, but daily entries of events and conditions, even cursory ones, provide a very full, somewhat dull, account of the voyage.

## SHIPS' LOGS AND JOURNALS

The log of a ship, when properly kept as it must be by law, is a detailed account of a ship's movements, courses and speeds, and includes signals received or sent, weather, winds, duties assigned, and encounters with other ships. A journal, as kept by individuals, is both less formal and more interesting. Cook's journals discuss almost everything encountered, in great detail and with remarkable insight. Officers had more time, and usually more literary ability. Nonetheless some of the most interesting journals have come from the lower deck, from a different viewpoint and with different experiences emphasised. Many journals were written for publication; others seemingly to fill in time or to release frustrations. Public perceptions of every voyage depend on its surviving journals. Cook was richly served, Tasman was not.

Compared with some later journals, what is missing in Tasman's case, in the seaman's journal which survived as well as in the official one, is comment, insight, the personal touch. Few individuals stand out in the journals of the voyage. We read that there was a trumpeter – and a trumpet – on each of Tasman's two ships, presumably for signalling commands at a distance, as in armies. Whether they played well or ill we do not know; the Maori apparently were not impressed. We know little else of any other crewmen except when either the violence of new-found and unappreciative peoples or the erosion of shipborne disease removed them. Two other existing journals of the voyage have the same deficiency. Compared with the reality of vigour, courage and competence the Dutch sailors and crews displayed, the journals are as flat as Holland.

With all his cares, and considering the conditions aboard, the commander probably had some help with his journal. One likely candidate was Abraham Coomans, appointed by the Company to act as secretary of the ships' council. One of two merchants on the expedition's council, his main concern was probably the trade goods and protecting them from the crew. Coomans would have had the time to write because he, unlike the other officers, would not be concerned with working or navigating the ship. Nor did he have Tasman's problems of command which invariably require much more thought than noise, modern movies notwithstanding. Whatever the assistance, the journal is definitely Tasman's. He signed it as an accurate record of the voyage.

Although copies of Tasman's journal differ slightly, it seems certain that the differences are only such as invariably occur when someone copies another manuscript by eye and hand. With Cook's we have not only his completed manuscripts but all the corrected drafts along the way. For the French and English exploration voyages as a whole we are well served by journal keepers, official and otherwise. Books and literacy had both increased. The growth of publishing meant there was a general public to serve – and to profit from. Officers and even some men before the mast took advantage of the exploration voyages to become authors, with real tales to tell. But they were sailing more than a century after Tasman. The world had changed, and in some ways the modern world had begun. The human links are closer than we think. Tasman was born the year Queen Elizabeth died; some who sailed with Cook were there to know of Victoria's crowning; and a few who watch sailing races today remember Victoria as queen.

The journal's chronology is not maritime, because in it days run midnight to midnight as on land. An existing journal of the voyage kept by a sailor used the common maritime chronology. On ships at sea at the time days ran from noon to noon, because when the sun was directly overhead, the navigating officers took their observations, fixing the time as noon. This interesting difference in the journals lends strength to the idea that Tasman's journal was not written by Tasman, or even a ship's officer, but by a merchant clerk.

In the journal the observed latitudes by which the ships were navigated seem fairly accurate. Comparing them with modern knowledge shows a persistent southerly error of only slightly more than half a degree; the navigational calculation of Tasman's officers was within fifteen or so statute miles of the true latitude, an excellent result given the conditions and the instruments. It was finding longitude which was difficult at that time. Later voyagers were very complimentary about the care with which Tasman gave his positions. Sir Joseph Banks, with Cook on his first Pacific voyage, said, "Thus much for Tasman: it were much to be wish'd ... that other navigators would Imitate him in mentioning the Latitudes and Longitudes in which they account the places from whence they take their departure to be situated; which precaution, usefull as it is, may almost be said to have been used by Tasman alone." Certainly Cook had found New Zealand close to where Tasman had said it was. Banks mentioning places of departure would imply the ability to get an accurate longitude from a ship steady at anchor, or from on shore.

This helped Cook later but Tasman had to face his position-finding problems with his own instruments and methods. Because 17th-century ships' navigators could not find accurate longitudes at sea, even if they knew where an island was, they still would not know how close or far away it was because they could not be sure where the ship was. And to be between a strong west wind and a sturdy island an unknown distance to the east brought a sinking feeling to the most imperturbable of navigators. Shipwreck in unknown seas on unknown shores with unknown terrors was the exploring crew's nightmare. On one of Cook's voyages over a century later a relatively easy solution, the use of chronometers, was successful in accurately finding longitude at sea.

The early days of the voyage were uneventful; one month and one day found them at Mauritius. In those days most landings were to get fresh food of various sorts, and invariably the ships needed fresh water. Where possible they got wood as well. The tiny fleet's stay was notable for the time Tasman's crews spent gathering firewood. These utterly essential needs of the old wooden sailing ships made New Zealand a penultimate stopping place. Good and unlimited fresh water, good and plentiful timber, myriad shoals of fish in the shore waters or rivers, great flocks of birds in the forests: all that New Zealand lacked were plentiful edible animals for fresh meat.

After Mauritius Tasman had not gone far south before he learned what great wool and wheat windjammers of 19th-century Australia would learn again: sailing southerly seas, where great westerly winds sweep unhindered round the world, was hard on sailing ships. On 10 October *Heemskerck*'s "mizzenmast was all in pieces." Craftsmen aboard the ship speedily, but not easily, repaired it. A week late the *Zeehaen*'s channel wales, from which the masts were braced, had to be repaired. Winds and seas had not finished with the expedition yet. On 26

October, *Zeehaen's* topyard broke and had to be replaced. As these ships and riggings were sound, breakages indicate very difficult conditions.

All through the voyage Tasman's two ships took great pains to stay in company with each other. Picking ships of much the same comfortable speed was important in any fleet, even the minimum fleet of two. By 28 October, the tiny fleet was south to a latitude of a little less than forty-five degrees, further south than Australia, and in completely unknown waters. They hoped to encounter land. When it was misty and the sea was smooth they would at intervals fire muskets, even sometimes big guns, listening for echoes indicating land ahead. None came. But occasionally they saw pieces of tree or weed floating by. They turned east in hope of clearer weather and a more promising outlook. and sailed eastward on roughly latitude 45 south. Even such directionless indications as drifting seals, or birds which normally rested on land, were avidly watched, and surface seaweed was hauled aboard to ponder. Tasman's men began to see such indications in late October.

Indications were only promises. But of what? A rocky islet or the great "southern land" they sought? That seeming chimera could be anywhere (or nowhere) ahead. At best there were slight hints on old and musty maps; at worst no clues at all. So what to do? Sail on and hope? Or try a different route? Land ahead meant tension in responsible officers; the great wide sea was relatively safe, near the shore one came near danger. If a ship were thought to be approaching land orders went out; care far beyond normal in navigation must be matched by consummate care in watchkeeping. Threats were brothers-in-arms to promises. On 27 October Tasman had announced a reward for the sailor first sighting a coast, a common procedure at sea. It added an element of competition, an inducement for the rank and file, themselves not unaware that results of poor watchkeeping could be lost ships and drowned men.

On 9 November the council decided to stay on latitude 44 South until they reached longitude 195 East. In the meantime watches were to exercise extreme vigilance, for the signs of land had convinced old hands of its vicinity. On 24 November a lookout sighted land, very mountainous and easy to see, about sixteen kilometres away east by north. Perhaps this closeness is why the journal does not mention whether he got his reward. This new-found island, now the most beautiful Australian state, finally came to commemorate this great voyage in its modern name, Tasmania. Tasman did not call it that. He knew the wiser way, and put in his journal: "This land is the first land in the South Sea that is met by us, and is still known to No european Peoples, so we have given this land the name of Anthoonij van Diemens land in honour of the Hon. Gov'r General our high superior who has sent us out to do this discovering ...." Van Diemen's Land remained the name of the island, and the convict settlement on it, until it was renamed Tasmania in 1853.

One of their first jobs was to call another council of both ships and firmly fix the longitude as well as the latitude of this land. The observations required great care and would have been done in calm water. Then Tasman's men examined the new discovery, proceeding around to the south and east, journal keepers making drawings of the shore which emphasised mountains as valuable navigation marks, and carefully describing the shore and such resources they found in brief landings.

KEEPING FOOD HEALTHFUL ON SHIPS

In the centuries of exploration by sailing ship the sailors had a very limited selection of food. Whether well cooked or not, and it practically never was, food on sailing ships if good was dull and if interesting was bad. Preservation meant salting, for meat and fish, or drying, for beans, peas, flour or oatmeal. Ships' biscuits were cooked very hard, baked twice to dry them out completely. They would keep for a long time, but eventually, and always, the weevils got into them. Some sailors said this was better than no fresh meat at all. Water, liquor, clothing, indeed almost all supplies were carried in wooden casks. Ships carried flour and rice and beans and corn in casks, as well as biscuits and salted meat and fish. Wooden casks preserved food fairly well, if they were absolutely airtight because of careful construction and caulking, and kept so by constant attention.

The sort of care food stowage sometimes required was arduous and time-consuming. Cook's ship *Resolution* at Ship Cove overhauled "the bread [4292] pounds of which [almost two tonnes] we found Mouldy and rotten and totally unfit for men to eat [3000] pounds more that few would eat but such as were in our circumstances, this damage our bread had susstained was wholy owing to the Casks being made of green wood and not well seasoned before the Biscuit was packed in them for all the biscuits that were in co[n]tact or near the insides of the Casks were damaged while those in the middle were not the least injured." It was a quite typical problem on a long voyage and, if the Admiralty had been unlucky or remiss in dealing with contractors, on short voyages too.

Water always went off after a time, especially in the tropics, and Tasman and Cook constantly sought good sources of fresh pure water. Present-day storage requires not only modern techniques but modern materials. Except for relatively soft iron, the vegetable materials wood, hemp for cordage and rope, and flax fibre in canvas were those used aboard the ship for almost all purposes. Wood was needed for repairs to the structure of the ship, or for the oars, the masts or the yards, and firewood was all they had for cooking. Craftsmen who worked with each material – blacksmiths, coopers, carpenters, sailmakers – were important men, and ranked as such, on the old ships.

Perhaps because preservation was such a problem, a rather messy alternative was often adopted. Food could be kept fresh by keeping it alive. In Mauritius, Tasman's ships loaded many he-goats and pigs. The he-goats were intended for meat; on some ships nanny goats, sometimes even cows, sailed the seas as living dairies for the officers. One nanny who first sailed around the world with Captain Byron, the poet's grandfather, later sailed twice around the world with Captain Cook. Nowhere in the journals of this Dutch voyage do we encounter a nanny, but there might have been one nonetheless. The mess and the dangers of pollution in carrying livestock and poultry on deck can be imagined. But if early sailors had had present-day knowledge of sanitation, no ships at all would have sailed.

Possible navigation of the future was very much in mind when charting anchorages and bays. But commercial visits seemed less and less likely the more the Dutch saw. Diligent searches found little of use but wood and water, and accounts of the island are not flattering. No one saw any sign of life except smoke and charred wood, evidence of the use of fire, although the shore party had heard sounds like gongs. There were tracks, but only tracks, of animals apparently as shy and cunning as the people. Their experiences did not enthuse them about islands in the south-west Pacific. It was a long way, in every sense, from Indonesia.

This first discovery certainly did not bear any resemblance to the "many inhabited places, in the pleasant climate and attractive sky ..." of which the Company had spoken so confidently when sending him forth to find them. Tasman must have been disappointed. Sailing along Tasmania could not compare with exploring the waters of the great civilisations of East Asia. With misgivings the expedition formally took possession of the island for the Dutch East India Company, although even this ceremony was not auspicious. The sea became so rough that finally the carpenter had to swim ashore alone with the requisite symbols. He set up the stake with the mark of the Company on it and "the flag above", leaving, as Tasman put it, "posterity and the Inhabitants of this land ... the above mentioned as a memorial." After only one more day examining the coast Tasman "caused the council and under-mates to assemble to which proposed [and] with it resolved, and having called out to the officers of the *Zeehaen*, to Set the course ... due east and to run on this course to the fully completed longitude of 195 Degrees ...." To carry out this decision the two ships left Tasmania on 5 December.

---

## LONGITUDE

In the 17th century the usual method by which skilled navigators found longitude was by measuring the difference between the angle of a line of bearing from a planet to the moon, and the angle of bearing of the same planet and the moon observed at the same time at a known place, for example, Amsterdam. It could not be used while at sea because the tossing of the ship prevented accurate observation and accurate measurements with the instruments of the day, so longitude could be established at sea only by dead reckoning. Dead reckoning means keeping a record of the direction and distance of every leg the ship sailed after the previous day's position.

In non-nautical language dead reckoning in practice means starting from a point on the map and drawing a line angled to represent the direction you are sailing. With the top of the page as north, if the line is to point north-east, as the ship is sailing north-east, it will run from the departure point towards the upper right of the page. Along this line the navigator measures a scaled distance to represent the distance travelled. This is found by multiplying the estimated speed by the elapsed time between the changes of course. This procedure is repeated at every change of course. The intention is to find how far east or west the ship has travelled. Observations taken daily at noon show how far north or south the ship is.

This dead reckoning method of finding longitude is certainly not precise. Time itself could be measured fairly correctly with sandglasses but speed was a problem for centuries. There were "logs" which measured a ship's speed by the rate at which a line was dragged along the deck by a piece of wood (the log) which had been thrown overboard. But these were not very accurate. Anyway, currents of which the officers naturally would be unaware when out of sight of land could falsify the position. The ship might be drifting southwards when by compass it was sailing due eastward. In that case progress would be south-eastwards, not eastwards; the ship would be further south and not as far east as calculated. The distance moved south could be found, by

Their passage of the sea now called the Tasman, often singularly unpleasant, was easy, perhaps because they had moved somewhat northwards to sail just north of the 42nd parallel. On 13 December the journal says laconically, "Towards noon Saw a large high elevated land, had it South east from us about 15 miles." But they were excited and a quickly collected council decided to "make said land, as soon as At all possible." But the closer approach made them cautious. "The great open Sea which comes shooting thereon with great hollow waves and swells" was rolling waves uninterrupted since they had fought their way eastward past Cape Horn over half the world around. Dutch pilots rightly feared one of the classic lee shores of the world, thought so dangerous 200 years later that no whaling ship would be insured which admitted any intention of working those waters.

Tasman quite likely saw at a distance the impressive bulk and height of what is now Mount Tasman, for "high elevated land" was an accurate description. The ships were within easy sight of several of the great peaks of the Southern Alps of New Zealand. But there was more to do and to see. On the 14th they turned to sail north-east within about three kilometres of the surf, "So close that one could see the Sea steadily break against the Land." Towards the evening of 14

---

the noon observations, but not the distance moved east. Or a ship could be carried forward far faster than estimated because of a strong stern-bearing current. Or vice versa; the possibilities of error were manifold. On the voyage to Mauritius the chart was about eight minutes out in longitude even though Tasman was sailing in an area with which his navigator was quite familiar.

Because of these difficulties, when opportunity offered ships' officers would use their instruments from land or an anchored ship in calm water, to calculate longitude. It was a fairly complex procedure, involving measuring the change of angle of bearing between the moon and different planets. Because the moon was changing its apparent position relative to the earth more quickly than was the chosen planet, the different bearings, or angles of sight, could be used to find distance east or west of another point on earth for which the angles at given times were known to the observer. In those pre-satellite days this implied the possession of written tables of this information for each day of the year. Compiling such a table required many observations and much time. But navigation had long since been so important to the great powers of Europe – and their huge trading companies – that this had been done. By 1600 Dutch navigators had worked out a system using the moon and Jupiter, comparing their figures to tables prepared in Venice. Visscher and Tasman at least would know that system.

In 1642 Greenwich was not accepted as zero longitude. Tasman estimated longitude eastwards from the meridian of the "Peak of Teneriffe" on the island of that name. This peak is sixteen degrees and thirty-nine minutes east of Greenwich. So to place Tasman's estimated position on a modern map a reader of his journal must add that amount to his estimated longitudes. The difficulty in finding longitude also explains why so many islands, and even land masses, were apparently discovered but the explorer could not say precisely where they were. Yet if the latitude was certain it was possible to go to that latitude and sail east ahead of the west winds and finally encounter the land you sought. "Sailing along a latitude" added distance, and success depended on the latitude being reasonably correct.

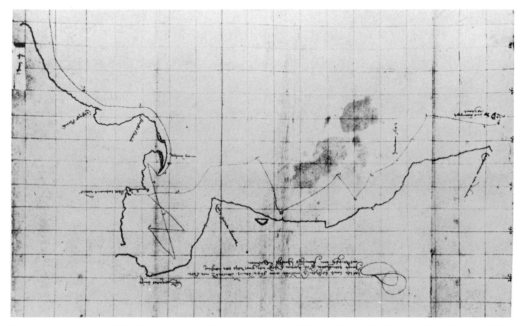

Tasman's navigator, Visscher, charted the west coast of New Zealand showing the Dutch ships' course as he had plotted it. Near the lower left hand corner of the chart there is a gap postulating the existence of the strait which Cook found later. *(Mitchell Library, State Library of New South Wales)*

December the ships came into sight off a low point, spending the night of the 14th drifting calmly well offshore. A light breeze on the 15th enabled them to sail around the point, now Cape Foulwind, encountering a great rock reef, far better met in full daylight. Although the weather was very clear they saw no people nor smoke.

On the 17th *Heemskerck* and *Zeehaen* sailed north-east until they came to a low sandy point, and unknowingly anchored off the north-west tip of the South Island, now Cape Farewell. As smoke rose from various places on shore, in the morning they sailed around the cape and its sandy spit with great anticipation. Visscher, in a shallop, went with another boat to find an anchorage near shore. As usual there was need for good fresh water. The exploration vessels anchored with high hopes in the evening and the crew saw many lights on land and "four vessels near the shore." When two canoes headed for the ships the two boats returned. The pilot-major reported finding no less than thirteen fathoms water, a good depth under a kilometre from land. Visscher and Tasman sketched the rough outlines of the area on clean parchment, and overwrote "Clean grey sand in sixty fathoms" on the first chart of a New Zealand anchorage, an excellent sheltered harbour now called Golden Bay.

And so at Golden Bay the first Europeans to set eyes on New Zealand met the Maori. Men in the two canoes began to call out to the sailors in "gruff hollow voice[s]." Although neither group could understand the other, they called back and forth for some time, the Maori too wary to come very close. A Maori blew an instrument, presumably a conch shell, which "gave sound like the moors' Trumpets." A sailor on the *Heemskerck* could play "somewhat on the Trumpet" and was ordered to blare his best in return. *Zeehaen*'s trumpeter joined in but the music apparently did little to soothe savage breasts, if any such were about. Darkness came, the Maori paddled away, and presumably relative silence returned to the bay. The Dutch ships lay at anchor with their crews on edge, officers quietly overseeing precautions, setting sentries, serving out "muskets pikes and swords sufficiently ready." Gun crews fired the upper deck guns and reloaded them painstakingly; now they were not likely to misfire if needed in the night.

Early morning brought another canoe to about a cable's length (approximately 180 metres) from the ships. The Dutch examined these new people thoroughly. Possibly they had help from telescopes, newly invented in Holland, for the descriptions are very detailed for such a distance. The most comprehensive portrayal hints of oriental experience. Perhaps it was the former member of the Japan Council, Tasman himself, who depicted Maori as "of ordinary height but rough in voice and bones, their colour between brown and yellow, had Black hair right on top of the crown of the head fastened together in style and form like the Japanese at the back of the head but a bit longer and thicker of hair; upon which stood a large thick white feather." The Maori were clothed; "some of mats, others Cottons, Some and almost all the upper body naked." Trade goods, knives and especially cloth, displayed over the ships' sides did not tempt the canoes near enough for paddlers to see properly. They seemed wholly unimpressed with the possibilities of trade; no display whatever tempted them near the ships. It is little wonder. Whatever the placatory display, most of us would hesitate to approach a spaceship too closely.

Many canoes were now in sight, one holding seventeen men and "projecting in front high and sharp" (presumably a tribal war canoe). Newly seen watercraft, "long Narrow canoes beside each other, over which some planks and other seating was laid ...", are always of special interest to sailors, and expert boatmen noted that the canoes were very fast. *Zeehaen* sent a small boat to meet the local canoes. A canoe rammed the boat and the men in it attacked the quartermaster Cornelis Ioppen with what looked like "a blunt pike" and clubbed the six others aboard, killing three men outright. A fourth, badly wounded, died later. The quartermaster and two more sailors escaped with the help of the ship's sloop. This event perhaps delayed visits to New Zealand until the mid-18th century philosophers devised the "Noble Savage."

When some Maori pulled one of the dead Dutch sailors into a canoe his enraged shipmates opened fire, regretfully reporting no hits from many shots. Not unnaturally, the Maori paddled swiftly to shore and the Dutch "raised our anchors and went under sail, because [we] could not expect to make here any friendship here with this people, nor Would water or supplies be obtained." Eleven more canoes came out and the gunners shot at them, hitting at least one man. The Maori fled. Two canoes set a type of sail the Dutch described as "tingang sails", presumably an East Asian type of triangular sail, which the Dutch would know from their Indonesian experience.

As soon as convenient the ships' council was convened and decided, as "this morning is a teacher to us, to hold this land's inhabitants as enemies"; not unreasonably they named the anchorage Murderers' Bay. Dutch feelings are easy to understand. The account of the events is Dutch, but they had nothing to gain and much to lose by initiating violence at this early stage. Seeking new lands for commercial purposes gives no motive whatever for abusing natives, certainly at the outset, for new peoples would be either customers, suppliers or both. The Company's attitude was clear and the great Company was not taken lightly by its agents. "The barbarous people whom [you] may meet and come to speech with, [you] shall make contact with properly and amicably." If self-servingly mercenary it was merciful too, for detailed and very definite instructions laid down that the captains must be forbearing even in the face of theft, certainly not the case in Holland in 1642.

The Dutch ships sailed towards the North Island, giving the water they were crossing the name of Abel Tasman Passage, "because he is the first who has traversed this passage." It seemed that they were in a great bay of a substantial land, and Tasman wrote in his journal: "this land looks like being a very beautiful land and we trust that this is the mainland coast of the unknown south land." New Zealand was now uncovered to the world, for parts of it would now be on the world's maps, presuming that at least one of the ships got home. Both did, and Cook came a century and a quarter later to a land he knew was there.

The Dutch stayed about six days at the western entrance to Cook Strait, held there by the wind. While experiencing Cook Strait weather, later notorious, they sheltered from a north-west gale under D'Urville Island. The officers noted tides which indicated a strait. Visscher's chart has an indefinite opening and the journal records the suspicion: "since the flood comes through from the South east: so that there might indeed be a passage ...." The weather was too fierce and it remained a conjecture, for they left without finding it. If there had not been a strait, upon going into the bay they might have become "embayed", that is, not have had room enough to tack out against the strong wind. Tasman was wise to be careful, exactly as Cook was off Dusky Sound later. To lose a ship at New Zealand was then a sentence of death.

In these rough conditions the crews of *Heemskerck* and *Zeehaen* celebrated the first Christmas in New Zealand; there were "two pigs killed for the crew, and the Commander ordered besides the ration, a tankard of wine to be given to every mess ...." Very special food and drink for Christmas has the earliest possible New Zealand precedent. Winds next day were not favourable for eastward exploration and the Dutch set sail to go west and north. Thus Tasman missed finding Cook Strait, prolonging belief in a great southern continent.

Cloud concealed Mount Egmont as the ships passed what is now Taranaki Province. Otherwise it might have become Mount Visscher! The tiny fleet occasionally saw high land as it sailed northwards, but most of the coast appeared to be sand dunes. Finally they reached a group of small islands which they named the Three Kings (Drie Coningen), "because We came to anchor there on three Kings eve." They needed fresh water and vegetables but the islands did not look very promising. Tasman sent boats inshore but no one landed because natives appeared, looking and acting all too like the "murderers" for whom a bay had been named in the south. These too talked with loud rough voices; they even threw stones. No sailor wished to fight for water, at least not yet.

Two thoroughly armed boats set off with casks next day only to be thwarted by strong shore currents, for when they did find plentiful fresh water they

*Heemskerck* and *Zeehaen* at anchor in Golden – then Murderers' – Bay, with various sketches of Maori single and, (in the foreground) double canoes. It is very much a composed picture; no Dutch artist at Golden Bay reached any point giving these particular views of ships, canoes or Maori. *(Hocken Library, Dunedin)*

could not get to it. The officers – in indecision – called a council. Decision duly came; to sail east to as far as 220 degrees of longitude. There the ships would turn and go north and west to the Hoorn Islands, discovered by the Dutch in 1616, by the same expedition which that year discovered and named Cape Horn. Journals spoke of food and water there, and peaceful people.

On 6 January the Dutch left New Zealand waters. Pushed further north by the wind than they intended, they discovered Tonga, and after an interesting welcome there they moved off to encounter Fiji. Tasman's great voyage was thus not devoid of discoveries even though he found neither Tasmanian Aboriginals nor Cook Strait. From Fiji the two ships sailed right around the Solomon Islands, without seeing them, and on to Batavia by June 1643.

Tasman's discovery of New Zealand was most unsatisfactory. It was brief, clouded by distrust, violence and death, and the Dutch commander felt hard done by. Nonetheless, from now on people knew that at a certain latitude and longitude one could expect to find a mountainous populated land and that there

## COUNCILS AND CONFERRING

All national navies and merchant marines used councils of some sort to obtain agreement on courses of action, and hence better acceptance, when faced with difficult choices. Only men of supreme confidence and leadership ability, such as Drake, avoided using them or at most used them to rubber-stamp policies already decided. A captive Spaniard in Drake's *Golden Hind* observed that "he takes advice from no one. But he enjoys hearing what they say and afterwards issues his orders." Few are Drakes. Most commanders called councils of officers, sometimes in hope of good advice and somewhat more often from a wish to share responsibility for consequences.

Besides holding councils, consort ships of all nationalities often conferred to compare navigation data. In practice they accepted averages of the navigators' conclusions, depending on odds to ensure reasonably accurate results. Consort ships communicated by sailing close enough to converse with speaking trumpets. But this depended on the weather. In very bad weather ships floated letters, "duly waxed and closely wrapped with a tarred cloth", from one ship to another in wooden waterproof cases. A roaring sea threatened safety as well as drowning voices. When consulting during rough weather in the South Atlantic, Marion's two ships collided, the damage preventing further investigation of the island group nearby. More important, the need to repair the ships caused the long stay in the Bay of Islands which may have been the fundamental cause of Maori attacking and killing Marion and his boat crew.

On Tasman's ship, Pilot Major Visscher, at his captain's bidding, put forward a plan which involved staying in 44 degrees south as far as 150 degrees longitude; if no sighting had been made by then they should turn north to 40 degrees latitude, then east as far as 220 degrees longitude, as closely as dead reckoning could estimate. This should bring them out to the east and south of the Solomon Islands and New Guinea, where they could sail with the trade winds. Tasman sent a letter to the *Zeehaen* on 9 November, suggesting the council should meet to discuss the voyage. On the 11th the sea relaxed, "whereupon the officers of the Zeehaen came to our ship." The council decided to stay in latitude 44 South as far as 195 degrees East, approximately the eastern border of New Guinea on their chart, which they assumed to be reasonably accurate. This was exactly the sort of consultation councils were for, with several experts discussing and deciding on a course of action to recommend to the expedition's commander.

Calling councils implied that consort ships kept at least within sight of one another. This was much more difficult than it sounds, and all ships had meeting places and times arranged in case of separation. On Cook's second voyage Furneaux, commander of his consort ship, became separated twice and was obliged to sail to "the appointed Rendezvous". Those who sent ships out in company tried to select apt "running mates" but often failed, for a ship's speed is an amalgam of potential speed, built into her, and her captain's skill and drive. Burney, on Furneaux's *Adventure*, complained that, "our Ship in her best trim is not able to keep up, or carry sail with the Resolution, at this time we fall bodily to Leeward being quite Light & so crank that we are obliged to strike to every Squall, and so unmanageable that there is no getting her round either one way or another." Poorly matched ships – and Cook's next two were well-chosen, no doubt after he complained about *Adventure* – nullified the purposes of a consort. These were assistance in case of difficulties and increased likelihood of reports of the ships' achievements getting home.

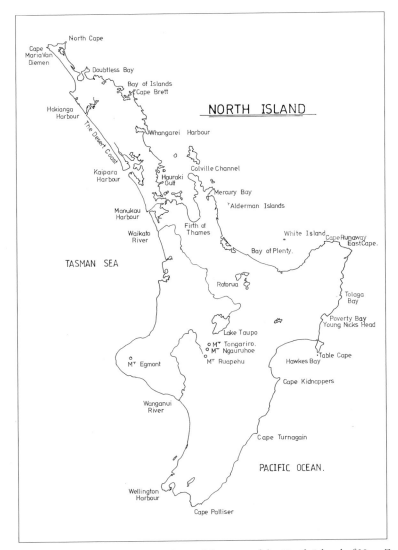

Relative positions of the main physical features of the North Island of New Zealand.

were good anchorages there. What extended south, north and east was another matter. For all that the world knew from Tasman's voyage, New Zealand could have been a peninsula on a vast southern continent, and it was exactly this supposition that Cook set out to verify or disprove. His world's "discovery" was Tasman's; that world's exploration did not start until Cook's voyage.

As a feat of seamanship and navigation Tasman's voyage was remarkable; only ten men were lost, including the casualties at Murderer's Bay. The Company recognised that success and each sailor was given a month's pay in cash and the pilots two months'. But the Company was not happy: Tasman did not accomplish much at New Zealand; indeed there was little he could have done. The Maori had no gold nor anything to offer the Company in trade.

But there is nonetheless something to remember; the Maori killed Dutch sailors yet Tasman displayed forebearance. He did not take revenge by bombarding the villages, and his few inaccurate shots seem singularly half-hearted by the standards of the 17th-century North Sea. Yet by later standards his exploration seems half-hearted too. He had, complained the Company's report, "left everything to be more closely inquired into by more industrious successors." The East Indies Council thought that Tasman had been "remiss in investigating the situation, conformation, and nature of the lands discovered, and of the natives inhabiting the same ...." Tasman's optimistic "trust" that the new land, a "fine country", was part of the great continent in the south was not accepted by the Council. The "fine" was clearly right; the "trust" was wistfully wrong.

Nor was the Company really satisfied that the expedition had found a passage to Chile and Peru. After all, from their point of view, if Tasman had sailed further east he might have run into the massive southern continent he was sent to find. Yet if the Company had but realised it, Tasman really had found the way to Chile, to Peru, and round the Horn to Europe. Unfortunately the route did not pay until New Zealand and New Holland were developed as wheat and meat producers, the rewards of which did not go to the Dutch. The Dutch East India Company did not send out any other great expeditions, for they did not pay quickly nor directly; the Council saw more profit from trade in the eastern seas.

The expedition was over. The captains and the crews departed, talk died down and memories began to fade. Possibly, even probably, aging men regaled their drinking mates with weather reports of the deep south, and tales of how one could, and why one should, avoid the natives of New Zealand. But other than that it was finished, except for the name Tasman on the world's maps. We know nothing about Visscher after 1644, but Tasman returned to Company service and led an important charting expedition between Australia and New Guinea. He began to drink heavily and for a time found disgrace before reforming and winning respect as a merchant in Dutch East Indian society. He died in 1659, owning much land in Batavia itself. At the end he remembered Holland and to Lutjegast, his native village, he left money for its poor.

To the Dutch, and hence to Tasman, the world owes the name New Zealand. Present-day Australia was already called New Holland. Zeeland was the other great province of the United Provinces of the Netherlands and was not to be forgotten. The second province to be honoured thus acquired the more permament memorial, for New Holland is part of distant history. Tasman Sea, Mount Tasman, Abel Tasman National Park, as well as Tasmania, commemorate Tasman. Cape Maria van Diemen, the northern point of New Zealand, indirectly preserves the memory of van Diemen, who deserves to be remembered. It was his drive and vision that sent the explorers on their way.

CHAPTER FOUR

# *A Master of Navigation*

For over a hundred years, from the brief visit of Abel Tasman to the arrival of James Cook, the world left the Maori of New Zealand alone. Their lack of anything even resembling rich trading goods – as well as apparent indocility – for a time guaranteed immunity. There was simply no good commercial reason for coming to New Zealand. Or indeed to anywhere near it, except to explore. Only when distance and emptiness made the area seem suitable for banished undesirables did Europeans actually settle the south-west Pacific. Even then the reputation of the Maori kept New Zealand free of settlers for a long time.

There was a lull in sponsored European exploration until after the great Seven Years War ended in 1763. Some of that restless continent's nations were distracted by civil war; foreign wars kept others busy protecting what trade and colonies they already had. Even as Tasman was sailing home from New Zealand his Company was revising its plans for more exploration in the South Sea, as "these plans of ours were frustrated by the machinations of the Portuguese over here (with whom we were compelled to renew hostilities, and, to vindicate the company's right, to employ our forces against them ....." European quarrels spread quickly, as the endless bickering in Europe played to a new audience on a Pacific stage.

There were some exceptional voyages, Russian expeditions in the north in the 1730s and Roggeveen's search for trade in 1722 or Barlow's in 1700. But for all this time Pacific exploration, or at least discovery in the Pacific, was largely incidental to buccaneering voyages like Dampier's in 1708, or wartime raids such as Anson's in the 1740s. Trade of the the Dutch, English or French East India Companies, and even the Atlantic trade of the Americas, carried by English, French and Spanish private ships, nearly always had to sail in convoys under the national navy's protection. The great convoy system, reborn to guard against submarines in the First and Second World Wars, came to perfection in the 18th century.

Such trade was making some nations rich. We ought not to be too censorious. It is not unnatural for countries to wish to profit from their overseas contacts. Trade is an honourable institution; to protect that trade is a natural reaction. Governments in modern New Zealand or Britain are intimately linked by commerce, if at times only through the operation of the law. Today even ordinary citizens expect government protection for their well-being as well as their safety. 18th-century governments, believing national prosperity depended upon trade, were careful to protect it for their own citizens; we do much the same, more quietly.

Nor was it at all unnatural, before the development of modern liberal Europe, for peoples to wish to profit from contact with another place or race. Only since the Second World War have nations shown any desire to lose from their contact with others; foreign aid is a very recent phenomenon. Except for war subsidies to allies it would have seemed strange indeed to 18th century statesmen. Nations were meant to stand on their own feet; if fate favoured it then possibly on the land of others. If this worked to their disadvantage it was because they were not organised, soldierly, nor numerous enough to prevent it. Until well after the Second World War moral qualms about these attitudes affected only a few philosophers, or occasionally less ambitious priests of some church or other. The main reason for exploration, apart from glory to discoverers – as humanly vain as statesmen, scientists, actresses and professors – was ambition to increase the wealth and power of the nation by finding the islands and continents, the best routes and channels, the best winds and best watering. Our attitudes to such ambitions, insofar as they have really changed, would have seemed laughable.

In spite of all those deplorable human failings there was a ferment of change then too. New ideas, gaining their strength and forming their base on what we may loosely call the scientific attitude, began to make their influence felt. England and other European nations had formed organisations such as the Royal Society. Their leaders, scientists and laymen fascinated by the progress of science, promoted exploration not only to find new routes for trade or to make the seas safer for sailors, but simply to know more about the physical world, and specifically its lands and oceans. Allied closely to this was a desire to know more about the diverse peoples of mankind, to examine them as individuals and as cultures. Entering a field long the prerogative of the Church and philosophers, science intended to examine life's motives and means.

The new wish to know did not ignore non-human life. The desire to understand how natural dispensations worked meant the rise in importance of the naturalists. Such people wanted plants and animals from around the world, not as curiosities but objects of study. Many in the new Societies were interested in the science of language; new lands meant new tongues to master and ponder. Astronomy reaped rewards from distant positions thousands of kilometres from home, examining the sky from completely different vantages. The development of science, not new but much more important, became a motive for exploration. Unusual characters such as Dampier had earlier acted in much the same way, but without the training and knowledge of the scientists who sailed with Cook. Bent and interest, even assisted by powerful observation and description, do not replace training and knowledge.

Britain chose Cook to explore because of his utter competence. Like Tasman he had come up through the ranks though, unlike the Dutchman, comparatively old at eighteen when he went to sea. Nine years later he joined the Royal Navy, a lowly ranker but a thoroughly trained seaman. Cook learned his trade in a rough but able school – in Whitby ships down the North Sea's English coast to London, in stormy waters. Explorers sail through unknown shoals; constantly shifting sands provide new shoals almost daily along coasts of the North Sea. Cook also sailed the Baltic for two years, a shallow enclosed sea, and when exploring he sailed many such waters. Survivors knew their trade well; the great explorer had had the right beginnings.

Cook advanced rapidly in the Navy, partly because he was usually lucky in his officers but mainly because his competence impressed percipient captains. Admiral Lord Colville spoke early of "Mr Cook's genius and capacity." As a result some captains not only promoted him but also taught him navigation, for example, in special individual lessons. Good pupils tend to get good teachers. Other captains assisted him by posting him to the right places at the right times. Although Cook survived naval battles, that was not how he earned his fame. Nor was it how he gained the chance to explore with such distinction. His abilities, superb eye and judgment in surveying and charting, his interest in mathematics, his pertinacity in study, made up only part of the man. What had him sent into distant oceans was his command of men, of method, and of himself. If genius is really the infinite capacity for taking pains then Cook was truly a genius; but humble men followed him and great men employed, admired, befriended and honoured him. Their discernment and his successes ensured that the world revealed its last great secrets.

James Cook would be remembered for his published maps even if he had never sailed the Pacific. He thoroughly charted much of the coastline of Newfoundland; although this island province of Canada is only about the size of the South Island of New Zealand, it has a coastline 9600 kilometres long, and some of the safest harbours of the world. Now there is very little reason for any but local fishermen to enter them, but in those days diets, ships and wars were different, and Newfoundland was important. Cook's charts of much of the coastline of Nova Scotia and of the Gulf of St Lawrence around and up the St Lawrence River to Quebec were in common use for decades. This gigantic river drains much of central North America, including all the Great Lakes. Cook worked early, as later, on a grand scale.

Many of his charts were done to help the Royal Navy take the British Army to attack the French fortress of Quebec, sited where the St Lawrence River narrowed enough for cannon to prevent enemy fleets using the river. Cook made a vital contribution to the undreamt-of British coup, bringing the huge ships of the line up past Quebec through waters until then known only to local pilots. This feat, combined with minor charting of the eastern Australian coast, the charting of New Zealand, and then charting during the exploration of the seven thousand kilometre coastline of British Columbia, affirm Cook's primacy in charting.

We can see his priorities clearly. In the cramped space of the *Endeavour* he found space for a map room and no less than four cabins for draughtsmen. In charting he was a perfectionist, but as in all else he was practical, grounding his thoughts on his own observations. Occasionally he drew inferences from indications; never did he base conclusions on inferences. Writing about one of his charts he explained this clearly. "I shall point out such places as are drawn with sufficient accuracy to be depended upon and such as are not ... some few places however must be excepted and these are very doubtfull and are not only here but in every other part of the chart pointed out by a prick'd or broken line." Much of Cook's navigational data has not yet been superseded.

Cook was man as well as surveyor; he married a handsome woman as well as drawing handsome charts. It was a happy marriage, although responsibility must have weighed heavily on his wife in those three- and four-year absences. The explorer came home to a child, more than once, who ran away from the strange man who kissed its mother and then tried to kiss the new face too. Once he came to the grave of the little girl they had both wanted but whom he had never seen play. James Cook was singularly normal, although perhaps more courteous and reticent than most famous men. His journals show that normality included being an observer of human nature, as keenly interested in behaviour of men and women of his own culture as of cultures newly encountered. His journals, so widely read, did much to immortalise his name and work. Yet if he had lived, the tribute to his authorship he would probably have enjoyed most was that his old father, two or three years before his eightieth birthday, "had learned to read, so that he he might gratify a parent's love and pride by perusing his son's first voyage round the world!"

Energy, driving willingness to work at whatever task was to hand including writing, air of command, superb navigational skills, ability to assess the danger of coastlines and the future of harbours and to chart both well, thorough interest in the health and welfare of his men, devotion to duty: all meant that Cook's exploration would not be as sparsely recorded as Tasman's. From the mind and hand of Cook himself, as well as those of many able people with him, came prodigious amounts of charting and writing. All that occurred seemed to catch his eye and mind, flow on through his pen, creating so much material that it has been studied and discussed ever since.

Although Cook did not explore inland, his charts of New Zealand and various islands, his curiosity about the natives, and his comparisons and insights about their early connections with Tahiti and other Pacific islands combine to make him pre-eminent in the field. And he foreshadowed New Zealand's future. His assessment of the resources of the country made him believe that it would make a remarkably fine place for British emigrants to settle: "all sorts of European grain fruits Plants &c$^a$ would thrive here. In short was this Country settled by an Industrus people they would very soon be supply'd not only with the necessarys, but many of the luxuries of life." Mount Cook rightly casts a large shadow.

Superbly equipped in mind and character, Cook had a physique to match them. "A tall, large-boned, powerful man, with strongly marked features": so a European writer described him. Physique and character united impressively. A young Maori felt the effect of Cook's bearing, recognising the "supreme man in that ship" by his appearance and his quiet authority. An impressive exterior is half way to an air of command. Yet there was nothing feigned about this. Cook could bear extreme physical hardship and did, as sailor and captain, yet his reaction to hard conditions and danger was that more foresight and better organisation would have either avoided or vanquished them.

English exploration in Cook's time was spurred mainly by the hopes and ambitions of 18th century science. This does not necessarily indicate great altruism. 17th and 18th century science was looking for knowledge which could be useful, rejecting any which seemed to be based on metaphysical explanation. Newton, for example, argued that the mechanism of the natural world must be governed by rational laws to be discovered by experiment and observation, and that theory must be built on facts seen and experienced, not on such things as the will of God or universal goodness.

Such plain doctrine found in Cook, although he was not a scientist, a practising disciple. New knowledge discovered by actual sight, accurate measurements and accurate description, aptly suited his downright common sense. Detailed observation of what went on in nature, or in the behaviour of

The artist, John Webber, captured one side of James Cook's character in this rather severe portrait. The captain could be stern when it was a question of enforcing his food regulations or indeed any rule affecting the welfare of the ship. But to have sailed with Cook became a badge of honour among sailors and surviving veterans boasted of it well into the 19th century. (*National Art Gallery of New Zealand*)

human beings, presumed that changes in categorisation, theories or general principles could only be deduced from masses of accurate information. Once deduced, theories or principles had to be checked against experiments or, at the very least, by thorough re-examination in similar circumstances. Cook, a tremendously energetic worker and persevering through the greatest difficulties, believed fervently in accurate observation and even more in accurate reproduction in publication. He proved himself a natural master of the methods and the attitudes. Lord Morton of the Royal Society and the Lords of the Admiralty had happened upon an almost perfect human instrument for scientific Pacific exploration.

Luck is one lever of success. Cook, an instrument of the Admiralty, had the luck to coincide with great improvement in instruments of observation. Vastly better navigational tools had appeared in the 17th century but the 18th century improved and added to them. It was an age of great mechanical craftsmen, basing their work on precision in mathematics, a science rapidly developing. New or refined instruments, vital to the scientific revolution, were being engendered by that revolution itself.

Cook however did not depend on his own instinct or observation to make *Endeavour*'s a scientific voyage; that is not why the Admiralty chose him. One of the Royal Society's official observers, he was there as leader, the captain, the decision-maker. For science, the Royal Society sent scientists. Chief among them was Joseph Banks, a gentleman of great gifts and energy, for at twenty-four years old he was a highly competent farmer and landowner, the source of his great wealth. Clever, capable and adventurous, immensely interested in science, he persuaded the Royal Navy to take him on what his presence made a gigantic botanising expedition. Banks was youthful, outgoing, overflowing with cheer, often arrogant; Cook older, taciturn, experienced, thoughtful, quietly confident. The possibilities of clash in these two very strong personalities was great. Yet they maintained good relations for nearly three years on a small crowded ship, sometimes under great strain. Even though Banks's untimely wish to botanise sometimes irritated Cook there was only one real disagreement, which reflects great credit on both men.

To accompany him Banks took a secretary, two artists (one of whom, Sydney Parkinson, was also a botanist), two footmen, two servants, and two large greyhounds. This is how wealthy gentlemen travelled; Banks was as fit and as tough as Cook himself. To assist him he recruited at a social occasion the brilliant Swedish botanist, Dr Daniel Karl Solander. This more or less accidental association meant that strange plants from New Zealand – and very strange indeed some were – would be introduced to European scientists by men capable of explication and description. It also meant Solander's immortalisation by a 19th-century New Zealand missionary-cum-botanist, William Colenso, who, seeking marine fossils, "was rewarded with a truly elegant species of *Patella*, which, not finding described, I have named *P.Solandri*, in commemoration of Dr. Solander." The voyage and its hopes for plant collection won Banks the friendship of George III, and royal support for exploration and science.

Society was excited by all this, but most people were very glad Cook was there. He was the practical man in these matters; one who would prove or disprove the theorists' speculations and theories. His observations were based on his own curiosity. He wished to learn, not to confirm preconceptions, much less to discuss what he had not himself observed. His perfectionism unwound the intricacies of observed data by reproducing conclusions in mapping or writing, coming to understand by phrasing it for others to ponder.

His writing is thoughtful and thought-provoking; comparison of Cook's journals with Tasman's is as of sun to moon. Objectivity was basic in the great explorer's personality. But he was no cold fish; his temper saw to that. So did his kindness. A Maori child experienced it and never forgot: "He was a very good man, and came to us – the children – and patted our cheeks, and gently touched our heads." Cook's writing shows insight, and empathy with the Polynesians of the South Pacific as well as the Indians of Eastern and Western Canada.

New navigational techniques always fascinated Cook, and he did not rest until he mastered them. Like any intuitive master he looked after his tools of all kinds, animate and inanimate. A healthy crew he saw as fundamental to success, and on a sailing ship with large, heavy and writhing sails to handle, and ponderous anchors to haul by muscle power, he was absolutely right. Under his eye crews tried all manner of things to stay healthy. Cook successfully held scurvy at bay with cleanliness and greens, but he was not omnipotent. Batavia's tropical fevers defeated *Endeavour's* efforts; Cook never took men back there.

Sailors had their own thoughts about Cook's discipline and diets. One gets to know the great captain well in the journals of his officers and men. That so many have been published, and so many at the time, indicates the interest Cook and his achievements aroused. Many sailor-authors refer to their commander's instinct and intuition. In Cook, as in nearly everyone, these qualities were based on study, thought, knowledge, skills and experience. An experienced motorist driving in many conditions and places will do the right thing reactively; it is not instinct but reflex which operates. So with Cook. He applied his years on the North Sea shoals to shoals in the Pacific; applied his immense knowledge of the capricious weather of Newfoundland and the North Sea to New Zealand conditions. Lore learned mapping Canadian harbours left traces in New Zealand, and his methods of crew management in the southern oceans had been inculcated by good Atlantic and North Sea captains.

On his first voyage Cook did all the things Tasman was supposed to do. He set about his tasks with a mature man's confidence; he was just a few months beyond his thirties. Although relatively few years an officer he was already a seaman old in experience and responsibility, and this maturity won respect and affection from the peoples of the Pacific. Technically he was supreme: surveying the surface, sounding the depths, draughting meticulously, reporting thoroughly. The Lords of the Admiralty had found a treasure and realised it. Like Tasman, Cook found no rich nation, but that was because there was no rich nation in the South Pacific.

The ship the Admiralty bought for the voyage was renamed *Endeavour*. The ships of his later voyages were renamed too. All those Cook took into the Pacific, his own or consort, were aptly named, a roll call suitably expressive: *Endeavour, Resolution, Adventure, Discovery.* They were all of a type suited to the purpose, cats built at Whitby. *Endeavour's* distinctive feature was somewhat unorthodox rigging. It caused some trouble for she headed up into the wind, wearing out spritsails set to prevent it. Cook had learned his seamanship on Whitby cats and lived in the town for years; he knew not only the ships but the shipbuilders. His early experience, and the thought which he lavished on any project, would have led him to favour that type of ship.

The Navy Board had suggested the "choice of a cat-built vessel for the said service" because "their kind are roomly and will afford the advantage of stowing and carrying a large quantity of provisions, so necessary on such voyages." In addition to the normal crew, Cook's expeditions had to carry abnormal tonnages of provisions for many extra people on extraordinarily long voyages. Sailing ships tried to start with at least a few supernumeraries in case of scurvy, but the kind of men who would make sailors. Presumably artists, botanists, and astronomers do not have abnormally large appetites, but their presence – to say nothing of Banks's hounds – was supernumerary. Banks's party of nine had a vast amount of baggage, including "botanists', artists', and naturalists' equipment to last two years – cases of jars for specimens, pots and presses for plants; canvases, easels … machines for catching and preserving insects; spirits to preserve small animals, wax and salts to do the same for seeds: and two large greyhounds." Enough indeed to hold an exhibition.

The first task of Cook's *Endeavour* voyage was to astronomically observe the "transit of Venus" at Tahiti, not half so exciting as it sounds. Afterwards he was to search for the great southern continent, which perhaps Tasman had missed

## COOK'S WHITBY CATS

Cats were sturdy, blunt and cheeky ships, flat-bottomed to sit safely on tidal flats when necessary, roundly roomy to make a profit carrying cheap coal from the northern mining counties to London. Immensely strong flat-bottomed little ships still lie on the sands of Whitby harbour when the tide is out. It takes a strong ship to lie safely on the bottom and in Cook's time the best were built at Whitby, built to stand up to North Sea winds, waves, weather and shoals, to keep the coal going south in the winter. In the coal trade strength and storage were more important than speed. The design of cats followed the same principles as that of Dutch flutes, and Tasman had taken one of those capacious sturdy vessels when he sailed to find New Zealand.

These qualities and characteristics of cats were exactly those essential in an exploration vessel. Cook, with his Newfoundland experience, saw this clearly. The evidence suggests that the Navy Board, which as the supplier of ships did know something about them, had reached the same conclusion as Cook. The Board had been disappointed by the relative failure of the Byron and Wallis voyages in frigates, which were sharp-bottomed ships, built slim, sleek and fast to function as the scouting "eyes of the fleet." Sharp-bottomed ships needed deeper water and fell over when the tide went out. Not unnaturally, their captains kept cautiously out to sea, a course of action which hinders charting shorelines and assessing harbours.

Besides the actual sailing of the ships, there was the probability that repairs and the certainty that normal maintenance would need doing far from home and dockyard facilities. Cats had the shape and strength to be sailed up onto beaches deliberately, when the tide went out, to be hauled over one way and then the other for the repair and cleaning of the hull to be done from the exposed sand. Copper sheathing to keep the wooden hulls clean of sea-spread growth was not yet general. It was more probable than merely possible that reefs, rocks and the ravages of shipworm might make major repairs necessary, as Cook had to do to *Endeavour* in Australia on his way home from his first visit to New Zealand. On long voyages thousands of kilometres from bases this capability mattered.

by not sailing far enough east from New Zealand. If Cook found it, he was to assess the inhabitants and the land and claim it for the Crown should it be suitable. If there was time he was to go on to New Zealand and "carefully observe the Latitude and Longitude in which that Land is situated, and explore as much of the Coast as the Condition of the Bark, the health of her Crew, and the State of your Provisions will admit of ...."

After a successful visit to Tahiti, especially for young and vigorous sailors, Cook sailed his ship south to about latitude 40 and then westward. On not finding the southern continent he moved north to the latitudes of New Zealand and headed west. On 7 October 1769 the boy Nicholas Young, "who was at the Mast head call'd out Land, I was luckily upon Deck, & well I was entertain'd ...." Banks recorded these words, and wishful, thought it was a continent; Mr Cook, factual, thought it was New Zealand, "which we stood directly for." The captain's first words about it in his journal are quite commending of the new land; "We saw in the Bay several Canoes, People upon the shore and some houses in the Country. The land on the Sea-Coast is high with white steep clifts and back inland are very high mountains, the face of the Country is of a hilly surface and appeares to be cloathed with wood and Verdure."

First contact with the land's inhabitants was to be almost as unfortunate for the English as for the Dutch. The Maori tried to seize the ship's boat when Cook and his companions landed and walked towards the house. When a Maori seemed about to hurl a spear at the four boys looking after the boat he was killed by sailors from a second boat after shots in the air had not deterred him. Captain Cook, some distance away on land and beyond controlling what happened, was extremely upset by the shooting. The next day started better; when they landed again Tupaia, the Tahitian, found "the language of the People

This pleasant painting by Thomas Luney is of "a cat-built Whitby barque" lying in Whitby harbour. The ship is said to be the *Endeavour* and, if so, Cook did his thinking and writing in the cabin whose windows we see in the stern. *(National Library of Australia)*

was so like his own, that he could tolerably well understand them, & they him ...." This helped matters briefly, although Tupaia warned that the natives "were not our friends."

This was only the beginning of Tupaia's services in New Zealand. A Raiatean and Tahitian, priest and navigator, he had volunteered to sail with Cook in order to escape a difficult situation in Tahiti but also, one supposes, to learn of the world beyond Polynesia. He learned much and taught as much again. The captain took him on board "at the request of M$^r$ Banks", indeed at the expense of Banks, who wrote, "I do not know why I may not keep him as a curiosity, as well as some of my neighbours do lions & tygers at a larger expence ...." Cook thought Tupaia "a shrewd, sensible, ingenious man, but proud and obstinate, which often made his situation on board both disagreeable to himself and to those about him ...." On balance his knowledge proved more useful than his personality was troublesome.

Maori now came across the small river to be given presents and trouble flared again. "We made them every one presents, but this did not satisfy them they wanted but every thing we had about us ...." A Maori tried to steal the astronomer's sword, Cook ordered him to be fired on and he was "wounded in such a manner that he died soon after." Cook was much upset and tried to capture some Maori and then "by good treatment and presents endeavour to gain their friendship." The Maori did not understand the European intentions, naturally enough, in spite of Tupaia's reassurances. Sailors attempted to seize some Maori from a canoe and as they tried to escape Cook had a musket fired over their heads, hoping they would surrender. Instead they attacked the English boat and two or three more of their number were killed. Cook's good intentions were paving a road to somewhere, and no one wished to walk it.

This was all most unfortunate to say the least, and in his report a downcast Cook rebuked himself sternly for misjudgment: "I am aware that most humane men who have not experienced things of this nature will Cencure my conduct ... nor do I my self think that the reason I had ... will att all justify me ...." Banks called it "the most disagreeable day My life has yet seen ...." But, although upset, Banks knew that force was a necessity at times, and that humans were most unlikely to be very different in the southern hemisphere than in the northern; he had thought it "nescessary for our safeties that so daring an act should be instantly punishd ...."

*Endeavour's* sailors picked up three Maori youths attempting to swim ashore and they rapidly became quite cheerful. As soon as possible they were put ashore with lavish gifts. A few Maori men, hearing of the good treatment given the youths, came on board *Endeavour* and traded their paddles for Tahitian cloth, apparently valuing it highly. It was bark cloth made from the aute or paper mulberry; this was a tropical tree although a few did grow in the extreme north of New Zealand. Three men stayed aboard and in the morning canoes approached very cautiously. Tupaia translated into English the Maori assurance to friends in the canoes that the English did not eat men; until then Cook and his crew had no thought that the inhabitants were cannibals. The exchange caused much argument and doubtless lessened the attractions of New Zealand for those who accepted its implication.

During the visit of *Endeavour* Parkinson painted a picture of a Maori war canoe. It seems to have about the number of paddlers that would be able to work effectively. But when war canoes went on raids they often carried extra men between the two ranks of paddlers or even down on the floor. *(Hocken Library, Dunedin)*

The ship now left Poverty Bay, so named because it supplied the expedition "no one thing we wanted." The south-western point of the bay was called Young Nick's Head, a twist of the name of Nicholas Young, the lad who first saw that feature of New Zealand. *Endeavour* coasted along south-south-westward. New Zealand seemed moderately high and inland even mountainous, but with many woods. There were "all the appearences of a very pleasent and fertile country", and many signs of habitation, such as smoke or houses. A few Maori were fishing and one group of canoes, on showing hostility, had to be warned away by firing a big gun. There seemed to be no safe harbour.

Everyone wanted water. So had Tasman and his men. Sailing ships usually did, often not because casks were empty but because their contents were putrid. *Endeavour* stopped at the first opportunity but several canoes came out aggressively and had to be warned away from watering boats by gunfire. Fresh water was foregone. Next day the crews were able to trade with the Maori, usually cloth for dried fish. The sailors called this local food "stinking fish", possibly a clue to palatability if not nutritional qualities. Then men in one of the canoes seized Tupaia's servant boy; the ship opened fire, killing two or three Maori, and the boy leapt into the water and was rescued. Like the Dutch before them, the English were finding New Zealand inhospitable.

Cook named the great bay they were in Hawke Bay, after the First Lord of the Admiralty who appointed him to command the expedition, and the prominence at the south end of the bay Cape Kidnappers, after the Maori who stole the boy. *Endeavour* proceeded southward but gave up hope of seeing much more in increasingly barren country. Cook turned back at a cape he named Cape Turnagain. Once north of all they had already seen, the Maori were more friendly. Cook could occasionally buy sweet potatoes and they had no trouble gathering wild celery. What marred the area was the difficulty in watering; there seemed to be few rivers and the beach surf was high and dangerous.

Cook's emphasis on crew health, at least partly under orders from the Admiralty, was not entirely popular, for it altered the diet of very conservative seamen. The captain insisted that every morning wild celery was to be boiled with portable soup, the early equivalent of Oxo or Bovril. Even if sailors liked neither the work or the reason: "in the morning some hands were employ'd picking of Sellery to take to sea with us ... and I have caused it to be boild with Portable Soup and Oatmeal every morning ... because I look upon it to be very wholesome and a great Antiscorbutick."

The Maori here traded actively for English linen and Tahitian cloth and coveted glass bottles. They seemed to see no use for spikes or nails, although later Cook found that Maori at Queen Charlotte Sound did. A northern Maori lad, who years later described his revered Cook, had no conception of heating and shaping iron but had put the nail he had been given in "the point of my spear" and "used it to make holes in the side-boards of canoes." But there were other values than pure utility. In spite of these practical uses the accidental loss of his nail devastated him for completely emotional reasons; it had signified his personal contact with the admired "chief of those demons."

The Maori were becoming less and less troublesome as each side learned how to cope with the other's ways, and Cook was now having more free time to look around and to think. He and the astronomer, Green, were able to make exact observations for latitude and longitude. He noted in his journal that there seemed to be no animals except the Maori dogs, for though he heard of land rats he did not see any. Cook admired the flourishing and well designed Maori gardens, looking at the work and attention put into them with a Yorkshire farmer's eye. Remembering his open-air boyhood in a beautiful district of England, he commented on the varieties of trees and plants and especially birds. The botanists and naturalists were in a sort of heaven, with novelty all around.

Cook remembered to write of it all, and the Maori remembered him too. About seventy years later a merchant spoke of their mementoes of Cook, spikes and nails that had lasted, and of the beautifully romantic scenery "of Opotoumu (Opoutama), enhanced by the cherished associations of the immortal navigator." A missionary too, William Colenso, in 1841 met a very old chief who claimed to remember Cook's visit "although he was a very little boy then." At the time of Colenso's visit the Maori at Tolaga Bay still showed people a well which Cook had his men dig to water his ships.

After leaving Tolaga Bay the ship rounded East Cape and began tracking along the northern shore of the North Island, seemingly more flourishing and fertile. We can almost imagine the events as we follow much of his route by his naming practice. Occasionally Cook named a feature to commemorate its discoverer, as with Hicks Bay. More often a name evokes the eventful voyage in new waters; Cape Runaway reminds us that here a number of canoes full of heavily armed and apparently threatening warriors were scared off by a cannon fired to do only that. Or emphasises the uniqueness of some feature; White Island was so named because it is white. Bay of Plenty flourished then as now. As they proceeded further west and north Cook's humour showed itself in his naming, calling an island The Mayor Island, perhaps because it seemed imposing, and a peculiar group of great rocks still further north the Aldermen Islands, or the Court of Aldermen, in honour of the council of London. Banks and others amused themselves by "giving names to each of them from their resemblance thick & squat or lank & tall to some one or other of those respectable citizens."

The clear relationship of each group of excellent plantations to the site of their pa caused Cook to question Tupaia's explanation of pa as places of worship. Cook now realised they were fortifications. Here too the *Endeavour* saw, coming out from Whale Island, the first double canoe they had observed in New Zealand. A sailor described it as "built after the model of those at Otahitee, but carved and decorated according to their own peculiar manner ... she carried a sail of an odd construction ... made from a kind of matting, and of a triangular figure ...."

They moved on, Maori threatening from their canoes again, but in spite of that Cook determined to find shelter to observe a transit of Mercury, important in itself but also ensuring a very accurate longitude. He found an excellent harbour near the north-east tip of Coromandel Peninsula, sheltered from every direction and laden with fish. Astronomer Green, with Cook as helper, managed very well according to Cook: "At 8 M$^r$ Green and I went on shore with our Instruments to Observe the Transit of Mercury ... Observed by M$^r$ Green only. I at this time was taking the Suns Altitude in order to asertain the time." Green's tale is slightly different, but if the captain wants to help that is that. Besides all this astronomy they heeled the ship over at low tide to scrub its sides. This was to remove shellfish, worms, and various other impedimenta that literally attached themselves to wooden ships. Although sheeting the bottom with copper had just been developed, *Endeavour* was not so honoured.

Every stay in harbour brought Cook's diet regulations into action. "Afterwards sent the other two boats to pick sallery for the ships Companys breakfast." Celery was not the only treat; fish and wildfowl swarmed in the region. Neither sailors nor explorers confined themselves, as we would likely do, to what would have seemed familiar: geese, ducks and pigeons. Any food in feathers was fowl in earlier times. Cook's officers and men ate shag, gulls, terns and albatrosses, in fact whatever fowl or fish they could catch. After months of salt beef Mr Banks found boiled shag very fine eating. But then Banks had a more catholic appetite than most. Years after his travelling was over he confided to a friend: "I believe I have eaten my way into the Animal Kingdom farther than any other man." Even though he admitted having drawn the line at monkey, partly from fellow feeling, New Zealand provided no hazards and some delights for such an eclectic appetite. Banks thought New Zealand lobsters (crayfish) "the largest & best I have ever Eat."

At Mercury Bay a Maori was seen stealing a roll of cloth; Lieutenant Gore specifically aimed at and killed the thief. This was the last Maori life sacrificed by *Endeavour's* crew. Cook was angry about the incident but it seemed that other Maori thought Gore quite right to avenge himself directly. Banks, earlier so upset at the first Maori death, although he had been first to shout for punishment and had himself fired at the sword-snatcher, pointed out that death was the penalty for major theft in England. No complaint and no action from the Maori followed and trade was resumed. One can presume feelings in another culture much too easily. Somewhat later a lieutenant had a Maori flogged for theft. This did not bother his companions, and on his rejoining the others he was beaten up by an elderly chief.

From Mercury Bay Cook went inland to visit a Maori pa. Nearby he encountered mangrove trees, a clue to northern New Zealand's climate. An old

## MAORI PA

The construction of fortified pa began probably during the 14th century, and pa with ditches, palisades and fighting stages existed throughout the country by 1500 A.D., although mainly in the more populated north. Some four to six thousand pa were constructed, an almost unbelievable task for a total population of possibly 125,000. Population figures for the individual pa range from thirty to 300 or more. Earlier small independent groups lived in several places, depending on seasonal resources. Most had a base settlement where they spent the winter, living on provisions gathered and stored for the purpose. Temporary settlements were made at various places where fish and shellfish were caught and dried; where birds, including the giant moa, were hunted and preserved; and where fern root was gathered and dried. Some base settlements were later fortified, especially in the south where they tended to be more permanent than in the horticultural north where the base village had to be shifted every few years as the slash and burn horticulture impoverished the land.

The slow increase in population may have put pressure on resources – fern root as well as good kumara land – and the need to protect not only growing and gathering areas but the produce from them may have led to the development of fortified stores and fortified bases. The reasons behind the relatively sudden increase in warfare are not clear. The first settlers brought with them not only weapons but the contemporary Polynesian proclivity for conflict and revenge. Early New Zealand was not peaceful; the 12th century inhabitants faced violent death. Nonetheless the small population and large country probably meant only occasional instances of personal violence rather than organised fighting. Traditional stories often deal with insult and reprisal, and presumably early society had its share. At some stage, mainly in the more heavily populated horticultural areas of the north, the groups became larger and strongholds developed. They varied greatly in size and purpose, some being settlements with defences, others refuges used only in times of attack.

Cook was impressed with the fortified pa he saw in the North Island. At Wharetaewa Pa at Mercury Bay he noted the ditches, scarps, and palisades, the fighting stage nine metres high and ten metres long, the terraces and outworks which formed successive lines of defence, above all the superb defensive position, "built upon a high promontory ... in some places quite inaccessible to man and in others very difficult ...." He added: "Many works of this kind we have seen upon small Islands and Rocks and Ridges of hills on all parts of this Coast besides a great number of fortified towns, to all appearences Vastly superior to this I have described. From this it should seem that this people must have long and frequent wars, and must have been long accustom'd to it otherwise they never would have invented such strong holds as these, the erecting of which must cost them immence labour considering the tools they have to work with which are only made of wood & stone." Between building their defences and growing, gathering and preserving food, the early Maori can have had little time left for actual fighting.

captured fort convinced him that the Maori must be very effective warriors, both in attack and defence. The fortresses were "very strong and well choose [sic] post and where a small number of resolute men might defend them selves a long time against a vast superior force ...." Maori seemed to have no projectile weapons like bows and arrows, much less guns, but threw three metre darts and stones, and used spears, lances and clubs. The captain must have thought of battles at the massive castles of his Yorkshire. The weapons showed that iron was unfamiliar to the Maori, and indeed they had little interest in it except occasionally for nails. This was to change half a century later; axes, guns, ploughs and knives were to become their hearts' desire when the whalemen and the missionaries demonstrated such tools' utility and supplied them.

The visitors would always try, where possible, to make friends with the Maori children. Often they would have been greatly amused by what was being whispered among the youngsters. Once the children said that ships' bread, the infamous hardtack, was hard and sweet and very like pumice stone, and red meat was too salty and hurt their throats, suitable comments on salt beef. But the Maori paid compliments too. Years later an old man remembered vividly how they had been affected by Cook's "perfect gentlemanly and noble demeanour." There is no paradox here, no conflict between his nature and his ability to command; fortunately for discipline he also had high standards and a temper. Indeed the Swedish botanist on Cook's second voyage, Anders

A fortified village in the Bay of Islands which had been deserted by the time Sainson, with d'Urville's expedition, sketched it in 1827. The open coastal settlements of the moa-hunters had given way to fortified hilltop sites either as settlements or refuges. Fortifications varied greatly, sometimes not more than a fence, sometimes a ditch added to natural defences such as cliffs, sometimes terraces as well as double palisades, with ditches in front and ramparts behind. Warfare was as pandemic in the New Zealand which early explorers saw as it had been in medieval Europe; the response was the same – to live on hilltops behind palisades. But the 19th century saw the introduction of firearms and a consequent shift back to low ground and palisaded villages with meeting house and marae. *(Hocken Library, Dunedin)*

Sparrman, wrote of Cook's handling of *Resolution* after striking a coral reef: "I drew no small satisfaction from remarking the celerity and the lack of confusion with which each command was executed .... I should have preferred, however, to hear fewer 'Goddamns' from the officers and particularly the captain, who, while the danger lasted, stamped about the deck and grew hoarse with shouting."

Reefs were one thing, ordinary life another. Captain Cook was thoughtful too, and gave two handfuls of seed potatoes to the Maori of Mercury Bay. They successfully planted and tended them, the first people to have potatoes in the country, although several other tribes also make that claim. At Mercury Bay too Cook had the name *Endeavour* and the date cut on a tree, and hoisted the Union Jack over New Zealand for George III. Granting its validity, New Zealanders and New Englanders were once fellow subjects of the Crown. But it was time to go. Mercury had transitted; the ship's hull was clean and the crew healthy; *Endeavour* moved on north. As Cook turned the Coromandel Peninsula he named the tip of it Cape Colville, for the admiral for whom he had charted so much of Newfoundland's coast. When sailing down the east side of Hauraki Gulf it became obvious that Maori on the west side of Coromandel Peninsula had heard about Cook's ship. "Several of the People came on board upon the very first invitation; this was owing to their having heard of our being upon the Coast and the manner we had treated the Natives." All went peaceably.

The river at the head of the inlet Cook named the Thames, for in many ways it resembled the English river. As the expedition had been instructed to assess resources, small boat exploration along the Thames led Banks, Solander and Tupaia to white pine trees or Kahikatea. They found "a tree that girted 19 feet 8 Inches [6 metres] 6 feet above the Ground, and having a quadrant with me I found its length from the root to the first branch to be 89 feet [27.3 metres], it was as streight as an arrow ...." Such a tree would make good planks, and the Firth of Thames white pine country produced masses of planking seventy years later. Cook liked this part of the new country. Although he did not spot spacious and sheltered Waitemata Harbour, he admired the area of modern Auckland.

They moved on steadily northward. On 27 November the ship passed a remarkable cape, a pierced rock off its extremity forming a natural bridge. Cook called it Cape Brett, after Sir Piercy. Even a rock, much less a Lord of the Admiralty, might resent such a pun, but the commander seemed to think that naming things might as well be fun. Just two days earlier he had named the one large and several small islands in a group the Hen and Chickens, and another remarkably unimpressive group the Poor Knights. His naming has stood up amazingly well.

At the Bay of Islands Cook described the local Maori nostalgically. "Backsides Tattou'd" reminded him of Tahiti. At first the Bay Maori were a nuisance; they tried to steal the ship's buoy, seemingly almost an obsession with Maori. Frightened away by cannon fire, they were perhaps impressed by Tupaia's scolding about behaving themselves, when the Tahitian told them much they did not know about guns, gunpowder and Europeans. Warnings seldom prevent aggression bolstered by natural boldness, and especially if aggression is a reaction to unknown intentions. A skirmish when Cook, Banks and Solander landed to examine the island near their anchorage showed the danger of over-confidence. Lieutenant Hicks brought the ship's broadside to bear, fired the four-pounders and dispersed the crowd. This reminder of yet-to-be-braved terrors enabled the commander to return with boats loaded with celery, after having made friends with many Maori. They seemingly forgave the incidents, perhaps realising their own contribution.

Flogging, the Royal Navy's maintainer of order, and in Cook's case used only when other measures failed, punished three sailors for "leaving thier duty when a shore last night and diging up Potatoies out of one of the Plantations ...." No doubt Cook hoped that the Maori would note that he kept his own people in order. Gradually relations seemed to become better; those Maori in the south end of the bay were very friendly. Cook and Banks landed to look at the country, and thought it beautiful, with parts highly cultivated and all of it well populated.

Bay of Islands waters teemed with fish of many kinds, and the Maori enjoyed exhibiting their skills with hooks and nets. As the whaling world came to find, the Bay was a penultimate base. Sheltered harbours, all with excellent holding ground for anchorage, also had plentiful supplies of suitable wood and water. The Maori provided both trade and entertainment, in many cases hard to tell apart. Like ships' masters from all over the world Cook waxed enthusiastic about the Bay of Islands. Bad weather held the ship so he began to chart and sound the anchorages and coves. But as the summer was getting on. he did not have time to finish an accurate survey of such a complicated body of water. He left the Bay with some difficulty because of very light and variable winds and *Endeavour* hit a rock, although without damage. The crew at first thought it was a whale and it is still called Whale Rock.

An almost compulsive cartographer, the captain was determined to fix the position of landmarks as closely as possible, partly because of instructions, mainly because he liked to do things right. As *Endeavour* moved north he succeeded in getting extremely accurate observations in spite of little co-operation from the weather. The ship's performance, sturdy old Whitby-built collier that she was, impressed everyone, for the bad weather seemed unseasonably nasty and unreasonably prolonged. Now they were almost at the north end of the North Island, for Cook could see right across it, forecasting they would find the ocean just over there, or something just as flat. He could see no green hills, the hallmark of New Zealand, and thought that the distant sandy ridge "lies open to the western Sea." For a few days the ship drifted north-eastward out of sight of land, but on the 14th the lookouts could see the northern capes again. Heavy swells from the west showed them clear of any sheltering land in that direction. At times they were close enough to North Cape to see a village and a few Maori, but the strong easterly current and winds soon swept *Endeavour* out of sight of land again. They could do nothing but wait for better weather.

On the 24th *Endeavour* closed the Three Kings to carefully fix its position. The next day, Christmas, they feasted on "Goose pye", made from gannets, 127 years after Tasman's New Zealand Christmas. And the pie was not all. "In the

Evening all hands were as Drunk as our forefathers used to be upon the like occasion", Joseph Banks rejoiced. But next day "all heads achd with yesterdays debauch." In spite of self-inflicted pain they were, by the 26th, in the Tasman Sea directly west of the Bay of Islands. Yet by longitude the ship was charted only about 144 kilometres west of the Bay; the northern end of New Zealand obviously was very narrow. As Cook could now say of the very tip, "the land

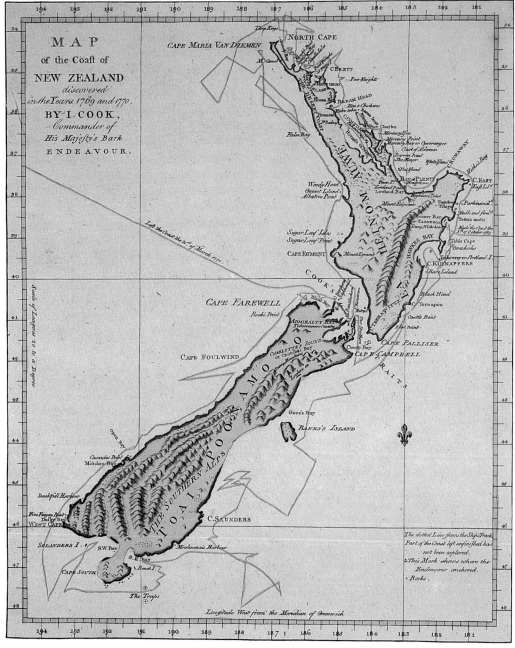

This Cook/Parkinson chart of New Zealand shows the route of the *Endeavour* around the island country. (*Alexander Turnbull Library, Wellington*)

here cannot be above 2 or 3 Miles broad from sea to sea", and he could not forbear adding, "which is what I conjecter'd when we were in Sandy bay on the other side of the coast."

More gales blew the *Endeavour* westward, then north-eastward, forcing *Endeavour* through a battering series of tacks and zigzags. Come what may the captain intended to fix the position of Cape Maria van Diemen properly. From the frantically tossing ship on New Year's Day 1770 he could see both that historic cape and North Cape beyond it. In spite of such conditions, Cook's latitude for Cape Maria van Diemen was only two minutes and his longitude only four minutes in error, a remarkable achievement. He could now go south. So away they went, willy nilly, complaining with much reason about the weather. In the New Zealand summer that supposedly semitropical latitude had put forth "a gale of wind ... which for its strength and continuence was such that I hardly was ever in before. Fortunately at this time we were at a good distance from land ...." Like Tasman he was wary. As they sailed along, west winds pushed enormous seas into the sands; New Zealand's notorious lee shores were rapidly building a reputation. Cook was discovering the dangers of the west coast of New Zealand, which Tasman had appreciated as he approached the south island. The west coasts of both major islands are classic lee shores, very dangerous for square-rigged sailing ships, for once too close there is no way for such craft to beat to safety against the winds. Winds and land destroy ships, not the sea. Cook knew this well enough: "the great sea which the prevailing westerly winds impell upon the Shore must render this a very dangerous Coast, this I am so fully sencible of that was we once clear of it I am determind not to come so near again if I can possible avoide it ...."

A few days later and somewhat closer in, Cook saw the opening of Kaipara Harbour. He missed seeing much of the coast, but from Tasman he knew that most of it was desolate and inhospitable. "The desert coast", he put on his chart. Critical or not, he took little time examining the land before turning north again to check the coast he had missed. When the weather cleared he found himself still in sight of Cape Maria van Diemen. Southwards they headed again and all mutterings were not under the breath. The next day *Endeavour* was in sight of Hokianga Harbour, just close enough to see dangerous breakers on its bar. By the 9th Cook was north again, abreast of Kaipara, and conditions at last eased to pleasant sailing. A good stretch south-eastward, coasting land much more beautiful and pleasant, more reminiscent of the Coromandel, seemed progress. By evening the southernmost land in sight was a very high mountain exactly like the Peak of Teneriffe. Noting it as "of a prodigious height and its top is cover'd with everlasting snow", Cook named it after the Earl of Egmont, First Lord of the Admiralty. One wonders if he were tall and white-haired? The land around it seemed pleasantly contoured and well wooded, fires showing it inhabited.

Not too far to the south the land swung away sharply to the east. and Cook ordered eastward helm to follow the coast. Now *Endeavour* was sailing the great inlet in which Tasman and Visscher had fought tremendous storms a century and a quarter earlier. Cook would have known for certain that this was so if the Dutch had not passed with the great peak concealed in cloud, for they would doubtless have mentioned it. Taranaki, as the Maori called it, towered proudly in clear weather as *Endeavour* passed, its foundation plains rich in the sunshine. Hilly to mountainous land sloped down to a serrated shore.

As usual *Endeavour* needed wood and water. On approaching a promising little harbour she was caught in a tide, and had to be pulled clear with her boats, the work spurred on by the sailors' realisation that being marooned in New Zealand would be far worse than being prisoners in France, a fate seamen had outfaced only a few years before. The weather was good, with little wind – in one of the windiest straits on earth, if they had but known – and so the boats towed the ship around the south-west end of a nearby island, watched by an audience of Maori, evoking thoughts of Tasman. By afternoon in a very snug haven on the north-west side of an inlet, they looked across to the inhabited island. Cook named this beautiful little harbour Ship Cove.

Some Maori attacked them by throwing stones, but Tupaia settled them down, bringing a few of them on board to receive presents. The Maori view of European goods was better here than usual further north: next day Maori were back with dried fish to sell. They liked this food, although even the iron-stomached Cook thought it revolting. He bought some for the ship to encourage trade. The Maori here as further north seemed at least as interested in theft as bartering and Cook fired small shot at one of them. A stinging rebuke, this was otherwise harmless, merely providing unusual speckling on a conventional buttock tattoo. The shot seemed to settle things down for the Maori became friendly. They told Tupaia that no such ship had ever been there before, which Cook took to mean "that they have no Tradition among them of Tasman being here for I beleive Murderers Bay ... not to be far from this place ...." The English saw this as a hopeful sign for peace.

If ships needed wood this was a trees' heaven; "the land here is one intire forest." Nor was that all. The Sounds area of New Zealand has superabundant water, in the sea, on the land, and often enough in the air. All ships found it a wonderful watering place, the sea providing healthful food in plenty too. As at most New Zealand stops the nets gathered in hundredweights of fish. *Endeavour*'s sailors liked fish and had salted huge catches of fine specimens at Mercury Bay. But perhaps that was because one of the varieties was "exactly the same as is caught in England ...." Sixty years later a Russian expedition, *Vostok* and *Mirnyy*, very proud of following in Cook's wake, found things somewhat changed. The surgeon of the *Mirnyy*, Galkin, as opposed to much other evidence, did not think fishing very good in the area. "The New Zealanders actually brought us very little fish, and our own fishing was unsuccessful even though we took great pains with it ...." His approval of Queen Charlotte Sound, as it was by then, was not very enthusiastic. He thought it a bearable visit only because "during our five-day stop, we had managed to make certain repairs to the sloops ... while our tireless and skilful Academician Mikhaylov had increased his collection with his depictions of New Zealanders and of many views." Galkin obviously thought a good catch much to be preferred to a good collection.

Ship Cove was also a place to put the ship in fettle. *Endeavour* was hauled hard over on each side in turn, to lean in one direction and then the other. Swearing sailors – for it was dirty hot work – cleaned and retarred the sides of the hull as far down as possible. Masts needed repair, seams recaulking or checking, sails inspecting and mending. Other skilled men had much to do too:

Maori fishing in Queen Charlotte Sound during the visit of the *Endeavour*. They appeared to use a type of fish trap. *(Alexander Turnbull Library, Wellington)*

the cooper to check and tighten the casks to guarantee the precious food and water, botanists to dry their specimen plants, astronomers to brood over their observations, the blacksmith to repair the ironwork of the tiller. Those not craftsmen were kept busy loading and smoothing ballast, or cutting grass for the sheep and goats in this miniature community in action. Visits to shore were restful only in the sense that change is said to be. And there was one special task we are unlikely to think of: spreading gunpowder to dry. Ships in distant waters did it when opportunity allowed. With packaged ammunition we forget that gunpowder required much care. Most of us have been figuratively adjured at one time or another to keep our powder dry; the idea is correct enough, for if gunpowder gets damp it will not explode. But it dries reasonably effectively in sunshine, and usually if not invariably it becomes explosive again.

Cook did not make his Jacks dull if it were avoidable. On 21 January, Sunday and a beautiful day, all sailors had leave to go ashore. This did not happen very often, and it certainly could not in any country where sailors would desert. Cook was sure the sailors were not likely to desert to the Maori; cannibalism, suspected for some time, was confirmed by observation at this anchorage. Banks noted carefully the ample proof. When travelling in a boat to another cove Cook and Banks happened to meet Maori who had captured a canoe-load of enemies, killed and eaten them, and in pantomime they showed the unwillingly fascinated Europeans how they ate the flesh. So much evidence convinced the two Polynesophiles there was no doubt whatever about what happened. Banks, although as sickened by the cannibalism as the sailors, nonetheless let science triumph. "Some of the Natives brought along side in one of their Canoes four of the heads of the men they had lately kill'd, both the

Hairy scalps and skin of the faces were on: M^r Banks bought one of the four ….” A preserved head bought on the spot would certainly attract attention to Banks's Natural History collection.

Both men were horrified at confirmation of what they had for some time accepted as probable. Nonetheless each made some attempt at a scientific attitude towards this aberration by their beloved Polynesians. Tupaia, the real Polynesian, was utterly horrified and condemnatory, looking on Maori cannibalism as a disgrace to all Polynesia. “Tupia who had never before heard of such a thing takes every occasion to speak ill of, exorting them often to leave it off; They however as universally agree that they eat none but the bodies of those of their Enimies who are killed in War, all others are buried.” Sailors with the officers listened avidly to the discussion. Shocked and shaken sailors would not desert in New Zealand as they had on Tahiti. Delights of the flesh were not so attractive when they were not the same delights and it might be your flesh.

Much of Cook's fame rested on the health of his crews. Ship Cove gave opportunity to find and feed greens to the sailors, as usual mainly wild celery mixed in with portable soup. But sailors did not always eat the vegetation they collected. They often accompanied Banks and Solander in their forays to observe nature and accumulate specimens of various kinds to carry home. If sailors may have done some observing, indeed one “other ranks” journal says so, it is certain they did much carrying.

Sailors also had to take the captain on his numerous excursions around the inlet. Cook much admired the heavily wooded countryside although pointing out the shortcoming: the magnificent trees were “fit for all purposes excepting Ships Masts ….” Their wood was too hard and heavy. Banks disagreed with Cook about this for at more than one place in his journals he argues that the heavy wood can be lightened, as “with the Pitch Pine in North America, the timber of which this very much resembles … the North Americans know how to lighten by tapping it properly & actually use for Masts ….”

The forest had other delights than potential masts and spars, being almost literally full of wildfowl. New Zealand birds thought then they had no foes but man, and ignored *Endeavour*'s deserting rats, in the long run a more persistent and pervasive enemy. Man began the slaughter though; sailors killed wildfowl for food, scientists for study. Man's appetites and appreciation are broader than rats'. Although not many varieties of birds graced New Zealand, Englishmen acclaimed the country's bird song as remarkable. So did the Russians. Fortunately they could make the most of nature's simple pleasures, for some famed Pacific – or at least Tahitian – diversions seemed unpromising here. Russians first met Maori women when they visited Cannibal Cove and were not impressed. In this they disagreed with many men of other European nations.

Birds of any kind are all very well; men are not necessarily so. In Cook's time commander, scientists and sailors alike were very interested in the Maori, not all for the same reasons. There was much to be fascinated by, even though sailors did not find Maori women as handsome, clean, or eagerly complaisant as Tahitians, in spite of their markedly attractive voices. Banks, who had an eye for women, was critical too: “The most disgustfull thing about them is the Oil with which they daub their hair … & consequently smell something like Greenland Dock when they are trying Whale blubber.” The Russian expedition sixty years later agreed. But in at least one way, and Cook's sailors commented on it, the Maori were more advanced than most Polynesian women. They ate with the men. Tahitians could not; nor, as a few of these men noticed on a later voyage with Cook, could the Hawaiians.

To *Endeavour*, and later the Russians too, the Ship Cove people seemed to be poor in comparison with northern Maori. Canoes were small and relatively unornamented. In 1820 when *Vostok* and *Mirnyy* called, they were welcomed by two well handled and beautifully carved canoes. The commander of the expedition, Captain Bellingshausen, believed the Queen Charlotte Sound canoes neither as big nor well made as those described in northern New Zealand. But when Sound canoes were pursuing or pursued, the men stood up to paddle, something not reported elsewhere, perhaps because of less sheltered waters. Craft handled that way certainly would go faster, but at greater risk of capsizing.

When *Endeavour* was there the visitors saw no gardens or cultivated patches of any kind; Banks therefore inferred they lived "intirely upon Fish, Dogs; & Enimies." In fact it was worse. Their main vegetable was fern root, made edible by baking and pounding; once "edible" is conceded, you have heard everything positive there is to say. Banks had views about this too: "a class of Plant, which in Europe no Animal, hardly even Insects will taste ...." But he acknowledged that the condition of the Maori indicated a healthy diet, whatever one thought of the food. Cook's ships introduced both animals and new vegetables to the local Maori, and within twenty years visiting whaling ships may have introduced more. The Maori adopted potatoes quickly. In 1820 Russians discovered a fine plantation of good European potatoes, and were able to gather "so much wild cabbage and celery on the shore that all the officers and men could have shchi [cabbage soup] from a single cook-up." Bellingshausen left more seeds – turnips, carrots, pumpkins, peas – which the Maori promised to use.

Probably because of the relative temperatures, southern Maori did not want Cook's Tahitian paper cloth. He thought their "extraordinary fondness for English broad Cloth and Red Kersey ... shew'd them to be a more sensible people than Ma[n]ly of their Neighbours." With only fish to sell, poverty perhaps made the southern Maori sharper. Not only did they trade eagerly for warm English cloth, but "they seem'd to have some knowlidge of Iron for they very readily took Nails in exchange for fish and some times Prefer'd them to any thing else which was more than the people of any other place would do ...." Within two generations these Maori learned the value of forged iron goods, though very few ships had called. In 1820 the astronomer with *Vostok*, Simonov, found an axe the most precious gift that could be given to a Maori. "Receiving *this* precious object, the headman exclaimed, '*Toki, toki!*'; and his face expressed his joy. Now, he exhausted his means of expressing his feeling of gratitude towards the captain, calling him *hoa* [friend]. So it was that we learned that *toki* means axe."

Simonov became the Banks of this later Russian expedition. A very able ethnologist and physicist as well as astronomer, he not only made a great contribution to the expedition but built his later success at home upon it. This publicised New Zealand and began the Russian interest in studies of that country which has continued to the present day. Simonov's discussion of the different values placed on objects by Maori and Europeans was very interesting. For example, a broken handle of a copper candlestick, simply junk to Europeans, to the Maori was valuable as a ring. Inversely, Maori bone fish hooks, collector's items to Russians, could be bought for small pieces of red ribbon. Maori valued nephrite tools, but even so one sold a beautiful chisel for a scrap of writing paper.

In 1820 the Maori at the Sound were guileless compared to those at the whaling base at the Bay of Islands. But already they had learned that anything associated with "Capinny Cook" was a tourist attraction. They showed the Russians the very tree to which *Endeavour* was moored; in turn a generation later they took men from the survey ship *Acheron* on the same pilgrimage to, as Hansard called it, "this interesting monument of this greatest of England's navigators." The *Acheron's* men found the tree scarred with initials, but with none older than 1807 because the bark's growth constantly erased such cries for immortality by association.

In the even more innocent time of first European visits Cook spent his time exploring, not trading. Occasionally, having dropped off the scientists to examine plants, all complaining of the paucity of new varieties, he took a guard of sailors with him to climb the surrounding hills. He could see great distances and it seemed that only open ocean lay eastward of New Zealand. On 23 January, probably from Kaitapeha, a hill on Arapawa Island, he saw what he

Ivan Simonov, with the Russians at Queen Charlotte Sound, was a very competent astronomer. He delighted in setting up his observation post as close as possible to the traces of that set up from the *Endeavour* by his boyhood hero James Cook. *(Courtesy of the Soviet Embassy, Wellington)*

"took to be the Eastern Sea and a strait or passage from it into the Western Sea ...." The South Island stretched away to the south-west. New Zealand, then, was two distinct bodies of land, almost certainly two large islands. One end of Tasman's "bay" was a strait dividing islands, as Visscher thought probable. Cook's officers persuaded him to call it Cook Strait.

Two days after this revealing hike the captain climbed another hill, this time with Banks. "We found ... a parcel of loose Stones of which we built a Pyrmid and left in it some Musquet balls, small Shott Beeds and what ever we had about us that was likely to stand the test of time." If no one meddled with them, the proofs of *Endeavour's* having been in the cove were more or less permanent. On the 29th Cook climbed the western point of the inlet's mouth, getting a north-west view of nearly fifty kilometres. He named several islands within sight. A new cairn of stones received a silver coin, musket balls and beads but to make England's case thoroughly the carpenter did as Tasman's had done and erected posts with the ship's name and the date cut on them. At the watering place one of the posts flaunted the Union Flag, then the crosses of St George and St Andrew. A third cairn was set up on the island of Motorara. To the Maori Cook explained all this as something to show ships which might come that *Endeavour* had been there. This might well have unsettled them; probably one *Endeavour* in a lifetime would seem enough. But they all got presents when in the name of the King his loyal officer took possession of the adjacent lands. Cook "dignified this Inlet with the name of Queen Charlotte's Sound ...", and the health of George III's queen was pledged "in a Bottle of wine." He used the possessive: to him the Sound was Queen Charlotte's, but is now Queen Charlotte Sound.

Cook, with Tupaia interpreting, talked at length with an old Maori, confirming that there were two islands of New Zealand, the South Island, *Te Wai Pounamu*, the Water of Greenstone, and the North Island, *Te Ika a Maui*, the Fish of Maui. Cook's rendering of the Maori was probably close enough. After an unusually long spell of beautiful weather, on 1 February came one of the Sound's unbridled downpours, silencing the birds and perhaps even the scientists. The storm carried away some of the ship's casks, even breaking one of the hawsers. It seemed time to leave.

Once out of the Sound Cook took the ship eastward well into the strait. As they sailed through it Cook named the North Island's southernmost point Cape Palliser, for one of his early captains, not only a constant friend and admirer but an influential patron. After a near accident at The Brothers, and missing the entrance to Wellington Harbour – for even the most carefully competent cannot see everything in complicated new territory – *Endeavour* steered south, on her way to the great ocean again. Not quite; old beliefs, chimeras or not, die very hard. Many on the ship, including sound officers and able scientists, argued that this seeming ocean might be just a gigantic bay, that the northern island might turn east as part of a continent. Cook satisfied them, sailing north until they came to easily identified Cape Turnagain, which they reached from the north in their early New Zealand days. By this deviation, nuisance or not, they completed the circumnavigation of the North Island and satisfied even the continental school it was an island. On that coast *Endeavour* encountered Maori who at once asked for goods, proving they had heard of strangers with a great ship, indicating once again communication between tribes.

Diversion over, the continent tucked away at least temporarily, *Endeavour* sailed south, viewing the South Island out to starboard. In the afternoon of the 15th, not far from a long peninsula, "Four double Canoes wherein were 57 Men Came off to the Ship" to look at them. At this time double canoes seemed to be used more frequently in the South Island than in the North, and in both islands more usually than by the end of the century. Cook called these canoemen the "lookers on" because they would not come near the ship, a quite understandable reluctance.

Another false trailing, this time south-east, where officers thought they saw land, interrupted general progress south and westward. On the 16th the lookout reported a large island near the coast, which Cook named Banks's Island, noting it populated. With a safer sea they might have been close enough to see it was a peninsula. On the 17th they ran eastward again, checking sightings of "land." Cook, on deck at the time, "was very certain that it was only Clowds", but nothing "could Satisfy Mr Gore but what he had saw in the morning was, or might be, land ...." Cook was not one to leave behind him the half-seen continents other explorers left on charts. Such illusions expensively entertained sponsors of voyages sent to check, but that was all. Cook, a chartmaster whose middle name was thorough, would have no part of this; "nobody should say he had left land behind unsought for orderd the ship to be steerd SE."

Returning westward, after no signs of "Mr Gore's imaginary land", Cook wondered whether he had missed a gap in the coast by sailing south and east. Perhaps they had sailed past a second strait? He did not know for certain, in spite of faith in the old Maori's account of *Te Wai Pounamu*, that the South Island was one island, until he came up the western side a few weeks later. On the night of the 25th *Endeavour* was off a high bluff whose name, Cape Saunders, honours the quietly competent admiral under whom Cook had served at Quebec. The cape is part of Otago Peninsula at modern Dunedin, but no one on *Endeavour* saw the concealed entrance to the excellent Otago Harbour, not discovered until the schooner *Unity* entered it in 1809. In his journal Cook mentioned "a remarkable Saddle hill laying near the shore ...." Unfortunately Saddle Hill, an historic landmark, is now losing its beautifully singular shape to provide construction material, even though there is good gravel and stone on every side.

It was late February, and in the south late summer storms were no more than timely. Gales lashed *Endeavour* for a few days, forcing her south and east. At the first chance Cook returned north to miss as little as possible and then again south-westward. At latitude 46 Cook wrote of a heavy swell from the south-west, "which makes me conjector that there is no land near in that quarter." But there are interesting entries about whales and seals, forerunners of the New Zealand whaling and sealing industries seventy years later. (Cook's journal was carried aboard one of the first British whaleships in the Pacific.) By noon on 4 March *Endeavour* had been blown north to Cape Saunders again, and she turned to follow the coast southward.

At the south end of the South Island, among small islands, the great seas rolling in from the south-west battered them. As a result they missed noting Stewart Island as a separate entity, although suspecting that it was: "the Southernmost Land makes very high and has the Appearence of being an Isld between which and the main seems to be a strates but as we had no convincing Proof of their being such I shall not Pretend to say ...." They eventually worked their way south of Stewart Island, frightened by "a very fortunate escape" between two ledges of rocks. Cook "named them the *Traps*, because they lay as such to catch unwary strangers." Now they were able to see New Zealand, even Stewart Island added, as no continent. "The total demolition", wrote Banks, "of our aerial fabrick called Continent."

On approaching the mainland they passed a small island, really a high-thrust gigantic rock, which Cook named Solander's Island for *Endeavour's* capable scientist. From here it appeared that perhaps Stewart Island was not an island after all, and Cook, uncertain, resolved to chart it as undecided. In that deceptive area it was almost forty years before Foveaux Strait, separating the South and Stewart Islands, was properly explored so mariners could know its dangers. For two days storms forced *Endeavour* south, but by 14 March they could see very high land again. Cook turned in towards a promising bay but they could not enter before dark. As the wind was strong they needed light to find safe anchorages; Cook, as careful as resolute, turned northwards. His glimpse of the harbour in approaching dark brought us the name Dusky Bay.

For the next eight days favourable winds and weather allowed charting of the west coast. In such conditions the views are some of the grandest in the world. Hardbitten crewmen quite as much as the more impressionable scientists and officers thought "mountains piled on mountains to an amazing height" very moving. The artist Parkinson saw "the shore of the land ... as wild and romantic as can be conceived. Rocks and mountains, whose tops were covered with snow, rose in view one above another from the water's edge ...." *Endeavour's* captain was not completely immune to romance. Cook liked the mountain scenery, but he overlaid everything with realism hard won in his Newfoundland days. His sense of responsibility brought conflict. He named a fine-looking harbour Doubtful, and refused to enter. "I saw clearly that no winds could b[l]ow there but what was either right in or right out. This is, Westerly or Easterly ... we could not have got out but with a wind that we have lately found does not blow one day in a month: I mention this because there were some on board who wanted me to harbour at any rate without in the least considering either the present or future Concequences."

The scientists were extremely disappointed at not getting to land, for they could see glaciers, although not recognising them as such. Banks never quite forgave Cook, whose responsibility for safety of ship and crew keen botanists sometimes forgot. West Coast landings are tricky even today, with seas as immense as shelter is rare. *Endeavour* had little choice but to press on. Shortly she was off that arc of coast first sighted by Tasman; no doubt his journals were consulted. Cook named the cape Tasman had first encountered Cape Foulwind. Like Tasman he commented on the dangers. Once, in a calm but with "a large swell from the WSW rowling Obliquely upon the shore ...",

Cook was afraid that he would have to anchor to save the *Endeavour*. But by the next evening, the 23rd, they reached, unscathed, what was soon to be named Cape Farewell, the north-west point of the South Island.

Cook summed up the West Coast of the South Island (neither coast nor island yet capitalised names) as a very dangerous coast, wind-scored, wave-beaten and displaying "as far inland as the eye can reach … the sumits of these Rocky mountains …." New Zealand narrowly missed having southern "Rockies" as well as southern "Alps." Further north Cook noted mountains further inland, with fertile well-watered land between them and the coast. North from Cape Foulwind the land was simply wooded hills, seemingly uninhabited. *Endeavour* saw no Maori on the whole west coast.

Now somewhat north of the main westerlies, Cook encountered exactly as Tasman had done, an easterly wind keeping them out of Tasman's "great bay." They tacked a whole day without gaining easting. At a time when only the wind moved deep-sea ships their officers needed patience. Plans and performance depended on variables further beyond their command than a soldier's, artist's, artisan's or merchant's were. Even the more than usually vigorous Drake had known the wind commanded sailors. But seamen did not necessarily like the commands; the wind Cook cursed was descended from one which sent Tasman away without discovering Cook Strait. Banks, although no sailor, felt the tension: "the Sea is certainly an excellent School for Patience." Cook's wind changed as winds always do, if one can wait without starving or thirsting too much, and on the 25th *Endeavour* managed to reach islands just west of Queen Charlotte Sound. They swept in happily on the wind of which Tasman had been rightly nervous, for he did not know about Cook Strait, although suspecting it existed. Cook knew and did not fear embayment.

Now *Endeavour* had circumnavigated both islands of New Zealand. A degree of triumph, and much relief, made wild little coves seem like home. Now officers, crew and scientists slept soundly at night, relaxed on a ship not tossing, creaking, groaning and squeaking. And there was the usual New Zealand measure of supply; no shortage of sweet water, good wood nor fish here. Nor of "anti-scorbuticks" either, and brighter sailors had found by this time they could win an approving smile from Cook by ostentatiously carrying greens up the gangplank.

*Endeavour*, snug in a bay between Stephens Island and Cape Jackson, found plenty of good supplies. No Maori lived nearby but supplies were what mattered, people often an unwelcome distraction. Depopulation seemed relatively recent; when exploring the anchorage, now Admiralty Bay, Cook found deserted huts. The captain insisted on exploration wherever the ship was at anchor, both to guard against surprise attack and to add to hard-gained knowledge. As usual Cook climbed "an eminency" to win perspective, and far to the west saw a great indentation, modern Tasman Bay. The views would be superb in fine weather, some as fine as any in the world. But views gave no answers, solved no problems for commanders of small battered ships at the far end of the world. Reaching the Antipodes had been an achievement, to reach home safely would be no less. They had done what they had come to do and it was time to go.

But which way to go home? If by way of Cape Horn, sailing far to the south, Cook would see whether or not there was a southern continent in habitable latitudes. And this was his real choice: "to return by way of Cape Horn was what I most wished ...." But in the depths of winter it was dangerous. As Banks wrote later, "our Sails & Rigging ... rendered so bad by the blowing Weather ... were by no means in a Condition to Weather the hard Gales that must be expected in a Winter Passage thro' high latitudes ...."

By this time supplies were a problem; *Endeavour* was out of sugar, salt, oil, tea, and tobacco, and for six months had had no bread. They needed a route to give them supplies much sooner than either Cape Horn, or south of Australia for Cape of Good Hope. They were not yet certain that to go that way to Good Hope meant battling great world-girdling westerlies all the way. But they were learning. Cook observed that "to the North of 58° down to 40°, 35° or 30° the Westerly winds prevail, this is to be understood of the great Ocean for where Lands intervene this may not hold good." The decision was for the East Indies. This meant, if they went far enough west, encountering the unknown east coast of New Holland – modern Australia – and being able to explore it on the way home. Determined to do even more than he had already done, Cook was setting new standards. The decision was taken, and on 1 April *Endeavour* left New Zealand. By evening they could barely see Cape Farewell to the east; by next morning New Zealand was well behind them, covered with showers and cloud. "Aotearoa" it would always be.

Cook left a New Zealand fitted accurately on the maps of the world, its situation "settled by some hundreds of Observations of the Sun and Moon and one of the transit of Mercury ...." The captain listed some areas of his chart not entirely dependable. His practice he later made clear, saying of shores seen near Chalky Inlet on his second voyage: "this part of the Coast I did not see in my last voyage, indeed we have seen so little of it now and under so many disadvantages, that all I have said of it must be very doubtfull." Yet most of what he did and most of his names are still part of New Zealand life. There were few errors. His two biggest mistakes were Banks "Island" and thinking Stewart Island probably part of the mainland. The narrowness of his chart's South Island is an effect of visual distortion from looking across flat land to distant mountains: the heights draw the observer's eyes, making plains falsely narrow, a phenomenon often seen at Calgary in Canada.

To counterpoise such penalties of being human, Cook's fixing the position of Cape Maria van Diemen so accurately, in spite of gale conditions, with the hardships, hazards and hindrances they impose, was a triumph of will and skill. He modestly reported after *Endeavour*'s voyage: "altho the discoveries made in this voyage are not great, yet I flatter myself they are such that may merit the attention of Their Lordships ...." Their Lordships thought so too, especially when Cook spoke of fatigues and dangers faced "with that cheerfulness and alertness that will always do honour to British Seamen." The Admiralty knew that cheerful alert crews bespoke competent captains, and that a captain's complimenting his crew showed confidence he and they had been successful.

New Zealand now was known to be two main islands, well watered, forested and temperate, with grand mountains, contoured hills and fertile land. Like early

Virginia, it appealed to Europeans because, amid differences, so much was familiar. All this meant the likelihood of a major continent in the high latitude south much lessened, although not disproven. Cook would do that later. New Zealand's climate ensured good adaptation for European plants, animals and people. Native birds and fish flourished, but animals were strangely rare, dogs and rats the only mammals *Endeavour's* people saw. Strange trees from the luxuriant forests seemed heavy for maritime uses, yet all observers suspected that good mast timber would be found, as indeed it was. Cook thought New Zealand flax would make good cordage and canvas, and it does. But all these things could be obtained in Europe or America. The only specifically New Zealand product which seemed valuable to Europeans, if only as souvenirs, was greenstone. Unfortunately the Maori valued it so highly that trade profited little. Tasman's cunning instructions to be careful not to show how much Europeans valued gold would not work for Cook with greenstone, already highly prized.

Cook thought European settlement certain and recommended the Bay of Islands or the rich forest area along the Thames. Banks seemed to prefer the latter: "the River Thames is indeed in every respect the properous Place we have yet seen for establishing a Colony ...." Maori opinion about all this would have to be reckoned with. Cook liked the Maori, yet agreed with his shipmates that they did not compare in sophistication or political development with Tahitians of the golden paradise. He realised the Maori's warlike qualities but underestimated the possibility of treachery and other unpleasant characteristics of all humankind. The captain was so much an 18th-century man, not quite realising the implications of the common humanity of all peoples.

*Endeavour's* shipload of talent described New Zealand habits, customs, and economy fully. Journals comment on what the Maori ate, including human flesh at times, how they caught fish, how they built houses, canoes and fortifications, and ornamented them with remarkably artistic carving and design. Scientists and officers observed daily life, how music related to dancing – which all praised as particularly rhythmical – and especially mourning the dead and what that told of religion. Cook decided that the South Sea Islanders on different islands seeming so alike was "a sufficient proff [sic] that both they and the New Zealanders have had one Origin or Source, but where this is, even time perhaps may never discover." Even more an argument now than then, origins are greatly argued. But Cook was right. The Maori came from islands where many of their people remained; language itself has shown that. But they came, so they must have come by boat, by extraordinarily skilled voyaging. Cook would have loved to meet their navigators.

What England thought and did about Cook's success need not concern us, except that now a hero he accepted command of two ships, *Resolution* and *Adventure*, for an even greater voyage. He came back to New Zealand in 1773, this time from the west as Tasman had. His route became the great 19th century clipper run, down past the Cape of Good Hope to the great west winds of the "roaring forties", then east to Australia or New Zealand, bringing immigrants and breeding stock, taking home gold, wool, wheat and the disillusioned. But all that was nearly a hundred years ahead; in 1773 New Zealand was to be the base for exploration to discover or disprove a third southern continent in temperate latitudes.

On the way out to the Pacific, ice was encountered well south of South Africa and separated Cook's two ships. *Resolution* reached south-western New Zealand first, entering Dusky Bay after an abortive trip into Chalky Inlet. Upon finding an almost ideal anchorage *Resolution* remained for over a month, marks of her presence still visible 200 years later. Although cartographers improved their maps of New Zealand and discovered the south-west mountain country's extensive resources, Cook's second visit was not to explore. But indirectly it led to sealing and whaling in the south, these industries entailed exploration, and the outlines of southern New Zealand became known in detail to New South Wales soon after that colony's founding in 1788.

The Dusky anchorage was safe whatever the winds and waves out at sea, the air pure though all too often bearing rain. As in Queen Charlotte Sound, the visitors found plentiful fresh water and wood, two vital supplies, but also abundance of fish, wildfowl and seals to vary diet. They also found wild celery, the crew prepared for this titillation by the old hands of *Endeavour*. They were still in good health: "After such a long continuence at Sea in a high Southern Latitude it is but reasonable to think that many of my people would be ill of the Scurvy, the contrary however happen'd ... Sweet Wort, and Marmalade of Carrots being given to such as were of a scorbutick habit of body ... we had only one man onboard that could be call'd very ill of this disease ... we must allow Portable Broth and Sour Krout to have some share in it." Cook insisted on other precautions too: cleanliness, good ventilation, and measures to ensure the men's quarters stayed dry. His obvious care and unfailing attention added to the good morale which some physicians thought preventative in itself. Using his Canadian experience very successfully, Cook brewed "spruce beer" as a liquid equivalent of wild celery. Sickness of several kinds rapidly disappeared, perhaps because of such cheering medicine.

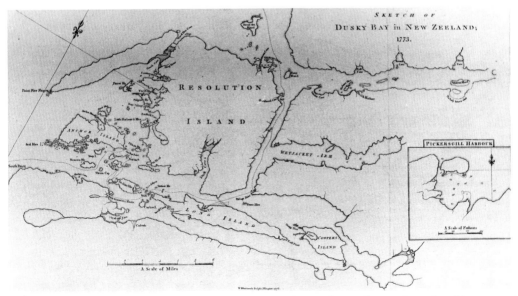

A chart of Dusky Bay done by Cook in 1773. *(University of Canterbury Library, Christchurch)*

The English found southern New Zealand's food plentiful and good. Clerke, referring to "the happy tautness" of his jacket, said, "Dusky Bay, for a Set of Hungry fellows after a long passage at Sea is as good as any place ...." All the same there was work to do. Cook surveyed much of the complicated area, his finest surveying on his Pacific voyages. The chart is attractive as well as accurate, for he had there the quiet needed for concentration. In 1791 one of Cook's midshipmen, George Vancouver, completed this charting on his way to what is now British Columbia. He did well, replacing "Nobody knows what", scrawled on Cook's chart to mark an uncompleted area, with "Somebody knows what" on his own.

The southern sounds were very lonely, in spite of the luxuriant growth and lavish supplies of good foods, with few Maori around and those very timid. They did not appreciate music, at least as presented, or indeed any of the new strange ways of the sailors. But Cook finally established relations with one Dusky Bay family, apparently fugitives from Maori communities of the east coast. The group had no permanent habitations. Cook liked them very much. "Of the same race as those in the other parts of the Country ... these indeed whether from custom or a more generous disposssion make you presents before they receive any, in this they come nearer to the Otaheiteans than the rest of their Country men." He gave little higher praise than that.

Following Cook's practice of stocking the Pacific with useful animals, *Resolution* liberated geese in Goose Cove. Usually he left pigs, as further north in New Zealand, and sometimes goats and cattle too, as he had in Pacific islands. Possibly the farmer's son in him realistically assessed the possibilities of the area, and even with special approval the geese did not thrive. None was ever seen there in later visits; wekas probably ate their eggs. At Dusky Bay Cook saw "the largest Seal I ever met with ... it is probable that it was a Sea-Lioness, it certainly very much resembled the one drawn by Lord Anson ...." Seals were the wild native mammals at Dusky Bay, and Cook was enthusiastic about them: "I went with a party a Seal hunting, the surf was so high that we could only land in one place where we killed Ten, these animals serve us for three purposes, the skins we use for our rigging, the fatt makes oyle for our lamps and the flesh we eat ...." One of the scientists successfully "tried braising the flesh with cherry sauce ...", but the origin of the cherries is not certain.

On 19 April *Resolution* weighed anchor but it was not till 11 May that officers found a way out through a new passage, now Breaksea Sound. Just out from Dusky Bay they encountered a waterspout which "first appeared in the sw at the distance of two or three miles [4 km] at least from us ... and pass'd within fifty yards of our stern without our feeling any of its effects. The diameter of the Base of this spout I judged to be about fifty or Sixty feet [18 to 21 metres], that is the Sea within this space was so much agitated and foamed up to a great height from which a tube or round boddy was formed by which the Water or air or both was carried in a spiral stream up to the Clouds." After that the rest of the passage to Ship Cove was anticlimactic.

In the Cove Furneaux and *Adventure* were settling into winter quarters. Reunion pleased Cook but settling down did not. Idling in winter quarters was not his style, and he was the commander. Both ships were fitted for sea and by 7 June steered east through Cook Strait to find the long-sought Great South

Land. Skill, perseverance, and endurance found no continent; it was not where a century of home-bound geographers said it had to be. Cook decided that if it existed at all it must be "within the Polar Circile [sic] where the Sea is so pestered with ice, that the land is thereby inacessible", a not inaccurate forecast of the discovery of Antarctica. Cook's firmly stated belief, by which he lived and served, was that "it is the business of Voyagers to pass over nothing that may be usefull to posterity ...." On his own voyages Cook occasionally had been further south than the northernmost points of Antarctica, but never in the right longitude to encounter land. The gods had frowned; some discoveries were denied him.

Beating heavily the long way north, sailors and scientists spent happy weeks at Tahiti before sailing westward. Keeping north to avoid his former route, *Resolution* and *Adventure*, like Tasman's *Heemskerck* and *Oostcappel*, rediscovered Tonga, another Polynesian culture for which they had been somewhat prepared by Tasman. Cook stuck to his belief that Polynesians were of one origin but he perceived important differences. This should not have been too puzzling to a thoughtful English seaman; his men shared the North Sea with Norman sailors, men of the same northern origins whose cultures grew gradually but greatly apart in six hundred years.

Then it was south to New Zealand again. By late October the ships were off Cook Strait, on the Pacific side. Spring gales blew *Adventure* from company again. Pressing on with a sharp lookout for his companion ship, Cook again narrowly missed discovering Port Nicholson, Wellington's superb harbour. Although they reached the inward passage the weather, notoriously fickle and violent, prevented his entering. He never got back to do so. At Queen Charlotte Sound the usual bustle took over: repairs, provisioning, scientific studies of people and plants. New scientists not only took up where *Endeavour* left off but sceptically reworked old information – as intellectuals tend to do. The captain did a little local exploring and a great deal of planning for his next sortie. And all the time he worried about *Adventure* in a way modern communications make unnecessary.

A few weeks later Cook put his last ewe and ram ashore in Queen Charlotte Sound. Within three days they died, presumably from eating some poisonous plant. "Thus every method I have taken to stock this Country with Sheep and Goats have proved ineffectual." In June he landed two goats, and Furneaux put a boar and two sows ashore in Cannibal Cove. In the Sound later Cook saw one of Furneaux's sows with some Maori, and was told the second sow and the boar were with others but the goats had been killed. Subsequently a botanist saw a black boar on Long Island, presumably Furneaux's: "there is little fear but that this Country will soon be stocked with these Animals, both in a wild and domistick state." One can still shoot "Captain Cookers" in the New Zealand bush.

The Maori at every anchorage had been well entertained by the animals running around on the ships. When a young boy, strutting in his gift shirt, was knocked down by a ram, "he told a very lamentable story against Goure [Kuri], the great Dog (for so they call all the quadrupeds we had aboard) ...." Anywhere in the country adult Maori seemed to enjoy the contacts and knew all the tricks of bargaining. On the North Island Cook gave pigs, fowls, seeds and roots to a chief, who seemed more interested in an iron spike: "however ... at going away, he very well remembered how many [pigs and fowls] were brought before."

Finally, though fighting reluctance for once, Cook's driving sense of duty took over and on 25 November *Resolution* left once more, watching all the time for *Adventure*. Five days later Captain Furneaux sailed into the Sound. Given the speeds then available to sailing craft, he had missed his commander's ship – and his commander's direction and support – by a very small margin.

It turned out to be a most important and unhappy visit for Furneaux. Just as *Adventure*, repaired and reprovisioned, was about to leave, an unexplained dispute broke out with the Maori at Grass Cove, where sailors reaped hay for shipboard animals. A boat sent to collect wild greens for the crew did not

The *Resolution*. This fine ship performed two great voyages for Cook and brought home his successor after the great captain's death. Like *Endeavour* it was built as a Whitby cat, with all the inherent virtues for exploration such an origin provided. *(Mitchell Library, State Library of New South Wales)*

return. The search party did not discover an accidentally stove-in boat, as expected, and for which the carpenter had some "sheets of Tin" in the launch. Instead they found "such a shocking scene of Carnage & Barbarity as can never be mentioned or thought of, but with horror." In the next cove they found "a great many baskets (about 20) laying on the beach tied up ... full of roasted flesh ... & a hand, which we immidiately knew to have belong'd to Thos Hill, one of our Forecastlemen, it being marked T.H. ... with a tattow instrument." Ten seaman had been killed, cooked and eaten. The search party destroyed canoes, and fired a volley at some Maori, but deciding "that we could expect to reap no other advantage than the poor Satisfaction of killing some of the Savages", left without marching into the woods. Without doing more Furneaux set sail for Britain as instructed.

Cook returned to the Sound in October 1774, after an important season of exploration had completely demolished any lingering belief in another middle-latitude southern continent. He knew *Adventure* had been there when they found trees cut with saws and axes, and saw that an observatory had been set up. Officers heard confused stories of shipwreck and killing, which made Cook "very uneasy about the Adventure". Later, after giving "Pedero" a suit of clothes and wooing him into "a communicative mood", they learned "that soon after we were gone, she arrived, that she stayed between ten and twenty days and had been gone ten Months ... that neither she or any other Ship had been stranded on the Coast." Cook was made "easy about her, but did not wholly set aside our doubts of some disaster having happened to some other strangers."

Whatever his worries Cook did his work. On this visit he found Tory Channel, later to play such a part in 19th and 20th century shore whaling. Even if he had suspected how important this new-found waterway would turn out to be, events on his return to the ship spoiled the captain's pleasure. The very capable astronomer of the expedition, William Wales, found that the original charting of the area, by Cook himself, had been forty minutes too far to the east. Naturally a pre-eminent surveyor and navigator did not like admitting a mistake. After thorough checking, he had to do so, and did so with courtesy, saying of Wales that his "abilities is equal to his assiduity ...."

The great explorer could afford to be courteous. In general his charts were so good that in the mid 1960s a young Navigating Officer of the Royal New Zealand Navy, even with his modern electronic devices mastered, told his admiral, "Give me Cook's chart, sir, and at any time I would take a ship around the coast of New Zealand with it." Cook was honoured in his own time too and across international boundaries. The Russians, who admired both the Royal Navy and Cook, paid him a tribute on their brief visit to New Zealand in 1820. Astronomer Simonov made great efforts to set up instruments and make all astronomical observations from exactly where Wales and Bayley had made theirs for Cook. To work on the location linked with the great English explorer was something he valued, and though unable to carry out his plan fully he thought it worthy of remark. On his return from the second great circumnavigation Britain – indeed the western world – recognised a debt to Cook. A major achievement was completed, proving chronometers could solve the longitude problem. In London the Admiralty promoted Cook to post-captain, a rank marking most unusual achievement for someone who had started as an able seaman. Once post-captain, if you survive you will eventually become an admiral, although you might not serve actively in that rank. An accolade which probably pleased him as much was his being elected a Fellow of the Royal Society; this was in addition to the praise for his paper on scurvy which won the Copley Medal. The Yorkshire farm boy now talked with his king and was consulted by his admirals. Given more time the Pacific might have won him a peerage, not martyrdom.

Cook's stay in England, his honours and his problems, need concern us little here, for we are writing of New Zealand and not the explorers. His honour, a pension in fact, of a captain's berth at Greenwich Hospital he had accepted

## CHRONOMETERS

As one would expect of exploration voyages, the journals constantly discuss the estimated position of the ships and the difficulties of navigation. Latitude, the distance north or south of the equator, was relatively easy to find by Tasman's time. Various forms of the cross staff, usually a backstaff, could be used from the deck of a ship. The most advanced of these in Tasman's day were the "reversed Jacob's staffs", and the calibre of pilots on this expedition would mean they had the best instruments available. By the 18th century new instruments, sextants and quadrants, were accurate and easy to use for finding latitude. But it was not latitude, distance north and south, but longitude, distance east and west, which was the problem.

Longitude could not then be found from ships at sea, for on the great oceans there is always a swell, if not waves. Contemporary instruments for finding longitude were useless except on solid land. This meant that explorers lying off a newly found island in a tossing ship, unable to land to make observations because of surf – not uncommon conditions – would not be able to give an accurate longitude for the island. The difficulty about observations for longitude was overcome in Cook's time by the building of highly accurate chronometers, large watches or small clocks, by watchmaker John Harrison, in the period from 1729 to the 1760s. As the earth spins at the rate of fifteen degrees per hour comparison of times will tell a navigator how far east or west of the known point he is. Two such clocks as Harrison's could be used to compare the time on board the ship with the time at a point of known longitude.

This is done by advancing one clock each noon to the precise noon shown by latitude observations and by leaving the other clock set at London time, for example. If the ship's clock is at noon and the London clock at 4 p.m. then the ship is four times fifteen degrees west of London. This had long been known. The problem was that the accuracy of the observation depends on the clock set at home port time being accurate to within seconds per year. This precision was finally obtained by Harrison and his success was of major importance to long-distance navigators until modern radio, radar and satellite assistance in turn replaced the chronometer method. French watchmakers paralleled the developments in England and equipped French explorers with excellent chronometers too.

Before chronometers were built to such high standards, when explorers discovered a new land they could find its longitude from the solid shore by observation of angles between planets, and other astronomical phenomena. Once it was reported and charted, persons all around the world would know the precise location of the new land, the distance east or west as well as north or south of their own homes.

only if it were recognised that he was available for service. As a result, and as the obvious choice, he was to command a third voyage of Pacific exploration in 1776. Cook's last ship the *Discovery* was another Whitby ship. The cat design and construction had proved as suitable as Cook and the wiser heads of the Admiralty had assumed. *Discovery* was eventually to be commanded by Captain Clerke, who had been on both earlier expeditions; he was to sail her home with the dreadful news of Cook's violent death in Hawaii and on the way was to die himself.

The third voyage took place when England and America were at war; the American Revolution had started. But by this time James Cook's uniqueness was so recognised that Benjamin Franklin, American ambassador to France, sent instructions to all American ships that if they encountered *Discovery* and her consort, they were to be allowed to pass unmolested. As those were different days from ours, the French gave the same orders as the Americans; honour counted then. After the modernising effect of the French Revolution, Captain Flinders, explorer of Australian waters, was captured by the French and held for years, losing his chance for further discovery.

James Cook, on this third great voyage, returned for a fifth visit to Queen Charlotte Sound in February 1777. He remained there for a fortnight in *Resolution* without anything remarkable happening. The local Maori appeared but although they knew and trusted Cook they would not board the ship. This shyness meant, Cook suspected, "that they were apprehensive we were come to revenge the death of Captain Furneaux's people." Omai, a Tahitian, in *Adventure* during the "melancholy event", was now with Cook on his way home, which probably increased Maori apprehension. Cook tried to reassure

John Gore, with Captains Wallis and Byron, crossed the Pacific twice before Cook saw the immense ocean, and then several times more as an officer on all three of Cook's South Sea voyages. Gore, as captain, brought the *Resolution* home. *(Nan Kivell Collection, National Library of Australia)*

them, but took sensible precautions, such as armed guards. He believed such precautions no "more necessary now, but after the sacrifice which the Natives made of the boats crew ... and the French in the Bay of Islands [in 1772] it was impossible, totally, to divest our selves of apprehinsions of the same Nature."

Meanwhile the usual jobs of refitting, provisioning and making observations went on, as well as brewing spruce beer, although only two crewmen of the complements of both ships were ill. Among occasional visitors was Kahura, said to have led the party which massacred the *Adventure* crew. He seemed, wrote Cook, "to be more feared than beloved ... many of them ... importuned me to kill him ... if I had followed the advice of our pretended friends, I might have extirpated the whole race, for the people of each Hamlet or village, by turns applyed to me to distroy the other ...."

Although perplexed and worried, Cook ignored the fate of Furneaux's boatcrew, determined to preserve good relations with the Maori, and claimed to have done "all in my power to assure them of the continuance of my friendship, and that I should not disturb them on that account." He may have been right to do so; he may just have been tired. Retribution by Cook would probably only have hardened a cultural attitude. The Maori of the area felt no guilt, as Bellingshausen found upon questioning them two generations later. However that may be it is certain he was not the old Cook, but a strained and unpredictable man, part stranger to his oldest and closest friends. Nonetheless he carried out his usual activities, giving away goats and hogs, making more observations, writing of the natives, asking questions. One curious piece of information he gained was about a ship which the Maori said preceded his *Endeavour*, and which brought venereal disease to New Zealand. Its identity remains a mystery.

This was to be Captain Cook's last voyage, both by his own decision and by fate. The mission was one which had killed many and broken more. He was on his way to seek, from the west, the fabled North-west Passage around the north of North America, from England to China and Japan. His valiant attempt failed, as it was bound to do; he had not been able to find a non-existent southern continent either. But at his northern winter base in Hawaii he was killed, unfortunately by some of the very Polynesian people he so admired and loved. His temper had flared during a quarrel of relatively minor nature with people in a land he had opened to the world, where he was originally, and some say still, revered as a god.

If James Cook were to be a god it should not be a Polynesian god explicitly, but one for all navigators and explorers. His defects were few. Only in most unusual circumstances did rare instances of rashness or harshness flare, revealing crushing pressures caused by superlative responses to challenges insensibly set by superiors. He was human too. But his qualities, though not superhuman, were at least extraordinarily above the ordinary. He is admitted by all to be *the* Explorer. If there were to be *the* Discoverer doubtless it too would be Cook.

Considering Cook's contribution to geographical knowledge in four of the ten separate provinces of Canada, it is strange that he is so often seen as most directly connected with New Zealand. He was not; and his connection with Australia was very slight. Yet the chief Pacific memorials, apart from majestic Mount Cook in New Zealand, are in Canberra and Melbourne. That one of the explorer's possible dwelling places is now re-erected in Melbourne is particularly remarkable, because only for a few hours at best did Cook catch fleeting glimpses of the Victorian coast. Canada, even England, admire his qualities but take them for granted. In New Zealand he is honoured as he deserves, for his forecast of Europeans flourishing in that country has been amply justified. And through him and in every way with his blessing, the Maori began their entrance into the modern world.

CHAPTER FIVE

# *Resurgent France*

The French first came to New Zealand in 1769, in search of a green land with plentiful fresh water, for de Surville, their leader, had read about Tasman's Staten Landt and hoped for relief from the scurvy ravaging his crew. Looking for New Zealand came easily to the French, for they in particular believed in a continent in the south. Frenchmen had made a landfall in 1504, at the very beginning of the 16th century, in a large southern land with presentable natives, two of whom were taken back to France. In the late 17th century a French descendant of one of the Indians brought the ancient voyage to "Gonneville Land" to the world's attention. The evidence now seems to experts to show that Gonneville Land was part of the coast of South America. Navigation in the 16th century was not very precise because observations were seldom accurate, and most returning voyagers could not say with certainty where they had been.

A few French had sailed the Pacific with Magellan, and many French sailed with English and Dutch buccaneers against the Iberian trade monopolies. Even the government of France argued that it was just to make war on the Spanish and Portuguese in the Pacific "until the said Spanish and Portuguese shall suffer trade to be free." Buccaneering did not last long and it produced more legends than either wealth or history, although William Dampier, an English buccaneer who partially explored the western coast of Australia in 1699, left interesting journals. But buccaneering taught the French there was profit in trading with Spanish colonies.

For some years French ships, claiming that alliance with Spain gave an ally commercial rights but often willing to fight if they could not deal, came round the Horn into the Eastern Pacific. They traded with the Spanish colonists in South America, doing what Francis Drake and John Hawkins, who began as traders and ended as heroes, had done in the Caribbean a century earlier, making forbidden trade legitimate by claiming need for supplies or the need to dispose of spoiling goods or starving slaves. New times, new ways; by the end of the 17th century the French were calling their expeditions "voyages of discovery". Tens of French ships thus got into Spanish waters legally, and then traded. Few made any real money. One of these voyages did prove that no Atlantic southern continent existed when in 1707 the *St Louis* sailed directly between Capes Horn and Good Hope across the South Atlantic.

The first French ship to cross the Pacific was Frondat's, in the same year. Shortly several captains crossed the Pacific from South America to go home by way of the French territory in India; Bougainville, in the 1760s, was not the first French circumnavigator. The French nursed hope that the Spanish would grant trading concessions to stop their sending further discovery expeditions into the South Sea but at the end of the War of the Spanish Succession in 1713 Spain again banned all foreign shipping from her imperial trade. And she enforced the ban. In 1716 Spain sent a successful expedition to capture foreign shipping trading along the South American coast, and afterwards policed her regulations reasonably well. Nonetheless this trade's importance – and some successful voyages – reawakened French interest in the Pacific.

In the 18th century France lost her North American and Indian possessions to Britain, and was interested in finding others. This would involve exploration voyages. More particularly, astronomers influenced the government. Like English astronomers, they were interested in the transit of Venus, the phenomenon which directed Cook to Tahiti on his first voyage. Transits were

## FRENCH INTELLECTUALS' INFLUENCE ON EXPLORATION

In the 17th and 18th centuries France was as interested in science as England. Many administrators, scientists, politicians and political writers, and especially "les philosophes", working in informal alliance, created the climate for French Pacific exploration. In France the "philosophes" were as influential in the mid to late 18th century, organised or unorganised, as the Royal Society was in England. There was much borrowing from English trends. One geographic book, the *History of Navigation to Southern Lands* by de Brosses, became influential. The author used material from English, Dutch and French voyages. The *History* was a milestone throughout Europe, ahead of anything written in English or Dutch. De Brosses believed that the earth must be balanced by a reasonable spread of land amid the great oceans; this argument may have influenced Alexander Dalrymple, the English philosopher of discovery. The Frenchman did not insist there was necessarily a southern continent, for enough substantial islands could provide balance. But he insisted there had to be land in the south balancing the land in the north.

De Brosses's arguments for exploration were imperial and economic, that colonies were a source of wealth and strength, valuable as bases for mastery of the sea. Colonies settled with criminals would strengthen the nation's empire and also reform the criminals, providing a second chance. This proved an accurate forecast of several colonies in Australia, and de Brosses was linked with that country in another way. Firmly believing in Gonneville Land, in writing about it he developed the new name Australasia; nor was that all, his original mind also coined the name Polynesia, "many islands." De Brosses thought the French base for Pacific exploration should be east of Europe, in Mauritius or India. It was sound argument. Sailing south from those places, as Tasman had, moves the ship into the great west winds blowing south of Australia; Cook used them to reach New Zealand in his second and third voyages. De Brosses's book was widely read, debated, imitated and pirated.

Exploration was certainly not all based on commercial or political imperialism. In fact some French intellectuals, especially Rousseau, applauded the loss of the French Empire. He thought all colonialism harmful to native peoples, for in his view all "Indigènes" lived in perfect societies. But whatever people thought about losing the empire or Rousseau's idealisation of people of whom he knew little, such arguments affected French exploration. After the Seven Years War this naivety persuaded the government in Paris to support Pacific voyages to see how humanity made out in Arcadia.

important astronomical events then because of their connection with developing navigation. More than scientific interest, however, triggered the resumption of French exploration. The French East India Company's dissolution in 1769 had two main effects: many of its sailors went into the French Royal Navy; others, some with private means as well as maritime skills, became available to find new rich trading lands.

Such an officer, Jean-François-Marie de Surville, attracted support for a Pacific expedition to look for trade; exploration came about almost as a by-blow. He built a ship, the *St Jean Baptiste*, about twice the size of Cook's *Endeavour*, and in 1767 took her to India, intending to trade in the Indies. When officers heard that a rich island had been discovered somewhere in the Pacific (undoubtedly a rumour about Tahiti, discovered by Wallis in the *Dolphin* in 1767) the chief investors – de Surville one of them – decided the ship should go on a voyage of discovery.

De Surville seemed to ignore the news of Bougainville's voyage, for that voyager reported Tahiti as most attractive but not wealthy. With gold, or even trade, the French explorers hoped any attractive land would rebuild the French empire, which except for some small islands had been taken from her in 1763. At any rate the *St Jean Baptiste* set sail towards an unknown but already fabled destination. Unfortunately the merchant overcame the commander in de Surville. Although heavily laden with rich trade goods the ship was not well provisioned, in both cases highly optimistic decisions.

De Surville himself had an excellent record at sea; a highly skilled sailor, he had done well in wars against the British. In spite of a tempestuous although short-lived temper, his men liked and trusted him. He sounds to have been something like Cook, but his temper did not mean strict, or even sufficient, discipline on the voyage, in spite of having some very capable officers. Three of them, Labé, second-in-command, Monneron, the supercargo, and L'Horme, the second lieutenant (or ensign), are particularly important to us because they kept journals. Crozet, Marion's second-in-command in *Mascarin*, kept an excellent journal now available as a book.

In 1769, as Cook was approaching Tahiti to observe the transit of Venus, *St Jean Baptiste* sailed from Bengal to another French settlement in India for bullocks and kids for provisions. When taking on firewood and water at a further French Indian port they embarked some soldiers as additional men. Finally the ship departed and sailed south-south-east through the Dutch East Indies. On 19 July the ship emerged in the South China Sea. At Trengannu they found a rather scruffy city, not the riches they expected. But they were able to secure supplies in exchange for opium and knives, a rather modern combination certain to cause trouble. The French liked the island, believing that only the influence of the Dutch prevented the French developing a good trading relationship.

In the seas between Formosa and Luzon they bought supplies wherever they could, mainly pigs, yams, potatoes and the local liquor, bashi. Dampier had named the the nearby Bashi Islands after this powerful brew, whose potency impressed his exceedingly tough crew. But on this French visit Supercargo Monneron, who looked after business matters, thought it not so bad: "this beverage sometimes produces intoxication; but ... it puts the natives in a sweet

114

"Watering" a ship was immensely important. Sailing through the tropics meant a large consumption of water. Here Sporing, one of Banks's artists on Cook's *Endeavour*, shows sailors filling barrels with fresh water and floating them out to be towed by boats to the ship. *(University of Canterbury Library, Christchurch)*

humour." Monneron was a Norman; perhaps he was comparing bashi to calvados, said to have given Normans their legendary prowess in arms. At the Bashis de Surville kidnapped three of the islanders, when attempting to get deserting sailors back. This was a hard-hearted action, although de Surville treated the shanghaied men very well, probably better than he treated French sailors. It was a hard century. Blacks in their tens of thousands were being taken to slavery in both Americas. Nor were colour or culture the determinants. White sailors in European ports were press-ganged into a form of slavery little better, and taken as far from home.

According to Labé's journal, by this time he was very worried about the efficiency of command and administration in the ship, specifically navigational decisions and the obvious shortage of food. We know the second-in-command's worries but not the reasons for de Surville's decisions. Here Labé's diligence as a writer preserved his memory well. Our views of voyages depend largely on men who wrote journals recording their own points of view, with sometimes glimpses of other opinions about quarrels, arguments or council decisions. Nor do we necessarily read all that was written. Fire, neglect and sinking remove journals; we cannot know what we have missed from those which did not survive. The world is fortunate if one journal remains, and extraordinarily so if several do. Journals from all ranks have largely formed the world's opinion of Cook and his voyages; de Surville's voyage was well recorded by journals from three of his officers and the commander himself.

Labé had been right to worry about the navigation. By 7 September no one aboard *St Jean Baptiste* knew where they were. De Surville was confident about latitude but knew his longitude was hopelessly awry: "I do not know where the currents have taken me. I think it is to the north-east … As far as my longitude is concerned, I am not altering it, for fear of altering it the wrong way." By this time all aboard were watching eagerly for signs of land. A dreadful period in the Doldrums, a windless area along the equator, saw them drifting for days at a time. Labé had plenty to worry him now: "Here we are in these notorious doldrums …. Our crew is suffering a great deal from the heat, and they have only their bottle of water to drink each twenty-four hours … I am really worried that sickness will affect them – I mean by that scurvy." His worries soon became reality.

As far as one can tell, de Surville went through the Solomon Islands, just missing New Ireland and Bougainville Island, sailing south-easterly, across

## SCURVY

Most of the early ships arriving at New Zealand had scurvy aboard. De Surville's and Marion's voyages were plagued with scurvy, the former very seriously. Scurvy, we now know, is a deficiency disease. But scientifically this was not conclusively demonstrated until 1917. The deficiency is of Vitamin C, but that vitamin was not isolated until 1928. The affliction hit sailing ships on long expeditions because they were away from fresh food for long periods. That was the factor – time. Scurvy was a land disease in Russia and Canada, with their long winters, and was a curse to armies and the fur trade, for each relied greatly on preserved food. Fresh vegetable matter, especially citrus fruit, turned out to be the key for long-distance travelling. And a key was needed, for scurvy was a revolting and deadly condition.

A French doctor, in the Pacific thirty-five years after de Surville, tried to depict the diseased men: "Swellings covered by black scabs appeared on various parts of their bodies, the skin revealed small wine-coloured stains at the root of the hairs; their joints stiffened, their flexor muscles seemed to shorten and held their limbs half-bent. But nothing was more hideous than the appearance of their face: to the leaden complexion of the victims of scurvy was added the prominence of the gums jutting out of the mouth, which itself showed ulcerated spots. The sick gave out a fetid smell, which, when you breathed it, seemed to attack the very root of life. I have often felt my strength ebb away when I approached them." In the intermediate stages of the disease many ships were lost because sailors were too weak to work, and the old sailing ships had little mechanical assistance in working sails or windlasses. In case of scurvy, sailing ships tried to start with at least a few supernumeraries, men who would make sailors if required.

By Cook's time medical men were beginning to see the problem, but were still some way from a practical solution. In Britain at least they had decided to test different foods as preventatives. Not long before, a Dr James Lind wrote a fine book on the disease and argued that a proper diet was the answer. In an oddity of history the early 17th century seamen had known that eating citrus fruit prevented the disease, yet somehow that knowledge had been lost. Sir Richard Hawkins, a cousin of Drake, had thanked God for placing "so great and unknown a virtue in this fruit, to be a certain remedy for this disease."

Cook, not knowing this, at the direction of the Admiralty and the King himself, fed

Bougainville's course. Finally they made landfall in another of these islands. De Surville did not realise that these were the islands Mendana had discovered a century or more earlier; by this time his longitudes were out approximately two degrees and thirty minutes – about 270 kilometres – and not correlating with Mendana's journal. The expedition desperately needed water, even food, but they had trouble with natives when they anchored near the present Surville Island, and could not safely land. Things were so desperate Labé wished to kidnap local men for sailors and so they carried off one youth who showed them where to get water and a little food.

Sailing ships needed many men. Sailors handled sails, huge expanses of very heavy canvas, buffeted and flung about by heavy winds. The sails had to be controlled by brute strength, and it took fit men. Scurvy- or plague-ridden ships were in danger, usually not because the crew had died but because they simply could not do this heavy work. In turn the men needed much food and

some rather strange foods to his crew. The achievement of the Whitby captain was to use his single-minded discipline to force compliance from conservative sailors. They did not mind fresh meat, fish, or civilised vegetables, potatoes and onions, but they certainly preferred salt meat to boiled wild weeds, sauerkraut and spruce needle beer. But where those were all that was available, that is what they ate. They muttered at his parallel insistence on cleanliness and fresh air, but they followed his orders. With Cook they could like or lump; a very few liked and the rest lumped. But no one died of scurvy.

Clerke, one of Cook's chief officers, thought freedom from scurvy "was certainly owing to the Extraordinary indulgencies of Govern$^t$ of Crowt, Wheat, Malt &c &c together with the strickt attention paid by Capt Cook to the Peoples Clenliness." This no doubt helped, but it was fresh vegetable foods that worked the miracles. Cook's long-suffering sailors, as many of them regarded themselves, breakfasted on wild celery, with enough of something or other familiar boiled with it to help it down. And the French, in the years of Cook's voyages, ate such greens too. Crozet described several useful plants, including a wild celery, and said, "We ate a good deal of these plants … which had a very salutary effect on our scurvied people …. The savages expressed great astonishment at seeing us eat these herbs." Wild celery is a true celery whereas scurvy grass, which Cook used in default, was not really a grass at all. The name was applied to several different plants but usually to one known, while it survived in New Zealand, as Captain Cook's "scurvy grass." It is *lepidium oleraccum*, a kind of cress; the Maori called it nau. Once very common in New Zealand it was so eaten off by sheep and cattle that it was thought to be extinct. It is not – quite! Recently a specimen has been found growing on a remote cliff near Kaikoura.

Cook made his contribution, and this was recognised. His paper on the "means of prevention and cure of scurvy" was proclaimed the best of the year, and worthy of the Copley Medal. The Yorkshire farm boy now talked with his king and was consulted by his admirals. Given more time the Pacific might have won him a peerage, not martyrdom. Spreading knowledge or persuading captains to be as punctilious as Cook were quite other matters. It was another century before all sailors on all ships could abandon their well-justified fears. What scurvy left as its memorial is the name "limey" for English sailors, even Englishmen at large, a memorial to the Admiralty's and Board of Trade's too-long-delayed insistence on lime juice every day for every sailor at sea.

water. Tasks easily done by healthy able-bodied sailors still had to be executed after poor diet and sanitation, hardly moderated by extremely basic medical care, had caused ill health and casualties. So every ship sailed from home with extra men if it could; in turn this placed pressure on supplies and space, and so on, ad infinitum. Praise of Cook for his attention to health is not misplaced.

De Surville continued, no land in sight, south-south-east through the Coral Sea towards the New Hebrides. Unknowingly but nearly within sight of them he turned south-west and missed those islands. If currents had moved the ship off course he might have hit New Caledonia, still undiscovered. But there was no such good fortune. By this time searching for anywhere with food and fresh water, his thoughts turned to Tasman's Staten Landt. On 22 November 1769, because of sickness in his crew, he finally decided to turn toward New Zealand, hoping to find "a place of refuge where we can rest awhile."

De Surville and Labé, who agreed with him and from whom we hear the story, obviously were thinking of New Zealand's fertility as described by Tasman. Mountain streams of cool sweet water seemed almost fantasies to men drinking slimy liquid from watercasks several months in the tropics. But de Surville and Labé had experienced what they saw as treachery in the Solomon Islands, and from Tasman knew it was possible and even likely in New Zealand too. De Surville had little choice, as Monneron saw it: "we put our course to ... New Zealand, where it was absolutely necessary to go in order to get our crew well again." By this time the sailors were so scorbutic that the ship was in danger. Not only the ship and health; men's minds were at risk. Scurvy was horrible almost beyond describing.

This leg of the journey went well. New Zealand was much closer than their maps indicated. At half past eleven on the morning of 12 December 1769, the lookout saw land just south of Hokianga Harbour, whence they sailed north looking for an anchorage. By the 15th they reached Cape Maria Van Diemen and turned North Cape soon after. Shortly they encountered Maori, who sold them fish. On the 17th they anchored in what they called Lauriston Bay, after Monsieur Law of Lauriston, one of the owners of *St Jean Baptiste.* Cook had already named it Doubtless Bay. The harbour is not a very good one, and the ship was in some danger. They lost two anchors, one of which has fairly recently been found, and is on view in Kaitaia in the far north of New Zealand.

At this very moment Cook was only a few kilometres away, having been forced out to sea by heavy weather. Going in the opposite direction to de Surville, he turned North Cape to proceed down the west side of New Zealand, missing by a day what would have been a pleasant encounter, and a valuable one for the French. If the two ships had met the French would have learned where Tahiti was, how useful and relaxing it could be, and might have identified it with Davis Land.

Even more important, the French would have learned much about New Zealand, concerning provisions and Maori behaviour. De Surville was pleasantly surprised by how friendly the Maori were, not seeming to object in any way to the French coming ashore. The strongest sailors collected supplies of firewood and fish. Fresh water and ubiquitous greens quickly restored the rest: "we found in abundance some excellent anti-scorbutics – wild parsley and two kinds of cress .... It is wonderful how these herbs made our crew convalescent in such a

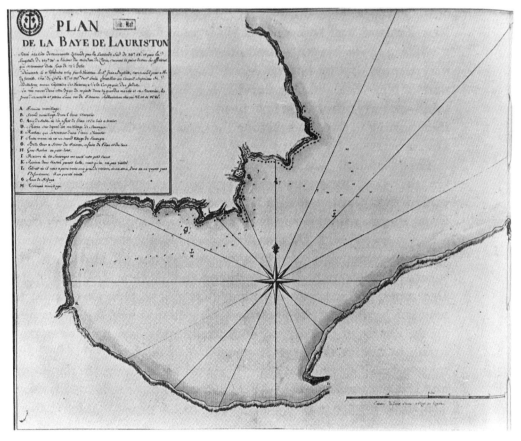

This inlet de Surville named for his sponsor Lauriston, not realising that only days earlier James Cook had named it Doubtless Bay. *(Alexander Turnbull Library, Wellington)*

short time …. One sailor, in particular, whose body was swollen all over, and whose mouth was absolutely rotten … by eating nothing but these herbs … got well enough to go on the voyage." But healthy men did not find New Zealand food nearly so commendable. "Fish was the only food used by the Natives that we could eat …. Their chief food is the root of the fern …. They warm it, beat it, and use it instead of bread." Fern root as bread was something to write home about – for a scientist, not a French sailor. But the visitors were wrong; the Maori had a range of foods, many most palatable to newcomers.

French behaviour made it obvious that the visitors were not staying very long and this may well have kept Maori tempers in check. De Surville instructed his men to take nothing without permission, and tried to ensure that no one broke Maori custom, wherever he could find out what it was. But the sailors did not necessarily approve the custom. Like Cook's men, the French were shocked by their realisation of Maori cannibalism: "He gave us to understand that when there were but a few enemies left on the battlefield they cut them in pieces and divide the pieces among themselves, to eat them …. I cannot say if they eat this horrible food raw or if they cook it."

On the 31st the Maori dragged away one of de Surville's small boats. After strenuous attempts to get it back failed, the French burned a number of huts, stole a canoe as evidence of having been in New Zealand and captured a Maori. They took him aboard the *St Jean Baptiste*, no doubt hoping, as de Surville had earlier, to "take away a native of the country in order to get from him what information I could about this place." Then the expedition left the bay for Spanish America, leaving for seed stock "some wheat, some rice, and some field-peas ... two little pigs, male and female, a Siamese rooster and a hen." As Cook had too, they found dogs and rats the only animals in New Zealand.

FRENCH AND ENGLISH

The French are very often given credit for getting along with indigenous races better than the English, or British in general, do. There is very little evidence for this outside North America and it is certainly not true in Asia or in Africa. There is not the slightest indication in France itself that the French co-exist better with Basques and Bretons than the English do with the Welsh and the Scots, and there is no real evidence that the French in Tahiti understand the Tahitians better than the British did the Fijians or the Maori.

Both these European nations have given much of their civilisation and culture to other races around the world. The British relationship in India has on the whole been a good one. Naturally enough the Indians did not wish to be ruled by foreigners but they respected the culture and kept many in responsible positions in the Civil Service and Army; in some ways British traditions are still followed in the Indian and Pakistani Armies more strictly than in the British Army. To much the same degree this adaptation was repeated in former French colonies.

The idea of a special French empathy arose in North America. There it was always claimed that the French succeeded with the Indians while English colonists did not. This is probably true. But it was based on circumstance, not differences in French and English – or more accurately in the context, British – culture. In Canada, the French and the Indians became partners in the fur trade. The French needed the Indians as suppliers and the Indians the French as buyers and marketers. But such a relationship was just as successfully operated by the Hudsons Bay Company, trading goods for furs in Western Canada from 1670 until the present day. This great company, staffed in the field largely by Scots, had as much influence with the Indians in the west as the French had ever had in the east.

It is true that the English-speaking group further south, now Americans, experienced conflict with the Indians. The reason was simply that in agricultural and ranching country Indian hunting cultures were a problem and a disadvantage. Whites were equally a problem and disadvantage to the Indians, displacing them, not working with them. In the north circumstances were different and so the relationship was too, for the fur trade required co-operation.

The view that the French fraternised more successfully with their Indian allies fails to appreciate that when the British took over from the French in Quebec and had to defend that part of the world against American land-seeking aggression, they had as much Indian support and sympathy as the French ever had. Indeed, at that time some Indian tribes moved north to Canada permanently. From a native race's point of view, circumstances altered perception of Europeans much more than the relatively minor differences between French and British culture: in New Zealand it was a French, not a British, crew which was massacred in the earliest days of exploration.

Introduction of new animals and new crops by explorers and whalemen had altered this scarcity of land mammals by the turn of the 19th century. Even so, in remote areas such as Queen Charlotte Sound in the 1820s, Russians found no change in this, in spite of Cook's introductions. Galkin, the surgeon of the *Mirnyy*, apparently saw no animals except dogs and rats. Polynesian dogs were a distinct breed and the Maori gave a pair of them to the Russians. "But these proved unable to adapt to us even after two weeks on board the sloop, constantly trembled, hid, would eat nothing, and finally died."

De Surville's treatment of the Maori at Doubtless Bay had been excellent. History has been hard on him because of his captive, and especially because the Maori he kidnapped was the very one who had helped the French during a great storm. The surgeon pointed out that he was the chief who "had so generously offered his hut and provided our people with food." Lieutenant L'Horme "was touched with the greatest compassion on the arrival on board of this poor unfortunate one ... making signs to me that he was the man who brought me some fish at a time when neither myself nor the ones who had the misfortune of not being able to get back to the vessel had any food to eat." Naturally the captive was treated well but he died on 24 March 1770 of scurvy, not the broken heart some romantics claimed. Yet Supercargo Monneron believed "sorrow, without doubt, contributed to his death ...."

To use a non-nautical metaphor, the rest of the trip was all downhill. Scurvy plagued them again. They could not put ashore at the Juan Fernandez Islands because of storms, and so set out for Peru. On the South American coast the weather was bad and de Surville's boat foundered in the surf while going for assistance. "M. de Surville and the two sailors ... could not get rid of their

FIG. 17.—Whole plant *Pteris aquilina*, showing creeping rhizome.

A drawing of the New Zealand fern, from a book written by Marion's first officer, Julien Crozet, shows the massive root system which provided food for the Maori as well as for Pakeha travellers in distress. *(University of Canterbury Library, Christchurch)*

121

clothing, and the three of them were drowned." The command devolved on Labé, leaving him plenty of problems. The Spanish suspected that *St Jean Baptiste* had come to flout their trade laws; indeed it was true, so the French officers destroyed many documents. *St Jean Baptiste* did not leave South America until 1773, being detained three years; by the time she reached France almost half her crew had died and many more deserted. The expedition had been a financial disaster.

De Surville was a much better leader than results indicate, but the expedition's planning was faulty, especially hopes of commerce which caused stocking of goods where supplies would have been more useful. But there were accomplishments, and new knowledge. The contact of the Maori with another European culture, and the resulting literature, contributed to the study of mankind; the canoe represents Maoridom in France; and in his trip from New Zealand eastward de Surville crossed ocean not sailed before, showing there was

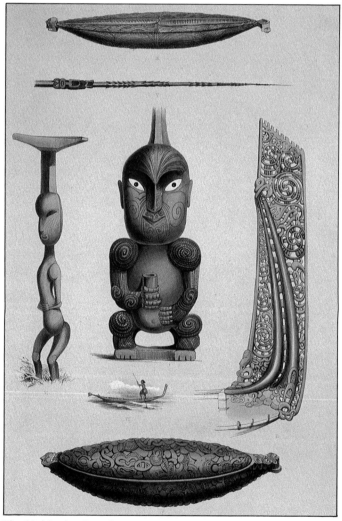

The highly developed artistic ability of the Maori was best displayed in their wood carving. *(Hocken Library, Dunedin)*

no continent there. Apparently the French thought they found one at New Zealand's Lauriston Bay. L'Horme's opinions about Maori weapons were based on human reactions which would only occur "if New Zealand is a continent, as it appears."

Although the kind but kidnapped Maori chief did not reach France on *St Jean Baptiste*, another Polynesian had already done so. Bougainville, a French military man and sailor, fought against the British naval and military expedition to Quebec in which James Cook won early recognition. After the war Bougainville became caught up in the exploring frenzy and commanded an expedition to Tahiti, before Cook. For some reason this voyage had apparently made little impression on de Surville. Bougainville never came anywhere near New Zealand but his voyage affected that country. Ahu-Toru ( the spelling varies), a Tahitian, had gone to Paris with Bougainville and spent eleven months there. When it was decided to return him to Tahiti, various French men and women donated money to purchase implements, animals and seeds for the island. The King of Spain even authorised a brief landing in the Philippines, a rare exception to Spanish exclusiveness. So it was with much support that Ahu-Toru departed France to return to Tahiti by way of Mauritius.

It sounds simple but any such voyage was a major exercise. Naturally the French hoped to accomplish more than merely returning Ahu-Toru, just as the British intended for Cook's third voyage, taking Omai to Tahiti after years in London.

Looking westward down Waiapoa or Frenchman's Bay from beside the little stream, indicated by the rushes on the right of the picture, where the French purportedly buried the bottle containing a document claiming possession of New Zealand for Louis XV. *(Shaughan Anderson and Bay of Islands Maritime Park)*

In Mauritius was a local naval man, Marc-Joseph Marion du Fresne, who like de Surville had served the French East India Company. When this was dissolved he suggested a plan to combine the repatriation of Ahu-Toru to Tahiti with a voyage of exploration. A wealthy man, he was willing to help with finance and an expedition was set up, financed in a rather complicated way which included a state subsidy. Marion was to seek the great southern continent, Gonneville Land, to assess its suitability as a French base. Naval forces there could protect French communications with India and destroy those of Britain. Not yet decisively defeated in the struggle for empire, the French were looking to the next round.

Marion's expedition would sail south of Australia to New Zealand, roughly on Tasman's route, calculations obviously paralleling Cook's thinking about his second voyage. The ships were to visit Van Diemen's Land and New Zealand before crossing the Pacific to Tahiti in 1772.

Marion du Fresne had joined his first ship when only eleven. After much experience in privateers, he rose to command rank at twenty-one. On his most romantic assignment he sailed the *Prince Conty* to Scotland to assist in bringing Bonny Prince Charlie back to France after Culloden. His service in the Seven Years War won him a respected decoration and promotion to the rank of captain. Having been a prisoner of war at various times, Marion could speak English. After the war he took part in several trading voyages, and such broad experience justified his description as a sailor "suitable for all kinds of voyages." He was thought brave, energetic and sometimes rash. Those who too easily trust others often seem rash – and usually are. Marion's trust was to be cruelly rewarded.

The expedition's main ship, the *Mascarin*, was a flute, a transport vessel very much like the *Zeehaen* of Tasman, and chosen for the same reasons as Cook's Whitby cat. But like Tasman's voyage and Cook's second circumnavigation, this was to be a two-ship expedition, and the *Marquis de Castries* at sixteen guns was rated, as *Endeavour* was, a sloop-of-war. Yet she was a flute too, quite like Tasman's *Zeehaen*. So the expedition was equipped much as Tasman's was, although 130 years had brought some minor technical improvements.

Julian-Marie Crozet, the second-in-command of Marion's ship, had served with him before. He wrote a very fine journal of the voyage and, like Labé, thus entered history. On his way home from the expedition Crozet met Cook at Capetown and the two competent and perceptive sailors became friends, but unfortunately their conversations are largely unrecorded. Forster, scientist on Cook's second great expedition, said only that at dinner in *Resolution*'s cabin Crozet "entertained us with many curious particulars relating to his voyage."

Marion's two ships sailed from Mauritius in October 1771, the commander worrying about the health of Ahu-Toru, for when they left smallpox was epidemic. Unfortunately the Tahitian had become infected and an early November landfall at Madagascar did not save him. He died two days later. The unfortunate Tahitian had not infected the crew and the ships kept going; although Ahu-Toru's death had removed the real basis of the expedition, undoing their many commitments would have been difficult and unpleasant. The expedition topped up provisions at Cape Colony and sailed from there on 28 December 1771. Delays at the Cape had lost them precious time. Starting southward at the end of December is really too late; late October would be

Polynesian visitors to Europe did not always have a happy homecoming. Omai went to England with Tobias Furneaux in the *Adventure*. He was lionised, but on his return to Tahiti found that an adventurer's natural response to applause abroad is regarded as conceit by those at home. *(Hocken Library, Dunedin)*

none too soon. The Dutch had put great emphasis on the time of Tasman's departure southwards.

Two weeks south-east of the Cape, driven by the prevailing westerly winds, they sighted a group of islands, the first of several islands discovered. These they named the Austral Islands, now known as Prince Edward Island and Marion Island, of the Republic of South Africa. The discoverers investigated whether these were in truth islands or the promontory of a southern continent; while consulting within shouting range, obviously risky in rough seas, the young captain of the *de Castries* ran into Marion's ship.

Tasman's captains had managed to avoid collision during councils by skill, caution or luck. Because of the damage, the French ships gave up closer investigation of the islands and left believing they might have seen part of the Southern Continent. Conditions allowed only temporary repairs to *Mascarin* and speed had to be reduced. On 19 January they hoped penguins and seals meant land was close; on the 22nd they saw icebergs and two more islands, now the Crozet Islands, for the *Mascarin*'s second-in-command. A young officer's journal says that "all these things persuaded us that we had found the continent." According to him, Marion intended to go as far south as 54 degrees to search for it, "but the demasting of the flute put a limit to his plans." The damage to *Mascarin*, requiring major repairs, was to have even greater consequences.

Marion claimed possession by placing a bottle containing a document on the island, still known as Possession Island. At this time they were only five hundred or so kilometres from another French expedition under Captain Kerguelen, whose discovery, Kerguelen Island, is still on the map. On 10 February Crozet estimated their longitude by "readings of the distance from the sun to the moon" (that is, by lunar distances). He made it 90 degrees east of Paris; this was a difference of 8 degrees 30 minutes from his own dead reckoning, perhaps as much as 350 nautical miles in that latitude, and shows how rightly de Surville, Tasman and others worried about inaccuracy of longitudes found by dead reckoning. Crozet found the latitude was 45 degrees 36 minutes South.

---

## WILD FRUITS AND VEGETABLES

The Maori used the limited number of edible plants and fruits which New Zealand provided, and many early explorers tried the native foods. A karaka tree berry, Wakefield thought, "is sickly and dry; but the kernel forms an important article of native food .... The natives gather the berries when ripe; and after separating the pulp of the fruit from the kernel by steaming them in large *umu*, or ovens, they collect the kernels in baskets and soak them in a pool, dammed up in a running stream. They are allowed to remain in soak until they ferment, when they are fit for use. As they require no cooking, the natives use them extensively for travelling .... Their odour is so offensive that I could never prevail on myself to eat them; but I have known many Englishmen who had acquired a taste for them ...." Karaka kernels were very poisonous when raw.

Some of the foods were much better than that. In the South Island Brunner recommended the root of the cabbage tree, called the ti, if baked in a Maori oven. "The root of the ti ... is generally from three to four feet long [one metre], and of a conic shape, with an immense number of long fibrous roots attached to it ... natives, whose tools consist of a pointed stick, and their hands, consider they have done a glorious days work if they manage to obtain five ti roots in the day. It requires an immense oven, and to remain twelve hours baking." The result was quite presentable.

Brunner also found some berries appetising and useful. The berry he called moko, which no one else mentions but which sounds rather like the tutu, was "very palatable when you have obtained the proper knowledge of eating them ... gauge your mouth so that your teeth will only crush the berry without breaking the seed, which has a most nauseous, bitter taste." Brunner found sweetness too: "the fruit of the ekiakia ... called by the natives tawara ... is very luscious, more like a conserve than a fruit; the honey

Turning somewhat northwards to head for Van Diemen's Land, the French – second European visitors to this island – sighted it on 3 March. Unlike the Dutch, they managed to contact the natives. They soon realised the inhabitants lived primitively, and described an existence little above that of animals. The visitors tried an unusual way of making friends, meant to reassure the natives that apart from colour the French were very like themselves. The plan worked; two naked volunteers were accepted by the Aborigines as friends and the French landed peacefully. Calm did not last. As other boats came to shore the Aborigines naturally began to fear the constant reinforcement. There was a quarrel, the sailors had to fire in self-defence, and in the end at least one inhabitant was killed.

Marion's expedition found difficulty, as Tasman had, in discovering fresh water. They decided to sail for New Zealand, and by staying somewhat north of Tasman's route had easy going. On 25 March 1772 a snow-covered peak rose gently out of the horizon. Marion named it Mascarin Peak, not knowing that Cook had named it Mount Egmont, nor that the Maori called it Taranaki; much less that later New Zealanders would call it "Mount Egmont *or* Mount Taranaki". Turning north, away from the direction of Murderers Bay, the ships sailed past the North Island to the Three Kings, where Tasman's journal gave hope of water and wood. Disappointed, they cursed Tasman somewhat unfairly. "This

of the flax blossom is also in season, called korari, and, when mixed with fern-root, also makes a species of confectionary." Along the west coast, Brunner believed, "the liquor of the tutu berries ... has here a much finer flavour than in most other places, and may be taken freely without injury." The juice of the tutu berries was obtained by placing them in a basket, the liquid seeping out from the pressure of the berries' weight. An 1846 list of the vegetable products of New Zealand called tutu, "the native wine ... when boiled with rimu, a sea weed, forms a jelly which is very palatable; when fermented it makes a sort of wine, and it contains so much colouring matter, that it may be used as a dye." We can assume that explorers seldom used it as a dye.

Oil from titoki berries was squeezed out of the dry seeds left after the fruit pulp and juice had been removed by tramping on the berries in special baskets. Raupo, or bulrush, seed were sometimes cooked and eaten; the taste was excellent, the process tedious. Brunner found at Lake Rotoroa a fresh-water mussel "called the kaiehau, which, boiled with the roots of the raupo, or bulrush, makes a palatable dish, and was the favourite meal" of Te Rauparaha. It was less rewarding to prepare tawa berries and hinau fruit, for they were not appetising and Europeans at least found cakes made from hinau meal most unpleasant.

There is no record of Maori beginning to eat celery grass because Cook's men ate it. Indeed Crozet described a number of edible plants, including a wild celery, and said that when the French ate them the Maori "expressed great astonishment ...." Arthur Harper may have been eating plants that the Maori, possibly very sensibly, did not use. He found that "though there are several edible plants, they are not very nourishing, nor can I honestly say very nice. However, a hungry man must eat what he can get, and I have often been glad of even a small feed of Piki-piki fern (*Asplenium bulbiferum*) ... and the curled, crozier-like shoot is quite passable when boiled for an hour." As explorers were often very hungry, they learned to eat what was edible and like it or be silent.

navigator has made some very erroneous statements …. Tasman is quite incorrect when he assures us that on one of these islands there is a river, and that good anchorages can be found there." Disgusted, the captains turned for the mainland but had difficulty in finding good water at the northern tip of New Zealand. Lieutenant Roux of the *Mascarin* wrote several despondent journal entries: "a little stream was found, the water of which however, was not very fresh … no fresh water could be found there … brought off some water from the river, but it was brackish, and good for nothing." The quality of water was important, for it had to stay drinkable for weeks.

Gales battered them, and they lost several anchors when they tried to find holding ground. They managed to recover those of *Mascarin* but the inept du Clesmeur, captain of *de Castries*, made another serious mistake. Vital equipment was lost permanently, even though *Mascarin* "despatched the two longboats and a third boat to dredge for the anchors lost by the *Castries* …. Nothing was found, and this because … they had not taken the precaution to buoy their anchors." Eighteenth-century hempen cables frequently tore free at the anchor ring, leaving the anchor hooked in the bottom and the ship dragging free a useless length of cable. Cautious captains fastened a buoy to the anchor with a separate length of line, locating the anchor whether still fast to the ship or not. Anchors were expensive and massively forged iron hooks impossible to replace on early Pacific voyages. Ships carried spares but not many; anchors are neither a weight to ignore nor the shape to stow easily.

By now almost desperate, the French abandoned the unbuoyed anchors and turned North Cape hoping for better conditions down the east coast. The wind forced them out to sea and they missed de Surville's Lauriston (Doubtless) Bay and instead came upon the Bay of Islands further south, a much better anchorage. Maori greeted the ships and some came on board, a few even sleeping there overnight. On 4 May, to the crews' great relief, the ships anchored in the Bay just south of Okahu Island. Crozet had brought a Tahitian vocabulary compiled by Bougainville and enlarged by Ahu-Toru. "At first we did not know how to talk to these savages, but by chance I bethought me of a vocabulary of the isle of Taïty which had been given me by the Superintendent of the Isle of France. I read several words of this list, and I saw with the greatest surprise that the savages understood me perfectly." Marion himself was somewhat of a linguist, and had learned enough Tahitian from Ahu-Toru to be able to talk with the Maori himself, an advantage over de Surville and Cook. On the other hand, having an interpreter there, as Cook had in Tupaia, was almost as good, and perhaps at times better, for then there was cultural understanding too. The French – as did Cook – thought it remarkable that peoples so far apart as Tahitians and Maori shared the same language.

Crozet, still thinking of the "southern Continent", speculated that it had but been broken by earthquakes, with only scattered island groups remaining, inhabited by former continentals sharing the original language. About a century later another Frenchman, Augustus le Plongeon, argued from evidence he claimed came from Mayan sources, that a vast and productive Pacific continent had broken up in an earthquake. And in the 20th century the American James Churchward produced several books about, and a map of, this transient

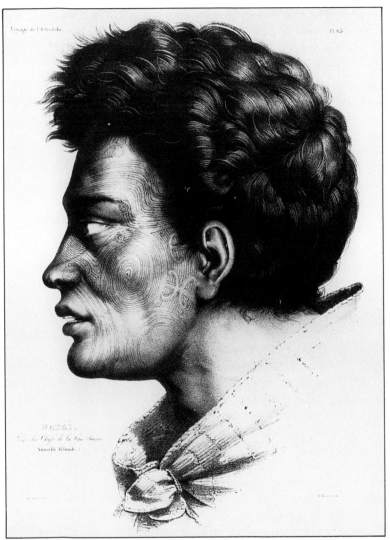

A later French artist in New Zealand painted many portraits of strikingly vital Maori, so many of whom had impressed Marion and his officers. This depiction (the French spelled his name Natai) emphasises the points Europeans constantly made about the hair and strong attractive features of the Maori. *(Hocken Library, Dunedin)*

continent he called Mu, which had left the widely scattered Polynesian islands with their closely related languages. As with Crozet, there has been no progress beyond speculation.

Conditions at the new base were much better for the French: plentiful fish and sweet potatoes available; water, wood and calm anchorages easy to find; and seemingly friendly inhabitants. They took the chance to explore and to visit, for whenever they could they sought the opportunity to examine Maori ways of living. "Amongst other things we noticed, their houses excited our admiration, so neatly were they constructed ... of stakes placed a little apart from each other, and strengthened by switches or small poles, which are crossed, and which interlace ... an outer covering, consisting of a layer of moss thick enough to prevent the rain and wind from penetrating ... is supported by small lattice-work, very neatly constructed."

In the Bay of Islands observation of Maori life would be relatively easy. The area was heavily populated and the Maori eager to trade and converse. Sailors and officers visited their houses, saw what people wore and ate, studied "their occupations, their work, their manufactures, and even their amusements." The Maori studied the French too. If Europeans thought Maori to be thieves, the Maori thought Europeans were niggards. If Frenchmen did not like fern root, Maori also had their preferences. To French amazement, Maori "were given some white wine, of which they drank a little, believing it was water, but having tasted it, they declined drinking it, making signs that they preferred the water." But in spite of cultural differences New Zealand, which did not toss about as *Mascarin* and *de Castries* did, seemed pleasant enough.

In such conditions, and after a tough voyage with a damaged ship, men will relax and lower their guard, at least temporarily. Good leaders prevent deterioration in discipline. Cook rapidly livened up *Adventure* when he found captain and crew settling into winter quarters. That Marion's ships seemed in no hurry to leave may have been an elemental mistake. Lieutenant Roux had no doubt that the Maori "firmly believed we were going to remain there always, for every day a large quantity of articles were taken ashore from the ships." Marion's crews established several camps in the Bay of Islands: one for the sick near especially good water; one as a stores and communications centre; another at a convenient place to get wood for repairs. French officers also spent much time visiting, exploring, and making notes for their journals, but although boats moved freely they did not chart the bay accurately. Marion seemed to enjoy being at the Bay of Islands; he probably hoped for long-term friendship between the Maori and France. In contrast with Cook, he was looking for immediate trade prospects and was not interested in groundwork, in charting the harbours for future trade or settlement.

On brief visits explorers seldom really assess the possibilities of a country, unless the inhabitants wear gold bangles. Cook tried, and seems to have been best. He inspected the forests and the flax, he noted seals and whales, he talked of European settlement: all became important in New Zealand. Nevertheless, especially in Crozet's superb journal, this French expedition left a fine early study of Maori life; the journal described the country in some ways better than Cook's did. Of the Maori the French approved. "These islanders are generally of tall stature, well proportioned, of a very agreeable figure, with regular features, and seem very agile ... in a word they are fine men ... everything we have seen ... tends to prove that they are a fine, courageous, industrious, and very intelligent race."

Crozet thought they were of mixed ancestry, perhaps like Bretons, Franks and Normans in his homeland. He believed the "three kinds of men" were distinct in colour and also in facial hair growth, but that each kind was good-looking. Some officers had reservations about Maori treatment of women. Roux said the Maori "paid no attention to their women; indeed, they offered them to us, and seemed hurt because we refused ... their daughters or their own wives." This was not what most explorers found, and Crozet, in the same expedition, understood it quite differently. The Maori "gave us to understand by signs that we must not touch the married women, but that we might with perfect freedom make advances to the girls. It was in fact not possible to find any more approachable."

Friction developed soon enough. The French view of French property was not shared by the Maori, and irritations and fears began to build. But the French still admired the Maori. "Had we departed about this time, we would have brought to Europe the most favourable accounts of these savages; we would have painted them in our relations with them as the most affable, the most humane, and the most hospitable people on the face of the earth. From our accounts philosophers fond of praising primitive man would have triumphed in seeing the speculations of their studies confirmed by the accounts of travellers whom they would have recommended as worthy of belief. But we would all of us have been in the wrong." Good relations were not to continue. Worry about thieving was compounded when a black slave escaped from the French, for his knowledge would help the Maori if they were plotting.

The officers persuaded Marion to "always have with him a small detachment. He was therefore generally accompanied by two or three officers and some soldiers." Roux and Crozet cautioned him but Marion, in spite of his lifetime of war service, had faith in humanity and accepted protestations of friendship at face value. Crozet thought the Maori "turn and turn about, sweetly affectionate, hard and threatening, never long in the same temper, but always dangerous and treacherous." He claimed to have "mistrusted them and always noted with the acutest sorrow how M. Marion took these savages into his confidence." To Marion, Maori visitors were visitors and never spies; as he was doing good he would not believe others might repay with evil. Roux thought Marion "convinced that if we did the Natives no harm they would never try to injure us." Rousseau had a distant devotee, but not for long.

On 12 June Marion went fishing and neither he nor anyone with him came back by nightfall. Worry would not find them in the dark, nor was there necessarily need to worry. He was the commander who made the decisions, and might have accepted an invitation from a friendly chief or gone to visit another camp. But the next morning a boat sent for firewood failed to return, and this time a sailor escaped and swam to the ship. The boat had been ambushed and all the rest killed.

The force sent out to search for Marion found that, like the boat's crew, the commander's party had been ambushed and killed. Lieutenant Roux, a critic and no sycophant, expressed feelings which seem to have been general. "We soon felt the extent of the loss we had experienced … it was irreparable. M. Marion was a gentleman … with all the qualities of a first-rate seaman he combined the greatest gentleness of disposition and the utmost frankness. No one was better fitted than he to bring about a state of peace and harmony, and … maintain good discipline on his ship …. After his death mistakes became as frequent as when he was alive they had been rare." Marion was mourned – and then revenged.

Du Clesmeur now became commander, for the captain of the consort ship was the senior officer. He gathered the available men together, then reinforced the second camp. Crozet was sent to evacuate the camp for

131

cutting masts; when bringing his men back to the ship he ordered the first shots the French had fired at Maori. "I found it advisable and necessary for our safety that I should make these unhappy people understand the superiority of our arms. I had the rowing stopped, and ordered four fusiliers to fire at the chiefs, who appeared more excited and animated than all the others. Every shot told, and this fusilade continued some minutes. The savages saw their chiefs and comrades fall in the most senseless manner." Roux beat off attacks on the camp at Moturua Island, and next day he inflicted heavy damage and casualties on the Maori village. Gunpowder was teaching and the Maori was learning very quickly. Fifty years later, with their own guns, they would show how much they had learned.

The French could not simply leave, as Tasman and de Surville had; the ships were stripped down under repair. Crozet and du Clesmeur did their best to get the craft refitted quickly but in spite of all efforts it was a month after Marion's death before both ships were ready. On 12 July the French buried a bottle as an Act of Possession, and sailed from Treachery Bay. In spite of its name they left a garden to improve Maori life, thinking that "plantations we had made on Marion Island, of wheat, maize, potatoes, and various kinds of nuts, might be very useful to them." The French would certainly assume that usefulness. Crozet thought the Maori "confined their whole agriculture to two or three objects. They have no knowledge of any sort of grain and, excepting some small fields planted with potatoes, gourds, aloes-pite, and very small flax, the country appeared to me to be lying fallow, and producing only the wild natural growth .... I did not even meet with the least fruit, either wild or cultivated." Maori tradition credits Marion with leaving the Bay of Islands garlic. Certainly it grew there, and the whaleship *Fanny* bought some at the Bay in 1823.

No one yet knows exactly what happened to Marion nor how it happened. Forty years later, a Maori told the captain of a British ship about trouble over a stolen axe. Humanity as it is, no doubt European goods seemed desirable, and there would have been much to share if the ships had been taken. Maori also told of a clash between sailors and natives in which a Maori had been killed, and finally in the late 1820s, told Peter Dillon, a British captain with wide Pacific experience, of fights about a catch of fish. Surviving evidence of Maori activities before the massacre indicated a premeditated attack, conceived because they suspected the ships were staying permanently. The Maori quite naturally wished to be rid of the ships, to be free of the constant unpleasant minor incidents, free of the constant worry about tapu, free from the need to produce extra food. Tahitians sometimes asked European ships to move on after a certain time. If Ahu-Toru had lived he could have interpreted and perhaps mediated. Roux spoke for many in regretting "the loss we had sustained in the poor native of that island who had died on board our vessel from the small-pox."

None of these explanations sound quite convincing. A modern suggestion relates the death of Marion to Maori tribal politics, in which Marion meddled by his friendship with "intrusive Maori", forerunners of the takeover of the area by another tribe, the Ngapuhi. If so, Marion's mistake was not friendship but favouring the wrong friends. Probably the argument will continue as long as historians need to fit new insights to old problems.

The French sailed north-north-east, intending to turn west to look for Tasman's islands of Rotterdam and Amsterdam in the Tongan group. As it happened, in bad weather they sailed through the Tongan group without stopping. Then they headed for Guam. A large number of the sailors already had scurvy, a remarkable contrast to Cook's experience and tribute to his discipline and methods. On 23 August they crossed the equator and on 26 September the ships anchored in Guam. They went back to their home base by way of the Philippines, reaching Mauritius in early April.

The expedition had not been important. The southern continent was not discovered, for the few islands they had found were not, nor seriously thought to be, real indications of it. Naturally the death of Marion made people firmly believe that the Maori were ferocious and bloodthirsty; it was seen as confirmation of Tasman's and Furneaux's experience. But Marion's expedition told the world much about the Maori, more being learned in this prolonged stay than even Cook had done at Ships Cove. Fortunately Cook's several well-publicised voyages to New Zealand showed before long that Maori were not irredeemably savage.

# CHAPTER SIX

# French, Russians and Maori

New Zealand really entered the world after 1815. By the 1820s Russian, French and American naval ships were coming to New Zealand on official cruises, partly because of the fame of Cook, partly because of a general expansion of outlook and ambition, partly because of profitable whaling and sealing. The great world wars were over; a new commercial and cultural age, to be called Victorian, was beginning.

"New ages" had no chance earlier; from Cook and Marion's time until 1815, Europe was usually at war and its effects spread around the world. War raged, with changes of opponents and intensity, from 1793 to 1815, with a minor break in 1801-2. The American Revolution changed that old world and the French Revolution destroyed it. In Eastern Europe war's changes were causes of more wars, yet also produced a new world power, Russia, peer of the German powers and of Britain and France. In America the young United States was flexing ever-developing muscles. All these events echoed in New Zealand.

The Russians visited New Zealand before the French did after the great wars, but the French left much more writing. Their connection, begun with de Surville in 1769, lasted until 1840. The quality of the writing is important: the French at the Bay of Islands wrote of commercial and missionary-inspired change while Russians at Queen Charlotte Sound were, almost literally, in a backwater. Yet national attitudes provide useful insights.

As usual much, but not all, of the best writing comes from naval surgeons but other professions shone too. The Russian Simonov, for example, was an astronomer but also competently interested in ethnology. The voyage was the making of him; he collected a store of information and material fundamental to his long career as a major Russian scientist, very much as Banks had done. In the case of the French the commanders themselves wrote very fine books. This was all very fortunate, for although much of the physical exploration of New Zealand was either finished or under way, there was an infinite amount of cultural exploration ahead.

The wars over in 1815, France had again turned her mind to Pacific exploration. Louis de Freycinet circumnavigated the world from 1816 to 1820 in *Uranie*, but missed out New Zealand. *Uranie*'s contribution was to bring the abilities of Duperrey to the fore. On the way home the ship struck a hidden Falkland Islands reef and was completely lost. This happened in good weather; perhaps more culpable but safer, in that the crew were saved. For the French government this loss was the last straw; any proposal for a new expedition would certainly face strong resistance.

Louis Duperrey had been a good senior officer with de Freycinet, and now aimed to command an expedition to the Pacific himself. A native Parisian, in the Navy since boyhood, he was decorated and promoted to lieutenant-commander after he returned from *Uranie*'s voyage. By vocation a scientist, he studied the

## THE RUSSIANS WERE HERE

The Russian Imperial Navy visited New Zealand in 1820, stopping briefly at Queen Charlotte Sound. Amid much world scientific and diplomatic activity Russia had decided in 1818 to send an Antarctic expedition, which was to spend some time (it turned out to be twelve days) in New Zealand. On the way to the Pacific the Russians bought many instruments in England, and met the elderly Sir Joseph Banks, for a briefing as it were. In Brazil they bought wine and fresh meat to supplement, among other foods, their innovation, tinned pea soup. The expedition then went to South Georgia, on to Antarctica and eastward to Australia. The Russians were greatly impressed by New South Wales and in turn impressed the Australians with their courtesy and fellowship. The timing of *Vostok*'s and *Mirnyy*'s New Zealand visit was accidental; they set out from Sydney for the Tuamotu Islands but fierce winds in the Tasman drifted them eastward, finally to be storm driven into Cook Strait. Then, much earlier than they had planned, they spent a few active and productive days in Queen Charlotte Sound.

The leader, Faddey (Fabian Gottlieb) Bellingshausen, was a Baltic German. His family had served the Russian Crown for years; many Balts held high rank in the Russian Navy. Bellingshausen had been with Kruzenshtern's successful *Nadeshda* expedition around the world in 1803 to 1806, and received this new command because of his prestigious commander's backing. He was able to recruit very competent young officers and scientists. The results were empathetic treatment of Maori and perceptive reports of their life and environment at Queen Charlotte Sound. The Russians had frankly adopted Cook's shipboard hygiene and his sympathetically firm way of dealing with Pacific Islanders. To do things as Cook had was considered correct in Russian naval exploration, an attitude encouraged by the number of Cook's subordinates, such as Billings and Ledyard, who had entered Russian service.

Like Cook, Bellingshausen took some German scientists with him. Routes and timing were firmly set out, but not the science. Here he was at liberty to improvise. As a Balt working with Russians, Bellingshausen was keenly alive to cultural and temperamental differences, and he chose to emphasise native cultures and naval science. The Russians visited Queen Charlotte Sound as Cook had done, whereas the French and Americans visited Otago and the Bay of Islands. Setting the different national observations side by side provides comparisons and contrasts of Maori culture, and also of the Europeans themselves. Much Maori material from Queen Charlotte Sound went back to Russia, creating so much interest that Russia still has very active interest in Maori Studies. Excellent journals, substantial studies, and a fine collection of Maori material from the voyage grace the Institute of Anthropology in Leningrad. The Russian stay of one week in Queen Charlotte Sound was a brief period to have had such lasting effects on European science.

oceans and the earth's magnetic fields; after his own voyage Duperrey wrote much about science but never finished his own account of the expedition, a failure which led to underestimation of his achievements. Effective publicity is half the way to fame.

Duperrey joined forces with another prominent naval officer, Dumont d'Urville, to downplay the anticlimax of *Uranie* and to interest France in exploration again. Although a distinguished sailor, d'Urville was famed for something quite different. While Duperrey had been away with de Freycinet, d'Urville saw the Venus de Milo just after the statue had been unearthed in Melos, an ancient Greek town. He recognised the exquisite classical form of Venus Victrix and, failing to persuade his commander to obtain it, wrote such an eloquent report that the French Ambassador purchased the statue without waiting for more prestigious advice. Being decorated for this achievement, so early in his career, fired d'Urville's ambition to do "something great" for France.

Duperrey and d'Urville argued that they could explore at a reasonable cost. In fact, when after some years they persuaded the government to send them exploring, they managed so well that sailing around the world actually cost taxpayers less than if the ship had stayed in France. Duperrey's and d'Urville's arguments finally succeeded and in 1822 the government gave them the corvette the *Coquille*, a slow transport from Toulon, of 480 tons and manned by seventy men. Just as the sloop *Endeavour* was really a cat, the *Coquille* was not really a corvette, for sloops and corvettes were ships-of-war. But well supplied and officered, she was so successful that on her return she was soon chosen for another expedition.

Dumont d'Urville, as planned, was appointed second-in-command. Unfortunately Duperrey and d'Urville, both able and accomplished men, were very different in temperament and tastes. Duperrey was volatile, impressionable, but in bearing the very model of a French naval officer. D'Urville was cold, haughty, occasionally pompous yet at times slovenly: "he joined to the excessive soberness of a Spaniard the disdain of a beggar for his appearance …." D'Urville once received British officers greeting him on behalf of the government of New South Wales, not in naval uniform but in torn

A portrait of Dumont d'Urville probably done some fifteen years before his death. *(University of Canterbury Library, Christchurch)*

trousers, a gravely wounded straw hat and a baggy old drill coat. In contrast Duperrey dressed for an occasion. Two distinguished men of such different temperaments in one small ship meant difficulty. And so it proved.

In spite of this compromising circumstance d'Urville himself wrote a good deal about this voyage, as well as about his later ones; his books are masterpieces. Several other officers on the *Coquille*'s voyage wrote excellent journals, with material about the Bay of Islands, in the 1820s. René Lesson produced the fine journal one might expect from our experience of surgeons' writing. Such men had the ability, the training and, at least on fortunate voyages, the time. The talented Lesson won high rank in the Navy's medical service and wrote much about zoology, ornithology, botany and French antiquities.

The Bay of Islands that Duperrey saw was quite different from that of Cook and Marion. The whaling industry had arrived and the Bay was a whaling base, giving rise to the establishment of English missions. Samuel Marsden, the New South Wales chaplain who founded missions in New Zealand, argued not only that they would improve the Bay as a whaling supply base but also that missionaries would protect the Maori from the whalemen. There was more than special pleading to his arguments, for both whaleships and missions changed Maori life, coincident and connected with the large-scale introduction of muskets and gunpowder. Both whalemen and missionaries sent or took reports of Maori culture and day-to-day behaviour back to Sydney. Now the Anglo-Saxons would themselves be assessed by observers at least as unsympathetic as a whaleman to the Maori (especially the males) or a missionary to Maori beliefs and behaviour. The French on Duperrey's ship comment on results obtained by various missionaries, and we learn much about Maori warfare as well as their way of life.

Well officered and equipped, the *Coquille* sailed from Toulon to Gibraltar, Teneriffe and Brazil. Minor difficulties in Brazil dealt with, they sailed to the Falklands where they saw the wreckage of *Uranie*, "her keel, a few carronades buried in the sand, iron casks and all kinds of debris ... her broken carcass over a small chain of rocks." Somewhat depressed, they were soothed by an easy passage around the Horn only to find Chile in revolt and difficulty getting provisions because of the requirements of local forces. Fortunately a colonel of Napoleon's Imperial Guard, now a mercenary, was helpful. Poverty-stricken Chile they were glad to leave. Duperrey records one of the few bright episodes, *Coquille*'s officers hearing an elderly Spanish gentlemen describe "the great dinner la Pérouse had given to his crew, which had been attended by all the officers ...." The old man did not know of la Pérouse's death and was quite overcome.

They found Peru seemingly as unstable as Chile, although Duperrey witnessed the installation of the first president. In spite of the poverty of Chile and Peru some sailors deserted. On the way to Tahiti *Coquille* sailed through the dangerous Tuamotu Archipelago, discovering a small island. At Tahiti they expected the kind of welcome Bougainville and Cook had received; they found the place transformed by English missionaries. The sailors were furious, Lesson recalled, without recording whether he counted himself a sailor: "Those who were plagued by sensual visions were sorely disappointed, Bougainville's stories had given rise to such hopes that it was hard to see them fade away."

D'Urville, somewhat more sour, or perhaps sensibly refusing to want what he would not take, summed up the visit: "we had an opportunity to examine at our leisure the fair sex of Tahiti and I am in a position to affirm that it in no way corresponds to the alluring descriptions of the first navigators." But the Tahitians were still friendly. According to Duperrey a few "true daughters of Eve" were able to evade missionary scrutiny, and after the first week of the visit the Tahitians were able to "perform traditional dances which they are no longer allowed to indulge in ...." Blosseville did not care for the Protestant church services but admitted the bans on tattooing, music, and traditional songs and dances had improved Tahitian morals. Duperrey too commended the missions. Indeed, most of the French officers realised that the missionaries were not simply bigoted but rather anxious to save the natives from disease and other misfortune stemming from rougher elements in visiting crews.

*Coquille* sailed westward on 9 July. When she reached the longitude to turn south for New Holland, storms forced the French to change course. Tossed around and driven back, finally the expedition reached the Solomon Islands. As most explorers, the French crew did not think the Melanesians – their appearance adding to their reputation for aggressiveness – withstood comparison with Polynesians. Lesson's description was typically unsympathetic: "their black and oily skin, their unkempt hair covered with red ochre dissolved in fish oil forming a thick putty-like cover over their head, truly gave a strange touch to their complete nudity ...." After Tahiti this would not impress the sailors.

The French went on to a cool welcome at the Dutch East Indies; they had to use their letter from the King of Holland to get into the harbour at Caieli Bay at all. After some arguments they continued to Amboina where officers and crew had a much warmer reception. Like most ships in these ports *Coquille* was harassed by disease and soon headed for higher latitudes to find cool weather. By this time supplies were low, nothing but "old salted pork, half tainted; some biscuits, full of worms; and to drink, ferruginous water ...." And that was not all the trouble. Cockroaches were "in their thousands, they fouled the food, soiled the water and disturbed our sleep. They attacked everything not overlooking the inkwells which they emptied without leaving a single drop ...." One blessing was the newly invented tinned meat. Blosseville had cans of chicken and beans three years old and still in good condition. Rust spoiled a few cans but the main problem with canned food was scarcity, not quality.

The ship went right around Australia, calling at Van Diemen's Land and New South Wales before heading for New Zealand. She was thoroughly searched for absconding convicts and nine were removed. But they had taken on real passengers, two Maori returning home and a missionary, George Clarke, with his wife and year-old son. The French learned much from the Maori during the uneventful voyage. As they arrived at the Bay of Islands an English, an American, and an Australian whaleship came out; the Bay of Islands was now in full swing as a whaling base. Obviously European influence and enterprise were changing Maori life.

By the time of this French visit European preconceptions had grown beyond the wistful and wishful simplification of the Noble Savage, a thesis not regaining fashion until the 1960s. All the French journals have something interesting to

## TAHITIAN FANTASY

Tahiti was and is real, but fantasy added as much to it in the 18th century as it does today. It was even said a lost tribe of Jews lived there, probably because some English in the first ships remarked the light complexions of Tahitians. After all, who were as scattered as the Jews? Who else might one expect to encounter anywhere? Rumour dealt in delusion in this as in much else. Tahiti-of-the-mind was a land of luxury inhabited by people with all the graces and no grossness. Some French and Tahitians believe it still, with little supporting evidence.

In the 18th century there was even a theory that gold could be found in Tahiti. Monneron, supercargo of the *St Jean Baptiste*, thought so: "it was quite natural to presume that the island must be much richer than any of the other countries, as it is situated about 700 leagues west of the Coast of Peru and in ... the latitude of Capiazo, where the Spaniards get gold from in immense quantities." And it might be the rumoured Davis Land which had been encountered by an English buccaneer, without its exact location being known, and which was said to be tremendously rich in gold and silver.

Gold seems very pie-in-the-sea to us, who have not lived with Spanish treasure fleets forever in our consciousness. Every buccaneer had dreamt of them by night, watched for them by day, and the fathers of 18th-century explorers had known buccaneers. Treasure ships the Spaniards sent home from their American empire in the 16th, 17th and 18th centuries were constant incentives to English, French and Dutch maritime enterprise.

When the British ship *Dolphin*, under Captain Wallis, found Tahiti it was not the hoped-for gold but the people which caught the attention of the world. Here was the paradise that men had dreamed of since the Renaissance had brought classical thought and dreams back into western ken. And Tahitian society seemed to confirm the arguments of the new wave of philosophy, which made what was simple seem profound and what was a low standard of living seem a belief in inherent simplicity. Tahiti was not quite like those dreams, but it was the closest men had found. Here was life not chained to labour, love unconstrained by responsibility, sex apparently neither restricted by the fear of pregnancy nor restrained by the rules of religion. Food and water supplies were so plentiful and the climate so pleasant that ships, if their orders permitted, called for rest and refreshment. The latter was somewhat more likely. Little wonder then that sailors looked forward to Tahiti, nor that captains plagued by desertion in almost every port took strong measures when the ships were anchored in a "paradise". Naturally such level heads as Cook and Duperrey had some reservations about Tahiti; d'Urville, less tolerant of other mortals' faults, had a great many. Their close examination revealed that Tahiti was part of the fallible stumbling world all of us know.

---

say, Lesson in particular writing perceptively about the Maori. French journal keepers were more literate than most on Cook's voyages and far more so than those on Tasman's. Their thoughts about Polynesians seem more critical, in the true sense, than those of the English. This should not surprise anyone; Duperrey's voyage was half a century after Cook's, and Europe had seen much more savagery than nobility in the period.

Lesson was a man of wide learning and trained mind. In spite of his cynicism about humanity he used classical quotations to illustrate the universality of human experience. He had read many accounts written by early visitors to New Zealand, sometimes referring to them in his own journal, not always fairly. Especially interested in the Maori, he appreciated that their ways were under great stress. Although by the time of the French visit missionaries had not had much success, they were initiating a long-term process of change in attitudes. Both positive and negative changes increased stress: introduced European diseases and weapons were killing Maori but also indirectly causing much deterioration in tribal life, at the same time as beneficial introductions – pigs, potatoes and other meats and vegetables – were affecting the ways of work and of living. In train with such changes, personal relationships were altering too.

From the French we gain new opinions about the Maori – from a European culture, it is true, yet with a perspective other than the English one. As the common English view of the French would lead us to expect, there is much about food and women in every journal. But there is more than that and on the whole it is good-natured, incisive, and useful comment. This particular French visit lasted only fifteen days. We must be aware that, like Cook and Banks, and still more Tasman, these French visitors could give impressions only, and all descriptions, whether more or less critical, depend on the observer.

Jules de Blosseville's journal is exceedingly engaging, flavoured by the attractive personality and sound Norman common sense of this junior officer (Lesson thought de Blosseville "the finest character of a man I have ever met"). Bright, young, earnest, de Blosseville thoroughly prepared himself by reading travellers' books and missionary reports, besides all he could find about the voyages of Cook and Marion. He regretted not having long enough at the Bay to check all interesting points, but thought New Zealand would make an excellent convict settlement. Having been to New South Wales, he believed the English experiment of reformation by life in a new land worth copying; 19th century Europe's hope to reform as well as banish convicts is seldom recognised in today's South Pacific literature. De Blosseville died young, only thirty-one, as someone good is said to do. Even worse, he did so on the east coast of Greenland, dying there being only marginally better than living there.

Almost all published French, English, American and Spanish discussion of early New Zealand is as fair as it is frank. Nearly always the comments reinforce one another, and only occasionally an idiosyncratic view intrudes. In total, readers find interesting and probably reasonably accurate depictions of contemporary Maori culture. Although these men were not modern anthropologists, many were learned and most were thoughtful. Few, if indeed any, were less than well-meaning; the romantic 18th century view of the Pacific, very like today's publicity myth, prepared them, where not objective, to be subjectively kind. Nor were all observers writers. Le Jeune, the expedition's artist, prepared twelve plates of New Zealand scenes or people. Although of interest, he is not ranked with some of the artists who sailed the Pacific with Cook.

The French arrived in the Bay of Islands on 2 April 1824, to be greeted by a crowd of Maori canoes approaching from all directions. When Hongi, the great war leader of the Bay area, or other chiefs visited the ship they brought warriors and women to dance for the sailors. By now Maori were not a danger to craft, except indirectly, such as when prostitution caused either carelessness

A Maori canoe in the Bay of Islands during the visit of Duperrey in the early 1820s. The water appears to be calm but even so the posture of many in the canoe implies remarkable stability – probably artistic license. Notice the fortified pa directly in the background. *(University of Canterbury Library, Christchurch)*

on duty or infection. Such danger faced both ways. Venereal disease had long been present in the Bay, but it had arrived with sailors.

At this time the Bay of Islands tribes were almost constantly at war. We have many descriptions of Maori warfare, and critical assessment of their attitudes about it. "The inhabitants of the N part of New Zealand seem to respect the missionaries; but they do not accept their rules of conduct ... the state of hostility in which they take pleasure incite them to take from our arts only the means to destroy one another .... Gunpowder and firearms ... are the main articles they request in exchange for the produce of their soil ... obtaining what they need to carry out their unspeakable plans is the sole reason for the safety which the Europeans find among them today." At least so thought Duperrey.

Such statements, for equivalents were made by most of the early explorers, predisposed other visitors to fear the worst. Surgeon Galkin of the *Mirnyy*, one of Bellingshausen's Russian ships, described his first sight of New Zealand. "At length we caught sight of the high, wooded shores of that country. Mount Egmont soared proudly above them, and its summit, eternally covered with snow and reflecting the sun's rays, presented a majestic and delightful spectacle." But delight fled from recollection. Fires on shore, assumedly lit by Maori, recalled to Galkin's mind what he had read of Maori cannibalism: "Perhaps, (we thought), they are even now roasting creatures like themselves on those fires .... So we approached the land where Captain Marion and several English and French sailors had been eaten by the natives." This dread was widely shared, and when the Russians arrived at Queen Charlotte Sound even the friendly welcome did not remove it. On that first night – indeed during the whole visit – Bellingshausen took precautions. The commander did not apologise, in spite of the seeming friendliness, for his care, because "of the well-known and perfidious character of New Zealanders, who wage a constant war on one another and consume the flesh of enemies." It is true he was anchored not far from where Furneaux's sailors from the *Adventure* had been killed and eaten; even so, such remarks of Bellingshausen, Galkin and Duperrey sound overly condemnatory, especially as they come from Europeans of the Napoleonic era, who must have known of the atrocities of French troops in Portugal, Spain and Russia, and the retaliation in kind.

But all went quietly, and next day the Russian ships bought 250 pounds [114 kg] of fresh fish. In turn they entertained Maori aboard with food and drink, surprised by their aversion to alcohol. Maori often stayed on board and "they would eat with us, and indeed ate our rusks, peas, gruel, and sugar with an appetite. Salt beef did not appeal to them at all ... rum and wine they could not drink." The Russians did not abstain, and songs Maori sang seemed to the probably maudlin sailors to be very like their own songs, even though they were many steppes from home.

Visitors tended to sympathise with the Maori. D'Urville thought "the tricks which Europeans have so often played on New Zealanders, the shameful manner with which the good faith of these men has been betrayed by whalers, have made them extremely suspicious in conducting business." Maori were sometimes cheated, but any individual only once; early visitors found both men and women perfectly capable of holding their own in a bargain. More importantly, they could not be exploited as Indians in North America were and are, by appetite for drink. For some decades the Maori resisted alcohol. As did so many voyagers, the Russian astronomer Simonov compared the natives of New Zealand with the natives of New Holland; predictably the Maori came off best. Indeed, comparing the races Simonov paid Maori the highest compliment a student of the classics knew: "an entirely different people from the natives of

Captain Bellingshausen, an extremely able officer of the Imperial Russian Navy, led his two ships into Queen Charlotte Sound for a brief visit in the early 1820s. Their observations about the Maori and Maori society add an interesting counterpoint to those of the English and French. *(Courtesy of the Soviet Embassy, Wellington)*

New Holland ... New Zealanders struck us as a people with the fire of intellect in their eyes, martial pride in their bearing, and pleasant facial features. Some of them reminded me of ancient Romans I had seen in prints ...."

Few visitors had prepared themselves for New Zealand by reading the classics. D'Urville, in a search for relevant information, had read some of Samuel Marsden's reports. He agreed with Marsden's accepting fidelity, affection and sensitivity as Maori characteristics, yet the French officer refused to see perfection even in the romantic Pacific: "these peculiar people are violent in all their feelings and carry everything to excess, their love and devotion as much as their hatred and revenge." Like Duperrey, he thought much of the co-operation was self-interested. Tui could certainly be ingratiating, and when dressed up to visit ships was often taken for a tattooed Englishman. D'Urville believed the chief to be "always guided by his one motive, he hoped to obtain from us a lot of *powder and muskets.*" Missionaries constantly condemned, and rightly so, this trade in weapons and yet it is true that the musket did not increase Maori propensity to war but merely enabled them to fight with greater ease and effectiveness.

D'Urville pointed out that in Maori society "the authority of the masters over their slaves is absolute and they have the power of life and death over them." He also observed that some of the slaves became very attached to their owners, in many ways part of the new tribe. But a child of the French Revolution, though well born himself, looked askance at Maori family pride and consciousness of rank. Maori pride was of some economic importance. Ships' masters and traders had to be careful not to deal or fraternise too much with slaves because it angered Maori of superior rank. Russians noted this too. *Vostok*'s Midshipman Novosil'sky spoke critically of Maori consciousness of rank and station. High birth appeared to matter much more in New Zealand than it did anywhere in Europe, even in those years of reaction against revolution. "On meeting us, they would inform us at once of their own station, and enquire as to ours. These noble savages readily understood our system of naval ranks, immediately comparing those of captain, lieutenant, and midshipman with corresponding ones in their island."

Russians in the South Island saw little other European contact with the Maori. At Queen Charlotte Sound in 1820 the Russians had no reason to discuss whaling but French officers at the Bay of Islands thought crews of whaleships a menace to New Zealand and one said that Maori crewmen on English whaleships were harshly treated. He overstated his case by generalising, whatever individual examples there may have been; some Maori rose to officer rank in British whaleships.

Naturally enough certain idiosyncracies of Maori culture caused more comment than others. Frenchmen thought peculiar the extreme value placed on the loyal chastity of Maori wives, when unmarried girls had their sexual liberty and prostitution flourished. In early 19th-century Maori society a very liberal attitude about sex as such existed side by side with conservative attitudes about marriage. In the days before birth control this made sense; wherever there was inheritance of rank or goods, especially rank, then true heirs were important. This did not apply to prostitutes, usually slaves, who danced on the ship in the evening, partly entertaining, partly advertising. Maori slaves could marry into the tribe, their children being full members of the tribe, albeit of low status. In some ways this was more benign servitude than the northern hemisphere slavery of the day, and gradually died out as the missionaries preached, persuaded and even purchased, to free the slaves.

Galkin of the *Mirnyy* was one European who did not agree about the sanctity of Maori marriage. Galkin liked the Maori. "Throughout our visit we observed no vices in them beyond a certain cunning in trade …. It is true that, for an axe, they were ready to sacrifice their wives' chastity (which they in fact value very little); but we could not know whether or not they held this to *be* a vice …." This does not bear out observations in northern New Zealand where, according to visitors' reports, marriage was very highly respected. Galkin did point out what all thoughtful Russians understood. "It would not be surprising if the fifty years that have elapsed since Cook's stay in the Sound have resulted in a change in their character." This insight might, one supposes, be applied to cunning in trade, chastity of wives, and to various other behaviour. And it is possible that Galkin sometimes failed to distinguish "wives" from a man's other female relatives, such as unmarried sisters or his cousins or his aunts.

Sex may not have been such a problem in Queen Charlotte Sound as in the warmer north. Galkin noted that the men with him on his visits to local settlements apparently were not favourably impressed. "Our sailors spat, and marvelled that the English could have been anything but indifferent to such women." In spite of, or perhaps because of this, Russian sailors were generally and genuinely friendly, treated the women well, and gave them little gifts.

Russian sailors on shore in Queen Charlotte Sound. *(Courtesy of the Soviet Embassy, Wellington)*

Humanity being as it is, not all sailors thought as Galkin did. Young Midshipman Novosil'sky, with the eyes of yearning youth, looked more favourably on the women than most of the visitors. "The women are plump, and not tall. The married women soon lose their freshness, but the young girls are sometimes quite pretty .... Some of the New Zealand maidens, indeed, might vie in beauty with European girls and despite their tattooing and dark faces ...."

Visitors enjoyed Maori dancing by either sex, although there were a few reservations. D'Urville seemed to think Maori love dances part of general Maori directness of expression: "nothing could be more lewd or more obscene than their movements, gestures and poses; moreover everything made one think that the songs that accompanied them were, to say the least, quite as lascivious." Love dances were certainly to excite desire, war dances to incite violence. D'Urville described the effect the war dance had on Tui: "in spite of our being present and the constraint that he tried to exercise on himself, his face lit up, his eyes rolled round in their sockets, his knees jerked convulsively, his tongue protruded from his mouth ... he was at one in heart and mind with the movements and the words of the warriors." Nor did every visitor admire

## MUSIC

On his brief visit to New Zealand Tasman found that the Maori seemed completely uninterested in Dutch trumpet music. In this regard experience differed, probably depending on the visitors, the visited and the quality of music offered. In most cases Maori would dance and sing readily and happily. On his third voyage's arrival in New Zealand, at Dusky Sound, Cook found the few local Maori somewhat shy about visiting. Perhaps it was because he entertained them by ordering "the Bagpipes and fife to be played and the Drum to be beat ... nothing however would induce them to come a board ...." It could have been taste rather than simply fear, for the Bay of Islands Maori loved the violin played for them by one of Marion's French sailors. Apparently the sound of the first and second strings in particular filled listening Maori "with astonishment and joy". They had, it seemed, quite specific tastes.

Two generations later, at Queen Charlotte Sound, although Maori freely came aboard *Vostok* and *Mirnyy*, the Russians encountered the same scepticism about their wind and percussion instrumental music. The Maori were not favourably impressed by the sailors' drumming and fifing, which the Russians expected perhaps because of their avid study of Cook's voyages. The Maori had instruments somewhat like the fife but no percussion instruments, unless one counts warning gongs and tapping sticks. This seems strange because the rhythm of Maori dances was remarkable, and when singing in canoes they beat perfect time with their paddles. One would have thought that drums, used in dance and song in other Polynesian islands, would have been at home in New Zealand too. There was some indication of change in this regard; at Dusky Sound they had preferred the drumming to the fife's shrilling and the bagpipes keening. And Simonov at Queen Charlotte Sound, somewhat patronisingly, noted that when "the New Zealand Chief himself wished to try out both; the flute would not obey him despite all his efforts, whereas the drum, under his blows, produced disconnected but loud sounds, which highly pleased him." Chiefs, by nature or because of the security of rank, often seemed more enterprising and inquisitive.

everything about Maori music. Anderson, the skilled and responsible naturalist on Cook's third voyage, thought that the music, at least that to which Maori men danced, "consists rather in mere strength than melody of expression."

Astronomer Simonov's comments verified English and French accounts of the compelling, dramatic effect of Maori haka on Maori warriors. One visitor was having his portrait done, "but the wild cries of his countrymen suddenly announced that a dance was on, and our friend was quite unable to stay put ... and joined the dancers, his muscles moving, eyes flashing: he went into a frenzy. By the end of the dance, every participant in it looked like a hero celebrating victory over his foes." Galkin too, indeed every Russian, approved Maori dances and dancers, and gained a lasting benefit from them. "Our sailors imitated them excellently, and later, by the South Pole, where daily perils cast the spirits down, they would occasionally cheer up the whole ship's company by means of their imitations."

All French and Russian journals complimented the Maori on good qualities, as Europeans saw such things. Lesson described some of the ship girls rescuing an old lady from a drifting canoe. "The first to dive in, with rare courage, was a crazy, cheerful girl whom the seamen called Nanette, whose irrepressible gaiety was the delight of the hammocks. This event gave us a favourable opinion of the good nature of these poor girls, whose corrupt morals made us blush ...." All European sailors, nearly all of whom could not swim, admired the facility of Maori of both sexes in the water. But only the physician Dieffenbach in *Tory* described how they swam. "The New Zealanders, men, women, and children, swim well, and can continue the exertion for a long time; in common with the North American Indians, they swim like dogs, not dividing the water, as we do, with the palm of the hands, but paddling along with each arm alternately."

In what seems European condescension, Lesson, in spite of admiring their bravery and skill, was amusing at the swimming girls' expense. "Their arms and breasts were tattooed like those of seamen with the names of their lovers, the name of the ship and the date of its visit to the Bay of Islands. By inspecting their bodies one could place the itinerary of ships putting into port, of which these living medallions kept a record as long as they lived." Perhaps he had never been to Marseilles or Portsmouth.

Of the girls' sexual behaviour the Russian, Galkin, seeing Maori of a somewhat less sophisticated area, favoured a theory other than simple prostitution. He implied, although somewhat uncertainly, that Maori women did not return gifts, whereas Maori men always did. If you gave a man a gift you would get one in return, but would not if you gave a gift to a woman: their bodies may have been all the women had to trade, or to give less commercially, for a gift. Women themselves, perhaps slave girls, were sometimes offered as gifts. Bellingshausen refused the offer of "a reasonably young woman" and criticised ships before him as having "encouraged [the Maori] in the pursuit of such shameful trafficking."

Sexy girls were one thing in New Zealand; blatant ferocity was something else, and frightening too. The French noted it among the warring tribes of the Bay of Islands region. Although he was doubtful about the effectiveness of the Church of England and the Wesleyans, Lesson believed missionaries would be a beneficial influence: "as far as I am concerned a religion which enlightened these

"Haka performed on board the *Astrolabe*". Maori men and women danced to entertain and impress men on ships of all nations, usually in their own groups but sometimes, as pictured here, together. The haka's vigour made it one of the Maori dances with which Russian sailors, who learned it at Queen Charlotte Sound, warmed themselves near the Antarctic. *(University of Canterbury Library, Christchurch)*

tribes would be in my opinion the greatest benefit this frightful race could receive." He compared the Maori with "gentle and inoffensive Tahitians ...." and feared the missions in New Zealand had "completely miscarried, and instead of being in absolute command ... the missionaries bow their heads and are humble and submissive before these ferocious pagans." In this plain-spoken surgeon's opinion, weakness seemed forerunner to woe.

A medical man, Lesson was generous about human failings but also sharply sceptical. A missionary promised that if he returned in ten years he would find great changes. Lesson laughed. "Mr Clerk will have managed to gather up a few piastres, or he will have been eaten by his catechumens; these perhaps are the changes there will be." Lesson thought missions unlikely to succeed, because "the New Zealanders, immovably fixed in their tendencies and beliefs, would blush to occupy themselves with growing crops or breeding animals ... plundering traditions are opposed to any kind of improvement." This was not entirely accurate; coastal Maori were growing potatoes and "running" pigs to supply ships. Neither was it necessarily inaccurate. Lesson went on, "To change them one would have to take possession of their territory, build fortresses, and forcibly impose a code of civilisation." This was indeed what happened, depending on one's view of civilisation.

Neither Lesson nor any other Frenchman was uniformly critical of missionaries. Nearly all mentioned Thomas Kendall with approval. He, as one said, "behaved with more tolerance and talent than the other missionaries. He has respected the opinion of the natives without showing distaste for their customs …. He is not obliged to be on his guard …." Approval from French sailors, if mission authorities ever heard of it, was the last thing to soften the disapprobation which his colleagues felt for Kendall's attitude to female Maori.

The French were not at New Zealand only to examine Maori and missionaries. When chances occurred d'Urville did some cartography, comparing as carefully as time allowed the real Bay of Islands to Marion's chart of it. And on 17 April *Coquille* and her sailors left the Bay of Islands to sail north, making their way north-east and then north-west to the west of Fiji. They encountered Rotuma and found the people to be pestiferous thieves. In spite of this the sailors liked them, because "our hearts, still frozen by the memory of the fierce Zealanders, warmed up among these kind islanders … here, the native, trustful, happy, clean, lightly clad, was bartering his surplus vegetables for our shining trinkets; there the ferocious man, disfigured by a cruel tattooing, carrying the head of his fellow-man in his hand, had asked for powder and arms …." Obviously Lesson had found New Zealand stimulating but not attractive.

The French ship sailed north through a patch of the Pacific recently explored, and then through islands north of Australia, reaching New Guinea on the 24th. The area was very unhealthful and by the time they were into Dutch territory the usual dysentery and fevers had appeared. In spite of illnesses, on 3 October they reached Mauritius, formerly French but now British, to be warmly welcomed by people with memories of France. By January they were at St Helena visiting Napoleon's grave, shocked to find his neglected home turned into a stable, resenting dishonour done to "the place of refuge of an Emperor

New Zealand's farming future can be seen in these "establishments of the missionaries" as seen by d'Urville's artist, Sainson, in the 1820s. *(Hocken Library, Dunedin)*

sent by Kings into exile", a remark the Emperors of Austria and Russia would not have appreciated.

In the Straits of Gibraltar by March, the *Coquille* dropped anchor in France on the 24th of that month. Away for thirty-one months, voyaging 75,000 miles [120,000 km] in well over 500 days actually under sail, Duperrey neither seriously damaged his ship nor lost a single life. Public awareness of exploration rose. The expedition had made some discoveries, although none of real consequence: Marakei in the Gilbert Islands, Mokil and Losap-Nama in the Carolines and Reao of the Tuamotus. But much capable charting improved the navigation of the world and observations in several fields of science, especially botany and geology but also anthropology and biology, deserved the wide acclaim received. Another result of the voyage was a French Catholic mission to the Pacific in the early 1830s. Duperrey's praising the work of Protestant missionaries in Tahiti made many French Catholics think their Church should not fall behind. The expedition also enlivened the penal reform movement in France. As Australia would probably stay British, the reformers looked to New Zealand for a penal colony.

In his writing about the voyage as well as his commanding of it, Duperrey was demonstrably an able, upright and modest man prepared to do his duty. Lacking the flamboyance of Bougainville and the excellence of Cook, no distorting admiration, much less fashionable publicity, was able to make him larger than he was. But that was sufficient: a competent man, a careful explorer and a courageous commander. He was not a great discoverer, for there had been less and less left to discover. He was an explorer; surveying, charting, and describing in detail lands found by the first voyagers, the discoverers. When all this is done, exploration is in the maps and minds of the world for all men and all nations.

So unalike in character, d'Urville and Duperrey had differences during the voyage which were more than "the normal outcome of restricting to narrow cabins officers full of energy and ambition but constantly in each other's presence. The antipathy between the leaders gave rise in turn to disagreements between their subordinates ...." This reflected badly on both, but mainly on d'Urville, a difficult man even though a more than competent navigator and scientist. Naturally it surprised many seamen that soon after the return of *Coquille* to France d'Urville was being considered as leader of another expedition. Because of the proposed commander's interests, botany would be the main emphasis of the expedition, but as well it was to explore the coasts of New Guinea, New Britain and the Louisiades. Finally d'Urville was promoted and given permission for his voyage, the instructions adding New Zealand, Tonga, Fiji, and the Loyalty Islands to the itinerary. The route was now standard: the Cape of Good Hope, south of Australia to New Zealand, and then north. In 1826 d'Urville was given the *Coquille*, well overhauled. He changed her name to *Astrolabe*, simultaneously and symbolically breaking with the last voyage and honouring the lost la Pérouse.

Happy with his ship, the commander was not so with his men, but in the event they served him well. An uneventful voyage out was enlivened by a stop in Tasmania, before they turned north along the Australian coast to Port Jackson. Because of some suspicion in New South Wales that the French had been looking for territory in Australia, the British were not as co-operative as previously. This time d'Urville went about in full uniform, impressively but diplomatically, as he did his best to persuade the authorities to help him with stores.

When *Astrolabe* left Port Jackson, the Tasman Sea provided stirring weather. On 10 January lookouts sighted New Zealand just south of modern Greymouth. As Tasman had, they went north, charting the coast more carefully. When they rounded the Farewell Spit to sail towards Cook Strait, d'Urville decided to anchor in Tasman Bay, which Cook had seen and named but not sailed upon. Here, much to his own satisfaction, he found that Tasman Bay was much bigger than Cook had thought, and was able to change Cook's map. He surmised correctly that the channel running eastward from the north-east corner of Tasman Bay led directly to Admiralty Bay. It was through this deceptive and vicious passage that d'Urville sailed *Astrolabe* with surpassing skill. Fittingly, the passage is now French Pass and the island it sunders from the mainland is D'Urville Island. The Maori name for this pass was Te Aumiti; one of Kupe's birds was killed there while exploring.

Once safely out to Cook Strait *Astrolabe* passed through peacefully, her officers listening to the captain pointing out Cook's minor errors. Niggling critical attitudes, ignoring others' difficulties, were precisely what had strained d'Urville's relations with Duperrey. His instructions told d'Urville to pass through Cook Strait and survey a few points along the north-east coast of New Zealand to verify what Cook had done so quickly. The ambitious commander planned to do much more than this, surveying all along the east coast of the North Island right up to North Cape. They sailed north picking up Maori when any came out to the ship. Two boarded near Cape Palliser and would not leave again until they could find tribal friends. This was not unreasonable, and they stayed with the ship for some time, the officers and crew learning what they could.

In his dealings with the Maori d'Urville was very responsible. At Tokomaru Bay the ship bought a number of pigs from the local chief. Good food makes a good mood, and d'Urville liked it here; the surrounding country with its Maori huts reminded him of villages in the Aegean Sea. His recollections of these ancient glories somehow prompted him to foretell a bright future for New Zealand. "These shores, at present without human habitation, except for a few isolated *pas*, will be alive with flourishing cities; these bays of unbroken silence … will be highways for ships of every type. And a few centuries hence … future members of the Academy of New Zealand would not fail to … argue laboriously about the narratives of the earliest explorers, when they found them speaking of the wilderness, the lands, and the savages of their country."

When *Astrolabe* rounded East Cape to cruise the north coast the weather turned, building enormous waves, driving her north-north-east. After almost giving up the survey d'Urville finally beat his way back to the coast and followed it as far as Cape Runaway. Complimenting himself on determination to overcome all difficulties of shore surveying, comparing himself favourably to du Fresne and Duperrey, he ought to have been reminded by this experience that Cook had faced even worse conditions, much bad weather and no one else's charts to fall back on. It did not; d'Urville was a rather unpleasant man. He was

A view of d'Urville's *Astrolabe* making its perilous passage through the dangerous waters of French Pass. D'Urville island is on the left. *(Hocken Library, Dunedin)*

also a superb seaman, but even so nearly lost the ship in a terrible storm near the Bay of Plenty. D'Urville finally worked *Astrolabe* around to the Hauraki Gulf, commenting that Cook's work was very inaccurate and that he hoped to do better. When they landed the French found abandoned huts and destroyed fields, wreckage of some local Maori wars, and must have thought of Europe's destruction only a decade earlier. D'Urville did improve on Cook here, as he had in Tasman Bay, for he spotted the potential of Waitemata Harbour, which serves modern Auckland, before they headed north.

On the way to the Bay of Islands the expedition bought pigs and potatoes from Maori along the coast, forewarned that supplies would be much cheaper than at a harbour whaleships frequented. Prices and progress, if not prosperity, had arrived in New Zealand. *Astrolabe* spent about a week in the Bay of Islands replenishing and refitting, the crew resting, roaming, relaxing, the more vigorous of them in seaport fashion. This French visit to New Zealand had been productive: a few new discoveries, some good charting, a great deal learned about the Maori and New Zealand's products. When the ship was well reprovisioned they weighed anchor.

A Maori wished to go with them, as much to save his life as to see the world. He was "a slave of the Kororareka tribe from childhood. After seeing his companions offered as sacrifices at the obsequies of the last *rangatiras*, he was afraid of seeing his turn come …." Kokako told other Maori who expected him to leave the ship with them, "that he was now a "Youroupi", and consequently very *tapou*." Kokako became a good seaman. D'Urville, confident of another voyage in 1828, hoped to return him personally. For some reason, presumably their small numbers, Queen Charlotte Sound Maori did not like their men going to sea with the Europeans. In 1820 the Russians were keen to take Maori to visit Europe, and some were willing, but the chief refused to allow it.

On the way north to Tonga *Astrolabe* narrowly escaped destruction amid some reefs, and lifeboat preparation was nearly ruined by the unsuspected amount and weight of souvenirs sailors accumulated in New Zealand. Before this was sorted out the ship had won clear to anchor safely in a Tongan harbour. D'Urville found time and perspective for perceptive comments about Tongan society. In spite of mutual goodwill, disputes flared about French deserters, the Tongans intending to keep all those wishing to stay; musketry-trained Frenchmen would be useful in the frequent civil wars. D'Urville managed to recover all his men but two. One of them, Simonet, became a successful trader and planter, as d'Urville found when he returned in 1838, years later than he had intended.

As *Astrolabe* sailed further north through various groups of islands lookouts watched for any traces of la Pérouse's expedition. At New Britain the officers learned that the choice of anywhere in that area for convict settlement was out of the question, and wondered why de Blosseville had even suggested it. Surveyors did some valuable charting as *Astrolabe* coasted New Guinea on her way to the Dutch East Indies. Among the islands they met the British whaleship *Castor*, with four Maori aboard, bound for the Bay of Islands. The new "Youroupi", Kokako, succumbed to homesickness, and joined the whaleship for home.

The stay in the Dutch Indies was not a happy one. Not fully recovered from illness, d'Urville could not endure heavy Dutch dinners or the dark island tobacco smoke swirling constantly from carved Holland pipes. And just after the ship left it lost its skilled and responsible carpenter who had gone around the world with de Freycinet in *Uranie* and Duperrey in the *Coquille*. Sailing with d'Urville, he died in almost retributive fashion. The carpenter cut down the wrong tree and from it ate poisonous instead of anti-scorbutic material; the forest had struck back.

*Astrolabe* now sailed right around Australia to Tasmania, the first French warship to visit Hobart. Here d'Urville learned that a flamboyant sailor and adventurer, Peter Dillon, had found the remnants of la Pérouse's ships on Vanikoro Island. D'Urville felt bound to investigate that instead of revisiting New Zealand and after doing so successfully they went north to the Caroline Islands and on to Guam. With much illness in the crew as well as fatigue approaching exhaustion, they sailed on to Île de Bourbon, French once more, and then to Capetown homeward.

Geographically and scientifically d'Urville's had been an important expedition. The charting was excellent, they had collected a huge number of insect and plant specimens, and the expedition had confirmed Dillon's statements about la Pérouse. In spite of these successes, d'Urville, whose personality negated much accomplishment, was neither lauded nor rewarded to his satisfaction. He had constantly made enemies. Although he lobbied to lead another expedition he was not given one for many years. Instead, for over five years he devoted undoubted ability and energy to writing up the voyage in a still-famous monumental publication.

Time passes; captains, kings and counsellors depart; their successors need projects. All these things happened in France in the 1830s. And so d'Urville's next expedition, after the great book was published, was to be even more important. In the mid-1830s d'Urville put forward a second circumnavigation through the Strait of Magellan to the Pacific, there to explore the Solomon Islands and search Vanikoro for survivors of la Pérouse's ships. The new king, Louis Philippe, thought that he should devote some attention to Antarctica. D'Urville agreed heartily; he wanted an expedition. This time he had two ships, sturdy successful *Astrolabe* and a 300-ton storeship, *Zélée*, rated as a corvette, well able to keep company with her senior consort. Preparations were standard except for a new type of tinned meat, another precursor of bully beef and Spam. Again the meat was good although some tins, not completely airtight, spoiled.

Heading south, the ships dropped off an ailing officer at Brazil, and went on to Magellan's Strait. About two weeks botanising, hunting geese and fishing preceded an easy trip through the feared Strait. Then the ships made the dangerous sweep southward, culminating in the discovery of part of Antarctica. The crew suffered much from scurvy. On returning north they called at Chile, and were told the English had annexed the North Island of New Zealand. From Chile they called at Tahiti and Samoa on the way to Vanikoro, to look again for traces of la Pérouse. In the western Pacific the French found citrus fruits which somewhat relieved the scurvy. Here too they approved of religion more than they did at New Zealand missions; pigs were very inexpensive because Moslems would not eat pork. After showing the flag in the Philippines they went south to Java, only to pick up fever and dysentery. These diseases ravaged and debilitated the crew as they sailed down the west coast of Australia and eastward to Van Diemen's Land.

Many French sailors died, others were so weak they could not work the ship. Replacement was difficult because few free sailors in Tasmania wished to go to the Antarctic. But south from Hobart they went, to discover land which d'Urville named Terre Adélie after his wife. From Antarctica the ships went north to the Auckland Islands, finding traces of whaling visitors, French among others. There was evidence, repeated in many lonely spots around the world, that in times of peace sailors of all nations tried to help one another. Shelter and food would be badly needed by shipwrecked or storm-tossed sailors: "many captains of whaling vessels ... seem to have built several huts like the one we used, and ... planted potatoes and other vegetables round them." From these lonely islands they went north to New Zealand, anchoring in Hooper's Inlet, Otago Harbour. By good fortune a French whaleship, the *Havre*, already encountered in Chile, lay anchored there, and sailors could gossip of mademoiselles and señoritas, and the captains of maritime news. Unfortunately there was more contact between the ships than the captains intended: "In the evening the wind blew strongly and in squalls; the harbour was so narrow that the vessel the *Havre* fell on us although it was cross-moored. We had to work for over an hour to get free; fortunately we managed not to damage her at all seriously ...."

D'Urville seemed much less upset by the collision with the *Havre* than by the condition of the local Maori. "These men were the same type of New

Zealanders whom I had seen on my earlier voyages, but they had certainly not gained by the contact with whalers. As a rule they were dressed in European fashion ... they appeared to have abandoned the old spirit of independence and those warlike qualities, which on my first voyage had seemed to be peculiarly characteristic ...." The notoriously difficult French gentleman was more than somewhat patronising about English "deserters", ignoring the rough and dangerous context of their lives as Otago whalemen. Apparently it was not only

---

"SPRUCE BEER"

An antiscorbutic which was relatively effective, and which the sailors preferred to scurvy grass and sauerkraut could be made on the spot in almost any wooded haven in the temperate regions. It was called "spruce beer", from its original source, and James Cook brewed it for his crews whenever time and suitable trees favoured the brewing. Cook had learned its value in Canada, where the Indians had taught the technique to the French in the winter of 1535.

In New Zealand at Dusky Sound, Cook's ships brewed it from local trees. "This Beer we brewed in the same manner as spruce Beer, that is we first made a strong decoction of the leaves or small branches of the Spruce tree & Tea shrub [rimu and manuka] by boiling them three or four hours, or untill the bark will strip with ease from the branches, then take the leaves or branches out of the Copper and mix with the liquor the proper quantity of Melasses and Inspissated Juce, one Gallon of the former and three of the latter is sufficient to make a Puncheon or 80 gallons of Beer, let this mixture just boil and then put it into the Cask and to it add an equal quantity of Cold Water more or less according to your taste and the strength of the decoction, when the whole is but milk warm put in a little grounds of Beer or yeast, if you have any, or any thing else that will cause fermentation and in a few days the Beer will be fit to drink, after the casks have been brewed in two or three times the Beer will generally ferment of it self." According to Cook the addition of the "tea shrub" moderated the too definite astringency of the rimu brew.

Most of Cook's officers and men found this drink acceptable, and some better than that. One officer was enthusiastic; "after a small amount of rum or arrack has been added, with some brown sugar, and stirred into this really pleasant, refreshing, and healthy drink, it bubbled and tasted rather like champagne." Besides these desirable qualities the name sounded more homely than kraut or wild celery, with their connotations of foreignness. Cook's men liked it, which is often half the battle with prevenient medication.

The dangers of disease and virtues of New Zealand as Cook had seen them in Dusky or Queen Charlotte Sounds seemed much the same to the Russians in 1820. As an astronomer from an extreme high-latitude continental climate, Simonov pointed out New Zealand's latitude was that of Rome or Barcelona. Its weather was further moderated by the sea; no wonder the Maori could have green vegetables in winter time. Simonov knew about scurvy, and mentioned seeing the New Zealand trees at Queen Charlotte Sound from which Cook brewed his beer. And the country provided more than that; the whole atmosphere fought scurvy. Most of the Russian seamen liked the Sound because, "notwithstanding the fact that it was winter here, the trees shone with fresh green leaves. While our people were filling casks with cold spring water – the spring rising from the hills like the purest crystal – others cast a seine and caught plenty of fish ...." All this was antiscorbutic.

equals and superiors he looked down on. D'Urville saw Maori degeneration arising from their contact with Europeans. "A few English settlers have begun to build ... one could see a dozen little *cottages*, each in its own garden .... Two of these dwellings had already been turned into taverns, frequented by the fishermen and sailors ... but especially by the natives, who came there to spend their money as soon as they got it." From this one sees that d'Urville's real culprit was alcohol, which the Maori had now apparently accepted. He foretold extinction. If the captain returned to Otago he would be as pleased as surprised to see the Maori recovery.

D'Urville had hoped to reprovision at Otago and was pleased with "a good stock of excellent potatoes." But he was not happy with the pork. "Our sailors found the meat so nasty that they would not eat it." Captain Jacquinot of *Zélée* spotted the cause – and the cure. "There are plenty of pigs about, but as they live on the shellfish ... on the beaches, their flesh acquires a very unpleasant, almost disgusting flavour. One has to keep them some time on board and to feed them quite differently to get rid of this repulsive quality." *Acheron*, surveying a few years later, thought the meat of the beachcombing pigs which ate "seaweed & whale's flesh" was unfit to eat.

Finally moving north, the expedition called at Akaroa, well known to French whalemen. While entering the harbour, *Astrolabe* was nearly wrecked by currents which "continued to carry us towards the cliff that forms one end of the bay ... the rocks which run round its base were not more than ten yards from the sides of our ship ... the certain loss of the ship as well as of most of the crew ... the *Astrolabe* was doomed to destruction, if at that moment the wind had not risen in the nick of time to snatch us from imminent peril."

This view of Dusky Sound from the sea was done from *Resolution* or *Adventure* by William Hodges, an artist with Cook's second great expedition. The visit began the practice of ships calling for wood, water and refreshment at the south-western portions of New Zealand if sailing south of Australia into the Pacific. Many of the early sea captains in that great ocean carried Cook's journals or navigational summaries of them. (*Mitchell Library, State Library of New South Wales*)

Thoroughly shaken, the sailors were pleased to see some French whaleships sheltering in the superb harbour.

Shelter apart, d'Urville did not think much of Akaroa as a site for a French colony. "When choosing this spot as the site for a future settlement, the French government only considered the beauty of the harbour, the facilities for defence, and lastly the wonderful resources it could offer our whaling vessels .... In fact, for a young colony to have any real hope of success ... the settlers must not only be able to count on living on the products of the soil, they must also be able to raise food crops for commerce. Further, a young settlement must have easy means of access to the interior so as to be able to expand ...."

One of his lieutenants was even more scathing about the residents than the location: "The few natives we saw made up three or four families, the men spending their lives lying about like hogs, sleeping off the effects of the brandy which they begged on board the ships ... the women, disgusting creatures, offering themselves without the slightest trace of shame to every sailor they met." Later, at the Bay of Islands, another lieutenant, Dubouzet, said that although Maori Christianity was merely imitative and not "a living faith", there was nonetheless benefit in European contact, for "it has made them a little less fierce, has put an end to cannibalism and has checked their unbridled desire for revenge that drove them to kill ... and often overshadowed the splendid qualities with which they are endowed." Another officer, also at the Bay of Islands, contrasted the French Catholic missionaries, "poor men" holding out "a helping hand", with the "rich, happy and with few exceptions fat and well fed" English missionaries: "money has made them forget the Gospel. The pious apostle has become a greedy tradesman." The opinion was better expressed than grounded.

With several whaleships in the Akaroa area, three French and one Danish, *Astrolabe*'s men met old friends from the Chilean coast. "M. Billiard ... of the *Courrier des Indes* ... paid us a visit with two of his officers ... they were old acquaintances whom we were specially pleased to see, because since then they had made a return voyage to France and so were able to give us news." From the Danish ship, and from some French ones too, several journals survive to add to historical knowledge of the whaling industry and the Akaroa area. After the French naval ships left and were proceeding northwards along the east coast they were insulted by an American ship's mistaking them for whaleships. Given the largely justified reputation of whaling vessels as smokestained and slovenly, this identification infuriated the well-kept warships. "The captain, who came on board, told us that he had taken us for whaling vessels and had come to greet his fellow whalers ... to tell them that he ... had secured a full cargo. We recognised the typical American vanity in all this and lost no time telling him that we did not belong to the craft."

At Poverty Bay the ships found a district greatly changed since their visit in 1827. "Young Nick's Cape ... is easily recognised from a distance by the white sand dunes which cover it ... surrounded by extensive plains which are very fertile and have already attracted a certain number of English settlers, who supply ships with provisions at reasonable prices." Otago, Akaroa, and now Poverty Bay; although miles apart each showed an increasingly European New Zealand. D'Urville, having seen the progress of New South Wales, was in no

The *Astrolabe* and some whaleships anchored in Otago Harbour in 1840. The low Otago hills seem somewhat glamourised and in the midground there is what appears at first glance to be a double canoe – possible but somewhat unlikely. (*University of Canterbury Library, Christchurch*)

*Astrolabe* in Akaroa Bay while d'Urville visited the French settlement. He found it now part of a new British colony and a thriving whaling base. (*University of Canterbury Library, Christchurch*)

doubt about New Zealand's British future. All he saw confirmed what he had said publicly about this after visiting the country twice in the 1820s.

*Astrolabe* and *Zélée* arrived at the Bay of Islands on 26 April to find British possession of the North Island established. The French could not officially recognise it without knowing the views of the government in Paris, nor did Commodore Wilkes of the United States Navy, also in the harbour at the time. D'Urville believed "this annexation will inevitably do great damage to the American and French whaling industry. Zealand harbours had always been freely open to whaling vessels of every nation. Not only had they found supplies of food, water and wood, but they had been free to stay in them ... annexation by England might affect all these facilities very seriously. It would inevitably bring onerous harbour dues .... Like myself, Captain Wilkes was without any instructions from his government. He had acted wisely in refusing to recognise an authority that might be contested, and I myself felt constrained to adopt a similar attitude." Most of these fears proved overdrawn, and in any case British possession was firmly grounded.

D'Urville was approached by Baron de Thierry, fearful his local land purchases might not be recognised by the new government. D'Urville satisfied him with a written statement, and by offering to help where he could. Unfortunately there was a cleft stick for the French. Pleading Thierry's case with Governor Hobson recognised British sovereignty, which d'Urville did not wish to do. He treated Captain Hobson respectfully, but as a naval captain of a friendly nation, not as a governor. But the keen scientist in d'Urville was not smothered completely by annexations and rumours of annexations. He managed to procure two kiwi to take to France. "The Paris Academy had expressed a wish to secure this curious bird .... But at every place I had touched in New Zealand my attempts to procure one had been without success. Chance, on this occasion, could not have served us better ...." What the kiwi thought of France has not come down to us.

D'Urville's ships left New Zealand on the 4th of May 1840, sailing north for Torres Strait. Both ships were nearly wrecked on a reef after passing through Bligh's Pass into the Strait, and though safe were considerably damaged. On reaching Dutch Timor they reprovisioned for the voyage to Bourbon and then home. Stopping again at St Helena, in the almost compulsive visit to Napoleon's grave, they found the great conqueror himself about to leave for his Imperial tomb, his permanent return to France.

D'Urville was honoured this time, promoted to Rear Admiral and given the Geographic Society's Gold Medal. Although he had not gone as far south in the Antarctic Ocean as some British sailors, he had discovered Adélie Land. His brief visit to New Zealand threw new light on cultural conflict and annexation, and his route from New Zealand eastward crossed parts of the ocean not sailed before. D'Urville was a much better captain than these relatively meagre results indicated and, in spite of promotion and the medal, once more he did not get all the credit due him for his efforts. He died quite young, in 1842, one of the first to be killed in a railway train accident, an early and grim example. In an odd sort of way d'Urville's death, as Cook's, happened while exploring a new world, and in each case the new world's attitudes and ambitions changed the outlook of the old world forever.

CHAPTER SEVEN

# *Pathways To God*

Missionaries were the first Europeans in New Zealand to venture any distance inland. Tasman had not landed; the explorers after him, courageous as they were, never went far from the sea. Aggressive natives were not a sailor's choice, and it seemed prudent not to venture beyond hope of rescue. Later whalemen and sealers had no reason to go inland; their provisions and their prey were at the shore. Nothing but curiosity could have lured them far from the coast, and set firmly against curiosity was fear. Maori war dances were fearsome enough to overawe even men who cheerfully faced huge bull seals on foot or whaleboat risks and whaleship work at sea.

Missionaries first arrived in New Zealand in 1814, landing just a few years after a dramatic event in race relations: the *Boyd* massacre of 1809. Relations had always been touchy between Maori and whalemen, although we must always remember that like all men, whalemen were a mixed bag. They came to New Zealand from several nations, on separate ships with unique captains. The Maori learned to look at different ships in different ways. If no ship was loved, most were tolerated; the *Jefferson*, Captain Barnes, was hated. Equivalently, the Maori lived in separate tribes with unlike chiefs. Perforce the whalemen looked at these tribes, and especially their chiefs, in different ways. Few disputes were so simple that all whalemen took one side of a dispute and all Maori the other.

A moderating influence was obviously needed in New Zealand. As the balance of power in the real world operated, such influence would serve to help the Maori, the weaker side. A far-sighted chaplain, Samuel Marsden saw missions as the answer. Marsden, Senior Chaplain in New South Wales, had become interested in the Maori after a visit to Norfolk Island, where he met that active patron of the Maori race, Philip Gidley King, later Governor of New South Wales. Marsden met individual Maori in Port Jackson too, most of them there on whaleships, some of them as whalemen. The down-to-earth chaplain came to believe that he was a man chosen to ensure that the Word of God was carried to those he saw as primitive, barbaric but attractive people. "The more I examined into their national character the more I felt interested in their temporal and spiritual welfare .... I knew that they were cannibals – that they were a savage race ... wholly under the power and influence of the Prince of Darkness .... But, as Saint Paul observes, 'How could they believe on Him of whom they had not heard, and how could they hear without a preacher, and how could they preach except they be sent?' "

This visionary chaplain, leader and founder of the New Zealand missions, was the son of a Yorkshire small farmer and blacksmith. The young Marsden fell under the spell of the evangelical movement initiated by John Wesley but remained in the Church of England, worked his way up through such means of education as he could find, and became ordained. Such a hard-earned achievement alone made him a remarkable man. But there was much, much more. Besides preaching a forthright and moving sermon, Marsden could raise and organise finance, and moreover he was an excellent farmer, a good shipmaster and business man, and of course a competent blacksmith. His whole life was founded on plain living, hard work and scorn of luxury and ease, in all this like that other great Yorkshireman, James Cook. Marden's practical mind assessed tangible resources for their worth to man, not delighting in them, as William Colenso did not many years later, for their worth as the products of the Creator of Nature and as displays of His omniscience.

Strong characters, particularly successful ones, attract opposition. Marsden became controversial in his time and later, because his belief in order was as strong as his belief in Christian virtue. He was a man of his time in both his weaknesses and his strengths. He sturdily defended his exceptional success as a farming landholder in New South Wales: "I entered the country when it was in a state of nature, and was obliged to plant and sow or starve. It was not from inclination that my colleague and I took the axe, the spade, and the hoe; we could not from our situation help ourselves by any other means, and we thought it no disgrace to labour .... If this is cast on me as a shame and a reproach, I cheerfully bear it ...." This down-to-earth attitude, literally so, shaped his approach to the New Zealand mission and resulting exploration; it also made for difficulties with those more ethereal.

With such presumptions guiding his perceptions, on his first visit to New Zealand Marsden walked through the natural beauty near the Bay of Islands: "the

Samuel Marsden: blacksmith's son, blacksmith, farmers, missionary, lover of good soil and admirer of hard workers. He wished well for the Maori and hoped that agriculture, craftsmanship and Christianity would bring them to a fuller life on earth and a just reward in Heaven. (*Hocken Library, Dunedin*)

land in general was free from timber, and could easily have been plowed. It appeared to me to be good strong wheat land .... This tract of country, taken collectively, would form a good agricultural settlement ... watered by several fine streams running through it ... skirted in various places by lofty pine trees and other timber." A farmer's view, but Marsden's missions became firmly established precisely because of such practicality in furthering faith. Work and resources to work with were to be the foundation of mission.

To finance his proposed establishment Marsden went to England and persuaded the Church Missionary Society to back it. He argued that the government and whalemen should support the missions, financially and otherwise, because Christianity would make New Zealand a safer whaling base. He prevailed. The whaling owners, particularly Alexander Birnie and Son, assisted the missions for years by taking missionaries and supplies to and from New Zealand, when possible without charge. And Birnie, for one, made "very generous provision for the comfort of the passengers during the voyage."

Marsden, the man as yet without a mission, recruited John King and William Hall to become the first missionaries, not clergymen yet both obviously sincere and venturesome, for they left good incomes in England. Their courage was exceptional too. Marsden had difficulty in finding anyone, he later wrote, who "would venture out to a country where they could anticipate nothing less than to be killed and eaten by the natives." The party reached Sydney in February 1810, with their wives and children, to be greeted by news of the killing of crew and passengers on the ship *Boyd*.

It seems that flogging a Maori chief, working his passage home on the *Boyd*, led to the massacre. Marsden was told later, on his first visit to New Zealand, "that Europeans were the first aggressors, by inflicting corporal punishment on their chief." His informant, a Tahitian, was married into the local tribe and had known Marsden in New South Wales. He spoke excellent English and, one supposes, might have been lying to defend his adopted people. But there was no misunderstanding. There were only four survivors, a woman and three children, and whaleship men in the area, ignoring the fierce Maori sense of dignity, thought a whole crew a high price for a flogging. Not unnaturally that reaction led whalemen to ruthless revenge on the local Maori town.

Marsden reported sadly to his superiors: "On our arrival at Port Jackson ... the melancholy news that the ship 'Boyd', of 600 tons burden, had been burnt, and the captain and crew all murdered and eaten by the natives of Whangarroo ... extinguished at once all hopes of introducing the Gospel into that country. Every voice was naturally raised against the natives, and against all who were in any way attached to their interest." So it was not until the end of November 1814 that the dedicated men and women – and some children and livestock too – sailed to New Zealand on the *Active*, a vessel Marsden had bought for the mission. So did a former schoolmaster, Thomas Kendall, whom many French, as we know, praised in the 1820s. Unfortunately his ability and energetic efforts were finally vitiated by associations with Maori women which were condemned as immoral by his colleagues on the spot and his employers at a distance. There were craftsmen aboard *Active* too, two sawyers and a smith, to build mission houses. One aim of the mission was to "civilise" the Maori by demonstration. Christianity was to be consequent, and hence subsequent.

*Active* had minor contact with the Maori and Marsden landed as soon as the difficult weather allowed. They went ashore on the Cavalli Islands, and a chief with Marsden, Korokoro, met friends. When his aunt arrived Marsden was astonished to see greetings somewhat like mourning, "the tears rolling down their sable countenances in torrents." Even more unsettling was seeing "women cut themselves in their faces, hands, and breasts with sharp shells or flints till the blood ran down in streams." John Savage, a voyager with much good humour and little reverence, landed briefly in New Zealand in 1805 and wrote the first book about the country. On seeing exactly the same greeting rites, he commented that "this custom must prove exceedingly distressing, if the male branches of a family were much in the habit of wandering." Marsden agreed with Savage's concern about the women, but found later it was "vain to attempt to persuade them not to do this, as they considered it the strongest proof of their affections."

The ship moved on. On 19 December 1814 *Active* dropped anchor right in front of the killing ground of the Boyd's passengers and crew. The chief Ruatara, who had accompanied them from Sydney, went ashore to discuss the visit with the local Maori before introducing them to Marsden's group. Through an interpreter, Marsden told them that the Sydney authorities recognised that unjust treatment provoked the massacre and would try to ensure that Maori serving on British vessels would be treated with dignity. The mission ship proclaimed new standards by refusing to allow Maori women to stay aboard all night. Marsden explained this to some of the women a few days later: "I told them I could not allow any of them to remain on board at night unless their husbands were with them ... the vessel was searched, and if any women were found they were sent on shore (sometimes not very well pleased)."

Marsden, conversely, stayed all night with the tribe which had destroyed the *Boyd*, accompanied only by a friend John Liddiard Nicholas, who described his feelings in a book he wrote about this exciting visit to New Zealand. During the evening Marsden told the Maori that white men would come with new grains and tools to make life easier for them. Sleeping in the village would show them that the Europeans had complete confidence in them. Lying near the chief himself, Marsden not unnaturally was subjected to feelings he later recalled in a report home. "I viewed our situation with new sensations and feelings that I cannot express – surrounded by cannibals who had massacred and devoured our countrymen, I wondered much at the mysteries of Providence, and how these things could be. Never did I behold the blessed advantages of civilisation in a more grateful light than at that moment. I did not sleep much during the night ...." Whatever his misgivings, Marsden's boldness paid off. He won Maori respect and retained it for the rest of his life.

On Christmas Day 1814, the mission more or less established, Marsden came ashore to preach the gospel for the first time in New Zealand, to be welcomed by Maori chiefs in British officers' uniforms, given them by the Governor of New South Wales. As Marsden looked at his Maori congregation – and perhaps the sailors too – he felt his "very soul melting" when he "considered the state they were in." His companion, John Nicholas, who had stayed ashore with him that first night in New Zealand, described the sermon in his book. He was impressed: "Splendid temples and costly decorations are not always the most

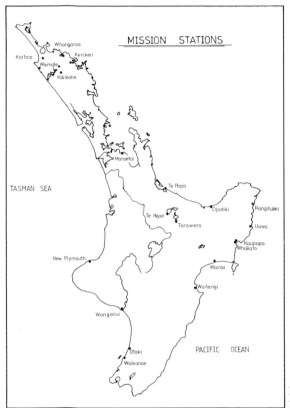

MISSION STATIONS

Whangaroa
Kaitaia
Kerikeri
Waimate
Kaikohe

Maraetai

TASMAN SEA

Te Papa

Opotiki
Te Ngae
Rangitukia
Tarawera
Uawa
Kaupapa
Whakato

New Plymouth

Wairoa

Waitangi

Wanganui

PACIFIC OCEAN

Ōtaki
Waikanae

Important early mission stations in the
North Island of New Zealand.

pleasing to the Deity; and I should hope that the orisons thus offered up by a
few Christians under the open air, and in the midst of their dark fellow-
creatures, were as acceptable in his presence, as if poured out with studied
accents in the most magnificent cathedral."

Even for the dedicated missionary there was more to do than preach. The
expedition and mission would have to be paid for. Marsden went inland looking
for good commercial timber for Sydney; *Active* would have to pay its way on
every trip if possible. Travelling inland was difficult. The area was covered with
great tangles of almost impenetrable scrub and bush, with here and there trees,
huge because of isolation. Some were kauri, up to ten metres around, usually
bare of branches to a great height, growing beautiful knotless timber, ideal for
masts and spars. A kauri spar had helped move Nelson's *Victory* to Trafalgar,
and Britain's naval pre-eminence ensured the safety of Marsden's mission and
thus underwrote New Zealand's British future.

Marsden and Nicholas did not explore extensively but it was a beginning.
Largely through lack of alternative, Marsden habitually travelled on foot in his
New Zealand exploration, occasionally in a canoe further south on larger rivers.
He was always the first white man the inland the Maori had seen, and they got
along well together. As we have noted, he assessed the countryside: the
population, quality of soil and water, potential of rivers for travel or freighting,
and waterfalls for mills to grind and saw. Compared to distances in Canadian or

Australian exploration these were short journeys, but important in their context, and certainly uncomfortable and risky. And at first the Maori seemed more dangerous than Aborigines or North American Indians, not because in fact they were, but because cannibalism cast a lurid shadow.

Marsden, or any other missionary who was the first European to traverse a district, had the motives of other explorers, if somewhat different aims. It was souls they sought; God, not science, fame nor Mammon that they served. They laboured, by teaching new principles, to develop souls, as other men worked to develop mines or farms or factories. To do so they had to find their pupils, and have routes to and good sites for their missions, while keeping contact with

## MAORI DISEASE

Arthur Harper, in the southern mountains in the 1880s and 1890s, found plant remedies for a multitude of ordinary medical problems, such as diarrhoea or constipation. The Maori knew of such uses for plant products, but apparently the belief that sickness was a spiritual rather than a corporeal matter prevented any curative treatment. The remedies were directed at what were largely mechanical problems: dosing, closing, healing wounds and poulticing. The belief that sickness, as opposed to injuries, was the province of the spirits often prevented much use being made of European medicine at first. By Dieffenbach's time conversion had begun to affect attitudes; he was welcomed as a surgeon and treater of battle wounds, whereas Williams had often not been well received as a physician.

Only slightly later the German missionary Johann Wohlers found the same attitudes prevailing in the far south. On Ruapuke the sick and dying were placed, just as Henry Williams had so often found them, well away from the huts in a rough shelter, to be left there, usually alone, with water and cold potato within reach. Elsdon Best explains: "The *tapu* pertaining to a sick person was the cause of this procedure. If left in the dwellinghouse he might die therein, whereupon the house would have to be destroyed, or at least deserted ... little care was bestowed upon a sick person, and the belief that sickness is caused by the gods prevented any use being made of medicines or simple remedies." In 1828 missionary William Williams wrote of the deaths caused by the introduced European disease, whooping cough: "Indeed there was scarcely a family to be met with which had not been visited by death. It seemed to be a prevailing opinion that it is a visitation from our God in anger to them for not observing the sabbath day etc." Later when influenza ravaged the population near his mission station Williams spoke to a chief who had lost his children: "I told him that to mourn over his children was right .... But we must remember the cause for which sickness came – it was sin .... All our bodies must die on account of sin ...."

Both the Williams brothers nonetheless spent much time helping the sick, giving medicine, and later during a smallpox scare carrying out mass inoculations: "There is an alarm among the natives about an eruptive disease with which a man is affected at this place, fearing it may be the small pox. I am glad to find it is groundless, but I propose to take the present occasion for vaccinating the whole population in this quarter." They probably used cow pox on the udders of their own cows for an initial vaccine, then using the lymph in the pustule to vaccinate others by an "arm to arm" method. It was not only the Maori who died from the epidemic diseases; in 1847 William Williams lost his son in an epidemic of typhus fever which swept the higher school in the Bay of Islands.

their resource base in Sydney. Effective missionaries were capable men; they had to be to survive, even more to succeed. They were not Cooks nor d'Urvilles, exceptional men to whom exploring was itself the end. Missionaries were equivalents of runholders or miners, with definite goals in mind. In some ways that end was as intangible as climbing Mount Cook or finding useless Crozet Island, but that neither nullifies the effort nor diminishes the determination.

In dealing with the Maori Marsden had but one principle. He believed, as firmly as Marion had, that if a man showed trust this would be shown him. Through his long and extensive New Zealand exploration this proved to be true, but Marsden did not have sailors with him to cause trouble. And this was a changing New Zealand, a half century later than Marion. On every exploration Marsden provided what medical care he could for those who needed it; unfortunately there were difficulties even beyond doubtful diagnosis and meagre remedy. Men, women, and children died, Marsden thought, because of tapu placed upon water or herbs or human contact. Naturally he felt that at least sometimes he might have saved them with what skill and remedy he offered.

Before Marsden ended his first visit he confirmed for himself what he had emotionally rejected, that New Zealanders were cannibals. "When I expressed abhorrence at their eating one another, they said it had always been customary to eat their enemies .... I am inclined to believe that these people consider the eating of their enemies in the same light as we do the hanging of a criminal ...." On his second visit Marsden was shown a tattooed head. When told it was the head of a chief killed in war and eaten, he saw it as ceremonial. "The dead body of the chief ... is cut up into small portions and dressed for those who were in the battle, under the immediate direction of the chief who retains the head." Maori sold the heads, and white men bought them, as Banks had, but usually for resale. European museums and collectors wanted them, and commerce flourished. Marsden saw fourteen heads displayed for sale on a table in the schooner *Prince of Denmark*. One old New Zealand hand mentions the "crime" of a slave, who ran off with his own head – after it had been tattooed to order, bought and paid for. Marsden tried hard to end such practices.

Those whom reformers hope to change somehow attain a magic virtue, known only to reformers, certainly not to themselves. Missionaries often saw what they wished to see, or at least an approximation. Marsden argued that Maori cannibalism was closer to a ritual than to an insulting revenge. He told the Church Missionary Society that, "it appears to have originated from a belief that Mowheeboo (or Maui-pu), the First Cause of all, sacrificed his son, and ate him. Their object is to satisfy their superstitious minds and to *appease the deity.*" This made it sound like a stronger version of the Christian sacrament, and is not at all what Maori gave as reasons to inquiring explorers. But it spurred the missionaries on.

Marsden explored much of north-western New Zealand to meet Maori and to find the paths between the tribes, to make converts and peace not war. And always he examined resources, for his mission was to pay its way as far as possible. Routes, resources and redemption; the end and the means interlocked. One of Marsden's expeditions set out to examine Kaipara Harbour on the west coast of the North Auckland peninsula and then explore eastward to Whangarei. If practical the route would shorten the journey from Sydney to the North Island's east coast, and avoid the wind-roiled seas at the northern tip. A local chief lent Marsden slaves as porters and guides. The Maori knew the country far beyond their own districts: "It is no uncommon occurrence for the people of the North Cape to travel throughout the country to the East Cape, a distance of two hundred (sic) miles, to make war." Tribes armed with new weapons, muskets, would range much further later.

Marsden saw the dangerous entrance as Kaipara Harbour's drawback. Otherwise it would be an excellent anchorage, and with local resources too. Its rivers were lined with "the finest Kauri spars ...." After examining the timber carefully they came to an inland Maori village whose people greatly feared the notorious warrior chief Hongi. Marsden offered to try and persuade Hongi to mend his ways, foreshadowing much missionary peacemaking. This promise so pleased the chief that he gave them two fine pigs, and canoes to travel upstream. At another Maori village this reciprocity was repeated; Marsden promised to intercede with Hongi and the chief gave potatoes. But in some areas such promises, even if workable, were too late. Hongi hallmarks showed a ravished land: empty homes, pillaged fields, burned villages. Yet many missionaries admired Hongi. Marsden himself described him as "uncommonly mild in his manners, and very polite, and well behaved at all times." Presumably your view depended on whether Hongi was likely to attack you. At last the party reached the coast, to be entertained by a village which had heard much about Marsden. They were most hospitable: "a woman immediately handed me a snapper ready roasted; others prepared me some fern-root. Being hungry, I relished my supper much."

Such exploration was different from that of Cook or Duperrey, who went to find out things for the sake of knowing; science was their driving force. Marsden looked for ways to travel and exist in New Zealand. He would never have apologised for offering the Maori both Christianity and technology; he was completely certain they were in dire need of both. The combination was what he called "civilisation." Forty years later Dr David Monro, doctor, politician, runholder, botanist and explorer thought the Maori still needed modernising, and did not believe the missionaries had succeeded in conversion either: "There is a great deal said about the Christianity of the natives. With the vast majority it is nothing but surface christianity ...." Opinions differed, but to be fair, Marsden was quite aware that the Maori had their own point of view. He made every attempt to understand it, as his journals make perfectly clear. Nor was he one-eyed about other Christians. Marsden suggested to New South Wales Wesleyans that they set up missions in New Zealand in the *Boyd* country, just nine years after his first missions. They did so and were harassed by Hongi, and at times despaired of their enterprise. But one of these Wesleydale missionaries, James Stack, explored widely.

Marsden's plan to have intelligent workmen modernise Maori by example worked only partially. Because techniques were to lead to conversion little sign of that appeared either. The mechanics were good men but had neither the education nor innate personality to become missionaries. And there were doubts about the whole approach. James Shepherd, a Wesleyan, thought that "the Gospel will prove the only means of civilizing the heathen ... I say

Evangelization precedes Civilization." And the Anglican William Williams later wrote: "I do most firmly maintain from experience that the progress of civilization does not contribute one iota towards the evangelization of a heathen people." Slowly the emphasis shifted to conversion through teaching and preaching, which implied travelling and exploring.

Change came for a number of reasons, but partly because of the arrival in New Zealand of Henry Williams, a man of unusual background and remarkable energy and character. He became an outstanding New Zealander and before that a good missionary. His pre-clerical background contributed to his development. As a Royal Navy officer during the Napoleonic and American Wars he had been trained to use order and discipline, but even more to value them. The young officer saw plenty of action and was given a medal by his own side and a wound by the enemy. As a result of the last naval action of the war, or so a fascinating story goes, his whole life was changed. In January 1815, when the war between the United States and the British was over but distant outposts had not yet heard the news, he was an officer on HMS *Endymion* when it defeated and captured the United States frigate *President.* A great gale struck during his voyage as one of the prize crew taking the American ship to Bermuda, and legend has it that Williams promised the Lord he would take up His work if the ship were spared. Whether this is exactly so or not, he became a missionary, and in New Zealand was assisted by his retired officer's half pay until the government ceased paying it to those in Holy Orders in 1827.

Both Henry Williams and his brother William, also a noted missionary, reared large families of able children. In 1846 Henry's son Samuel married his cousin, William's daughter Mary. William Bambridge, a teacher who had come to New

Henry Williams. A responsible leader at sea and on land, he worked hard to make Christian life a boon to the Maori, travelling incessantly to find the ways and to bring the light. *(Hocken Library, Dunedin)*

Zealand in Bishop Selwyn's party, wrote in his diary: "A long train there was consisting chiefly of the Williams' family. Awfully numerous. I think that New Zealand and Williams will ultimately be as closely connected as Wales & Jones." Mrs Selwyn estimated there were twenty-two Williams in Auckland for the wedding. Their descendants have played an important part in the development of New Zealand society.

Henry Williams served Britain as a fighting man from the age of fourteen until he was twenty-three, but it was his personal qualities which gave the ex-officer such stature in his new context. The Royal Navy's training helped, but above all his Christian faith buttressed his innate strength of character. Such qualities quickly made him the dominant figure among European missionaries and especially – and more importantly – with the Maori. He had his faults. Although he was self-disciplined and courageous, colleagues criticised his stern character and his overly definite views about right and wrong. That last criticism was made of the Saviour Himself. But it is true that, and with good example, Williams did not consider the personal costs of following what was "right." At the Bay of Islands he quarrelled with ships' captains, the immoral activities of whose crews he deplored. He did not hesitate to reprimand Maori, at the Bay of Islands or on his journeys. A Maori told Edward Jerningham Wakefield, a young Englishman travelling in the same area as the missionary, that Williams was "a *tangata riri*, or "angry man", who shuts his tent-door upon us, and does not sit by our sides and talk kindly to us, as you do: but he has the *Atua* [God] upon his lips, and we are afraid of his anger." Williams explored so he could better look after the natives. Wakefield's secular approach believed the Maori perfectly competent to look after themselves. Friendship thrives on the second gratitude.

Williams's absolute certainty of his rightness was not attractive. Not simply 19th-century Christian in its foundation, it has a very modern sound; arrogant certainty is widespread today within causes of diverse variety and validity. In Williams's case there was bound to be conflict as his good intentions set out to pave the road to Heaven. Fortunately he was an able and balanced man as well. William Colenso, who worked with him for years, said that, "Mr Williams, though a strict precisian, would be bound by no rules, not even of his own making; he was very imperious and distant, almost of repelling manner, and yet very kind hearted. However he was eminently fitted for his post at that early time in this then savage land." Courage that Williams showed in battle off Copenhagen and in a dashing naval affair at the Basque Roads, stood him in good stead in early New Zealand. He could not be ignored. And his character was such that neither captains and grog-traders, nor their Maori sympathisers, could despise him.

Gradually Williams won support from the Maori. The blunt and courageous ex-officer was the kind of leader they respected, and once he had their trust he became a peacemaker. To accomplish his ambitions as missionary and "diplomat" he travelled widely. Many of his journeys were not exploration in the usual sense, but one certainly was. Williams travelled on foot for over 400 km through rugged and completely uncharted country, up the Wanganui River, overland around Mount Tongariro by a way now known as the Desert Road, to Lake Taupo, Lake Rotorua and on to Tauranga. Maori knew and used the way for their purposes. Williams had to find if it suited his.

At much the same time a young Englishman, Jerningham Wakefield, travelled over the first part of Williams's journey and wrote of it in detail. His comments provide interesting counterpoints to the missionary's journal, particularly so in discussions of Maori, with whom both Williams and Wakefield sympathised. But sympathy can rise from different points of view. Wakefield's proclaimed purpose for exploration was "seeing for myself some of the natives unvisited by intercourse with savage white men, and unimproved by missionary labours." Wakefield, nephew of Colonel William Wakefield, the leader of New Zealand Company immigrants in 1839, bought Maori land against the opposition of the missionaries. Both groups, missionaries and Company men, looked forward to "improving" Maori, but in totally different ways.

Williams lived at the Bay of Islands but travelled widely on supervisory duties. In late 1839 he was at the Bay of Plenty, on his way south to check mission activity by Maori converts. Leaving Tauranga on 31 October 1839, he sailed down the east coast past Hawke's Bay, the district where the Williams families were to make so many notable contributions to this country, and continued down around Cape Palliser to Wellington Harbour. Cook had not entered the harbour. All he had "laid down" was the possibility, having heard from Maori that there was a harbour there.

The difficulty of finding Wellington Harbour was clearly apparent to Williams: "the natives observed we were going wrong, that our port was not round Cape Tarawiti but abrest of us ... an opening tho between some terrific rocks. Went under easy sail and were soon in a most splendid harbour called by the natives Poneke, quite a different place to what is laid down by Cook." He found that the immigrant ship *Tory* with Colonel Wakefield, both of the New Zealand Company, had been in the harbour already; the Company had begun sponsored emigration to New Zealand and purchased most of the usable land near the harbour. Some local Maori were not satisfied, which exacerbated the argument about Maori land sales raging between the Company and paternalistic missionaries. These arguments began before colonisation and lasted long after it.

On 9 November Williams sailed across to Cloudy Bay, noting shore whaling from deep small coves at the north end of the bay. Each cove had at least one whaling station, from which men pulled out in whaleboats to kill migrating whales as they passed or came into shallow water to calve. They towed the carcasses to shore, rendered the blubber down into whale oil and cut the elastic whalebone from the mouth to dry for sale to makers of corsets or buggy whips. Shore whaling stations were rough and ready places. Missionaries detested whalemen, deplored their corruption of the Maori, and debated the possibility of civilising the Europeans before they barbarised everyone near them. The Wesleyan missionary at Waikouaiti whaling station in Otago, James Watkin, wrote in his diary that "morality has no place in this part of New Zealand; to say nothing of religion." This was not a completely accurate picture of shore whaling, but most of the missionaries saw it that way.

Jerningham Wakefield, not a sympathetic observer, criticised the habitual and off-putting mission gravity. Many well-intentioned missionaries, concerned about violence and inequity in the world, seemed to lash out at laughter as a team-mate of sin. Wakefield felt their failing to relax with Maori hurt the missions; he thought missionaries seldom tried to enter into the Maori spirit of occasion – nor that of whalemen. It is an arguable point of view. On one river journey in company with several Maori canoes, he thought "the only chill cast on the innocent gaiety of the throng was the cold and untimely gravity of Mr. Mason, the head missionary … a face of which not a feature moved, a posture in which not a muscle changed, for miles and miles together. And his dress and attitude … black tail-coat, trousers strapped down, waistcoat and stiff cravat, black beaver hat and rusty kid gloves, could not possibly be agreeable …. He sat on one of the thwarts of the canoe, not above three inches in breadth, perfectly upright, looking straight ahead …. He seemed to keep his crew at a distance. No one sat or stood within a yard of him, and he hardly ever spoke."

Certainly Henry Williams was not like this, although as a former naval officer and a missionary he was used to being in control of situations – and displaying it. As Williams was to find on exploration, even strict supervision given by dedicated men did not guarantee that all would go well. Williams, like Marsden, was a leader, and each effective leader has his own way. Not a "gloomy Christian" himself, he was aware that converts could confuse gloominess with godliness. There were some extreme examples. In the case of one Maori chief, Wakefield "was much struck with the severe discipline which this curious specimen of a warlike and influential chief, turned into a stern religious pastor, maintained over his people … no shouts; not even a smile … one among the mutes, could refrain no longer, and laughed outright at some cheerful observation …. "Who laughed?" … and so Kai treated the assemblage to a long sermon on the sin of laughing …. Such was the intense religious enthusiasm of this extraordinary man; and such was the extravagance of speech and doctrine to which he was carried by it." Kai was an ill-timed guru with a ready-made flock.

Heaphy's painting of immigrant ships, like the one E.J. Wakefield came on, lying in Wellington Harbour. *(University of Canterbury Library, Christchurch)*

In the 1840s George Angas painted Te Awaitaia (the seated figure), a famous warrior who converted to Christianity and became a man of peace. Te Moanaroa, the standing chief, Angas said, "is an intelligent and enlightened man, and a friend of the Europeans". *(Hocken Library, Dunedin)*

Maori ceremonies for the dead were, and are, impressive. Tombs of chiefs, as here, were highly decorated and although of wood were built solidly, to last. *(Hocken Library, Dunedin)*

Of course, some missionaries were gloomy not from religious intemperance but from despair. Reverend James Watkin, who had come from dangerous service in Tonga, found life at Waikouaiti too much to bear. "Welcome to purgatory" was his greeting to the Creeds, who had come to relieve him, travelling with the surveyor Tuckett, the medical man Monro and the German missionary Wohlers in the *Deborah* in 1844. Wohlers himself was later to suffer the deep bouts of depression which seemed to plague so many missionaries. It was a hard life in a hard land.

Williams, fully aware of adjustment problems, sailed back to Wellington Harbour. Almost immediately he and a new missionary, Octavius Hadfield, were taken in a canoe to a point from which they could walk overland to Cook Strait and find a boat to Kapiti Island. They had the chance to discuss the problem of living in the true Faith and preaching the Gospel when no one wishes to hear, for on the way they had passed Te Koroiwa whaling station which "looked filthy and [had] a most disgusting stench from the putrid carcasses of whales." It was the nature of the job. A few years later David Monro looked at John Jones's Waikouaiti whaling station and remarked, "The whole beach was strewed with gigantic fragments of the bones of whales, and flocks of gulls, cormorants and other sea-birds and savage looking pigs prowled about to pick up the refuse." It was the attractions of Waikouaiti station which broke Watkin, and similar pigs which nauseated d'Urville.

When the two missionaries reached the coast opposite Mana Island Williams found transport, and was one of "nearly one hundred in the canoe" going from the mainland to Mana Island to visit the Maori under great chief Rangaiata. Intermixture of Europeans and Maori was well underway: "several Europeans were here who were civil. One in particular was very solicitous that we should take some rum, which gave me an opportunity to speak upon the evil of this practice ...." Undoubtedly there were evils in the "practice", especially as by this time the Maori, who at first rejected alcohol, were drinking. Or at least some of them were, and a few heavily. This being so missionaries did not endear themselves to either group if each time Williams accepted hospitality he preached on the evils of rum. In the south, chief Tuhawaiki encountered coolness upon hospitably offering the Bishop of New Zealand a drink of rum.

Soon afterwards Williams poured out his feelings after encountering some whaling men who "spoke of the cheat and folly of Missions." Some expressed their doubts strongly, suggesting if Christianity could "induce the natives to leave off war and make peace they would turn Missionaries themselves." Others did not care how long the Maori kept up the war as "it would be well if they were all killed." Williams may have been right – and he certainly thought so – in his judgment. "These were a wretched sample of Christians. Need it be said that they were under the influence of rum, but so it is, their nourishment is liquor and their language is blasphemy." For one who saw his duty and did it, this was somewhat discouraging. In the area Williams "found both natives and Europeans of this place in a very dark unrelenting state. Held service however with both parties. About 10 Europeans here."

While travelling along the shore they saw *Tory*, the immigrant ship, sailing near Kapiti Island, a Maori stronghold. Williams began to encounter Maori converted by Maori missionaries. Conversions heartened him, but some

Waikanae Pa and Kapiti Island, seen here, played parts in the adventures of Henry Williams and Octavius Hadfield just before Williams decided to make his great overland trek to Tauranga from the Port Nicholson area. (*Alexander Turnbull Library, Wellington*)

accompanying teaching worried him greatly, for he saw it as corrupting the truth of the message. Here too he met the great chief "Rapauraha, who we found to be more agreeable than I anticipated. He had none of the savage appearance of so celebrated and bloody a warrior and was a very intelligent man. He received us very graciously and entered fully into conversation upon politics and upon the necessity of laying aside his sad evil ways ... the Old Man presented me with a splendid Pig." The next day Williams believed he had persuaded Te Rauparaha to make peace with the Otago Maori. Rauparaha's retirement into respectability foiled a war party from the south led by Tuhawaiki who, saddened at missing a good battle, instead sailed a schooner to New South Wales to visit the Governor.

At Kapiti Island Williams helped unload horses from a ship into a large canoe. They were for Waikanae on the mainland, to convey Hadfield, carrier of the Word to the heathen. Hadfield, like Bumby, was a missionary whom Wakefield very much admired; judgments, not inveterate prejudice, inspired his criticisms of others. Williams then took leave of Rauparaha. He had decided to walk overland to Tauranga, and not go south to Banks Peninsula. The North Island needed him. "I felt it needful to run my course northward, from the disturbed state of things from this new war to do what I could to effect a peace ...." Along his way Williams tried, often successfully, to make peace between different groups of Maori. Like other explorers he found them very warlike, but hoped that Christianity would end conflict. It had not in Europe, or at least not great national wars. But it was a worthy hope, and on this expedition the missionary negotiated peace between two tribes, spurred on perhaps by crossing a battlefield where the Waikanae Maori had defeated Rauparaha.

Chiefs pointed out to Williams land they had sold for "a few muskets and casks of powder, also the land which they had not disposed of." In general the Maori knew very well what they were doing in selling land, and it was usually the best and most convenient portions which they kept for themselves. In Otago, where Symonds, the Acting Protector of Aborigines, nearly drove surveyor and Maori mad by insisting on going over and over the land with the two-miles-to-the-inch maps with them in order to avoid any misunderstanding, Tuhawaiki suggested a million pounds. He settled for £2,400 plus various reservations, which included the portions of the peninsula open to the sun and rich in kai moana, seafood. Colonel Wakefield said Tuhawaiki "entered into all the details of the sale, described the boundaries exactly by name and designs on paper, and conducted the transactions on the part of the Natives with the tact and readiness of an accomplished man of business."

Prices look ludicrous today because we ignore the inverse availability of land and desirable goods at the time. In other words, we foolishly put the deal into our context, by definition a false one. And Maori were especially careful about delineating and enforcing boundaries. Problems arose because purchasers were not careful enough in finding out who they should be dealing with, and because the settlers made the false assumption that all land which was not being "used" was waste land and should be made available for settlement. A similar assumption by the Crown led to war. In New Zealand the incomers were dealing with a proud race.

Some things went well. Williams was pleased by the many converts made by a Maori Christian missionary in that area. Converts are very often enthusiasts, and the shortage of missionaries, although some thought there were too many, meant that early converts taught and preached. Rauparaha's son, Tamihana Rauparaha, spread the Anglican gospel in the south. Ordained Europeans still baptised and gave other sacraments. Williams met nearby a Maori chief who knew several Christian hymns, but as he could not deal with the tunes he "therefore composed some of his own of which he gave a specimen, quite original. He afterwards commenced repeating the Morning Service .... I was much delighted with him and gave him a primer and two Prayer Books ...."

Williams was perceptive enough to realise the Holy Spirit sometimes took second place to self-interest in bringing light to the heathen. Christianity was making the Maori more peaceful, but at their own pace. Heu Heu, the principal chief of the lake, according to a traveller "told Mr. Chapman, at his last visit, that he would only have one more fight with the tribe at Wanganui, to settle his old grievances, then make a durable peace, settle down, and 'believe'." This traveller, a highly educated German doctor Ernst Dieffenbach, came on the *Tory* with Wakefield to assess climate, soil and natural productions as naturalist for the New Zealand Company. He wrote an excellent book about his experiences, including the first ascent of Mount Egmont. His empathy with the Maori did not exclude scrupulous observation and impartial assessment. Quite as much as Williams, Dieffenbach sought ways to bring them a new and better world, not of the spirit but of intellect and the flesh.

Divisions appeared to be deepening between Wesleyan and Anglican converts, which greatly saddened Williams. Many devout Anglicans still hoped for reconciliation and reunion but the opposite was happening. Doctrinal division had hardened by the time Thomas Brunner made his famed expedition to the west coast of the South Island only a few years later. In 1847 he was "astonished to find amongst the natives in these distant parts so much attention paid to their forms of religion, which is the Church and Wesleyan …. In some places there are only six or seven natives, yet they have separate places of worship, two schools, and they are always quarrelling about religion …." Not by any means were only these two sects divided. Protestant missionaries all disapproved of the Roman mission. William Williams wrote, "The Papists are increasing their numbers … sent into the unoccupied districts they would do much mischief … they are doubtless withheld by the great disposer of events until a purer gospel shall have been planted."

With more on his mind than doctrinal division, Henry Williams left Hadfield at Otaki, also to be in charge of Waikanae, for from the former it would be possible to "pass from one to the other with ease on horseback in an hour and a half and keep a general oversight to the settlements all around until he should have more assistance, which it is highly important should be speedily afforded to him." Williams then poured out his own worries in his journal, words, thoughts and hopes as typical of the 19th century as so many of Banks were of the eighteenth. "I determined therefore with much regret to proceed alone through the heart of the Island, a distance of more than 300 miles an entirely new rout [sic] over country not yet explored by Europeans. I regretted leaving Mr. Hadfield a young man with ardent zeal but in very delicate health alone in this extensive and most important field, which requires several Missionaries at different stations to meet in a slight degree the wants of this people."

The missionary was exploring to see "such extensive fields" and form plans for the harvest. It was souls he sought, and the best routes to where they were. His counterpoint in place and period, Jerningham Wakefield, had different and by no means inferior motives. He was discovering with a new eye, as one does a fortune-teller or a restaurant, which until "discovered" was known only to those with no influence to further their interests. Williams or Wakefield, or both, may have been misguided, but they found the way well enough on physical paths. And both revealed to the world what was found. Wakefield wrote an excellent book, and Williams reported through his Church to the wider community of England.

From Otaki Williams "commenced my journey", his great walk to Tauranga. Wakefield, within a few months, made almost exactly the same expedition from Wanganui as far as Taupo, the first and more difficult half of Williams's expedition. Wakefield's descriptions enliven what Williams briefly mentioned in his journal, just as a few years later Williams's brother needed his travelling companion Colenso's eye for animating detail.

Williams was not only checking routes to potential converts and to locations from which missionaries could work, but also sounding out Maori opinion on this. He spoke fluent Maori. His small party proceeded along the shore to the Rangitikei River, often encountering Maori. Turning inland, they toiled up the Rangitikei in canoes, an interesting experience for an old Royal Navy man. Boats and methods were unfamiliar and the conditions unnerving: "the current so extremely strong that the natives were obliged to push the canoe on by the aid of poles requiring the greatest care that our bark was not upset .... I kept up my eye upon our boat men who appeared quite composed and aware of what they were about ... myself perfectly quiet."

## MISSIONARY RIVALRIES

The disputation among Maori converted by the different mission churches was matched between and within the European churches themselves. The more tolerant attitudes of Samuel Marsden had been overwhelmed by the competition for converts. Wesleyans disapproved of Anglicans, both – and very strongly – disapproved of "Popery", and the Lutheran Johann Wohlers was quietly deprecatory about them all. Henry Williams's own view, naturally, was strongly Church of England. He "heard of some Wesleyan teachers baptising at some of the neighbouring places ... some other particulars also were mentioned plainly shewing the necessity of some duly authorized teacher being immediately placed among these tribes." "Duly authorized" meant Church of England.

The newer, younger missionaries were not like Marsden, who had left England before the lines between Church and Chapel were so clearly drawn and who had welcomed Wesleyans to New Zealand. William Williams thought Wesleyans "still a thorn in our side .... I much doubt whether their baptism ought to be anything accounted of by us." The Wesleyans felt just as strongly. Watkin, who had been visited by Bishop Selwyn at Waikouaiti, wrote that the Bishop pleased him "much as a man and somewhat as a Churchman." And because Johann Wohlers was not Wesleyan, Watkin did not tell him Tuhawaiki was seeking a missionary.

In this European equivalent of tribalism even the Anglicans did not always approve of each other. William Williams's wife Jane wrote in 1844: "Mr Cole the clergyman at Wellington belongs to the Society for the Propagation of the Gospel and reminds us more of some of the card-playing and dancing clergy of Southwell than any one we have seen in New Zealand – as light-minded as Mr Cotton without his cleverness. The latter I am sorry to say is a decided Tractarian and so I fear is Mrs Selwyn. The Bishop is a good man and a conscientious man and I am sure has an earnest desire to do his duty as a Bishop. His views and ideas do not in all things coincide with ours, but we pray that he may be led into all truth and preserved from Puseyite errors." But in 1847 William Williams himself wrote, "The more I see of the Bishop the more I feel that he is unsound at bottom and I have no expectation of seeing a sound superstructure. I relieved my mind before I came away by writing a letter upon intonation and candlesticks."

Infighting did not suit the situation in a new land. Nonetheless, most of the missionaries were unwilling to compromise to fit new conditions. Watkin had prevented any Sabbath whaling at Waikouaiti. William Williams favoured Watkin's view: "On Sunday last a small whale was driven on shore ... they proceeded to cut it up immediately without regard to the Sabbath .... I invited them to come to service but said I should not allow them to attend the candidates class [for baptism] for some time. However, they preferred remaining away which is a proof that they have a very inadequate idea of the extent of their offence." No doubt Henry felt the same. One lonely figure, the Lutheran Wohlers at Ruapuke, preached that if the Lord sent a whale or shoal of fish on a Sunday he should be thanked and use made of His bounty. This did not endear him to his colleagues.

Wakefield, on a river nearby at about the same time, described the process fully. The Maori forced their way up rapids using "long poles made of *manuka, toa toa,* or other hard wood, and charred at the lower end. They now push against the bed of the river in perfect unison, the poles plunging and lifting, while the canoe foams ahead, as though by clock-work. The helmsman also steers with a pole, balancing himself in the high peaked stern .... The canoes follow each other in single file ... and though a collision would in most cases render the capsizing of both inevitable, such is the skill of the natives, that an accident rarely occurs in going up the rapids."

In this part of his journey Williams found native teachers of Christianity changing ceremonies in ways to which he objected. Of one, Wiremu Neira, he said angrily that "his ceremony appears to be the washing of the head which has always been considered sacred by New Zealanders in warm water out of a iron pot ... a washing away of sin and a release from *Tapu* very much according to native custom. A perfect cheat of Satan and what an abominable perversion of baptism!" Generally speaking, Maori adaptability was not approved by the missionaries, who were not adaptable themselves; they wanted them to do things as Europeans did. William Williams was sometimes willing to compromise. An argument arose over the carved posts for the new church at Turanga: "the horrible figures they are accustomed to make, are hardly suitable for a place of worship .... I told them plainly that I could not approve of that which is disallowed in our churches at home ... the character of native carving remains but there is nothing to be objected to in the device .... It is gratifying to see so much labour bestowed upon such an object."

After landing again well up the Rangitikei, Williams's party plodded on, at first over rough well-rivered country and then along beach sand. From the beach they saw a startlingly beautiful view: Mount Egmont and Mount Tongariro, "both covered with snow in the height of summer. Two most magnificent objects ...." Next day the beauty of the peaks lightened the morning walk, and by ten o'clock they reached Putikiwaranui, on the Wanganui River. At this village two days later Williams negotiated a controversial acquisition of Maori land, claiming that they "all approved of their land being purchased and held in trust for their benefit alone." However well intended, his action, so in character, caused the decisive churchman much trouble with the New Zealand Company and the New Zealand authorities. On 8 January 1840 William Williams wrote that his brother had given "a most favourable report of the district over which he travelled, with one exception namely that Europeans are trying to buy the land in every direction, or rather to cheat the natives out of it .... Be that as it may, Henry has purchased a quantity of the said land for the Society, and the Banks of one entire river, Wanganui, which the Association had contemplated the purchase of, he has secured for the natives ...." Modern authorities realise that the Maori nearly always knew what they were doing, and also that they kept their bargains very well. Trouble came later when not all Europeans understood or kept theirs.

Wakefield disagreed strongly with Williams about purchase and did not hesitate to say that Henry Williams lied in his reports. The Maori showed Wakefield the agreement of sale. After he translated to them Williams's paper telling of the purchase, Wakefield asked the Maori whether this had actually been made. According to Wakefield they denied it completely. "I could scarcely believe for some time that such a deception could have been made use of by Mr. Williams, in order to prevent our completion of a bargain which we had commenced at Kapiti a month before his arrival. I could not see a single excuse for the action. It was by no means calculated to give these ignorant natives a high opinion of the character of the white man for honest and straightforward conduct; as they were kept uninformed of its motive, either real or apparent." The question of land purchases from Maori is always a sore one whether done by the New Zealand Company, the missionaries or by the Crown. A certain amount of confusion undoubtedly occurred because land ownership meant different things to the different cultures.

Whoever owned the land Williams said he bought, there was a great journey yet to be made. Williams left, with much evidence of goodwill in the Maori farewell. "Turoa and other Chiefs came to see us off. The Old man wanted to give me a fine pig, but the pig had the sagacity to get out of the way. I promised them that a Missionary would soon come to reside among them .... They requested that the Missionary might bring a wife as then he would be likely to stay with them." The contribution of missionary wives to missions has never been adequately recognised.

The travellers proceeded upriver by canoe, pestered by "musquitoes", but entranced by the scenery which provided so "many beautiful rich and romantic

This hut, upper left, and the two chief's houses pictured in the Bay of Islands during the mid-1820s d'Urville voyage, show the major features of Maori construction at the time: wooden construction and decorative carving, which were repeated in the churches they built. (*University of Canterbury Library, Christchurch*)

spots." After three days they spent Sunday at Ikurangi resting from travel, but active otherwise. Williams held a service, to which "a good congregation" came in answer to the "bell", an old musket barrel. Afterwards he responded to questions for hours, but was happy to do so for "they were very importunate for Missionaries to come and reside amongst them." It is hard to say whether a resident missionary would have increased or decreased the keenness, approaching zealotry, of some converts.

Next day Williams's party set out for Pukeika, on the way landing at a small but "very interesting and romantic" settlement. Williams was impressed by the splendid country and by the number of Maori, "very much delighted to see me the first European that has visited them." After conversion, he thought, their future would be bright. On reaching Pukeika Williams found it "a formidable place ... and the scenery was grand." The entire area must have been impressive, for shortly afterwards Wakefield thought a view "as majestic as that of the highlands of the Hudson .... Picturesque gardens and small settlements were perched on the banks, or halfway up the ascent; and many canoes, laden with food for the fishermen, glided gracefully down the river. As we met, kind greetings were addressed to the chief and his white man, and often a basket of cooked birds or other food was handed into the canoe." This sounds more appetising than the fare which Williams, Wakefield and Dieffenbach usually described. Their fervour when they speak of something tasty indicates its rarity. Dieffenbach complained that the food "consisted only of fresh pork and potatoes, without the luxury of salt or anything to give it a relish. As for myself, I bore it very well, although I generally found that the disuse of salt and the uniformity of the food caused one or two abscesses ... common amongst the Europeans on their first arrival in the island."

For food or otherwise, travellers seldom climbed up to the Maori settlements on the Wanganui's banks, unless sheer necessity forced it. The way up was usually "a rude but strong ladder consisting of trees and *kareao*, or supple-jack, reaching from the water to the top." Wakefield climbed up once, and his experience was not encouraging: "at length we reached the foot of one of the skyscraping ladders ... leading to the top of the cliff, here about 200 feet high [60 metres], while the river is not more than 40 yards [37 metres] broad. The natives clambered carelessly up, with heavy chests, and guns and paddles, and my great dog in their arms, while I was ascending cautiously, step by step .... At the bottom they had shown me the spot where 'two or three foolish old women' they said, 'had been smashed quite flat, having missed a step while going down in the dark to the canoes.'" Perhaps Wakefield openly demonstrated his reaction to the perceptive and humorous Maori, for the very next day he was shown a tomb, perhaps to cheer him up. "Here there is a beautiful monument in honour of a dead chieftainess. It consists, as usual, of a large canoe stuck upright, and is 30 ft [9 metres] high, ornamented with carving representing three figures standing one at the top of the other's head. The workmanship is most elaborate .... The two men who carved it told me it took them six weeks to complete. The bones of the person to whose memory the monument was sacred were pointed out to me up in a tree."

Williams, an old New Zealand hand, avoided such distractions. At the river stop where the Taupo trail began, Maori warned of "nearly a week's march and a very difficult one." Presumably his party "of 25 natives and 3 pigs" found the march difficult. Wakefield's certainly did. "Our path lay chiefly along the valley of the Wanganui, which keeps an average of two miles wide, and is intersected by a deep cleft in which the river runs. Many parts of the valley are clear, and in some places we passed over small plains of grass; in others, we plunged into the forest, and crossed steep ridges, apparently in order to avoid circuitous bends of the valley. We had forded the river five times .... This road must be perfectly impassable in winter, when the river is swollen by freshets." Dieffenbach found the going hard too, even with Maori guides: "travelling through the bush in New Zealand is rather a scrambling affair, and with a load is very fatiguing, and cannot be kept up for a long time. Fifteen miles I considered a very good day's work, even in the open parts of the island."

An important member of Williams's party found the trail more than difficult. "One of our fellow travellers (the largest of our pigs) fell down the precipice and broke nearly every bone. Detained for two hours while the boys cut up the pig. Our road was so rough that the pig drivers had to lift their charges over the numerous trees that laid in our way." Williams was in a hurry, with good reason, and any delay upset him. At times the Royal Navy in him came out, deploring what he saw as a false appreciation of time. "I was sorry to make so short a day as it was highly necessary that we should hurry on owing to the length of the journey to Taupo and there being no provisions but what the boys had to carry with us." Thomas Brunner, the South Island explorer in the same decade, went further and argued that the introduction of pigs had made Maori appreciation of time worse and not better. He argued that pigs had increased Maori wealth but decreased cleanliness and industry, and suggested that "goats would be more useful, and less troublesome in their potato gardens. The skins would serve them instead of dog-skins, of which they are very fond .... I took much trouble to impress the value of goats on them ...."

In spite of inter-cultural disagreements Maori porters proved invaluable. Wakefield's normally carried bundles of trade goods such as "blankets, shirts, tobacco, pipes, axes, powder and shot, fishhooks, beads ... a little biscuit, log books, and pencils ...", and three guns, as well as food. "The 'boys' were extremely handy in making up the bundles, which they strapped on their backs by belts resembling braces in form, neatly plaited of flax." Dieffenbach made a most favourable arrangement on one trip. As he put it, he "persuaded E Kake, one of the chiefs, to accompany me, who took a slave with him, and sent on before a female slave to one of his plantations which lay in our route, with an order to prepare maize-cakes for us to carry as provisions." Others got less service. Wakefield's expedition bought most of their food along the way, except such pukeko as Wakefield shot, a bird "of a dark blue colour, and about as large as a pheasant ... its flight is slow and heavy, resembling that of a bittern ... although my boy told me that it was *kai kino*, or 'bad food', I found one of them a very good addition to my meal of boiled potatoes." A welcome addition is a different matter to something which may save your life. In the absence of a large Maori population in the South Island the explorers there, only four or five years later, found wild birds vital to their provisioning.

A few years later Brunner from Nelson, culturally sympathetic but not uncritical, found his porters as essential as Wakefield's but much more trouble,

This picture of a settler "bartering tobacco for potatoes and pumpkins", just as Wakefield and Dieffenbach did, shows Maori kits and packs and the methods of carrying, loading, and unloading them. *(Hocken Library, Dunedin)*

and he spoke Maori too. He found that Maori required sensitive handling. "I counted fifty-four eels ... making a heavy load for three of us to carry. I was obliged to take the heaviest, to keep good humour amongst them, and to be enabled to laugh at them when they complained of being tired." Laughing at Maori might not have been as effective as laughing with them. Dieffenbach argued from his experience that "joy and mirth ... are always sure to find an echo in the susceptible heart of the New Zealander, and are also the best means to secure his good will and confidence." Not everyone would be capable of constant good humour, or mirth on demand. Nor were all porters equally efficient. Dieffenbach found local guides not always useful; in one case the Maori "knew the valley as little as myself, never having penetrated far for fear of the Nga-te-Kahohunu tribe, the former proprietors ...." Whether willing or not, Maori porters had to be dealt with carefully in all manner of matters. Tapu could not be ignored for Brunner, for example, completely depended on their co-operation and, whatever he thought about it, humoured them. Once the Maori insisted Brunner walk almost a kilometre for water although a stream, but tapu because of eels in it, ran within a few metres.

In dealing with the Maori, finding food, or anything else, Williams had the advantage of thoroughly understanding the language. When the missionary "met a small party coming from Taupo, they gave us a little news of wars and rumours of wars and were much surprised at finding a European in the wood and more particularly so when they discovered that he could speak to them in their own language." Williams had been startled too. As a convinced Christian he preached against superstition. And yet a day earlier a Maori in his party hurt his foot on a root and had claimed this meant that next day they would meet a travelling party.

By now the trail had fewer roots and ran through rather pleasant country, well watered and reasonably level, sloping to the foot of Mount Ruapehu. After a time they sighted Lake Taupo, still some distance away, and next day, the Sabbath, they rested short of Taupo and withstood their hunger. Fortunately on Monday they found wild potatoes, so restoring them that by four that afternoon they arrived "on the Great Lake Taupo, a magnificent piece of water about thirty miles [48 km] in length with various fine bays. We were received with much kindness and abundance of food handed out tho' almost all the men had left yesterday on a fighting expedition in consequence of a *Kanga* (native curse) having been uttered respecting a chief. These abominations have nearly ceased at the Northward." Williams, not surprisingly, believed missionaries to be useful and effective in northern New Zealand.

A day later the tiny expedition reached another village; here there was a "a good Chapel erected at the desire of Mr. Chapman. I began to feel myself drawing near home!! from the circumstance of having arrived at a place where one of our Missionaries had been." Heartened by this Williams relaxed as they travelled north on the lake, as much he could in a small canoe in rough water. Soon Dieffenbach too found Lake Taupo dangerous when winds were strong: "it being a large basin, and on most sides surrounded by cliffs, which are divided by gullys, the waves are frequently very high, and prove dangerous to the canoes, which have here no gunwhales ... this lake, they said; it is worse than the sea." Combining shallow canoes with high waves was everything the Maori had predicted, and he grudgingly admitted: "the natives had been right, as the

In this scene from Dr. Dieffenbach's travels we see across Lake Taupo to Tauhara Mountain and to where the Waikato River leaves the lake. *(Hocken Library, Dunedin)*

waves of the lake still rose high even from the moderate winds which we had had the last two days, and the canoe was very deep in the water."

But rough lake or no, Williams was nearer "civilisation", or at the least his own way of life, for a Maori from Rotorua arrived next day with a note from a missionary and, even more welcome, "a loaf of bread some tea and sugar and a bottle of porter." The party moved down the Waikato River, landing at some boiling springs, today the site of a tourist hotel. Williams approached a geyser to test the theory that it was the "abode of the God of the Lake." Advancing with caution, he quietly put down his staff near the fountain, when suddenly it jetted a column of boiling water. Williams had to flee, or as he put it, "retreat with all possible despatch." The Maori, worried about how angry the god might become, asked Williams to leave well alone. Heedful of such opinion, or simply sensible, he did not approach the jet again.

When Wakefield arrived he was more relaxed in his ways and took advantage of the springs as the Maori did: "cavities from 10 to 30 feet [9 metres] in diameter are filled with water of various temperatures; some nearly boiling, others tempered by the cold stream which runs through one part of them. In one of the latter we all had a delicious bath." A year after Wakefield, Williams and Dieffenbach visited Taupo, a printer and Maori scholar, William Colenso, one of the ablest of several able contemporary Anglican missionaries, reached the thermal area. Exploring the north-eastern North Island to catalogue plants, he was fascinated by springs near Lake Rotorua, partly because "on the very edge of the large boiling spring, several plants flourished in perfection." He saw with approval that, as at Taupo, bathers chose desired temperatures; "just within the lake, the water was warm; a little further on, it was luke-warm; and further still, it was cold; so that these natives have baths, of every requisite degree of heat, always ready, without any trouble whatever."

Wakefield was impressed by the very fine skin and good health of the Maori along the Wanganui River and inland, as compared with those further south. "I was told that this was owing to their constant bathing in the *puhia* or hot springs ... they have earned the sobriquet of the Waikoropupu or 'boiling water' tribes." Dieffenbach agreed. He thought Taupo and Rotorua Maori "excelled in their hospitality towards strangers, in prudent attention to their own affairs, in cleanliness and health, most of those who live on the coasts, and who have become converts to Christianity." When coming down from climbing Mount Egmont he pondered the Maori's good health and fine appearance. He saw some digging muddy ochre out of a river, which they mixed with charcoal to rub on their faces and bodies, and wondered if "the sleekness of the skin for which the natives are so remarkable ... may be owing to their frequent bathing and continual exposure to the air, or ... a characteristic feature of the Polynesian and other coloured races ...."

Exploring was debilitating work, its exponents out in all weathers, often both wet and cold from wind-driven rain or too hot from exertion. Arthritis and rheumatism, ailments thermal springs helped, were as well known to explorers as they were to sailors. A fellow naturalist and explorer, Allan Cunningham, Colonial Botanist of New South Wales, warned Colenso of the medical dangers: "an indifference to the ordinary, the necessary comforts of life, will entail an eventually premature debilitated frame of body and an absolute break down must take place …. In all your excursions among the natives, look to your necessary comforts, and never 'rough it' excepting in cases of necessity …."

Colenso agreed with Cunningham, but also realised how bad conditions contributed to inefficiency quite as much as to ill-health. "I have often been surprised at the great carelessness which I have shown towards rare natural productions when either over-fatigued or ravenously hungry: at such times botanical, geological and other specimens – which I had … carefully carried for many a weary mile – have become quite a burden, and have been one by one abandoned, to be, however, invariably regretted afterwards." Undoubtedly physical debilitation meant explorers missed discoveries. But they accomplished much in conditions it is difficult for today's observer to imagine; the botanists lacked most things a modern expedition would consider essential. Colenso, notwithstanding his modest declaimer, overcame his fatigue so often that Sir Joseph Hooker believed he discovered "more new and interesting plants … than any botanist since Banks and Solander."

Without spring-water rejuvenation, and near the end of a wearing and weakening march, Henry Williams was exhausted. Yet on the evening of the "spring day", as it were, the dedicated missionary was persuaded to climb "a very steep and high hill which was very wearying being at the close of a very fatiguing march." He was rewarded by finding in a fortress, fearing their enemies, a small band of Christian Maori. Several of the young men could read, and his fluent Maori enabled Williams to debate many intriguing points of Scriptural doctrine.

At break of day Williams's party moved on, stopping to break fast on a new bridge across the Waikato River, "formed with 4 very large planks cut out of the solid the ends of which rest on the rock in the middle of the foaming stream." Colenso, in upland Hawke's Bay a few months later, found the capricious nature of New Zealand streams threatened even strong bridges – and not only 19th-century Maori bridges, as we well know today. "A bridge of trees (and one of the best constructed native bridges I have ever seen) was thrown across the foaming torrent, which, though strongly secured together, seemed as if every rush of the bounding water would carry it away. A nervous person would scarcely have hazarded himself …." Even so, South Island explorers for decades to come would have paid handsomely to have bridges at all to deliver them from rude rafts, mokihi and cling-poles.

To his astonishment Williams learned that the Waikato River did not rise in winter, no matter how much rain fell. He attributed this peculiarity to water soaking swiftly into the porous pumice soils. Although still observant, he was near the end of his physical resources, no longer the young officer but a man of nearly fifty who had never spared himself. It turned very hot. By afternoon faint and almost ill, he thought of stopping despite his eagerness to reach friends and news and mail. But, just like the U.S. cavalry sweeping over the hill, or perhaps in Williams's case Royal Navy gunboats creeping over the horizon, a Maori brought him Mr Morgan's horse. In a couple of hours the four strong legs bore the exhausted missionary to Rotorua.

Williams went by canoe across Lake Rotorua's cool water to Mr Morgan's island house. At last he was back in the "quiet abode of the Missionary. A cup of tea was very refreshing and much needed. Here I found letters from my

William Williams: missionary, indefatigable walker and traveller, occasional medical man, and later bishop. (*Alexander Turnbull Library, Wellington*)

family and with much thankfulness heard that all was well." Fortunately the next day was Sunday, for Williams was "very weary and feverish and little inclined to move ...." His sense of duty drove him to take the morning service and, after resting all day, "in the evening baptised Mr.Morgans infant son." The connection between missionary exploration and their sense of mission was amply evident on this pioneer journey by one of the most successful. After resting briefly on Monday, on Tuesday he went to a nearby community to make peace between two tribes, albeit unsuccessfully.

Even a Christian can be impatiently reminiscent. Williams had been long from his family and his post. On the very next day they walked to Mangarewa, a day's journey from Tauranga and the coast. Thursday was wet but even this failed to dampen their will to be home. "Rain was falling in great abundance but as this was the last day all were in good spirits." Good spirits were auspicious. At two o'clock that afternoon, "while pushing my way through the wet bush I came suddenly upon my brother!! ...." William Williams, arriving at Tauranga three days earlier, had set off to meet his brother; reunion was heartfelt pleasure for them both.

By sunset the exhausted explorer had met not only his brother's family but his own son Henry. "I had much news to receive and much to relate and many mercies for which to be thankful. It was a truly joyful meeting." In a little over a week Williams arrived by sea at his own home to "the unspeakable pleasure of finding myself at home and all my family well after an absence of thirteen weeks." Next morning was the Sabbath, and "the quietness of the morning was peculiarly gratifying. I took afternoon service. This was indeed a day of rest and sweet refreshing." But the journey had been important, and its events and results were told to the Maori. After that he met with his fellow missionaries "with whom I had much communication upon the state of the natives to the Southward and that universal spirit of enquiry and the great spread of Christian knowledge which I had ascertained in a journey from the Southern extremity and thro' the heart of the Island. We lamented that so little could be done ...."

Williams was home again after a major trip whose hardship and sheer slogging he played down in his journal. Within ten days he was to play a larger part in New Zealand's history, when the Treaty of Waitangi was signed and New Zealand passed under British control. It was then that Henry Williams made his greatest contribution to the welfare of the Maori, for without his intervention the treaty might not have been signed at that time and in that form. No one in a position to know suggested a better option. In this Colenso also shared. Without the notes of that able printer and linguist, taken on the spot as the event occurred, historians would know much less about the context of the fundamental agreement. The treaty, in spite of ambiguities which caused later discussion to range widely, was almost certainly to be preferred to any alternative at or of this time.

Henry's brother William Williams was the real traveller, although not necessarily an explorer; some of his journeys were twice as long as Henry's main trip, but it was arriving which counted, not the way. William covered his Turanga parish, stretching from East Cape to Palliser Bay, and inland to Lake Waikaremoana, on foot. Earlier he made several journeys from the Bay of Islands, where for nine years he was in charge of the Boys' School at Paihia, among his manifold duties: "We preach we talk, we keep school and translate ... we lay bricks, we plaster, we plant, we salt pork, and occasionally hunt cows in the bush. We take voyages in search of provisions .... If we want a chimney we must make bricks and lime and build also."

In 1832 he went north to Kaitaia to explore the possibilities of native teachers. Williams thought an intelligent New Zealander "much better able than a foreigner to adapt his language so as to arrest the attention of his countrymen." Not all thought it wise: "the chief said it is very well for the Europeans to tell them that their souls will be put into the fire, but for the natives to do so is not to be endured." In 1833 Williams sailed for East Cape with Maori redeemed from slavery by missionaries and taught for eight months at Paihia. On the way he explored inland near the new Puriri station and crossed to Turanga. At Hicks Bay Williams and William Yate walked from Hicks Bay to Waiapu. Williams with his usual brevity called the cliff path "precipitous." Yate, like many of his future travelling companions, was more forthcoming – "I had to creep on my hands and knees by the sides of precipices so steep and dizzily lofty that one false step would have been death ... upon the rocks which frowned or the waves which roared below." Lack of fear improves an explorer; brevity does not.

From 1835 Williams took over the Boys' School, and taught for the next few years while editing the Maori New Testament, working with printer William Colenso. After finishing this work, at the end of 1837 Williams and Colenso set out on a sea trip to Tauranga and East Cape, and an overland walk from East Cape to Turanga on Poverty Bay. James Stack had joined them at Tauranga. Turanga impressed Williams: "The whole district upon which the natives live is a beautiful plain of rich alluvial soil about eight miles wide and from 12 to 20 [32 km] in length. It is intersected by three rivers which for New Zealand, are large …. It possesses many good advantages for a missionary station … the natives are all accessible at the distance of from 2 to 10 miles respectively from the spot which would be fixed upon as a station." Williams was interested in the supply of potential converts. Stack was more interested in the practicalities: "the landing of Mission stores would be attended with serious hazard and expense." Colenso was interested in history: "What a different reception we received compared with that received by Cook!"

It was now evident to Williams that several missionaries should go to the east coast, but most had reasons which prevented their going. Hadfield wrote that "all here are unwilling to go except the two Mr Williams." Taylor accepted the School so that William Williams could go to Turanga, and the family sailed for Turanga on 31 December 1839. En route they left James Stack at Tauranga, where Williams received letters from Henry "announcing his arrival at Rotorua,

---

## THE WILLIAMS BROTHERS AND THE TREATY OF WAITANGI

Henry Williams was possibly the European most influential in getting the Maori to sign the Treaty of Waitangi, and his Maori translation of it may have affected today's debates. His brother William too, as on 5th May 1840, "Conversed with natives about the Treaty with the Queen of England, sent hither by the Governor for signatures. The natives approve of the tenor of it, & several signatures of the leading men were obtained." The brothers considered they were protecting the rights of the Maori, and were annoyed and concerned when it appeared the Treaty would be set aside.

William wrote: "Many of us were actively engaged in procuring signatures …. There was even then a strong feeling of suspicion …. This we combated with success by a reference to the words of the Treaty, which were too plain and simple to admit of a double meaning … [Unfortunately documents written in one language to be translated  for acceptance by those who speak another language will often, if not always, be said to have double meanings]. The natives will apply to us, their oldest, & as they believe, their best friends. They will ask what course they are to pursue. Can we say? Your country belongs to England by right of discovery, & though the Queen of England had solemnly covenanted to secure to you all your lands and estates, forests, fisheries and other properties so long as it is your desire to retain the same possession, yet as christians you are bound to submit patiently? If on the other hand we tell them they are hardly dealt with, we are the promoters of rebellion."

The Williams brothers were horrified but not surprised when the various land transactions eventually ended in war. Both Henry and William had been scathing about some of the early European land deals, and had promoted the Treaty to protect the Maori. In spite of modern reservations about ambiguities in that document, which many discuss completely out of context, in the sense that the attitudes and circumstances of both parties to the Treaty are vastly changed, the influence of the Williams family appears to have been used sincerely to foster inter-racial understanding.

on his way from Cooks Straits." The next day William walked twenty kilometres to meet Henry.

After bad weather the *Martha* reached Turanga, and less than a month later Williams was off to Wairoa on Hawke Bay, a journey of almost three weeks. He recorded little detail of landscape or resources, except the resource which concerned him – "This seems to be the most favorable spot for a mission station, being two miles distant from the sea, having a population within the distance of two miles of 1000 persons; about 2000 persons at a convenient distance higher up the river, besides 1200 half a days journey to the south of the Wairoa & 1200 more a days journey to the north." Only most remarkable natural features draw any comment: "Here the river loses its name at a waterfall of splendid magnitude .... It is a remarkable fact that the rock over which the river falls is full of seashells, like that at Hicks's Bay, shewing that at a distant period it was a bed of the sea ...." Colenso described the fall and the fossilised shells on his 1841-2 journey.

Two months after arriving home William Williams set out for East Cape, a journey of four weeks. After wintering at the station, he spent October journeying to Ahuriri on the southern part of Hawke Bay, south by ship and back on foot. Penetrating inland by canoe he found that "This part of the country is exceedingly fertile being a plain of alluvial soil for some miles in extent and the natives say that after passing the nearest hills there is plain grass land the greater part of the way to Cooks straits, through the centre of the island. This will doubtless be a strong bait to Europeans but the natives need

William Colenso: printer, missionary, explorer, and naturalist, as seen twenty years after his major exploratory/botanical exploits. *(Alexander Turnbull Library, Wellington)*

not suffer on that account as the district is unoccupied." Williams travelled constantly, and not all trips are important or interesting.

After less than three weeks at home he was off again, inland to Rotorua, an important trip. William Williams was the first European to reach Lake Waikaremoana, and the first to follow the Maori track from Opotiki on the Bay of Plenty overland to Turanga. Colenso followed in his footsteps a year later, describing his travels in more detail. Exploration was just a tedious part of Williams's job of getting to the Maori. Even the lake did not receive much attention: "November 25. Continued on our journey to Waikare which is a romantic lake surrounded by rough mountain scenery. The part we have to cross is about three miles over, but the natives say it opens into another sheet of water which is larger." The party proceeded to Rotorua mission station, now not on Mokoia Island but "beautifully situated on the bank of the lake ...." From Rotorua they walked to Tauranga and then to Opotiki. From Opotiki to Turanga was generally a five day journey, but by making "a forced march all day" on Christmas Eve day, Williams, the first European to cross, managed in four. In October 1841 he walked to Wairoa again and met the Catholic missionary Father Baty for a debate in Maori. "This Priest is a very fine young man and possesses much shrewdness as most of the Jesuits do."

In 1842 Williams left with his family for the Bay of Islands on the *Columbine*. At Paihia they met the new Bishop Selwyn, and Williams worked on his Dictionary of the New Zealand language. They returned to Turanga in mid-August, and on 5 October Williams and a newcomer, Dudley, left for Ahuriri to meet Bishop Selwyn on his way north. "The country which the Bishop has traversed from Manawatu is described as being remarkably fine level grassland, wholly unoccupied by natives and watered by four beautiful streams." The party arrived back at Turanga on 25 November, with Dudley very ill.

At the beginning of November 1843 Williams joined Colenso on the *Columbine* for a sea trip to Port Nicholson (Wellington). The ship got as far as Palliser Bay before strong winds came up and forced her across the Strait to Cloudy Bay. Several attempts to reach Port Nicholson failed. Colenso wrote of the Cook Strait storm: "A never-to-be-forgotten day! battened down, lying-to, sea breaking over us, sick, and without all temporal comfort. The Captain declared it to be one of the severest hurricanes he was ever in." Three days later they reached the shore well up the east coast at Castlepoint. Williams noted "a little after 4 we left the vessel with Captn. Stratton and landed in safety at Castle Point." Colenso saw it differently: "10 persons in the boat, a dog, baggage and water casks and only 2 sound and one broken oar ... As we neared the shore, we found, to our almost despair, the coast presented a perpendicular line of cliff, against which the sea broke incessantly." They walked north to Mataikona, spent a week teaching, and walked up the coastal route arriving home on 21 December.

In April 1844 Williams set out for an overland trip to Auckland and the Bay of Islands. "Our guide was very communicative upon the subject of their former history, but he takes little interest in that which is of more importance." Missionaries had opportunities to learn tribal histories and legends, and to examine the original way of life; most were more interested in stamping out all traces of it. But they meant well. At Russell Williams ended up as peacemaker when Hone Heke cut down the flagstaff: "Heke and his people were very saucy .... He said that the Americans have urged them to cut down the Flag Staff."

Constant travelling by the missionaries was hard on wives, left behind to cope with family, illness, teaching, and local Maori. Possibly the worst was not knowing what was happening. In July Jane Williams wrote: "It is now above five months since we received letters .... My husband has been absent now nearly three months ... but as yet I have heard nothing from him .... Nor have we yet heard anything of our boys who left us in the month of March." Williams did not reach home until the beginning of November. Jane wrote: "He arrived at home on the first of this month but has only paid us a visit of three weeks and is now gone to the East Cape .... These continual separations form my greatest trial, but I try to remember that I am a soldier's wife and that when he is away he is on his Master's service. Still I cannot but feel it." Mrs Cook would certainly have understood.

There was no suggestion that Williams was enjoying his jaunts along the routes he and other explorers found for European travel. Trails were rugged and comforts scarce. Often after a full day's walk he catechised candidates for baptism, held evening prayers and classes for communicants, preached to the converted and talked to others, instructed native teachers and held baptism and communion services. He also held services twice, in Maori and English, if settlers appeared, as well as teaching reading and spelling and settling disputes over property or complicated points of scripture. No one ever said it was easy, and it broke lesser men.

By the late 1840s travelling was beginning to tell. "Fancy a clergyman being required to itinerate from London to Edinburgh and back on foot, & then to Southampton & back again ... and then when he is at home having charge, in addition to all other matters, of 300 candidates for Baptism & of 700 regular attendants at Bible Classes ...." But Williams tended to make light of the many difficulties. In November 1849 "a native sent by Mr. Colenso to carry a letter to me was affected with coup de soleil and died in three days. I used my general precaution of carrying a wet handkerchief in my hat & thus felt no inconvenience." In February 1850 "I had the misfortune to get a ducking. I was safely ashore on the opposite bank, but the horse made a plunge in trying to get up the bank & pulled me in after him." Jane added more detail: "the animal stumbled and fell dragging his rider with him under water. Of course he was much entangled but succeeded in keeping his face above water till he received assistance ...."

In August 1848 he wrote: "I cannot consent to remain as sole clergyman in priests orders for a parish 400 miles in length." Williams was trying to persuade Bishop Selwyn to ordain more priests, but having "no chance whatever with him in conversation, so I put down what I have to say on paper, as I did my letter on intonation, & then Irishman like deliver it with my own hands." In September Jane wrote to her son: "Having your Father at home for nearly 4 months has been quite a rare event ...."

Bishop Selwyn was what Jane Williams called "a most amazing walker." In 1842 he walked from Wellington to New Plymouth, then across the island to Ahuriri and up to visit the Williams family on Poverty Bay. This was only one of the long trips made by this indefatigable man. He travelled the length of the

PENITENTIAL TRAVEL

Travelling along the coasts of New Zealand by ship was by definition the lot of maritime surveyors. But missionaries, settlers, government officials and others with business at any distance found travel by sea faster and much easier than travel by land. And yet the ships were not like an English railway car or even canal boat or channel packet. It was all extremely rough and ready, and ready to be rougher any time.

A new missionary, Richard Taylor, arrived from England in 1839 and suggested that he and William Williams, who would help settle him in his new post, should travel down the East Coast in the small cutter *Aquila*. Taylor was unhappy with the cabin, the food, the weather – Williams mentioned no discomforts. It soon became apparent Taylor would find missionary work in remote areas required adjustments. He especially disliked the lack of privacy in Maori villages: "directly we sit down the people rush in and we are almost stifled with dust and heat and my companion is too good natured to desire them to retire to a distance. I tell him I hope antichrist will not walk in for he would not have the heart to command him to walk out." Taylor never really accepted all this as part of colonial travel. But at least he retained a sense of humour about the close observation of all that they did: "and when I brushed my teeth and gargled my mouth with water, the gurgling noise drew forth a burst of applause. I could not help laughing and almost dreaded to shave lest I should cut my throat ...."

Nor would jostling uncouth companions be the only embarrassment. Wohlers was later to remark of another journey: "At first it's a bit embarrassing dressing and undressing morning and night in the presence of women, but one soon gets hardened to that." The good man lasted decades as a missionary, and his "hardening" must have been meant figuratively, for his gentleness was legendary.

country, visiting Stewart Island and Ruapuke with Tamihana Rauparaha, who had been sent south by Hadfield. On Ruapuke Selwyn preached a sermon on contentment with one's lot; according to Pakeha traders on the island the Bishop's words were taken literally and production of pigs and potatoes stopped. Johann Wohlers, arriving soon after, found it hard to persuade his flock to industriously prepare for winter as their, and his, ancestors had done.

Although no explorer Wohlers had to travel through early New Zealand and he noticed things around him more than many missionaries did. He wrote of them in letters, in his memoirs, published in 1883 in German, and reports and journals for the North German Mission Society. He was devout and conscientious, but also humorous. At his first mission, in the Moutere valley near Nelson, Wohlers wrote, "the tui is the size of a thrush, but much more vivacious, slender in form and poise; its feathers are a glossy blue-black; under the chin hangs a little snowy white double bunch of feathers .... I have to overcome a certain emotional reluctance when it comes to shooting this creature. There is no bird in the world which looks more like a German missionary, clerically garbed."

On his way south on the *Deborah* Wohlers, and another missionary, Charles Creed, left the ship at Port Cooper (Lyttelton) to walk to the next bay to hold a service. On Mount Herbert thick fog forced them to struggle through scrub, bush, swirling waters and boulders, only to find themselves not at Port Levy but on the other side of the peninsula. Prayers in English and German – and Wohlers's flint and steel – obtained a warming fire. They were directionless, for Surveyor Tuckett had gone off with Wohlers's compass (and spent an even more uncomfortable night, wet and without a fire). Next day they backtracked up the glen, as Wohlers "tore with both hands, and opened out a way through the dense growth ...." On the tops fog was dense, and the night was spent on the steep slope supported by bushes. Next day, stumbling around the wilderness, Wohlers spotted a little stone wall he had built the first day. Now they knew where they were, relatively, but exhaustion meant another fog-bound night on the mountain. In the morning they found the right ridge, the fog lifted, and they saw not only Port Cooper but the topmasts of the *Deborah*. Wohlers decided the Lord was against a mission at Port Levy. Tuckett lectured them on bushcraft, even though his ill-gained compass had not kept him on the trail either.

At Port Cooper Wohlers met Tuhawaiki, thinking he looked like a horse dealer and a shrewd one. He made Tuhawaiki's Ruapuke headquarters his home, but Tuhawaiki never saw Wohlers there. Aged only forty, the chief drowned south of Timaru in November 1844, when a freak wave swamped his whaleboat. Wohlers continued south on the ship and finally was landed on Ruapuke, to spend the next forty-one years there, except for occasional trips away. In 1846 he travelled to remote areas of his parish, visiting Stewart Island once by ship and once by whaleboat. "These seaboats are built to keep on an even keel, whether on the crest or in the trough of the big seas, and they snuggle comfortably so that they are not easily swamped by a choppy sea. At times they slither along the slopes of the waves like a goat running along a sidling." On Stewart Island, the view made the trip worthwhile: "In the background are high mountains and the troughs of the valleys; on the other side, to the east, the immense ocean; to the north, in the near distance, a row of islets; further away the hills of Ruapuke stand glittering above the waves, and in the far distance the blue mountains of the Middle Island shimmer on the horizon; with Bluff Hill standing isolated, like the cupola of a dome."

In October of 1846 Wohlers travelled across the Strait to the mainland, visiting several small settlements on foot. The voyage across to Jacob's River (Riverton) was more exciting: "Things were on the rough side at first, for high seas were rolling into the Strait from the west ... most unruly. One after another washed over our heads, and there was one among them which could not have been any bigger without disastrous results ... lucky that the boat was manned by experienced and strong seamen." Wohlers walked overland back to Bluff, passing the two family settlement of Oue, where the European family operated a sugar refinery, a beer and vinegar brewery, and a brandy still, using ti stems.

The following year Wohlers visited Creed at Waikouaiti, travelled to Otakau, returned to Stewart Island and visited Tautuku, a whaling station on the south-east shores of the Strait, the northernmost settlement of his parish. The "extraordinarily attractive" setting was backed by impenetrable bush covering most of the hinterland. Wohlers found his journey meant: "wandering through heavy bush, over steep rocks and through deep gorges, and ... climbing over coastal boulders swept by heavy seas ...." In 1855, in a happier mood, he rode on horseback from New River to Jacob's River and described change and development. "The New River is navigable even for sea-going ships of ordinary size, but the skippers have to be thoroughly conversant with the waters at the mouth. Up to now, however, there is nothing for ships to do here, for the river comes from a wilderness empty of people .... Before it enters the sea, the Jacobs River extends itself into a large inland lake, into which several small rivers flow together. On the banks of these rivers are beautiful swampless meadows, on which a patriarchal pastoral life is just beginning .... The Europeans have begun stock-farming only of recent years .... In former times they went whaling, for which they still keep two vessels fitted out."

In the 1870s Wohlers carried on a lively exchange of letters in German with his countryman Haast in Canterbury and sent specimens and preserved muttonbirds, plus notes on the preserving. In his last letter just before his death, he wrote (in English, for once) to advise Haast: "scientific men must not be misled by random talk of the present Maori who do not understand the old traditions and whose fancy is led astray by talking with Europeans." Wohlers had intended to do good, and had achieved much; he had a mission and in more than one sense.

The aim of missionary exploration was to seek out souls to bring to God, paths to their homes and means to maintain the mission. It was hard labour for only an inner reward – and it is to be hoped that all received that. Maori finding the true ways of God depended on missionaries finding the true ways of New Zealand, in every sense of the word. They had to seek but they did find, and New Zealand is the richer for their seeking.

CHAPTER EIGHT

# *Happiness is Charted Havens*

Before Europeans could explore New Zealand conveniently they had to find and examine proper anchorages for the ships which brought them and moved them along the coast. Tasman's officers did the first surveying of New Zealand anchorages in what is now Golden Bay. It amounted to little more than a few soundings and a very imperfect chart, but considering the welcome they had been given that is not surprising. Because of their caution about the lee shores along the west coasts of both main islands, the Dutch maps were understandably sketchy. Their general view of such coasts, remembering that ships of their century were not easily worked against the wind, emerges from the log entry at the Three Kings Islands: "we anchored with the help of God ... in 40 fathoms, grey sandy bottom. May the Lord preserve us from danger and misfortune." Sailors preferred anchorages less dependent on God's mercy.

Later and happier visitors, with more workable ships, took the time to chart for those they knew would follow. Cook and d'Urville, and of course their officers, were the chief early surveyors, but all ships at this time produced some maps or charts, although for one reason or another not every one of these entered the public domain. Cook's former able seaman and midshipman, George Vancouver, was a master surveyor, both his minor work in New Zealand and his major work in British Columbia justifying that title. He and his officers charted Doubtful Sound, Facile Harbour and Pickersgill Harbour in 1791. There were others too. In that same year Captain Malaspina, an Italian in Spanish service, brought two Spanish ships to the south-west coast of New Zealand and found "it would be difficult to give a more perfect description of the ruggedness and elevation of this coast than that given by Capt Cook ...." Malaspina sent an officer, Felipe Bausa, to survey "Dusky Bay" – in fact Doubtful Sound – from a boat. The Spanish had insufficient time to make a proper survey, but they did enough to learn and emphasise the advantages of what they believed would "ever remain the port of welcome in this neighbourhood, offering as it does a more convenient, a safer and a healthier refuge."

In 1847 the Admiralty ordered "a full and accurate Survey of the ... Coasts and harbours of New Zealand ...." To do this their Lordships dispatched *Acheron*, the most remembered of the ships sent specifically to survey New Zealand's coastal waters. Although a paddle-wheel steamship she was fully rigged as a barque and could use sail when necessary – and it often was. As a Royal Navy ship-of-war she carried guns, but only four, partly because of her paddles. At 760 tons she was about twice the displacement of any whaling ship she might encounter near New Zealand, and much larger than brigs, schooners, snows and other small craft trading from Australia for wheat, timber, flax fibre and potatoes.

Paddlewheels are much in evidence in this picture of H.M.S. *Acheron* at anchor. *(Alexander Turnbull Library, Wellington)*

A stout but active Welshman, Captain Stokes, commanded *Acheron*. He had sailed in the *Beagle* with Charles Darwin under Captain FitzRoy, later Governor of New Zealand. Although *Beagle* is best remembered for its naturalist, it too had been sent to survey South America and the Pacific Islands. Survey ships were useful to scientists, as they kept stopping to chart harbours, which meant passengers could travel inland to study flora and fauna. Stokes had become a friend of Darwin and remained in touch with him. Remaining with *Beagle* for eighteen years, six of them in command, Stokes had become an experienced explorer, and he seemed the ideal man for such a detailed coastal exploration and survey of New Zealand.

Stokes wrote a two-volume book about discoveries in Australia which, with his notes and orders, displayed a considerate but vigilant officer, differing from Cook's views only in emphasising that officers were neither to lose their tempers nor use bad words. Cook himself could not have met that standard. Stokes insisted on certainty of punishment, not severity; in this he agreed completely with Cook. *Acheron*'s captain encouraged his men to write records of the voyage in hope that they would let him use them in his own proposed book, with proper acknowledgement of course. As an experienced author he kept careful notes and acted more as the commander of an expedition than of a steam barque. Much of the work of operating the ship was done by his second-in-command, Commander Richards. Stokes Valley and Mount Stokes commemorate the captain on maps and it was Stokes who tranferred Cook's evocative name "Lookers On" from the Kaikoura Peninsula to a nearby inland mountain. Unfortunately the name was completely abandoned later.

Captain Stokes brought his wife and little daughter on *Acheron* but sadly Mrs Stokes died on the voyage from fever contracted at the Cape. Reaching the Pacific was to have been a sort of homecoming for the captain's wife, the daughter of Philip Gidley King, a competent early Governor of New South Wales. This role, and an even earlier one as Lieutenant-Governor of Norfolk Island, King had used to build up connections with New Zealand, sending the Maori useful seeds and animals and encouraging the whaling, flax and timber trades. King's granddaughter, Fanny Stokes, five or six years old, survived this terrible loss of her mother, at least partly because the crew of the *Acheron* almost adopted her. She apparently remembered the voyage without rancour. Fanny was taken over by her relatives at Sydney, so Captain Stokes could concentrate on his exploring and surveying. As a married woman years later she generously sent part of the *Acheron* voyage manuscript to New Zealand to Doctor Hocken, founder of the Hocken Library in Dunedin.

One New Zealand Company surveyor thought Captain Stokes "a very odd mysterious man"; if he indeed was, it is probably attributable to his sad bereavement so far from the support of family and friends. He was obviously a man who needed company. Whether or not he had them for his whole voyage Captain Stokes had some enormous "bloodhounds" on board in Wellington Harbour. In this he did somewhat better than Banks, who lost two hounds he took in *Endeavour* long before reaching New Zealand.

*Acheron* had a fine corps of officers to carry out the manifold duties of an early surveying ship in waters so little charted that surveying was still part exploration. The surgeon, Dr Lyall, was an able naturalist, but much assisted in antipodean natural history by William Swainson, a painter who joined the ship

Captain John Lort Stokes of the *Acheron*.
*(Hocken Library, Dunedin)*

in New Zealand. Before photography, one qualification for appointment to exploring expeditions was the ability to sketch. Many of the people on *Acheron* made drawings and sketches; some are thought excellent still. But of the barque's one hundred men perhaps the most important to us was G. A. Hansard, supernumerary clerk. A member of the Hansard family identified with recording debates of Parliaments, fittingly enough, he kept the literary record of *Acheron*'s difficulties and achievements. Hansard played the role Abraham Coomans filled on Tasman's voyage, and similarly his contribution was not recognised for many years.

During the voyage *Acheron* spent some time in Australian waters. In voyages to early New Zealand most ships, whether exploration or trading vessels, called at some port in Australia, as Tasman's had at the very beginning. The Australian stops did not please *Acheron*'s men much, as they were not favourably impressed by the natives. There is a strong contrast between the opinion of Aboriginals given by journal keepers of the time and their opinion of the Maori. In this view they were supported by extant statements of Maori brought to Australia by whaling and trading ships. There was as yet no sense of shared injustice. On *Acheron* Hansard grumped that the Aboriginals had an unsatisfactory way of life from the beginning, one not improved by drunkenness and thieving habits they had picked up from Europeans. As a naturalist he was shocked by an Aboriginal hunt, in which they lit fires in a huge circle, leaving a flame-free opening in which hunters stood to kill the terrified animals. Naturalists were bound to deplore such wholesale destruction of flora, quite apart from fauna. As for the Maori, he thought the "tall, stately" men trod "the earth as if conscious [they were] born to subdue it", whereas the women, or at least well-born ones, "have elegant persons, and regularly formed features ...."

Finally, on 3 November 1848, *Acheron* left Australia for Auckland, still the capital of New Zealand. The officers were impressed by Auckland, not by the city itself for it hardly existed, but by the possibilities they correctly foresaw. Auckland was long emerging as the site of a major settlement. In 1801 Captain Wilson of *Royal Admiral*, while loading timber at Thames River prepared an excellent chart of its navigable portions, and of much of the Hauraki Gulf. In 1820 Captain Downie of *Coromandel* surveyed the waters of the harbour where he loaded his timber, now Coromandel Harbour. Samuel Marsden, pioneer missionary and explorer, was with Downie and the bustling missionary borrowed the ship's launch to enter today's Auckland Harbour, describing it as "a large river, in some places five or six miles wide." On the charts it still is a river. As well as Marsden, d'Urville and a couple of British captains had done some charting in the general area.

None of this had made Auckland a site for settlement, much less a capital. But the first Governor, Captain William Hobson of the Royal Navy, not satisfied with his out-of-the-way capital at the Bay of Islands, took Felton Mathew south to find somewhere more suitable. The first Surveyor-General, Mathew, a land surveyor, had done marine surveying and recognised good harbour sites as particularly important in planning settlement. Much of his time he spent surveying the coast for potential harbours. A delightful diary by his wife survives from his two month's surveying expedition around northern harbours, which she shared in the cutter *Ranger* in 1840. Unfortunately Mathew's maps of harbours have been lost or destroyed. Charting done on land by land surveyors could delineate coastlines even better than marine charting, and there was much co-operation between the professions. For example, careful and accurate surveying was of crucial importance in deciding locations for lighthouses. The siting of these landmarks, vital for men at sea, is not as easy as one might think at first thought – or glance.

On that trip Mathew recommended the Tamaki River area as suitable for settlement, although he admitted that "a serious impediment is that presented by the Bar at the entrance of the River which certainly renders it impracticable for large vessels." But small vessels could get in and for some odd reason he preferred the site to the Waitemata, which he described as "a secure anchorage, well sheltered, with great depth of water ...." In the end all these advantages made Waitemata the site of Auckland. In February 1840 Lieutenant Fisher and Mr Bean, the master of the *Herald*, which had brought Mathew to the area, made the first proper survey of Auckland and Waitemata Harbour, a "comprehensive survey of the harbour from the North Head to the vicinity of what they named Herald Island."

Wherever *Acheron* went the several surveyors charted harbours, shoals and shorelines from the ship's boats. Just as Cook had done elsewhere, at Auckland they set up a trig station – "a Pyramidal Surveying Mark" – where Devonport now is, for surveying the harbour. This was the beginning of the "Great Survey" of the New Zealand coast, from 1848 to 1855, actually begun in what is now Windsor Reserve, where a plaque commemorates it. The *Acheron* and later the *Pandora* together produced "250 fair tracings of various parts of the coast", surveying almost all the time, stopping the ship each half hour when under way and under sail. This meant the ratings had to shorten sail and then handle the cold wet deepsea lead line to take soundings. They always had to batten down and make ready for the heaviest storm every time they anchored off an unexamined coast. As New Zealand coasts are notoriously rough, lying at anchor involved tremendous rolling and buffeting, hard on ships and hard on men. Charlotte Godley, an *Acheron* passenger later on, remembered "a good deal of motion, from their stopping every half hour to take soundings, when of course the ship rolled as the sea took her." Often one finds in journals the comment that galley fires were lit, making one wonder how often they remained unlit, everyone existing on cold salt beef and hard tack. "Coaling ship" was dreadful: shovelling coal from an opencast seam, carrying full bags to load into ship's boats, pulling back through surf and then hoisting the bags on board. There it made everything dirty, upsetting both officers who liked clean decks and enlisted men who disliked cleaning decks.

Under steam or sail the survey went on steadily. Richards examined Hauraki Gulf and the Bay of Islands in the schooner *Albert*, no doubt named for the Queen's husband. One of the two second masters, Mr Smith, had supervised the dragging of the ship's decked boat – called the *Maori* – from the Tamaki River to Manukau Harbour, and surveyed those tricky waters. Excellent accuracy was attained in such forays, and some of the charting is still in use. Not being skilled in surveying, Hansard climbed Mount Eden while at Auckland to enjoy the view and decided, again correctly, that it was an extinct volcano. There were many Maori in the area and on their home ground Hansard contrasted born warriors of tremendous dignity, eager to prove their valour, with the Australian natives he had met. From Te Rauparaha, whom everyone found impressive, he quoted the old warrior's rejection of the virtues of peace: "I began to fight when I was no higher than my hip, and I will fight till I die." With such attitudes to overcome, permanent peace might be hard to enforce. Only a few years earlier Charles Darwin had written, "a more warlike race of inhabitants could not be found in any part of the world than the New Zealanders." British redcoats did not intimidate the Maoris; in one case a warring tribe had a good harvest of gourds and kumara and suggested the soldiers would make a fine relish.

Hansard admired the Maori but was not uncritical; for example, he did not think much of Maori living quarters. And at Wellington he objected to

A portrait of "Rangui" by de Sainson, d'Urville's artist, emphasising wavy hair and tattooing of the well-born male Maori and subtly pointing out the adaptation to European ways that trade goods made inevitable. *(Hocken Library, Dunedin)*

*Acheron*'s boats having to get water downstream from a Maori pa where "all moveable filth" was deposited in the stream and "the women constantly come there to wash their potatoes …." He also lamented the Maori's swarms of dogs, saying what Brunner had also claimed, that dogs were never killed except for the skins. Nor did Hansard miss what seems anachronistic today; the Maori were intensely acquisitive. As Hansard put it, and many contemporaries agreed, "their avarice makes them send everything to the market." Although they had resisted the drunkenness which plagued indigenous peoples in other colonies, they had a reputation for being "lavish in other expenses." The perceptive and analytical Hansard also saw changes: efforts so many Maori were making towards literacy; the increasing downgrading of tapu; and Maori allowing European medical men to cure and heal them in ways custom forbade. Nor did he fail, as so many did at the time, to see and comprehend percipient Maori worries about Europeans needing more land as farms prospered and spread.

*Acheron* arrived at Wellington only a week after the earthquake of 1848; in fact they had been sent there hastily to "afford assistance." In spite of her haste some surveying had been done on the way to the stricken settlement. Although England has had quite notable earthquakes, particularly in the 18th century, Englishmen tended to find them novel and exciting. Hansard described their effects fully, being especially curious about waves seeming to pass along land as if it were water. He marvelled that witnesses agreed that earthquakes stopped an atmospheric storm completely for as long as the earthquake continued, the

Jacky and Betsy Guard's house at the little whaling station settlement of Port Underwood in the Marlborough Sounds. *(Hocken Library, Dunedin)*

storm resuming when the tremors stopped. Hansard might have thought even this brief period of calm desirable, given their location: "calm weather is very extraordinary at Port Nicholson, where it seems eternally blowing." Whatever their reasons may have been, many of the officers thought Wellington much more interesting than the areas they had seen further north. And they could perhaps look forward to more earthquakes. Dieffenbach, one of the authors whose writing about New Zealand some of the officers had read, said that earthquakes were quite often felt at Wellington and "indeed, are often felt in the Middle Island."

Quakes were not only interesting but something of a professional hazard, and *Acheron*'s results could be negated by them. One in Wellington in 1855, "which raised the harbour bed hereabouts by five feet, rendered part of the surveys of Herd, Chaffers, and Stokes out of date." Herd had done a quick survey in 1826, on his way to Hokianga from his landfall in Stewart Island. Along Cook Strait by 1830 there were many whaling stations, whose boats found their way by oar as it were – at any rate without proper surveys and charts. The first chart of the Cook Strait area after that of Cook was the aforementioned one, drawn in 1826 and attributed to Captain Herd. He was a forerunner of Chaffers in more ways than charting, for the settlers Herd brought to New Zealand had been sent by the first New Zealand Company. Enthusiasm waned as they spent a month in Port Pegasus on Stewart Island, entertained by tales about the ferocity of northern Maori. In spite of this they went on, visiting Otago, Port Nicholson, the Bay of Islands and Hokianga, where they intended to settle, before giving up their project and going to New South Wales. The most lasting legacy of the expedition were good charts of these harbours by Captain Herd.

E. M. Chaffers was commander of the *Tory*, already mentioned as the 1839 immigrant ship which brought Dieffenbach, the Wakefields, Charles Heaphy and a company of lesser known New Zealand Company immigrants to New Zealand. Chaffers had been master in the *Beagle* with Fitzroy, Stokes and Darwin, and must have been a sound man. Presumably he had every chart of the area available, including Cook's and d'Urville's, and perhaps even the new ones from *Alligator* and *Pelorus*. He may even have had Captain Barnett's chart of Port Nicholson. Even so they picked up Dickie Barrett, a well-known whaler of the Sounds, to pilot them in. Immediately they began to survey the harbour and gradually charted other areas of Cook Strait, the northern part of the South Island and southern part of the North Island. Charles Heaphy made a very fine draft of the plan of Port Nicholson but probably he used Chaffers's work.

Captain Barnett of the little cutter *Lambton*, which had accompanied Herd's expedition, made the first widely used chart of Port Nicholson. Herd also drew one which apparently never reached the Admiralty. In fact the captains probably co-operated, and the charting and charts would differ only in draughting skill. Charts were certainly needed then. While d'Urville was actually in the area in 1827, a British battleship, *Warspite*, went through Cook Strait, commenting that "the Strait is not well surveyed ... the only chart of them being by Captain Cook of the *Endeavour* ... the conducting of a line of battle ship through such a narrow passage requiring ... the unceasing operation of keeping the lead going." That same month d'Urville also went through and did some charting.

A delightful view of Port Chalmers painted about 1850 from the anchored *Acheron*. *(Otago Early Settlers' Museum, Dunedin)*

Shortly after this John Guard came to found his whaling station, probably only the second established in New Zealand, after Preservation Inlet. In 1834 Mrs Guard and her husband in their ship the *Harriet* were wrecked on the Taranaki coast. The survivors were plundered by the Maori and some killed. The Guards were held as prisoners. Guard escaped in a boat, found a whaleship and went to Sydney to seek help and HMS *Alligator* was sent across the Tasman. Mrs Guard and the children were rescued, with some deaths and many inter-racial complications. But while it was at New Zealand the *Alligator* did not forget a primary purpose of the Royal Navy in the Pacific and accomplished a good deal of surveying around d'Urville Island, Port Gore and Queen Charlotte Sound. The name Alligator Head, at the side of Guard's Bay, is evidence.

*Acheron* next went south to Akaroa with W. B. D. Mantell, the South Island Commissioner for Native Lands. Several Maori chiefs, including Taiaroa of Otago, were on board to receive the purchase money for many acres of Maori land, freely sold after long negotiations. Hansard thought intertribal hostility apparent, especially with Taiaroa; long-standing enmity seemed more important than any disagreements about accepting money for land they were not using themselves. Mantell, who spoke Maori well, paid the recipients in gold coin and banknotes, and the only quarrelling which broke out was between the women of those who had not received much and of those who had. Human nature being what it is, the hotel keeper, Captain Bruce of whaling fame, did best of all; most observers thought that "of the 12 or 14 hundred pounds distributed that afternoon, full two thirds found its way into his strongbox."

A Maori village in Canterbury, Rakawakaputa, about the time of *Acheron's* visit to that colony. Note Sir William Fox's contemporary portrayal of Maori dogs. *(Hocken Library, Dunedin)*

Those interested in changes of Maori technique found delight in seeing Maori actually using their canoes. Hansard even saw a lateen sail, outriggers, and a double canoe being used! This was more than twenty years after John Boultbee drew pictures of double canoes in use near Stewart Island, where by Hansard's time they had been replaced by the more efficient whaleboat. Double canoes had long since been outdated in the north. The tiny French settlement at Akaroa, and the few Germans in the area, absorbed into general New Zealand ways, were very hospitable. Much more important were the excellent sheep being raised in the area, the forerunners of Canterbury lamb and the base of New Zealand's future. Captain Stokes acclaimed what he called the great southern plain of New Zealand, for he had not yet been to Southland. Rather romantically, and hence rather optimistically, he said it was "watered by a multitude of streams that like silver threads meandered on their seaward course." But his forecast of a bright future for the area was accurate.

Frederick Strange, the naturalist, his life in Australia inoculating him against dry weather and distance, responded to the Canterbury Plains. Taking ten days leave from the ship to explore, and following the Waimakariri River as far as the Torlesse Range, he found what he thought were traces of earthquakes, but more likely by his description a fairly recent rockslide. Seeing a rare kokako thrilled him and so did finding moa bones. Only days later in Otago, *Acheron's* master, Evans, found some distance inland the leg bones of a great bird, and assumed they were from a moa. Only a year earlier Mantell had found proof that moa and man had been contemporaries. In unexplored country travellers faintly hoped to see a live one. Not too many years earlier a whaleman, Jimmy Robinson, claimed to have seen a moa and never changed his story. As one can imagine, poor Robinson spent the rest of his life being told he had seen a vision or been drunk.

Strange scientifically described the South Island weka, the bush hen for which so many explorers felt the interest of appetite rather than intellect. At Pigeon Bay he found a beetle new to science, a somewhat unexciting duck and a brightly coloured lizard, which sounds like a gecko. Hansard's journal fully describes such finds by other members of the voyage. Not only was he fair about others' achievements but was somewhat of a naturalist himself, being almost certainly the man *Acheron*'s sailors knew would exchange a glass of grog for any interesting plant or creature.

While Strange was in the interior, Bishop Selwyn returned from the Chatham Islands and, hardly pausing for breath, set off to climb Mount Herbert. He took with him J. W. Hamilton, a remarkable member of the *Acheron* party, a geologist, skilled artist and draughtsman who spoke Maori fluently. Hamilton, with the ship at the New Zealand Company's expense, had New Zealand experience, and Stokes found him of help with *Acheron*'s charts, "besides making himself of use to the Expedition on every possible occasion." He had

## MOA BONES

William Williams, almost as interested in science as Colenso, shared his fascination with a giant bird. This had lived - and, some thought, still might - in New Zealand, and its past existence had been first discussed in a book by Joel Polack, published in 1838. A trader in New Zealand, Polack had been given some bones of a giant bird in the mid-1830s, when stranded in a damaged ship in Poverty Bay. In his book he stated that "a species of emu, or a bird of the genus Struthio, formerly existed in the latter island [of New Zealand] .... the natives added that, in times long past, they received the tradition, that very large birds had existed, but the scarcity of animal food as well as the easy method of entrapping them had caused their extermination."

A moa bone from the same area reached Professor Owen of the Royal College of Surgeons by other hands in 1839. From the examination of the femur the professor decided, after much thought and some indecision, that it was from a "struthious" ["of or like an ostrich"] bird. The Zoological Society of London worried about the bone not being fossilized, fearing a mistake or fraud. Nonetheless the discovery of the bone, with the conclusions drawn, was published in early 1840, and copies of the paper about the bone reached New Zealand in 1842.

In the meantime in 1838 William Colenso at Waiapu had been told of the moa and after constant inquiry was finally given bones which he recognised as coming from a giant bird, and of tremendous significance. On next encountering neighbouring coleagues Colenso found Williams and Taylor had discovered important moa bones in the area too, and had persuaded Maori to collect more. The missionaries agreed to send two femora and a tibia to Dr Buckland, a cleric, geologist and well-known scientist in England, whom Williams had known at Oxford. Williams's February 1842 letter to Dr Buckland contains the first written reference to the name 'moa', although Colenso's paper, completed in May 1842, used the name throughout. Williams wrote been secretary to Governor Fitzroy, Stokes's commander in the *Beagle*, which probably led to his being on *Acheron*. Hamilton knew Selwyn from earlier times and learned much from the Bishop, who had long since travelled through distant southern parts of his giant diocese.

Hansard found the local Maori leaving messages for one another scratched on flax leaves with a knife point, early instances of useful literacy. But neither numeracy, a traditional skill, nor the new literacy, made them into 19th-century English men or women. On one occasion some Maori women ran out from a village waving a welcome with their mats and blankets. Hansard quietly commented, "as the wearers had no other covering there was an unusually liberal display of charms usually left to the imagination." After some thought and much observation he decided some Maori women were relatively pretty but the majority, "reeking with putrid sharks' oil cap à pie, their faces bedaubed in alternate lines of red and blue, these venerable harpies presented an appearance truly diabolical." And in more than appearance, for like the devil he compared them to, they traded in temptation; when Hansard offered one tobacco she made very definite advances to him. Hansard fled because, like Russians twenty-five years earlier at Queen Charlotte Sound, he was repelled by women harbouring, in his view, far too many personal insects. He described in

in May 1842 to the C.M.S.: "I am sending home to Professor Buckland of Oxford, a box of ... bones of a gigantic bird ... upwards of six feet to the lower extremity of the back ... the probable height of the whole creature not less than sixteen feet [4.9 metres]." Buckland received the bones in January 1843 and took them to Owen.

Colenso in New Zealand and Owen in England both wrote scientific papers on the subject. The Maori had probably forgotten the exact form of the giant bird, and the bones, still being used for fishhooks, were ascribed to a fabulous creature called tarepo or moa. Colenso noted that the Maori "always obstinately denied" the bones were from a real bird. Legendary descriptions confuse the moa and the giant swan, also extinct. Dieffenbach, on his travels in New Zealand, was shown a tree by some Maori, near which, they claimed, "their forefathers killed the last moa." The missionary Watkin, in the South Island in 1841, recorded a fable "of immense birds which were formerly said to exist, and the bones of which are said to be often met with, but the oldest man never saw one of these gigantic birds ... ."

Bones were found by many South Island explorers: Evans, Master of the *Acheron*, found the "claws, foot, leg & thigh bones of a veritable Moa" in Otago and the officers debated "the present existence or non-existence of this gigantic specimen of New Zealand ornithology." Most argued that the moa was extinct: "A few however attached considerable importance to the Maori reports of its having been seen alive in the west Mountain forests of Middle Island."

"Moa" means hen in Polynesia. The giant New Zealand birds were probably named by moa-hunters with an ironic turn of mind. The name was remembered; where else had it come from? South Island Maori knew the bones were "moa bones"; but the bird itself had become myth. As a result moas created scientific debate in 19th-century New Zealand proportional to their size in the world of birds. Haast, Hector and Hutton, with other New Zealand scientists, devoted much thought - and perhaps even more words - to scientific description. They also argued their theories about the life, extermination and legends of the moa; it is a process not yet over.

shuddering detail how one old woman warmed her clothes until the lice crawled out to be caught and eaten. Great War veterans might understand her point of view.

Like so many Europeans before him, Hansard was utterly shocked by signs of cannibalism at one of Rauparaha's former camps, established when the old warrior besieged Kaiapoi. The captain might have told them of his 1835 Bay of Islands sojourn. Darwin said of *Beagle's* visit that "whilst at New Zealand we did not hear of any recent acts of cannibalism, but Mr Stokes found burnt human bones strewed round a fire-place on a small island near the anchorage ...." Hansard acquired a low opinion of Rauparaha, for here a local Maori told him of Rauparaha's men hanging a man by the heels to be butchered; "then Rauparaha make a beef." The conventional Englishman thought Rauparaha should be hung up too – on a gallows "loftier than that of Haimon."

Putting unappetising thoughts firmly aside, the explorers went on to Mount Grey and in its shadow enjoyed a gigantic stew of pork, pigeons, kaka, wild duck, quail, flour and potatoes. In contrast with so many then and later, they found no shortage of food at all; pigs in plenty supplemented wild fowl. Obtaining fowl could be a problem, as when a gun went off accidentally in one of the duck-hunting canoes and spattered Captain Stokes himself with some shot. Like his sovereign on occasion, he was not amused, but pointed out why in more detail. In this incident a modern New Zealand touch intruded. Although as undamaged as Stokes, a Maori chief, hit on the lip by one of the flying pellets, was indignant when everyone laughed. The chief sat unwontedly silent for a long time. Asked if he were thinking about his sore lip, he said, "No, I'm thinking of the compensation."

On the way home another chief demonstrated his rank, producing a very beautiful mere which blazoned, he said, a real chief. All the rest were slaves. To some extent his view corroborated early European opinion that the Maori divided into chiefs and slaves, with no one in between. Even this distinction was blurred. Darwin had noted: "Although among these savages, the chief has absolute power of life and death over his slave, yet there is an entire absence of ceremony between them."

At Pigeon Bay Hansard and some Maori discussed tattooing, already going out of fashion. But he had met a chief on Barrier Island able to make a complete drawing of his own moko without a mirror. When Hansard showed the drawing some 1400 kilometres further south it was recognised, and "the draughtsman's name" correctly given. And this although the southern Maori had never seen the northern chief. Darwin concluded that as tattooing was "a badge of distinction between the chief and the slave, it will probably long be practised. So soon does any train of ideas become habitual, that the missionaries [who strongly opposed tattooing] told me that even in their eyes a plain face looked mean, and not like that of a New Zealand gentleman."

In April *Acheron* moved from Banks Peninsula to Otago, seeing few signs of settlement along the way. A pilot greeted them at Otago Harbour to guide them in, a sign that civilisation had settled there. *Acheron* was to ensure the harbour's features were known to other ships, a facet of the publicity so important to real exploration and discovery. Charts were highly valued in those days. First, the ships were not as technically capable. Charting had to be thoroughly done because the 19th century, although one of startling scientific development, did not have today's technical knowledge or equipment. How the masters and pilots would have appreciated depth finders and radar! Second, the imports or exports carried on one large container ship today would have filled literally dozens of ships then. The far-famed American whaling fleet, 700 ships strong, which in the 19th century pursued and harried Moby Dick and his relatives, could not, all ships combined, carry as much whale oil as one of today's Japanese supertankers. Yet every entry or leaving of harbour, even by small ships, is an individual enterprise; each ship, large or small, must be piloted in and allowed room to swing at anchor. The book work was voluminous. One harbour visit today brings in the tonnage of perhaps ninety then, and so ninety bureaucratic or statistical entries would have been necessary then to one now. Fortunately for historians and shipping buffs it was faithfully done, at least in important ports.

Northern Maori had soon learned to charge for piloting ships to the best anchorages. Hansard concluded quite perceptively that they thought rich people fair game while the poor should be given what they needed. He often mentioned their generous hospitality, evident at Otago too, as well as that of the newly arrived Scots. Although Dunedin as yet had only about 120 houses, already the Taieri Plain was being cultivated, perhaps the reason that "Swedish turnips" were mentioned. Apparently the famous vegetable "swedes" of Southland and Otago had appeared, a savoured winter food for man and beast. But the local food varied. Hansard liked Nordic turnips but not another food Otago Maori provided, a stew of unplucked and uncleaned shags, plentiful then and now in the harbour.

*Acheron* soon went back to Piraki whaling station on Banks Peninsula to retrieve the naturalist, Dr Lyall, busy collecting specimens in the area. At the end of April the ship sailed from Akaroa for Wellington, on the way finding clouds at Cloudy Bay and self-consciously approving Captain Cook's name. Those charting either surveyed from *Acheron*'s decks or sent parties out with instruments to survey the coast. Somewhat later Commander Richards tells of surveying near New Plymouth "on foot, accompanied by natives to carry the Instruments. All the NW side of Cook's Strait is now completed ...." By April 1850 it was possible for the commander to claim that "as *Acheron*'s time is now drawing to a close, I suppose enough of N. Zealand will be considered to have been done for the next fifty years ...." Richards used a small schooner supplied by Sir George Grey to survey north from Auckland to North Cape. He had also done the south-west seaboard of the North Island from Waikanae to Taranaki. In both cases his instructions were "to do his best to acquire *correct* Maori place names." On occasion too, *Acheron* and its captain were able to take a stand on behalf of Maori who had helped the Europeans. Even so the Maori were swindled. Such a stand was the duty of anyone commissioned by the Crown, whether in the armed forces or in government positions, and on the whole they performed it. The Royal Navy was undertaking identical tasks in these same years on British Columbia's coasts the length and breadth of the Pacific away from New Zealand's, linked in this as by Cook's voyages.

Anchorages were particularly important at such places as New Plymouth on the extremely dangerous Taranaki coast. Evans, *Acheron*'s master, reported fully on the anchorage, suggesting a system of lighters and wharves to save establishing heavy moorings: "a boat may be launched from the beach six days out of seven, and the cargo boats worked five days out of seven on an average." It would need skilled seamen but the district had them. With some significance on this dangerous coast, Captain Stokes found that many Taranaki people were "Deal men", for centuries famous for handling small boats in the terrible surf on the North Sea's southern shores. Men from Deal built good boats as well as handled them and no better seaman settlers could be imagined for Taranaki. Were they chosen because of the surf or did they themselves seek the familiar roar of breakers on open beaches?

*Acheron's* officers not only surveyed landing places and harbours but sent explorers inland. Hamilton explored in Southland and in the North Canterbury hinterland, going over the Kaikoura Mountains with Lieutenant-Governor Eyre. Wherever possible *Acheron's* staff assisted shore-based surveyors working for the government, and they were to watch for suitable settlement sites. Hamilton was one who recommended the Canterbury Plains for the Church of England settlement.

*Acheron's* crew, and the officers in particular, probably books and certainly reports in mind, were very interested in the relationship of Maori and whites. Hansard noticed that many Maori women married white husbands and usually both of them lived happily with their good-looking and bright offspring. He speculated that Maori women were pleased to do so because of "more gentle treatment, good clothing, acquired habits of cleanliness and better food." Whatever the reasons for the original unions, many descendants of these marriages live in Marlborough, Southland, Otago and Taranaki today. Whaling brought the cohabiters together but by *Acheron's* visit to Port Underwood near Cloudy Bay the whales had almost disappeared, killing the industry in nearly every whaling area. Agriculture was to be the future and at almost any whaling station, working or abandoned, the ship could buy bread, fresh milk, eggs, poultry and pork. Whalemen had successfully blended much of their own culture with that of their wives, and the thriving children exemplified the successful mix.

In Queen Charlotte Sound *Acheron* was mistaken for HMS *Driver*, the first steamship to reach New Zealand. Just like the Russians a generation earlier the sailors picked up Maori artefacts at the Sound, more than they were able to elsewhere. And at Port Gore they encountered a bald Maori, something Hansard was astounded to see, and fairly rare even today. Nowhere do they mention having encountered elderly or middle-aged Maori who might have been children of Cook's, d'Urville's or Bellingshausen's sailors. It would be surprising if there were no bald men on those ships to leave their genes where inclination led them. Here at the Sound too they were able to compare favourably the taste of pigs reared inland with the flavour of pork from pigs which had scavenged the shore for dead fish, seaweed, shellfish and the remnants of butchered whales. Just as d'Urville had found at Otago, the shore-based pigs – as it were – tasted almost impossibly fishy.

*Acheron* proceeded to survey the north coast of the South Island, finally going west to the bay, now thought Golden but then still called Murderer's Bay from Tasman's experience of it. By misfortune or poor planning they reached there on Sunday, for the Maori were strict Wesleyans. As a result of doctrinal enthusiasm the ship's suppliers could not buy the usual poultry, vegetables and fish for the crew's sustenance and health. Here was something Brunner and Heaphy had encountered many times, as had Wakefield and Dieffenbach in the North Island. With convert fervour the Maori appeared as avid followers of one or other Christian creed. Here, with the split between Wesleyan and Anglican, Maori "conversation turns much upon points of doctrine." But Maori subtlety in disputation could sometimes relieve such situations. Once Dieffenbach encountered North Island Maori who refused to kill a pig or supply food on a Sunday, having "become missionaries of late", fired with the convictions of recent conversion. Fortunately one of Dieffenbach's Maori companions went off to a "a neighbouring Heathen pa … and came back in the afternoon with a pig." This caused an argument among the Maori, which a chief settled, for he, "although not yet a christian, was well read in his Bible, and proved to them that there was no commandment to refuse a hungry wanderer food on Sunday." *Acheron*'s sailors sadly missed such a perceptive chief, and went without fresh food.

There was better fortune with what *Acheron* herself required. Here, at the south side of the bay, they found the best New Zealand coal yet. A steamer in pre-petroleum days, *Acheron* had constantly to think of coal and it is not surprising that this survey party's interest in New Zealand's coal resources was greater than that of any other. Of course the old steam engines were relatively omnivorous; manuka wood was reasonably good engine fuel if coal was completely unavailable. Even so this dependence on coal finally meant the replacement of *Acheron*. The Admiralty thought the survey was becoming too expensive and, with some reason, blamed the steam engine. Where coal was available it had to be dug and carried to the ship, and whether done by sailors or civilians it cost money. Where there was no suitable coal, wood had to be cut, and this too was expensive. But given New Zealand weather and coastal hazards, sending out the *Pandora*, a small sailing ship, to finish the survey was a mistake. Already *Acheron* had showed the advantages of steam by towing an endangered sailing vessel safely into Wellington Harbour, and shortly she was to be saved by her engines from foundering in the gigantic seas off southern New Zealand.

*Acheron* worked in several of the harbours in the area before returning through the Sounds to the North Island. Visiting Nelson made the crew admirers of the thriving settlement there. The haven of Nelson, missed by both Cook and d'Urville, was discovered in October 1841 when Captain Moore of the schooner *Jewess* found the sheltered waters behind the natural boulder bank. Within a year or so Charles Heaphy had been there and, as a modern navigator sees it, his "delightfully engraved" chart is "a magnificent contribution to New Zealand's art and exploration as well as to its hydrography." Settlement, like the charting, had gone well. As had Julius Haast a few years later, Hansard, although not speaking specifically of Germans, thought the Nelson settlers "the most agreeable and warmhearted community they had visited in these islands." Both New Zealand cultures impressed him in that region. He was particularly pleased to see Nelson Maori profiting from contact as much as Europeans. In French Pass, on the way to the Sounds, Hansard saw very fine Maori carvings, both large and small. Several of *Acheron's* people seemed knowledgeably sympathetic to Maori ways and to evidence of Maori adjustment to the new world which had arrived without their willing it.

Across at Kapiti Island officers again encountered English whalemen with Maori wives, and whereas at Port Underwood they talked of what the Maori

## MAORI FOOD

In the North Island, even at the time of the earliest missionary exploration, pigs and potatoes were staple foods for European travellers. They mentioned birds and occasionally fruits but in general they did not eat Maori foods which had not been introduced by the missions or the whalers. In the south it was different, largely because the area was very lightly populated and people could still exist on what indigenous nature provided. This might have been more healthful. William Colenso found some mountain Maori whom he thought, from their general appearance and low death rate, much healthier than the lowlanders he usually dealt with. Yet he had found his new friends hard up for good food, as he saw it. "Poor creatures! At this season [with snow] they were all living on fern root, which the children were incessantly roasting and hammering; yet they were all very healthy."

Healthful it may be, but there is very little that attracts one about fern root. Even the modern natural food stores ignore it. The Maori had much more attractive foods to eat, at least in favoured districts. Perhaps Williams and Wakefield were less interested in food than was Thomas Brunner, Nelson explorer of the 1840s. Certainly no meals the North Island explorers described matched Brunner's choice on the Westland coast in 1847-8. "The rivers, large or small, abound in eels, hawera, upukuroro, haparu, patiki, parauki; the fruit of the ekiakia is then ripe, called by the natives tawara, and is very luscious, more like a conserve than a fruit; the honey of the flax blossom is also in season, called korari ... the natives also commence on the young potatoes and turnips, and make taro ovens of the mamakou, and of a species of ti, the stem of which is the eatable part, and is called koari; it is very sweet and pleasant to the taste." Brunner also described the preparation of the ti root after its baking in a Maori umu or oven, as we saw in Chapter Two.

Some of the Maori delicacies were not favoured by all the explorers. Colenso, at least according to his punctuation, was not favourably impressed with huhu grubs, describing them as "large, wrinkled, and of a dirty-white colour, with a black head. Some measure from four to six inches in length, and are proportionately thick. The natives call them, Huhu, and consider them a great delicacy!" With much the same reaction the officers and men of *Acheron* rejected the Stewart Islanders' muttonbirds, which were fat half-grown terns preserved as South Island Maori did birds and eels, by cleaning, boning, placing the flesh in kelp bags, pouring in boiling fat and sealing the bags. They are certainly an acquired, perhaps even inherited, taste. Muttonfish are shellfish. Hansard of *Acheron* saw "dark women" taking "muttonfish from their shells" to "string them upon strips of green flax, to be dried in the smoke of their wood fires." Heaphy said, "The muttonfish or *pawa*, although resembling india rubber in toughness and colour, is very excellent and substantial food for explorers ...." Muttonfish as a name has perhaps passed into history, but these seem to have been today's paua, for Best says paua are so tough that the Maori sometimes fermented them into a cheese-like consistency so that they could eat them.

women had gained, here they saw the advantages to the husbands. In front of a whaler's hut, "two or three dark women are busy extracting muttonfish [paua, an excellent shellfish] from their shells. Afterwards they string them upon strips of green flax, to be dried in the smoke of their wood fires." Hansard saw the Englishman dining, "waited upon by his wife ... tall, well-formed & having handsome, intelligent features ... [and] a beautiful baby, clean & well clothed ...." On the whole the English whalemen appeared to be "well looked after by their Maori wives ...." Another visitor emphasised that the wives were "extremely inexpensive too, their dress consisting of a calico gown and blanket, and their only luxury an occasional pipe of tobacco, the cost of which they fully repay by obtaining potatoes and fish, without charge, from their relations."

In October 1849 *Acheron* left Wellington to skirt the east coast to Auckland and the Bay of Islands. Prosperous Auckland so impressed the crew that they thought that many in Britain might be wise to emigrate to such a place. After repairs in Sydney they came back to Wellington. Shortly afterwards *Acheron* went down past Port Cooper, expecting its immigrants momentarily, and then on past Otago to Ruapuke, Johann Wohlers's small island mission in Foveaux Strait. On this visit steam power saved them from foundering in one of the immense southern storms of the area. The gale lasted five days, their coal down to a worrying level before sea and sky relented. When the weather relaxed *Acheron* went into Bluff to recuperate and various officers did some of the charts and pictures so valuable today. Minor expeditions went inland to cursorily assess Southland's possibilities.

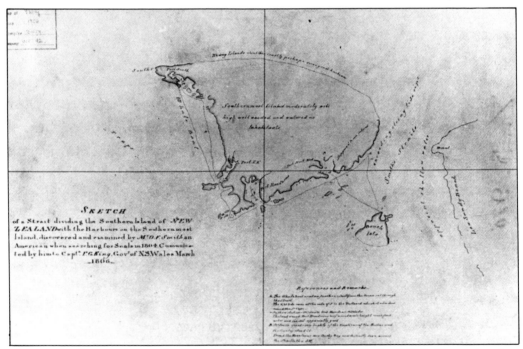

This "Smith Chart" is the result of the first exploration of Foveaux Strait. O.F. Smith, an American sealer, discovered the strait in 1804 and reported it to Governor Foveaux of New South Wales. *(Alexander Turnbull Library, Wellington)*

Very early charts of the area – and of a kind – existed. In 1803 or 1804 Owen Smith, an American sealer, had discovered Foveaux Strait. His chart, made from a small boat in a rough sea and naturally imperfect, portrays the main features quite recognisably. The chart still exists, in the Alexander Turnbull Library. By 1809 Smith's new passage was referred to as Foveaux Strait in Australian newspapers, named probably for Governor Foveaux of New South Wales. He was Governor King's successor, and had received Smith's rough chart. But perhaps the name accrued as sealers referred to it as Governor Foveaux's Strait, having the information but not its source from the Governor. For years the Admiralty called the strait Favourite Strait, possibly after the ship which brought Smith to Port Jackson with the information – and a huge cargo of sealskins – in 1806.

In April *Acheron* crossed to Stewart Island, where her experienced seamen admired excellent boats being built by an Englishman, mainly for sale to Maori. Muttonbirding was in full swing and not all Europeans approved, although this was no surge of modern conservationist emotion. It was aesthetic; a matter of taste, visual as well as gustatory. Hansard thought the birds, preserved in their own boiled fat in brown kelp bags, were "most disgusting objects with a rank rammish odour …." Visual taste had full exercise at the island. The officers enjoyed the chance to examine artistic tattooing revealed, after remarkably little urging, by an old Maori lady. Among several stories portrayed on her skin was a tale of an unfaithful husband who shot himself upon discovery, a remarkable work of art perhaps intended as a morality play for local society. If so it was not working effectively. The Maori complexions already ranged from light bronze to English fairness, which Hansard saw as a forecast of assimilation. And perhaps of attitudes too. A decade earlier Darwin had noted the northern chief who had hanged one of his wives and a slave for adultery: "When one of the missionaries remonstrated with him he seemed surprised, and said he thought he was exactly following the English method."

During a visit to the eastern coast of Stewart Island, at one stop the crew met a Maori who caught weka on the main island and turned them loose on a small island for later use: the beginning of poultry farming, or more accurately, as Hansard said, "in the true spirit of an English Game preserver." When *Acheron* took a weka aboard it soon jumped overboard and swam ashore; a woodland bird swimming in Stewart Island waters is a fowl of spirit and talent. Yet only one such fowl among many, for further south they saw seagoing penguins gambolling as awkwardly on beaches as the weka swam. There were seals about too, even a whale, a pleasant and fortunate sighting. By this time whales were rare in the whaled-out New Zealand waters; they are just beginning to reappear in numbers now, after 135 years.

Captain Eber Bunker, in 1791 the talented commmander of the first whaling ship to visit the area, had done some charting, including Port Pegasus. So indeed had Owen Smith. In 1809 that magnificent haven was surveyed properly by the first officer of the sealing ship *Pegasus*, William Stewart, after whom Stewart Island is named. Immediately afterwards *Pegasus*, under Captain Chase, went north to "Banks's Island" and "fortunately discovered before night came on that the island so called is really connected to the mainland by a low sandy

The *Deborah*, by an unknown artist. Captain Wing used her for many surveys and she carried Johann Wohlers to his mission in southern New Zealand. *(Hocken Library, Dunedin)*

isthmus ...." An experienced modern chartsman-author has wondered why a sealing vessel spent so much time charting.

In March 1826 Captain Herd in *Rosanna* came to Port Pegasus and obtained a copy of Stewart's chart of the harbour from Stewart himself, which he added to his own charts of New Zealand waters. And in 1844 another very active cartographer, Captain Wing, in his brigantine *Deborah*, brought the New Zealand Company surveyor Frederick Tuckett to the southern coast. Wing surveyed Bluff and the New River with Tuckett. Then the Company surveyor concentrated on land surveys and town sites and while he was thus engaged Wing charted the coast from the Catlins to the eastern approaches of Foveaux Strait in some detail. This fine coastal seaman not only did much charting of New Zealand waters but was still charting as Harbour Master on Manukau Harbour in 1886.

Bluff Harbour had been charted long before Wing's visit, by Robert Williams, a New South Wales convict who was also a skilled flax dresser and ropemaker. He was released, "a dangerous precedent" some thought, to be taken to New Zealand to find commercially harvestable flax for processing in New South Wales. Useful hard work was then thought to be reformative – and at the least the product might pay part of the penal system's cost. The party anchored at

Port William and went by boat across the strait, where they happened upon a large harbour, and probably were the first to discover it. Williams, obviously of many parts, presented in a well written report "a chart of the place as far as my abilities would permit ... plenty of water for vessels of burthen ... fortunately formed by nature to answer all our purposes for a large establishment." The convict exile was still able to say "our purposes" instead of "your purposes." His chart, sprinkled with decorative and flourishing flax plants, is in the Alexander Turnbull Library. Bluff Harbour was also charted nine years after Williams had done so, by Captain Edwardson, his schooner *Snapper* the first deepsea ship to enter the harbour.

By June *Acheron* was back at Wellington, subject to observation by the critical population. One lady thought the barque-rigged black steamer rather tublike, which in all honesty *Acheron* was, for in those days she was being compared to the strikingly beautiful clipper sailing ships, just reaching their highest development and fame. Indeed this observant lady thought much the same of Captain Stokes, "fat, with grey hair", though she did not compare him with a clipper. She came to revise her opinion of both ship and commander on closer acquaintance. On visiting the ship she found a competent crew dedicated to an important task which the officers, in a very modern approach, fully explained to the public whenever they could.

Soon the barque was away again, to Golden Bay this time. Here the surveyor Burnett led an overland expedition – which missed the most important coal deposits of the area. The notes of the survey trip somehow were saved when, in returning, the rough sea swamped their boat on the way to the ship. Burnett was drowned with three others, one a Foveaux Strait Maori boy who had resisted his family's pleading not to join *Acheron* for a life at sea. And the

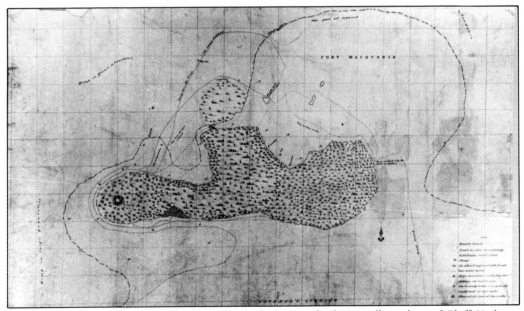

Robert Williams, a convict from the Australian colonies, made this excellent chart of Bluff Harbour when he visited there to lend his expertise to an assessment of the possibilities of the New Zealand flax industry. *(Alexander Turnbull Library, Wellington)*

officers and crew encountered tragedy vicariously as well. On the way back to Wellington the ship called at a whaling station whose owner's former wife had been a daughter of Te Rauparaha. Occasionally the famous fearsome father-in-law had dropped in as he took home, all neatly stowed in flax packs, some of his favourite "beef", a euphemism for an enemy's flesh. Even in 1850 the survey party, on an onerous and seemingly perpetual job, was armed; there was no certainty that the Maori encountered would be peaceful.

After nearly a month in Wellington *Acheron* set off for a complete circuit of the South Island, taking Bishop Godley and his wife as far as Lyttelton, so that the church itself would be in Canterbury before the settlers. Captain Stokes gave young Arthur Godley a puppy, "the grandchild of his own favourite pointer", and Commander Richards gave Arthur's father a pointer. From Cook's time on dogs were part of the complement of many a ship's company. On boarding ship Arthur had been met by the captain's bloodhounds and a large spaniel. Also on board was the Newfoundland dog Sailor, left behind in Wellington, who had recognised "his" ship when she entered harbour and swum out to meet her.

*Acheron* went all the way south. Stewart Island was not only for surveying but rest and recreation, in particular the officers' hunting expedition for wild ducks and weka. Superb fishing and fish of the Island waters were more to the sailors' taste. *Acheron* was held up for some time in Stewart Island but finally got away, taking a ship called *Otago* in tow, but not the famous barque *Otago* skippered by Joseph Conrad. At Port Pegasus they met Archbishop Selwyn in his tiny *Undine*, on the way to the Auckland Islands. The Bishop took his duty to visit parishioners seriously and at this time there was a settlement on the Auckland Islands, based on an English plan to revive whaling by locating it further south. A visit to Chalky Bay was marked by a tempest so black that at eleven in the morning it seemed as if there were an eclipse, followed by a violent rainstorm lasting several days. In fact the weather was so bad Hansard concluded that "no one could live here the year round." Yet in spite of such opinions Stokes recommended to the government that they ought to clear up the purchase of native lands as quickly as possible. In the far south many Maori seemed extremely interested in selling land and Stokes was keen to protect Maori interests.

At this time they met the famous Tommy Chasland, a half-Aborigine whaleman of immense strength and vitality, but most famed for remarkable eyesight. Many circumstantial stories seem to verify his ability to see further than most men using telescopes. He had another advantage over less far-sighted men, in both senses of the adjective. He had wooed and won to wife a Maori woman who was something of a tohuka, roughly "wise-woman" or sorceress, and who was known to have chanted karakia which imputedly calmed a storm and ensured her a safe voyage home to New Zealand. Chasland piloted *Acheron* as far as Dusky Sound, and needless to say did not mislead them.

At the great inlet the ship's company ate weka and in turn suffered from sandflies doing their best to eat them. This pest has not been conquered yet, and definitely had not when the surveyor E. H. Wilmot was inland of the area in 1897 seeking routes for trans-island roads. "Sunday here is a miserable day, entirely owing to those plagues the sandflies. One can neither read nor write nor sleep – cannot even sit down for a few minutes without torture. I think the idea of the Lilliputians tormenting Gulliver with their spears must have had its origin in a plague of the little wretches."

Hansard noted that kiwi in the area ate grubs and worms, kakapo ate grass and herbs and weka seemed to eat anything, including crabs, which gave them a fishy taste. Hansard's comment supports the assessment of other explorers. *Acheron*'s sailors used the ambitious dog Sailor to catch birds. "Sailor has taken to climbing trees wherever he discovers a bird …. Bolts off suddenly in the night – captures a woodhen – returns & lays it before the tent door, then again settles himself to sleep." Unfortunately he never learned to take live specimens. Amidst all the wildfowl they had observed, dogged, hunted, eaten and collected, they saw one mysteriously different, a bird "all colours." This might well have been a notornis or takahe, a giant flightless moorhen, eaten by early sealers. Described by Mantell but not sighted again until 1948 it is, needless to say, extremely rare.

In Milford Haven, now Milford Sound, with "cliffs towering on either side several thousand feet perpendicularly …", *Acheron*'s men enjoyed it when "the brilliant sunbeams refracted in the spray … all the rainbow's prismatic colours." All in all, Hansard thought Milford Sound "the most remarkable harbour yet visited by the *Acheron* in New Zealand." Not only Nature's beauty showed; the

---

## BIRDS FIGHT BACK

Dogs and other bird-killing mammals did not have it completely their own way; birds fought back as best they could. The kiwi would usually "kick and scratch or jump on the hand that is thrust into the hole to catch them", and presumably a dog's nose too. It was at least a show of defiance. And the weka's temperament led it to fight back. Harper claimed that "for downright impudence, too, the weka is unequalled, and no doubt this fact will help to preserve him against his new foe, the weasel … for if he sees the weasel first he will charge it …." Weka courage did not save them from skilled and persistent dogs, and this very pugnaciousness was a weka's undoing if it dealt with man.

The kaka, or brown parrot, could even sever snares with its beak, a frequent necessity, for it was the second most important game bird of the Maori, after the pigeon. Other parrots sometimes won, even against dogs. Many a dog found that the clumsy, rather stupid kakapo "can bite most severely …." Brodrick, a surveyor who travelled much in the bush, claimed he had known a kakapo "to sit in a hole under the root of a large tree and face a setter in such a determined manner that he could not get it out and was savagely bitten every time he tried." Harper, who would have known for he ate some of them, said that a kakapo "shows a great deal of fight before he surrenders." Even so, resistance did not save him or his species. This green and yellow parrot is now found only in Fiordland and Stewart Island. Heaphy, even in his days of exploration, thought the kakapo "nearly or quite extinct. This bird, of which no perfect remains are extant … was formerly to be met with abundantly in this district … and the natives attribute its extinction to the wild dogs. The European rat, which has spread over the whole of the country, in my opinion is more likely to have been the cause, destroying as it would the eggs and young in the lowly situated nests of the kakapo and kiwi."

ugliness of human aggression dwelt here too. They found tracks of some Maori of an almost unknown and very small isolated tribe known as the wild men of the mountains, refugees from persecution by the powerful tribes over the mountains. But writing in the 1890s, Arthur Harper, one of the surveyor-explorer-mountaineers of southern Westland, claimed that a chief of a defeated tribe led his retreating followers "into the inaccessible mountains between the Otago Sounds and Lakes, and there disappeared. Rumours of recent date point to the existence of this lost tribe even now, for fires are said to have been seen in the hills from the sea-coast ...." But it all remains a mystery to this day.

Now heading northward toward Wellington and official news, unbeknownst, Captain Stokes was near the end of his remarkable cruise. But by coincidence he had the chance to leave a name on New Zealand's maps that became part of the language to more than surveyors and sailors. *Acheron* called at Jackson Bay as they surveyed their way northward up the coast from Milford Sound. From the anchorage in the bay the entranced sailors could see a great mountain in the distance. So majestic it seemed, so obviously paramount, that Captain Stokes named it Mount Cook for his predecessor.

In spite of the strains of storm and the constant exertion crew and officers were in good heart. So was the ship; the boiler and hull were in fine shape. In April, after examining the *Acheron* thoroughly in Wellington Harbour, the Captain reported her sound for another three years. Other authorities, with other pressures and reasoning, intervened. In spite of the undoubted success of

A photograph of Pembroke Peak and the rock formation known as the Lion taken more than half a century ago at Milford Sound in South Westland. *(University of Canterbury Library, Christchurch)*

the survey, and all the good material sent home to the Admiralty, Captain Stokes received new orders: *Acheron*'s officers were to go home to England on another ship. The survey would be completed by HMS *Pandora*, a sailing ship. Stokes, well aware of the value of his work, which had been carried out "on the two great principles of economy and despatch", suffered "annoyance & mortification at being thus suddenly suspended from my command, and ... turned out of my ship at a moment's notice." Understandably, he spent much of the voyage home "shut up in his cabin", though he managed to survey the Chatham Islands' higher points on his way past.

All this may have been caused by the difficulty in getting coal for *Acheron*. Stokes, enthused about the future of steam, probably was overenthusiastic in his use of it, at least as the Admiralty saw it. The change was a foolish decision; there was urgency about the survey and *Pandora* took four years to finish the job. Stokes thought *Acheron* might have finished in a matter of months. There has been no doubt about the quality of *Acheron*'s work. The tubby little steamer and her crew had been successful, and even modern methods and resurveying have not replaced some of the charts surveyed by Stokes. As one modern surveyor sums it up, "the charts they produced were the result of long hours of hard work, skill, seamanship and keenness of observation."

*Acheron*'s successes were recognised. Naturalists had accumulated botanical and avine specimens of all kinds. Doctor Lyall, surgeon and naturalist, based a distinguished career partly on his acclaimed paper discussing observation of kakapo, and his collection of plants went to Kew to be used by Sir Joseph Hooker, who had sailed with Lyall to the Antarctic on *Erebus*. Many New Zealanders recognise his giant buttercup, *Ranunculus lyallii*, under its incorrect but common name, Mount Cook lily. Charles Forbes also wrote much about New Zealand geology. Commander G.H. Richards and the Master, F.J. Evans each became a Hydrographer of the Royal Navy, a mark of distinction. Captain Stokes could remember achievement on a cruise so shadowed by the loss of his wife, and then what seemed dismissal. He remarried and lived a happy life with no small accumulation of honours, as a Member of the Council of the Royal Geographic Society, an Honorary Member of the New Zealand Institute and in due time an Admiral.

Stokes worried about the Maori's future, his chief concern their inordinate "love for money" and, arising from this unwise emotion, their eagerness to sell more land than was good for them. Stokes thought more highly of Southland's possibilities than the surveyor Tuckett did. So the naval captain used his influence to have Mantell sent south to buy land for settlement, trusting an honoured public servant to deal honourably with Maori who established ownership. He hoped that *Acheron*'s visit would chart for New Zealand not only better communications but a better future for both its peoples.

Whatever the measure of Stokes's and *Acheron*'s worth they were swiftly part of New Zealand's past. *Pandora*'s main task was to do what *Acheron* had not had time to do. But the new ship would work and report in her own way. She spent much time charting Manukau Harbour, much more important than today because small vessels sailing from Australia to Auckland could use it, sparing themselves the long haul up around North Cape. *Pandora*'s officers suggested some interesting schemes at times. Her surgeon argued that eventually "the Waikato would be joined to the Manukau by a canal – which could be built at trifling expense." Estimation of people's worth seemed much less optimistic, and no more accurate, than of canal construction cost. An officer of *Pandora* also reported that Dunedin was populated by "very narrow-minded and quarrelsome sort of people."

In the main *Pandora's* trials were those of *Acheron*, writ somewhat larger because she was smaller, her laybys longer because she had to wait till, in Drake's phrase, "the wind commands me away." Stokes and his officers knew all about the dangers. Commander Richards was shipwrecked not once but twice during his *Acheron* voyage, on survey side trips in schooners. Coal may have been dirty compared with the white wings of sail but with coal calm was not as much a curse as storm. And *Pandora* had her dangers, her officers their doubts. In March 1852 she carried away her anchor in a gale in Kaipara Harbour and beached herself. The crew threw equipment overboard, trusting it would be washed up on the beach. It worked. By morning "good and valuable instruments such as chronometers and watches along with cocked hats, pigs, swords, and dogs" were scattered along the sands, messy but recoverable. Kaipara Harbour had been charted by Captain Wing in 1836 and in 1840 by Captain Chaffers of the *Tory*, but they had not imagined anyone examining the shore in such detail. Fortunately, and somewhat miraculously, in the early light the ship too was found beached almost as high and dry as the impedimenta. With much effort they warped her out into deeper water. After repairs at Sydney *Pandora* was back to her New Zealand duties by September.

*Pandora* settled into her routine of inshore charting. She was only a little brig of about 300 tons, a mixed blessing. Her surveying took longer, partly because she lacked the reliability of a steamer but mainly because she concentrated on detailed harbour soundings whereas *Acheron* often worked offshore. Although her commander, Byron Drury, lacked Stokes's drive, *Pandora's* work was ably done.

By 1855 the great survey of New Zealand was over. *Pandora* had filled in the gaps, even including "the islets called the Snares", discovered by Lieutenant Broughton in the little "armed tender", *Chatham*, from which the Chatham Islands got their name. She was *Discovery's* consort in the 1790s, when George Vancouver, former able seaman and midshipman with Cook, stopped at Dusky Bay to finish the charting his great commander had not had time to do. Actually both these ships discovered the Snares separately but it was Broughton's chart which was sent to the Admiralty.

This was not the end of charting, for it never ends in a commercial and civilised land. Supporting troops during the Land Wars, many of the warships did local surveys. When the gunboat *Avon* struck a hidden rock in the Waikato River, Charles Heaphy did a survey justifying his reputation as an explorer of Nelson province. In the days of peace visiting Royal Navy ships maintained their charting skills by performing useful tasks. *Wolverine* surveyed Port Nicholson and *Rosario* Tauranga Harbour during visits. Availability of charts was a problem; early European settlers cursed their scarcity. One ship searched eleven days for the entrance to Otago Harbour.

Having charts aboard did not always help; many were not reliable. One by Thomas McDonnell, though a lieutenant in the Royal Navy, "is most remarkable for its hideous inaccuracies and gross distortions." Admiral John Ross, who knew charting and New Zealand waters, thought that chart so inaccurate, not because of McDonnell's incompetence, but because he emphasised areas where he had land for sale. In other words, as Ross said, it was a "salesman's chart", suitably "salted" to attract custom. Few other charts had such a basis. Charts were so important that people used what they could get, and men with surveying skills did what they could to help. Many land surveyors, such as Heaphy, did a quick survey of the harbour before they surveyed a proposed town.

The importance of frequent harbour surveys cannot be exaggerated. Charts must be up to date because harbours, in that they constantly change, are living things. Bottoms fill and channels close as drainage pours in silt, a particular hazard in agricultural areas, where the harbours are usually at or near the mouths of rivers sweeping down the topsoil casualties of cultivation. Captain R. Johnson, Secretary of Marine and nautical advisor to the Government in the 1870s, did an impressive number of surveys. Gradually harbour authorities undertook the supervision of local surveying. By the turn of the century surveys were becoming fairly routine, moving beyond original exploration to become simple updates of earlier charting.

Inshore and nautical charting is, even if seemingly never-ending, the completion of discovery and exploration at sea. It is useful publicity revealing the results of exploration for constant use by a world which needs mankind's productions, the means to move them, and the knowledge to make movement easy, safe and swift.

CHAPTER NINE

# *Sound Titles*

Surveyors, sailors and sheepmen, rather than missionaries, explored the south end of New Zealand. As in the north, the few missionaries sympathised with the Maori, but problems were different in scale and intensity; there were no Maori-Pakeha wars in southern New Zealand. Few Maori meant less possibility of major conflict. As a result southern missionaries generally did not oppose Maori sales of land as strenuously as the churches had in the North Island. And for most European newcomers there was the pleasure of familiarity. Southern New Zealand's appearance was very much like Scotland's, and with huge areas of apparently empty fertile land besides. Men came in from the British Isles and sheepmen came over from Australia to make use of it.

Exploration by sheepmen in Marlborough, looking not only for runs but for routes to market, was duplicated in the Wairarapa. The creation of farms around Invercargill and Dunedin was certainly matched near Auckland and New Plymouth. But two things lent extra interest to southern exploration. One was the early discovery of gold. The other was the possibility of huge open untreed ranges or runs, more like most of Australia than like the North Island, except for small areas in the Wairarapa and Hawke's Bay. Another difference shaping action was the chain of huge mountains along the western side of the South Island, affecting Otago, Canterbury and Nelson provinces. The search for good sheep country and the search for good gold country was, will it or not, combined with discovering lakes and waterfalls and climbing mountains to find passes. All this made for exciting, arduous and dangerous exploration; people occasionally just disappeared. In some places it was easier because explorers could use horses. In others distances were greater and travellers had less Maori assistance than in the north, especially in supply. In the far south problems and solutions often were as much like Australia's as like Auckland's, or even those of Waikato, Taranaki or Nelson.

Sealing men and whalers did the first exploration, much of it simply round the coast as a form of charting. Some of this was important. Foveaux Strait, missed by Cook, was finally found by an American sealman, Owen Folger Smith. And in 1809 a sealing schooner called *Unity* entered the commodious and sheltered Otago Harbour, which *Endeavour* had not seen. Early missionaries came south because whaling and sealing interacted with the Maori in ways needing legalising or control, depending on whether the actions were in sex, trade or employment. The Europeans needed, as the whaling stations near Wellington demonstrated, to be weaned or frightened away from drinking, hard living and cursing. Many had been living for years with Maori wives without benefit of marriage, and Christian weddings and baptisms seemed called for. Bishops followed, Pompallier by sea and Selwyn by land. Bishop Selwyn's arduous and well-described walk in the 1840s was hardly exploration, but he, like the churchmen further north, was finding the best way to his flock. Early southern missionaries came because of sealing and whaling, and hence stayed near the sea, for even the Maori lived along or near the coasts. Only later did anyone go inland, and when they did the Church followed, setting up parishes which still exist.

There had been other visitors. Captain Herd of the *Rosanna* charted Otago Harbour in 1826. Dumont d'Urville had stayed briefly in Otago Harbour, and discussed only the whalers and the Maori – and the pigs – of the harbour itself. The Weller brothers examined basing agriculture on their whaling stations in Otago, and sent a Mr Dalziel, with Scottish farming experience, to explore farming possibilities inland. The Scot inspected country around the Taieri and Molyneux but did not think much of the rivers, the land and especially the harbour. Wellers abandoned the idea, but others did not. Johnny Jones,

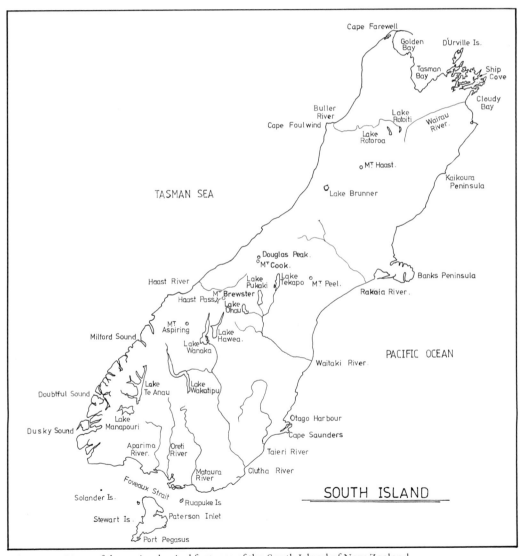

Relative positions of the main physical features of the South Island of New Zealand

222

another whaling owner, set up a farm at Waikouaiti to the north, the foundation of extensive landholdings. But farming, at least livestock running, developed faster at whaling bases further south. Captain Howell at Riverton had begun livestock enterprises which would make him, at his peak, reputedly the largest landholder in New Zealand. Pastoral and agricultural possibilities in the south were beginning to be appreciated.

In 1842 Captain Mein Smith, Surveyor-General to the New Zealand Company, in the small cutter *The Brothers*, explored land and harbours on the east coast of the South Island, intending to go far enough inland to assess all possibilities. The expedition took three months and reputedly did very thorough work, except perhaps further south. Unfortunately Mein Smith lost everything when *The Brothers* sank during a squall. Although he compiled a report from memory, it suffered accordingly. Deep southern exploration had been perfunctory, for Smith did not go into forested areas. A boat is hardly the best carrier from which to examine land suitability; and Smith did not see Otago's agricultural promise. The Surveyor-General did say a town could be built near the entrance of Otago Harbour, and like all early visitors he wondered at the wealth of bird and fish life there. Plenitude of birds and fish was not duplicated in people. Maori might be counted in dozens, not hundreds, and Smith thought no more than twenty Europeans lived there.

More exploration would have to be done on land. Dr Edward Shortland, the new New Zealand Government's Protector of Aborigines, came to Otago in 1843 to interpret for a court of inquiry dealing with various parcels of Maori land. With that settled, Shortland looked at Maori life in the south, visiting Moeraki, Purakanui and Waikouaiti. Augustus Earle, artist, writer and naturalist, went with him to Moeraki. At Waikouaiti Shortland had been astonished to find a piano and someone who could play it well; now he and Earle saw moa bones a whaleman had collected on a beach. Being on excellent terms with Johnny Jones, the highly successful whaleman capitalist whose piano had so impressed him, Shortland went on his ship with Jones to inspect his southern stations. From there they went on to Jacob's River, now Riverton, where the whaler John Howell was developing agricultural and pastoral enterprises. When he returned to Otago Harbour, Shortland decided to explore overland southwards to where he had been with Jones. He and Earle left the site of modern Dunedin, travelled the coast to the mouth of the Taieri River, then headed inland to the Taieri Plain. From Maori there he learned that most old Maori tracks were unused because whaleboats, cheaper than double and more seaworthy than single canoes, were now the favourite Maori transportation. Disappointed, the small party headed back to Otago Harbour.

After his extensive examinations of representative sections of the southern part of New Zealand, Shortland thought that "the only respect in which the northern parts of New Zealand can be preferred is that of climate; but this, although undoubtedly milder, is not so much so as might be supposed … from the consideration that the northern and southern extremes of land are separated by 13° of latitude." Shortland was right. In European terms the south's very temperate climate enabled production of all European foods, and even crops for which most of Europe's climate is too harsh. Until 1843 and Shortland's visit, very little was actually known inland. People stood on the top of Bluff Hill, indeed constantly did so to watch for whales, and could see the plains of Southland stretching off northward and eastward. But somehow they had done nothing about them.

In 1844 Shortland left Otago Harbour to travel to Banks Peninsula overland, something not done before. On the way he met a Maori chief, Huruhuru, who "drew with a pencil the outline of four lakes, by his account, situated nine days' journey inland of us … nearly due west of our position [on the Waitaki]. One of these named Wakatipua is celebrated for the "pounamu" (greenstone) found on its shores, and in the mountain torrents which supply it. It is probably the "Wai-pounamu" of which the natives spoke in reply to the inquiries of Captain Cook and Mr. Banks, who supposed it to be the name of the whole island …. The other three lakes … had formerly inhabitants on their shores, who frequently went to and from Waitaki to visit their relatives. Huruhuru … described the country through which the path across the island passed." The chief described extensive grass plains in the inland country, and told of the Te Puoho raid on the southern Maori from the north. The map is an important demonstration of Maori knowledge of the interior, made necessary by war and the importance of greenstone. Oddly enough on his lonely walk Shortland met another solitary footworn traveller, Bishop Selwyn heading south. The bishop took the meeting in his stride, confessing only that he "was not a little surprised." Selwyn was on his way to examine the southern people's innate and immaterial resources, intending to bring consolation for the consequences of approaching civilisation.

Finally, after the evidence was in, the New Zealand Company decided to found their New Edinburgh in southern New Zealand. At first the site was to be located near today's Christchurch, but Frederick Tuckett, sent out for an on-the-spot look, recommended Otago. He thought that for Scots it would be like home. A kind enough thought too, for Tuckett was an aggressive individual, belying his belonging to the Society of Friends. An excellent surveyor, fastidiously accurate and honest, he was appointed Principal Surveyor of Nelson in 1841. Three years later, commissioned to find the best place for the next settlement, he did not like Port Cooper's prospects because of doubts about close settlement on the Canterbury Plains. He moved on to Otago in the *Deborah*, and disembarked to look at the Moeraki district. He liked the area but not the harbour.

Tuckett walked to Waikouaiti to meet the ship, delighted with the district's pasture land and Johnny Jones's farm. On climbing over the high hills as he looked for a land route to Otago Harbour, he worried about the lack of good land in the immediate area but approved of the harbour. If there was fertile land just to the south then Otago would be better for farming than Canterbury. Upon examination the experienced surveyor concluded the area's land was suitable for close settlement whereas Canterbury's drier soils best suited runholders with capital for stock. Tuckett's decision about Otago was a fateful one, and in the long run thoroughly justified. He seems to have been right about the Scottish appearance of early Otago, for his friend and associate, David Monro, gazing at the country south of Dunedin a few weeks later, reacted nostalgically: "the swelling bare hills which rose around us reminded me very much of some of the pastoral districts of Scotland, Peebleshire, for instance

An early view of Port Chalmers on Otago Harbour. We look directly across the site of the modern container terminal. *(Hocken Library, Dunedin)*

...." Beauty, memories, homesickness, a new land and the old land in one. After a thorough examination, Tuckett chose Dunedin as the site for settlement.

Tuckett had not, like Bishop Selwyn, walked all the way south, and as he proceeded south by sea a whaleman on board assured him that the land inland of the Moeraki coastal hills was excellent. As this was true it indicated that, contrary to general belief, whalemen actually knew something of what was inland. For there is little evidence that whalemen did much exploring. They would hear tales of inland areas from their Maori wives, would have heard of the great lakes there. But apart from occasionally accompanying in-laws on trips, for example up to Mataura Falls, where lampreys ran at certain times, they seem to have stayed along the coast. John Boultbee, a sealer in the 1820s, travelled in the farthest south, and recorded his impressions thoughtfully. But with no effect then. His diary, with its shrewd comment, did not return to New Zealand until recently. Knowledge without publicity is of no use to the world.

Not every early resident hugged the coast. Tuckett learned that one whaler, Edwin Palmer, went by whaleboat for at least eighty kilometres up the Clutha River, and that another whaler had gone further up the Mataura. It was a whaleman who suggested to Rhodes his Levels run in South Canterbury. Reluctance to go inland was not simply boatmen's skills shaping a preference for sticking to their craft and using available water. Dense rank vegetation made overland travel difficult and unpleasant; occasionally wild pigs could make it dangerous. Besides, they would not have escaped water. Dozens of swamps in early Southland, now drained and fertile flatlands, made travel not only difficult but dangerous.

Early reconnaissances found good land inland, south and west of the mouth of the Clutha. In what is modern Southland, Tuckett went up the Aparima River for three or four kilometres. From there, as far as he could see "north-east, certainly beyond Tuturau, the land appeared to be one continued prairie, not low and flat nor much broken, but a fine swelling surface, slightly elevated, just such a surface as is most compatible with beauty and utility." If Tuckett could see today's beautiful and highly productive Southland, he would find his forecast utterly justified. Lime, time and work has made a retrospective triumph of understatement of his calling the area, "a fine grazing district." Millions of grazing sheep and cattle, recently deer too, have proved him right, far beyond his vision.

One of Tuckett's companions, the homesick Scot David Monro, having admired the Taieri Plain, certainly productive now, looked westward and "saw a great extent of country of an upland, but not mountainous, character ... its surface is singularly broken, lying in rollers or like the sea in a heavy swell." Further south, near the site of modern Balclutha, Monro realised that "an immense surface of country, admirably adapted for sheep grazing, waits here the introduction of stock ...." Tuckett did not go far inland but men were beginning to be tempted. The Maori told them tales of inland marvels, especially of four large lakes. At Colac Bay other Maori gave Tuckett useful and detailed information: "there is one river between this and Preservation Bay, with a bar entrance not accessible to boats; its source said to be an immense lake, from the head of which one may walk to Jackson's Bay in two days." This, told as he understood it, is roughly accurate.

Southern New Zealand seemed a rich area for settlement. Indeed it has turned out so. The land the Maori sold to the New Zealand Company, the Otago Block, was surveyed by the time the settlers arrived in 1848. For a while Dunedin was Otago, for few townsmen sent by the Company resisted keeping the settlement

Frederick Tuckett was a dour, uncompromising but immensely capable and energetic man. His surveys of southern New Zealand helped shape the lives of generations of people on farms and in towns and cities. *(Hocken Library, Dunedin)*

compact, cohesive and controllable, Cargill's dream of "concentration and contiguity." But gradually farms spread out, tracks between them became roads, bridges and culverts spanned the numerous streams. At any distance from Dunedin itself roads were tracks, and travel by land was almost exploration. Travellers sometimes strayed; it was risky to walk from Dunedin to the Clutha or north to Waikouaiti without a guide who knew the road. To Waikouaiti it was simpler to take a whaleboat. All through the late 1840s and 1850s people got lost in Otago and suffered greatly. The peculiarities of the New Zealand bush create risks even today.

By this time livestock men aimed to use these seas of grass. In 1846 Charles Kettle, a surveyor with North Island experience, came to survey the Otago Block. An enterprising man, Kettle later owned a Waitahuna livestock run, but at first he kept busy surveying within the Block's boundaries. By 1847 he found time to climb the Maungatuas, to see the Strath Taieri and distant Central Otago: "an immense extent of country stretching away into the interior of the island ... low, undulating grassy downs ... offering every inducement for the depasturing of sheep and cattle." This was all extremely encouraging and in February 1851 Kettle journeyed inland from Waikouaiti in exploration that matched earlier Wairarapa achievements. His party reached the Taieri Plain, followed the Taieri River north-eastward across the Strath Taieri. From hills there he glimpsed the Maniototo Plains, but turned to go out to the coast.

A month later Kettle and W. H. Valpy, the earliest sheepfarmer in the Waihola district, went from Lake Waihola to Waitahuna, following a Maori chief's directions. Valpy, whose father probably was still "the" Dunedin man of wealth, almost certainly intended further investment in sheep. The two men saw the valley of the Clutha River and beyond it mountains for many years after known by the name of the most prominent peak, Mount Valpy, bestowed by Kettle. It is tempting to believe that Australian goldminers later named the mountains the Blue Mountains after the haze hanging over them, so like that shrouding their namesakes in New South Wales. But colonists called them Blue Mountains, undoubtedly because of the azure film, for years before the diggers came.

In the same years in the northern part of the South Island stockmen such as E. Dashwood and Frederick Weld sought routes southward to the Canterbury Plains and new grazing areas in the interior. Moving stock along the coast was possible but slow and better routes were required. After great efforts, much danger and hardship, and some loss of stock, including the abandonment of a whole drove of sheep in 1850, E. J. Lee found a reasonable way across Barefell Pass from the Awatere to the Acheron and took a large mob of sheep that way into Canterbury in 1852. And in the North Island too, potential runholders were seeking out good locations, and sometimes suffering in the search. As usual they were in competition with surveyors to be the first to see new country. In 1852 John Rochfort, a newly arrived young Englishman engaged to join a survey party, set out from Wellington to Hawke's Bay, proposing to do most of the journey on foot. He managed to achieve this but went seventy kilometres without food on one occasion and suffered greatly from not knowing the tricks of the New Zealand travelling trade. On his arrival at his first Hawke's Bay homestead a Maori told him that of the few people who had previously crossed by that route "two had died of starvation and one had become raving mad."

W.B.D. Mantell depicted how the men carried food and equipment for a surveying or exploring party. *(Alexander Turnbull Library, Wellington)*

Further south there was activity too. Captain Stokes of the *Acheron* was favourably impressed by Southland. Intrigued by the promise of the interior, in April 1850 Stokes and Hamilton went up the Oreti River to explore, reporting that "a more desirable tract of country ... could hardly be found." Shortly afterwards Hamilton and another officer, Lieutenant Spencer, rowed up the Aparima River as far as Otautau, and in May these officers left Bluff to travel overland to meet the ship at the mouth of the Molyneux, now the Clutha River. *Acheron* not there, they pushed on to complete the first overland journey by Europeans from what is now Invercargill to Dunedin, greatly impressed by the luxuriance of "at least 600,000 acres of rich soil clothed with fine grass." Stokes recommended the purchase of the southern grazing districts by the Crown.

W. B. D. Mantell, son of the distinguished geologist and a fine scientist himself, and by this time Commissioner of Lands in Otago, was sent to do this. In 1851 with diverse and interesting companions of both races, he walked by land from Dunedin to Riverton, the first party to do so. Then he went further west and north to negotiate the new and important land purchase, as well as solve problems arising from earlier deals. On the way south Mantell examined the land and produced a clear and detailed report. He was extremely interested in the peculiar mosses of the Southland Plain, now almost disappeared. Mantell thought they showed promise as fuel, and might prove "to be of great value in a district so deficient in timber." These mosses often concealed deep swamps,

Lake Te Anau, photographed thousands of times since, but first depicted in 1852 in this sketch by C.J. Nairn. He and a companion called Stephen had gone inland to explore for grazing country and found good areas along the shores of Lake Te Anau, which they discovered and described. *(Alexander Turnbull Library, Wellington)*

some of such depth that tent poles over two metres long did not reach bottom. People who disappeared in Otago may well have sunk into these swamps: "in one part of Central Otago when drainage was carried out, the skeleton of a horse bearing a saddle came to light, and how many men and beasts were lost in them is unknown." The mosses reminded northern Englishmen and southern Scots of the "moss troopers", named after moss swamps in the border region of Britain. John Turnbull Thomson, of Border heritage, used "moss" as part of several place names when surveying Otago.

As Mantell examined Southland he recorded that grassland varied in quality. "I am inclined to attribute this varying quality of the grass not so much to a defective soil in those places where the present growth is inferior as to the herbage there having grown for years untouched by fire, exhausting the soil and rendering a longer period necessary for it to recover its fertility after the fires ... (tufts which remain show that the growth had been very heavy) ...." Resources varied in this south-western part of original Otago. Some had been introduced. North of Bluff Mantell encountered traces of wild cattle, descendants of beasts the whalers imported, and sufficient to satisfy cattle-shooting parties in the early 1850s. But another resource had built itself up for millions of years and now was wasting away. Mantell saw lignite already on fire and smouldering underground. He also saw lignite being eroded at "Waihoaka or 'grindstone stream'. This falls gracefully about 30 feet, shooting in 5 streams over a bed of lignite."

Men took trips about which we know nothing. Some important exploration was not recognised until the 20th century, when papers and diaries came to light, as families moved or the heirs cleaned attics. But enough was going on that we have sufficient information for at least an outline. In 1852 two white men, W. Stephen, of unknown occupation or purpose but who had come overland from Dunedin with Mantell, and C. J. Nairn, later a Hawke's Bay runholder, went inland, subsidised by the government. Mantell recorded that the two men had "resolved to start for te Anau lake in search of Mountain maids tomorrow. They have engaged Rawiri te Awha, a native of te Anau, and the only one who knows the way, and George Wera at £1 a week each without rations. I have volunteered to pay one of them." The "Mountain maids" referred to a beautiful female Maori ghost of the area, and explorers' oft-expressed wishes to encounter her.

The exploration party worked inland from near the site of Riverton to near Te Anau, finding some splendid grazing ground on the way; "first-rate pasture ... one of the finest tracts of natural pasture in the island." Indeed it has proved so. On the way to Te Anau, local Maori told the explorers that the Aparima River once flooded so badly after two days and nights of rain that two thousand people living along its banks were swept away. Invercargill's flood in 1984 showed the story may not be exaggerated. At Te Anau Nairn and Stephen were delighted with both lake and location. There is no doubt about what lake it was: "the length of the lake I cannot guess for it loses itself among the snowy mts to the north; from the mts to the southern shore I shd estimate at about 30 miles [48 km]; its width 15; it has a beach of 35 yds [27 metres]. The land of the Eastern shore is undulating with manuka scrub and high fern, flax etc., the soil very stony but well adapted for grazing."

Having found good grazing country and seen the famous lake the explorers turned for home, or at least home base. One substantial advantage of exploring upriver, as James Cook found on the majestic St Lawrence, was that some reward for the hard paddling upstream came from the leisurely floating down. Rivers in Southland are not extensively boatable because of rapids and shallows,

The mokihi or rush rafts, used by the Maori for centuries because they could be constructed of easily found materials, proved of great value to travelling Europeans. *(Alexander Turnbull Library, Wellington)*

but even such rivers are navigable enough for rafting downstream. Many explorers who tramped up, in, or along the rivers, forcing their way through scrub, criss-crossing streams and fording tributaries, floated back comfortably on Maori mokihi, rafts made from flax seed stalks, profusely erect in the river swamps. Such at least was the theory. Nairn and Stephen fought through "a long dispute with Natives who wanted to go down the river Waiau in Mokis." The Europeans flatly refused to float to the coast on a flax-stalk raft. They were more nervous than need be, as experience of many others showed, but there were real dangers in the swift and shallow rivers. Mantell, who had used mokihi, warned that "the principal danger arises from the innumerable snags, the slightest touch of one in such a rapid stream being sufficient to tear a moki to pieces."

Central Otago rafting provides longer and more exciting rides than anything a Foveaux Strait stream could show, as Nathanial Chalmers found. Chalmers had been in Otago briefly, then in Australia at the diggings. Tiring of that he returned in 1853 with the first shipload of sheep to be successfully landed in Southland, at the New River. He intended to take up land. For experience, and to scout out the best areas, he helped "Surely Surely" McDonald drove the pioneering mob of cattle from the Aparima to Dunedin. On the way he met Reko of Tuturau, and the old chief, in return for a three-legged pot, agreed to help him explore northward. The same pot can still be seen in Southland. Reko was very co-operative in giving information to potential settlers visiting his pa, and was probably the person who drew the maps and gave information about the interior to Mackenzie, the emigrant Scot famous for his ox, his dog and his wayward habits with other men's sheep.

After delivering this long-lived pot, Chalmers went northward in September 1853, with Reko as guide and another Maori, called Kaikoura because he had run away from there, probably to the district's benefit as well as for his own. The party travelled lightly, living off the country, Chalmers with a gun, salt and a blanket, the Maori with two spears and a large fish hook fastened to a stick for catching eels and weka. The gun provided many ducks, still common enough for easy shooting. The walking was usually easy but when Chalmers thought the grass and scrub "too long for walking in comfort I out with my flint and steel and set fire to it." Chalmers' party went up the Mataura and on the sixth day he "climbed a very high jagged range alone, and saw a lot of water and snowy mountains a very long way off in the distance about north-west." Back in camp Reko told him, "That water that you saw was the Wakatipu water." He assured Chalmers they would soon reach the river draining the lake, and cross it "by a bridge of stone." Next day they reached the river and crossed it, as promised, by a bridge of stone left as the river carved its gorge.

The tiny expedition pushed on in spite of Chalmers' battered feet, now of necessity shod only in flax or cabbage-tree leaf sandals, "the latter far and away the more durable." They reached Lake Wanaka "very tired but still getting ducks and eels ...", and when Chalmers ate them he thanked his foresight, no doubt Heaven too, for salt. At Lake Hawea Chalmers, not surprisingly as he was ill, "felt too fagged to proceed further." Although Reko assured him they were only two days' walk from the Waitaki via the Lindis Pass, the worn-out would-be runholder decided he "had had enough." They made a "korari raft" (the dried stems of the native flax plant) and paddles to deal with the Clutha "and paddled down the river so rapidly" that Chalmers "could hardly credit our speed." At the Cromwell Gorge he was frightened, but many years later remembered admiringly that "those two old men seemed to care nothing for the current." Once through the gorge they floated to the lower Clutha country and relative civilisation with ease. Chalmers was almost certainly the first European to see the three beautiful lakes, a fine if arduous achievement.

---

## WHO WAS MACKENZIE?

James Mackenzie, for whom the Mackenzie Country is named, became famous for stealing sheep from Canterbury runs and droving them south through unknown country, and as the discoverer of the two million acres of grazing land between the foothills and the Southern Alps. The best student of the matter concluded that Mackenzie stole sheep "with the idea of founding a run in his own name", not to sell to dishonest Otago runholders. It is even less likely that he stole to prove something about Canterbury's social system. In fact he was stealing sheep before the big Otago runs were even founded; there is nothing romantic about the man.

Mackenzie probably came to New Zealand in 1851 from Australia, having originally left Scotland for Scotland's good, and was described by a runholder, who knew him well, as a "tall, sinewy Highlander, and one who could talk Gaelic better than English." Men who knew him were seldom favourably impressed: "a big, raw-boned Highlander, rough as you make them – regular barbarian – there is no other name for him ... our friend began to undress and coolly to take off his nether garments to dry them before the fire ... and seemed to ignore the presence of a lady in the room .... This man was a regular scamp ...."

Mackenzie's route to and through the interior is not certain to this day, but it had taken skill and enterprise to work out its use for sheep, even someone else's. Keeping it secret violated the code of exploring, for the Maori knew the country but did not yet think in terms of sheep movement. The Maori chief Reko, so forthcoming with his knowledge of the interior of Otago for Thomson and other explorers, probably drew maps and told Mackenzie about the interior. Maori knowledge of the Mackenzie country came from often going there for the plentiful weka, ducks or eels, usually in the late autumn when these were fattest. An early settler in the area thought "there must have been abundant food in the stunted tussocks to support such a dense bird population, food such as grubs, slugs, caterpillars, and insects." Maori forced by low food supplies who went in midwinter sometimes came to grief and perished in heavy snow. They had not hidden their knowledge; the chief Huruhuru told Shortland "that there were extensive plains in the interior of this part of the island, similar to which we are now traversing ...." Shortland thought the area "no doubt well adapted to pasture sheep" and foresaw meat and wool transported to the coast and beyond.

The wonder is that the Mackenzie plains were not found sooner; the pass to them is a good landmark for vessels coming into Timaru. Mackenzie's dishonest exploitation of his secret knowledge caused his conviction and jailing for theft. An entirely unjustified Robin Hood myth has grown up about the man, a doubtful reputation of supercanine skill about his dog, and a more accurate one about his imaginative use of pack oxen.

Before Mackenzie had become notorious one of J. T. Thomson's surveyors in Southland saw plates and other furnishings sufficient for four people in his hut. This may have indicated collaborators. This has not been confirmed, and indeed one of Mackenzie's claims to fame, if that is the word, is that he – and his ox and dog – managed so much by themselves. In spite of his dishonesty and general unpleasantness he was obviously a competent stockman, an explorer for usable droving routes, and an individual of some enterprise and energy. People have given much credit for unusual ability to his dog but those who used the dog after Mackenzie was out of circulation found nothing really remarkable about it.

Mackenzie was of innovative mind. A contemporary, who did not like him, admired this quality: "Mackenzie's method of exploring with a bullock instead of a horse was original and ingenious, as he crossed rivers hanging onto its tail and he used it as a pack-animal to carry his provisions, blankets and tent." Oxen did not stray at night to the distances horses did, and they were patient and strong. The pack saddle "was fixed on with girths, the same as a riding saddle, and creels (baskets flat on the inside and round on the outside) were fixed on each side of the bullock. Waterproof covers were on top of the creels."

A quite typical New Zealand sheep dog in appearance, this dog called Friday, at least by the station on which he lived after his notorious master's capture, was said to have guided and guarded the sheep on the Mackenzie raids. In this case renown is based on reputation and legend rather than remarkable appearance. *(Mrs A.E. Woodhouse, Timaru)*

Mackenzie was finally caught in the act, captured, and after some resistance – and temporary escapes – was brought to court. Once he fled in the night, when his captors had kindly released his bonds so he could sleep. Mackenzie confessed later that if he had slept with his boots on he would have got clean away; without boots he was helpless on ground all prickly with matagouri scrub, the dreaded wild Irishman. Out of evil comes good for some. Mackenzie's raid and capture focussed the attention of potential livestock men on South Canterbury, and "various parties of one or two men secretly slipped away in the year '56 to explore the great sheep country in the south."

Writers have argued that "we must admire the boldness of his conceptions, the excellence of his mountain knowledge, the extent of his plainscraft and the daring of his explorations." There is some truth and sense in that. But a modern lawyer thought Mackenzie a "real genius" and hoped that a writer was "treating him kindly and not allowing either a family feud or a sheepfarmer's unreasoning predjudice against sheep-stealing to blind him to his outstanding qualities." The genius got caught. And few sheepfarmers would agree that it is less reasonable to wish to keep their legal means of livelihood than for lawyers to protect files or petty cash boxes.

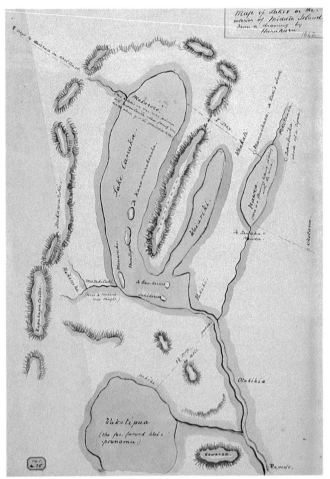

The three scenic great lakes of Otago from a drawing by Huruhuru, a Maori chief. *(Hocken Library, Dunedin)*

By this time intending runholders constantly travelled the interior of Otago. Edward McGlashan explored inland from the Otago Block in early 1854. Although he did not reach the valley of the Clutha he found extensive plains of excellent grass, and almost simultaneously R. A. Wight, penetrating to the north-west of Popoutunoa, found good wood and grass country. Combination of grass and timber was fairly rare in early Otago and was important because wood was essential for fuel, housing and fencing. Of what there was, much was lost by burning to clear scrub or dead grass. One such incident involved Chubbin, McFarlane and Morrison who were following up Maori reports of great interior lakes and had gone up the Mataura and finally reached Lake Wakatipu. "One of our party carelessly dropped a lighted match into a tangle of grass ... the flames spread with lightning rapidity, and soon a great fire was raging all around .... I led the packhorses in until only their heads were out of the water ....the roaring of the fire was so loud we could not speak to one another to be heard .... In fancy yet, after fifty years, I can hear the flames roaring and crackling and see the terror-stricken birds ... little native quails fared badly, and I should say that hundreds perished .... It was three hours before we got out of the 'bath' we were having." John Chubbin was a Manxman who came to New Zealand through Australia in 1855, and down to Otago. On a walking tour with a companion to select runs they chose country which included part of the land the sheep stealer Mackenzie had intended to stock with stolen sheep.

Carelessness with fires as shortcuts in clearing land was matched in other ways, and not confined to explorers or the outback, for even the government was keen for cheap and quick returns. In 1855 a mysterious Dr G. F. R. Schmidt, a German scientist and geologist, arrived in Otago from the North Island with grandiose plans to discover not only good sheep and cattle country but a practical route to the west coast. Perhaps taken in, perhaps merely gambling, the Otago government gave him some money. Schmidt went south to Stewart Island, up the Waikawa and finally disappeared forever, presumably in the dense tangle of the Waikawa Tautuku bush. Although the government had approved his mission, no one knows much about his motives or means. If he discovered anything no one is likely to ever know, and his efforts were as useless to world knowledge as those of an accidental voyage.

Doctor – if indeed he was – Schmidt was but an incident, or an accident, in the scramble to find and exploit resources. But few would set out heartily to build flocks and fences, herds and houses, without sound title to the land they found exploitable. As important as discovery, delineation is the foundation of title. Ever since the repeated springtime surveying of the silted wheatlands of ancient Egypt had created mathematics, surveyors have been primal travellers in new lands.

John Turnbull Thomson, of Northumberland, Singapore, Dunedin and Invercargill, once explained the urgent purposes of surveying in the colonies. These were to enable description and positioning of the resources of the colonies fully by the use of charts and maps. In a sense it was a slight step further than such exploration as Sir Julius Haast's, even if somewhat earlier. But it is very difficult to draw a line, if the profession will forgive the phrase, between surveying and exploring. John Turnbull Thomson is known to history as Mr Surveyor Thomson, but he did a great deal of exploring. Charles Edward Douglas is known to history as Mr Explorer Douglas, but he was employed to survey what he explored. It is a matter of emphasis; surveying emphasises the charting of what has been found, whereas exploring emphasises finding routes and resources worthy of charting.

One of the best of surveyors, John Turnbull Thomson, was born on a farm in Northumberland, although of a Lowland Scottish family. On his grandfather's farm, Earnslaw, north of the border, his grandfather James Thomson developed the Border Leicester sheep in the 1790s, to be big, bold and beautiful like the New Zealand countryside in which they flourish best. So even before birth the surveyor had an early connection with New Zealand, and the name *Earnslaw* is still used, on a steamship carrying tourists on Lake Wakatipu in Otago, where Thomson did so much of his work. He never forgot his origins. Lindis Pass, Mount St Bathans, and many others evoking North Britain as Thomson knew it, are still Otago and Southland placenames.

Thomson flourished, as many colonials did, because of sound North English and Scottish education. He passed the special course of mathematics in Aberdeen, which always served young colonials well. Then, at the age of a modern fifth-former, Thomson set off for Malaya to survey the huge estates of a large company. In Malaya young Thomson worked hard for four years, learning local languages and finding, to his great profit, an interest in differing cultures. His work, and a reputation for getting along with people, won such respect that the ancient and imposing East India Company, employer of Clive and Wellington, appointed him its surveyor at Singapore. At the age of twenty-one Thomson was a figure of some importance in the foundation of what today is a leading South Asian state. Creative drive in the area suited the young and ambitious surveyor. He won professional success and enough wealth to retire to his beloved Northumberland in his early thirties. Fortunately for New Zealand his health commanded a change of climate and his nature demanded creative work. New Zealand offered both and he landed in Auckland in the summer of 1856.

Thomson toured the provinces to pick his new home, and selected Otago for its cool climate and opportunities for surveying and development. Any provincial government saw such an experienced man as a catch; and "through the intervention of his friend, Sir Francis Dillon Bell, he was persuaded to accept the position of Chief Surveyor of Otago, which he retained till 1873." Otago then included Southland. This virgin and desirable territory was almost the size of Scotland; practically all of it, a wealth of resources, was uninhabited.

Thomson's descriptions of working conditions in early surveying, by themselves make his writing worthwhile. Because he worked mainly in pastoral Otago he was not frequently discussing the hardships of forest and famine that Haast often knew, although he encountered them at times. What Thomson portrayed were normal working conditions of early colonial surveyors, the conditions which any pioneer traveller faced, all the more interesting for being a distortion of normality rather than the daytime nightmares some explorers survived. Thomson's details of daily life and work evoke the period: "the Colonial Surveyor in these regions is clothed in fustian trousers and blue shirt, Panama hat, and stout hob-nailed shoes." Except for the hat, this does not sound too unlike what English labourers wore then. It was definitely unlike what Arthur Harper, thirty years later, said he wore on the glaciers and mountains of Westland: "I find the best costume to be flannel shirt, woollen jersey, and thick knitted woollen drawers – without trousers ... flannel or wool next to the skin, owing to the constant wet, and woollen garments underneath trousers are too hot for my comfort .... After a few months one may be said to be wearing a number of patches connected together by woollen material!" Coastal Otago was not so harsh as to require nor so lonely as to permit such self-preserving informality.

If Thomson's "Colonial Surveyor" smoked, and most did, he managed with "foetid negrohead through a 'cutty' pipe .... He has a hundred things about him; knives, needles, telescopes, matches, paper, ink, thread and buttons ... in all corners of his dress; and then his 'swag' contains his tent-blankets, and change of clothes. These with his theodolite he carries on his back, and walks away through bogs, 'creeks' and scrubs, at the rate of 3 miles an hour. He cleans his shoes once a month with mutton drippings, and he lives on 'damper', salt junk, and oceans of tea." Fires for tea could be risky. Arthur Harper, an explorer and surveyor in Westland somewhat later, came cheerfully into camp one evening looking forward to his "comfortable little shelter and dry clothes [but] found only a wreck. The batwing and a corner of the fly had been burnt .... In one corner a heap of ashes, a button or two, and a large hole in the scrub bedding, were all that remained of my dry clothes. This was the crowning disaster of an unlucky expedition."

Thomson was enough of the English gentleman to note that the New Zealand surveyor could not to be singled out from his chainmen. "In this land of equality he shares bed and board with his men, but they are not of the common sort, for 'the service' is popular amongst the enterprising colonists ...." These were men and this was work any farmer, hunter, or even weekender can understand today, with the thrill of "firstness" in it too. Thomson was describing conditions of work in the final stage of exploration, a very important stage, for just afterwards – and indeed before in some cases – came pioneer settlers actually mining minerals, running sheep and exporting wool. Their sweat, thought and energy paid the taxes with which infant colonial governments lured in skilled solid second-stagers to build an economy on the sweated gritty foundations early settlers laid. But flourishing economies can only be built on sure and safe title. That is why surveyors came so early to new lands – to become explorers perforce.

Thomson did his first Otago trip in 1856. A major difference between travel here and as Wakefield or Brunner knew it was that Thomson and his assistants could confidently go on horseback. Except for odd patches they were not faced with the bush dreaded by explorers and surveyors further north. Thomson was able to wear flannels and strong tweeds, watertight shoes, and forage cap. He carried his "blanket and spare clothing in an oiled cloth strapped to the pommel of my saddle. Here I also put my theodolite stand, carrying the instrument in its box on my shoulders. I had purchased a small hardy mare to carry me and my provisions; thus equipped I could be out alone for five days at a time, to reconnoitre right and left from the camp." They were lucky to have a horse each. Later surveyors, usually under-supplied, often had only one horse between them. John Holland Baker, who became chief surveyor for the shortlived Southland province, described the system of "riding and tying" in Canterbury. "First I rode for a mile or two, tied the horse up to a bunch of flax, and walked ahead, then the other man following came up to the horse, jumped on, and rode past me for another mile or two, and so on. It is surprising how much ground one can cover in this way." It is a good system; even the horse gets a rest periodically.

Without having to Ride and Tie, Thomson and his companion rode south to spy out the land, staying with such settlers as convenient, or in the primitive roadside inns. At Tuturau, a Maori village near present-day Mataura, he found that in 1837 the great Otago chief Tuhawaiki had defeated the Cook Strait Maori who had come down the West Coast and through Haast Pass. Reko, the chief at Tuturau, had already guided Nathanial Chalmers to Lake Wakitipu. Reko also told Thomson the route over the Lindis Pass from Otago to Canterbury, another example of Maori knowledge of which, naturally, all surveyors and explorers availed themselves. Knowledge of routes and resources was important. But each culture used the knowledge for its own purposes and had always to check and assess it completely for the different ends they had in mind.

Thomson described the visit to Reko's home fully, including a harrowing description of a slave girl and the life she led. As an honoured guest he was treated to a haka or war dance. Reko, who had fought in war, knew the haka well. "The dance, if such it may be termed, was done in a sitting posture, and consisted of movements of the arms, with grimaces and contortions of the face, extrusions of the tongue, and loud, savage whoops. At the time he had worked himself up to the climax of fierce ravings, he approached my companion with the most diabolical threatening aspect calculated to quail the stoutest heart. He stood as if to strike him dead, but my companion moved not a muscle: he sat still and met the excited, savage eye with calmness ... and the savage sank down before him, exhausted with his exertions. His countenance altered to its former good-nature, and he resumed his friendly position on the opposite side of the fire." In this description of the effect of war dances on Maori warriors, a generation later than even Russian accounts, Thomson depicts exactly what English, French and Russian explorers had seen.

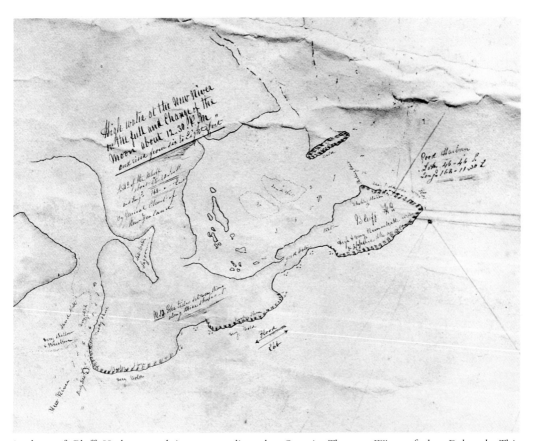

A chart of Bluff Harbour and its surroundings by Captain Thomas Wing of the *Deborah*. This captain left informative charts of very many New Zealand harbours, with marginal notes of local conditions of great value to other mariners. (*Otago Early Settlers' Museum, Dunedin*)

## TRIANGULATION

Much New Zealand surveying was done by triangulation, a system invented in Holland in the 17th century but perfected in 19th century British India to survey large completely unsurveyed areas. Several prominent New Zealand surveyors had worked on the Indian Survey, notably John Turnbull Thomson of Otago and G. J. Roberts of Westland.

John Baker, who had worked with Thomson, quoted a report written by that excellent surveyor when they were trying to straighten out problems with the Canterbury survey. "The initial station of the Foundation Surveys of Canterbury is on Mount Pleasant, an eminence situated above the harbour of Lyttelton. The true bearing from thence was supplied by the officers of the *Acheron*, Admiralty Marine Surveying Ship; this was in about the year 1849. In the year 1849, a base line was measured on the plains near Riccarton in length 20,469 links, and on this a net work of triangulation of 2 to 3 miles sides was carried from thence northwards to Oxford and southward to the Rakaia .... In the maps there is no proof that any attempt had been made to carry on the true bearing from the initial station ... and there is seldom any evidence of how the lengths and positions of sections were connected with the trig points ...."

Put simply, in triangulation the surveyor establishes a chain of triangles, starting from an observation point, for which he has the azimuth, the direction from North. From this point he carefully measures a baseline by chaining, and on this line, by observing angles of various landmarks, he surveys a triangle. He then carefully builds up a chain of connected triangles, based on the original triangle. The length of any side of any triangle can be computed. When this chain of abutting triangles is complete, the surveyor can compute the distance from either of the original points and the furthest point of the furthest triangle, or indeed any two points on the triangulation grid. The fine surveyor and explorer Charles Douglas admired the accuracy – and appreciated the struggle and effort involved – when Roberts had observed "the triangles of a major-triangulation which binds together with indisputable accuracy all the survey points north from Hokitika to Ahaura."

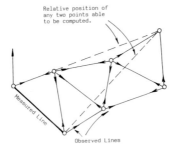

Triangulation.

Measuring the angles by theodolite, and then computing distances, makes full use of the most accurate instrument of the pre-satellite pre-laser surveyors, and saves the laborious and time-consuming chainmen's work, measuring distances on the ground by an enlarged version of the tape-measure. In some areas of early New Zealand the chainman's job would involve making his way through some extraordinarily difficult bush and mountain country. Geometry created to measure the flooded flatlands of the Nile, and then adapted in the flat wetlands of Holland, proved of great assistance in a country and countryside which could hardly have been more different from both if it had been created to be so.

Reko, highly intelligent, drew his guests a map of the rivers and lakes of Otago's interior on the dust of the floor. Thomson could record it only by heart, but it was particularly useful information. On completing his journey to Bluff Harbour, Thomson surveyed the site of Invercargill before returning to Dunedin. He had also observed the true meridian at Bluff and carried standard bearings from there outward; using a triangulation method "systematically calculated on the meridian and perpendicular", in three months he surveyed some two and a half million acres of land, traversing about 2400 kilometres of difficult country. Thomson enjoyed the southern hospitality.

The south was interesting. Just a few years later, when J. H. Baker extended triangulation from Bluff Hill up the Aparima and across the big plain near today's Winton, American whaleships still visited the southern coast. Like most tourists, whalemen paid well for especially interesting souvenirs. "Enbalmed Maori heads were enormously sought after as curios, especially if they were finely tatooed, and the American whalers in particular would pay large prices for them." One very skilfully tattooed Maori chief, Jacob, feared the "Yankee head hunters", collected his family and goods and disappeared "to the upper reaches of the Aparima ...."

From more prosaic Dunedin, Thomson began to survey North Otago in October 1857, first fixing the latitude of two or three prominent coastal hills as a baseline for his triangulation, Behe Waka at Port Chalmers, Puke Ivita near Palmerston and Big Hill near Oamaru. He obtained the baseline by calculation, using their differences in latitude; from this line he could determine all positions within sight of the hills. For a time bad weather prevented Thomson's making a major inland trip, but exploring when possible, he waited patiently. An occasional major trip up country, in one case 112 kilometres up the Waitaki River, let him form his plans. He crossed the Horse Range to the Shag River and another time went as far west as the Manuherikia River, which joins the Clutha at today's Alexandra. From there he saw south far enough to recognise mountain ranges he had surveyed. Striking eastward, but unable to cross the Taieri River, he turned north to the Shag Valley and followed it to the coast.

In early December the driving surveyor set out on what became his major exploration journey. Following the Waitaki River inland, then its Ahuriri branch, he crossed a low pass to the westwards, the pass Reko had described to him. He named it Lindis Pass, probably after a little hill on Lindisfarne Island near his birthplace. A day later he climbed Mount Longslip to obtain from the peak sweeping views over the whole Upper Clutha country, and back over the Waitaki lands he had traversed. Crossing the Lindis Pass, he went as far as Black Knob, which he had named from the other side, and renamed this magnificent outlook Grandview. In climbing such a peak mountaineers pass through whole climatic ranges within hours. But it is worth the shivering. From Grandview Thomson not only saw the great West Coast mountains but looked down over Lake Hawea and, west of it, Lake Wanaka. To the south-west a huge rock slanted upward from a peak which he named Mount Pisa.

Here Thomson wrote in his notebook, "at the head of Hawea about 40 miles distant is a very lofty conical peak which I call Aspiring." The Maori name was Tititea, or Shining White. Thomson probably did not know that. In surveyor's fashion, he used Mount Longslip to connect the great interior peaks, Mount

Surveyor Thomson named this mountain well. To aspire means to aim high. If it is for beauty then Mount Aspiring has achieved its aim. But it is a deadly mountain too and man has paid – and is paying – a heavy price for his triumphs. *(NZ Aerial Mapping, Hastings)*

Sefton and further west Aspiring, with trig stations along the coast on his map. Mount Aspiring – what a suitable name – is one of the world's truly beautiful mountains. Only rare montane shapeliness will seem pre-eminent among Southern Alps, and Aspiring is much used by mountaineering clubs to exemplify in practice what a mountain ought to be.

Humour spares no one, not even distinguished surveyors and distinctive mountain peaks. Two years later an "eminent surveyor and explorer", Edward Jollie, had "a large contract run survey" to do and a bright young assistant to help complete it. From the top of a high mountain they could see Thomson's mountain standing majestically to the north. "Mr Jollie did not belie his name, being full of fun and humour, and always cracking jokes. On looking round from the top of the peak near Shotover he said, 'Thomson has called that mountain "Aspiring"; we must call ours "Perspiring".'" It was registered as such; Noeline Baker, who wrote the book about Baker, "on a map in the Dunedin

Survey Office, dated 1858 ... found Mt. Perspiring marked .... From the general direction of the Matatapu River it seems as if it might have been Mount Matatapu." Jollie's mountain is now called Motatapu, and in spite of its attractive Maori name Jollie's assistant was right to regret that it did not stay "Perspiring." As he said, if it had "those early explorers might be remembered more often than they are."

From Grandview Thomson painted the view, sketching outlines of the peaks in his field book as well. At this time he merely gained an overview of the area, leaving it to James McKerrow, his able assistant, to complete the survey later. The area's beauty was self-evident and the Chief Surveyor foresaw future summer visitors flocking there. After walking as far south as the Clutha Thomson turned back to the Ahuriri and followed it to its junction with the Waitaki. On the way, from the Benmore Range's commanding altitude he could see junctions and patterns of many of the area's rivers, Tekapo and Pukaki, the Ohau branch of Waitaki, and where Twizel joined the Ohau. Thomson decided to go to Lake Ohau along the Ohau River. Today some people view Mount Cook from Lake Ohau's western shore; we do not know if Thomson did; probably he

## HELP   IN   NEED

The multitude of streams which Captain Stokes observed from Mount Grey, and others like them all over New Zealand, had all to be crossed and recrossed as the country was explored, surveyed, stocked and developed. There were risks in crossing almost every one of them in either island, but the greatest risks were in the southern rivers which rose and fell in swift response to the weather in the great mountains to the west. Draught animals, keen to preserve themselves, helped their riders or drivers as a consequence.

John Holland Baker, the fine surveyor who worked with Thomson in Otago for many years, was given some good advice by a cousin when he first began to take horses across rivers in Canterbury: "in any difficulty in a river never leave your horse. If you get washed off stick to his mane, and if you cannot clutch that, hang on to his tail, because a horse is never drowned unless he gets into a quicksand." Horses knew what they were doing. W. H. Rhodes, of the Levels, said that "horses were carefully trained to ford the rivers, as young or inexperienced ones were liable to lose their heads in an emergency." It was not lost heads that would have been the major problem, but missing tails. Hanging on to a big animal's tail seemed to be sound advice, and the famous South Island sheepstealer, Mackenzie, claimed he always crossed dangerous rivers by hanging on to the tail of his huge pack-ox.

The animal did not need to be large, as long as it were willing. The first donkey to reach south Canterbury went in with Charles Torlesse, a surveyor, explorer and runholder. A German boy with Torlesse, when crossing behind the cattle, "stuck manfully (and boorish-like utterly unconscious of danger) to the donkey's tail" and arrived safely at the other bank. A strong stubborn animal with a stout strong tail was obviously a great help in crossing South Island rivers. Getting stock across posed problems too. Rhodes said it was often hard to induce cattle to cross the rivers. Drovers developed a means which worked; driving the cattle round and round, then breaking the ring in such a way that momentum would shoot cattle into the river. The would have mentioned it if he had. What Thomson had wished of Lake Ohau was not a view of Mount Cook which differed from the view from Lake Pukaki, but a route to Jackson Bay on the west coast. Alternatives to sailing south of New Zealand to Melbourne were expensively sought by the Otago Provincial Government. No Ohau route to Melbourne ever developed, but a surveyor, T. N. Brodrick, discovered a pass in 1890.

Accompanied by a young runholder, Thomson went on from Lake Ohau to Lake Pukaki. The young man crossed a river in dare-devilish fashion. Thomson thought him foolish, and with years in the East behind him, had no need to prove his own courage. His disapproval of the young man crossing a stream in flood led to a small but wise homily. He thought want of moral courage, not physical, led New Zealanders to cross unsafe flooding rivers. Thomson, morally courageous, refused to follow the young man until the water subsided overnight. As it was, Thomson had some trouble getting across and to do so he went alone, leaving his horse behind. Horses could not always be trusted in streams, although the danger was not always direct. A mountaineer, Green, in the area much later to climb Mount Cook, was furious when "the horse on whose back

pressure of the river always sent some beasts far enough in that they would have to swim for it; this always led the whole mob across.

Not every beast or man reached the other side safely. One of the better known drownings was that of Dr Sinclair, no young New Zealander but an elderly medical man, amateur botanist, and long-time Colonial Secretary of New Zealand, drowned not many kilometres from where Thomson sensibly refused to cross. Accompanying Sir Julius Haast in order to indulge a botanising retirement, the elderly Sinclair foolishly tried to cross a dangerous river near Samuel Butler's station, Mesopotamia. His young companion, for Haast was busy surveying, could not save him. Haast's sincere praise also condemned Sinclair: "with almost juvenile alacrity he had climbed and searched the mountain side, showing that, notwithstanding his advanced age, his love for his cherished science had supplied him with strength for its pursuits, until at last over-taxing his powers, and not sufficiently aware of the treacherous nature of Alpine torrents, he fell a victim to his zeal."

The Waitaki was thought to be the most dangerous river. W. H. Valpy, a pioneer runholder, referred to it as "far-famed and long-dreaded Waitaki ...." Shortland once encountered the Waitaki in flood, "furiously rapid, dirty white, pipe-clay colour", and "almost a mile wide." The flood coincided with "a strangely hot, dry and oppressive, nor' wester ...." Floodwaters begin as thawing mountain snow, and changes downriver can affect the flows and dangers. Robert Bruce, who spent years in Canterbury, wrote reminiscently that "one might approach the Rakaia today and find it consists of three or four streams from twenty to one hundred yards wide, and not exceeding one or two feet in depth; tomorrow it will be a roaring sea a quarter of a mile in width, racing at a speed of five to ten miles an hour." And the problem grew worse, as Rhodes perceived. "The rivers in the early days were not so dangerous as they became after the land was broken up, for sixty years ago the tussock-covered country held the rain when it fell and was not so speedily dried up after a shower as it became in later years." Even in their pristine state the rivers were dangerous enough to make drowning the "New Zealand disease".

we had packed the flour, tea, sugar, and my extra clothes, took the opportunity of our attention being off to lie down in the deepest part of the stream and enjoy a delicious roll …. The tins in which the provisions had been enclosed were crushed and burst. The sugar streamed away for the gratification of paradise ducks …." Thomson, by this time an old New Zealand hand, had his share of mishaps too.

On this trip Thomson passed through country which Haast explored five years later. He climbed the Ben Ohau range a few kilometres past Lake Pukaki's head and saw one of the wonders of the southern world. "Mount Cook, the monarch of the southern mountains was full in view, distant about 25 miles [40 km], and towering 13,000 feet [4000 metres] above the sea. It was clothed in snow from its tapering peak to its base, and supported as it is by rugged precipitous sides surrounded by desert and utterly barren mountains and valleys; its appearance, however, calculated to excite the admiration of the lovers of the picturesque. For it possessed with its magnificence, so much of the appalling and forbidding …." Everyone seems to feel its singularity. Samuel Butler said, "If a person says he *thinks* he has seen Mount Cook, you may be quite sure that he has not seen it. The moment it comes into sight the exclamation is, 'That is Mount Cook!' – not 'That *must* be Mount Cook!' There is no possibility of mistake." But with all the majesty of this mountain there is, as Thomson saw, some of life's sordidness too. The pure grandeurs of rock and ice and height contrast strongly with the peculiar sand and "great glaring wastes of shingle", as the mountaineer Green saw them, crawling repulsively from mountain's foot to the water's edge.

This is the young Samuel Butler, who increased his capital by sheep farming in New Zealand so he could afford to become a novelist in England. *(Alexander Turnbull Library, Wellington)*

Thomson was the first European to describe the mountain from the Canterbury side. He also calculated its height, something which had been done from *Acheron* in 1851 by Captain Stokes. But Thomson did these things several years before Haast saw the mountain, although the latter's name is so closely associated with it. Thomson's zeal and capability made him a consummate surveyor and compared to current measurements, his figure for the height of Mount Cook is only 111 feet out. Water from Mount Cook's snow forms Lake Pukaki, and reaches the sea by the Waitaki River, the boundary line of Canterbury and Otago. Thomson, as surveyor of Otago, named many geographical features on this visit, including several mountains. Haast almost entirely ignored this anteriority, and renamed them during his employment by Canterbury. Nevertheless Thomson's map from this expedition became vital evidence in an important Otago-Canterbury boundary dispute. The boundary was to be the Waitaki River but when the line was first declared the river was yet unmapped. Thomson's recommendation that instead of the Ahuriri the Ohau (both branches of the Waitaki) should be the boundary was accepted.

On the way home Thomson's party encountered very rough country, and rough weather too. This is not uncommon in Otago winters even at medium heights. James McKerrow and his assistant John Goldie, surveying the Wanaka region a few years later, were caught by snow on their way to Dunedin, not very far as a kaka flies from where Thomson and his party had been. Goldie said he did not like it: "Monday night was a 'whistler', with a fall of six inches of snow, with keen frost … our horses, poor beasts, stood all night beside the tent

This particular view from the Cook River of great mountains' tops and bases shows that high rainfall and steep terrain produce not only snow for beautiful mountain peaks but also the erosion resulting in rather depressing river flats. *(University of Canterbury Library, Christchurch)*

without a morsel to eat, and before we saddled them in the morning, we had to scrape the frozen snow from their backs, and break icicles one foot in length from each side of their bellies …. Against a biting drift we made a start and reached the summit of the mountain by midday ….” And their horses were not shod! In Thomson's case, being snowbound for three days changed his mind about crossing the Hawkden Range into Central Otago and they went down the Waitaki. Not completely put off by the experience, perhaps remembering a Northumberland boyhood rather than Singapore surveying, Thomson reprovisioned his party to return to the Strath Taieri. After crossing the Taieri River he could see from the Rock and Pillar Range an Otago area now notable for both sheep and water power.

The advent of such an active surveyor as Thomson had not meant any slackening in private exploration. Late in 1857 Alexander and Watson Shennan set up a well equipped, planned and organised expedition in Dunedin: “horses were necessary, but there were none to be got, and it was only after a small shipment came from Sydney that I was able to procure the hacks required, and at very high prices. As soon as the equipment necessary for an exploring expedition was ready, I went south.” Leaving the Tokomairiro River, south of Dunedin, they worked inland to the upper Tuapeka, and here perhaps missed their chance; “I pitched camp one night in the gully afterwards called Gabriel's Gully, little thinking of the wealth that was buried only a few feet under the ground. Had I suspected the presence of gold, I might have given up searching for sheep country.” Unsuspectedly leaving the next decade of Otago's wealth and growth behind them they pressed on through some fair to good sheep country. “Most of the country had a beautiful cover of good grasses.” They had not come to accept the first prospect, and went on to Manuherikia River where it joined the Clutha. Here it seemed right: “from the top of the Knobbys I had a splendid view of the Manuherikia Valley, presenting a most beautiful landscape – quite a change from the country previously traversed. I exclaimed to my brother: ‘Here is the country we are looking for; a land well grassed and watered – a very land of promise. Here we will pitch our tent, and here we shall stay and make our home for good.’”

Exploring more happily now in spite of the lack of timber, they saw plenty of “native duck, quail, pukaki, wild pigs, wild dogs, and also a wild white horse.” Watson Shennan was concerned, and correctly so, about wild dogs: “rats and mice swarmed, so the wild dogs found abundance of food, and they often caught a duck asleep at night. Afterwards they found mutton was more to their liking.” Another settler, Alex Petrie, had his own fright: “wild dogs were numerous and had made tracks all along the river side. We put our tent across one of these tracks, and were wakened one night by hearing our dog growling. Looking up, I was confronted by a wild dog, which, on being struck at, went off. I got tired of this sort of life and returned to Waikouaiti.” Otago runholders fought a long expensive war against wild dogs, using poison, bullets, traps and even imported Australian hounds to save their livestock.

The Shennans explored the junction country thoroughly and finally, some distance up the Manuherikia, cut over the Raggedy Range to Ida Valley, crossed the Rough Ridge and Lammerlaws and found their way back to Tokomairiro. Shortly after they returned to the Manuherikia to establish on either side of it

WILD DOGS

Thomas Brunner blamed the wild dogs in the New Zealand bush for the extinction of or the threat to wild birds. Many of these were descendants of Polynesian dogs, distinctive because they did not bark, which were just beginning to interbreed with dogs from whaling stations and new immigrant settlements. The original Maori dog was seen by Europeans as "a sort of domesticated fox, quite black or white, very low on the legs, straight ears, thick tail, long body, full jaws but more pointed than that of the fox, and uttering the same cry; they do not bark like our dogs .... They would have been dangerous to keep where poultry was raised or had to be protected; they would destroy them just like true foxes." A South Canterbury runholder described hunting down a wild dog, "a pretty creature, white, with black or brown patches, of stiff build, with long hair and a bushy tail." The description sounds to be of the same animal. Unfortunately New Zealand wild birds were as easy prey as poultry.

Dieffenbach had pointed out that the wild native birds were in danger; "the introduction of the carnivorous dog and cat into New Zealand has had a curious and fatal effect on the feathered races." But the German naturalist blamed their becoming feral at least partly on Maori warfare. "On the breaking up of the tribes these animals were dispersed into the forest, which afforded nothing for their support but the birds, whose number has greatly decreased in consequence ...."

Brunner was quite certain about the dogs' role: "I caught three kiwi – one large and two small. There are two distinct species. This country used to abound with them, but they are now nearly extinct by the dogs of the bush." In another place he says the same about weka and kakapo. And, besides the spur of canine hunger, many kiwi were caught by surveyors' dogs to make meals for men. A very few years later wild hybrids from Maori and European canine interbreeding became a real pest as sheepkillers on the new South Island sheep runs.

the runs of Galloway, named after Shennans' home county, and Moutere, Maori for an expanse of land nearly surrounded by water. These fine stations are still operating, although much pruned from original boundaries. Conditions set for taking up a run varied little from province to province. When J.B. Baker, later an eminent surveyor, was thinking of doing so in Canterbury in 1860 these were the main requirements: "within six months [the runholder] had to stock it with one sheep for every twenty acres or one head of cattle for every hundred and twenty acres, and he had to pay a farthing an acre rent for the first two years, a halfpenny an acre for the next two and three farthings for the fifth and all subsequent years. If he did not fulfill all these conditions he forfeited the run."

Baker examined landholding in the years Samuel Butler was an active runholder and explorer. He could not remember who introduced them but when his cadetship was over Butler asked Baker "to join him in an exploring expedition and on December 24th, 1860, found myself at Mesopotamia .... Three of us sat down to Christmas dinner and our names were Butler, Baker and Cook, the latter being Butler's shepherd manager." On the expedition they "noticed quite a low pass evidently leading to the West Coast." On a follow-up expedition, "we reached the Rakaia River and the day after came to the foot of the pass we had seen. This pass, though discovered by Butler and myself, was afterwards called the Whitcombe Pass, after a surveyor of that name ...

drowned in fording one of the West Coast rivers." Baker now knew that what he wanted was not in that area. On an 1861 expedition without Butler he found some desirable undulating downs: "about 15,000 acres of good sheep country worth applying for as a run." Baker "put in an application … with a sketch plan of the position, which application was granted." Soon after he sold the lease for £300, "a good bit of pocket money for a couple of youngsters under nineteen." Baker had, with other sales of rights discovered, done quite well from his explorations, something most unusual.

In 1857-8 David McKellar went up the Oreti River in Southland, crossed the watershed and followed the Von River to Mount Nicholas at the central portion of Lake Wakitipu, which Reko had shown Chalmers from a distance. McKellar could not explore the lake because of high winds. Others saw the lake in 1858, and within a few months, in 1859, Donald Hay, an Australian, rafted up Lake Wakatipu to the mouth of the Von. From there he glimpsed the great northern arm of the lake. Before he left he explored the Kawarau valley and discovered Hay's Lake, now misspelt Lake Hayes.

W. G. Rees and a Russian, Nicholas von Tunzelmann, came to Lake Wanaka late in January 1860, by the Waitaki and the Lindis Pass. Von Tunzelmann was a Baltic German, like Bellingshausen. His father was a general in the Russian Army and Nicholas himself a godson of Tzar Nicholas I. After trouble over their children's schooling in Germany the family were exiled from Russia and went to England and later to New Zealand. Von Tunzelmann decided to settle in the south and he joined forces with Gilbert Rees. From Wanaka they reached the top of the Crown Range, named by Rees, and saw the spectacular view down to the Kawarau's gorge and round to the right to Lake Wakatipu, that today automobile passengers see from the highest state highway in New Zealand. Rees had given up in discouragement but von Tunzelmann set off for one more hilltop, "and when he reached it he flung up his hat and gave a shout of joy, for there below him lay the vast expanse of Wakatipu. They drew lots for the two sides of the lake." Rees got the eastern and von Tunzelmann the western side, with his commemorations, Mount Nicholas and the Von River.

Otago was fast becoming sheep country. David McKellar now teamed up with George Gunn to search for sheep grazing into the mountains between Lakes Wakatipu and Te Anau. In 1861 the explorers followed the Von and Mararoa, crossing the Livingstone Range to Lake McKellar, at the head of the Greenstone, and to Lake Gunn, the source of the Eglinton. Along the watershed they climbed a mountain from whose top they saw "the sea on the West Coast distant about fifteen to twenty miles, bearing about W. – upper Te Anau bearing S.W." Because they took bearings and allowed their achievement to become public knowledge (the trip was written up in the *Southern News* within weeks of their homecoming) this was genuine exploration; the map was filling in.

Official surveying was proceeding apace too. James McKerrow, who worked with J. T. Thomson and took over his western surveying when he moved to Wellington, surveyed over 800 kilometres of country from Lake Hawea to Foveaux Strait. He was a superb surveyor, according to such contemporaries as Baker, who had worked with him. The country McKerrow mapped was that of the majestic lakes and almost inaccessible mountain ranges of South Westland.

The young Scotsman conducted exploratory surveys of the lake district from 1861 to 1863, charting much of the area around Lakes Wanaka and Hawea. While surveying Lakes Te Anau and Manapouri he and his assistant, John Goldie, climbed Mount Pisgah and sighted Caswell Sound on the Tasman Sea in the distance; they thought they were the first to have seen the Tasman from inland Otago. As we have noted, McKellar and Gunn had done so in March 1861, but McKerrow apparently was not aware of the *Southern News* story. His worth and work are commemorated by Lake McKerrow.

The province of Otago engaged James Hector in 1861 to carry out a geological survey of the province. He hoped, and the province too, to discover a pass to the west coast. After all, he was the scientist of the great Palliser exploration of Western Canada. They had found passes making possible the projection, and then the building, of the Canadian Pacific Railway, the greatest railway construction project up to that time. Otago emphasised the necessity of a pass to the west coast, for rail or road, because the province hoped to establish a port there on which to base direct communication with Melbourne. This would cut out the long haul for ships in rough and dangerous waters around Stewart Island and up the east coast. They found no pass – and there were several death-dealing shipwrecks.

The search for a usable pass had been going on for some time. The Maori knew passes, but what was needed was one suitable for heavy traffic, and not prohibiting road building. G. M. Hassing, with a companion H. S. Thomson, who in 1859 became a Wanaka runholder, advanced past the head of Lake Wanaka up the Makarora for thirty-two kilometres through almost impenetrable

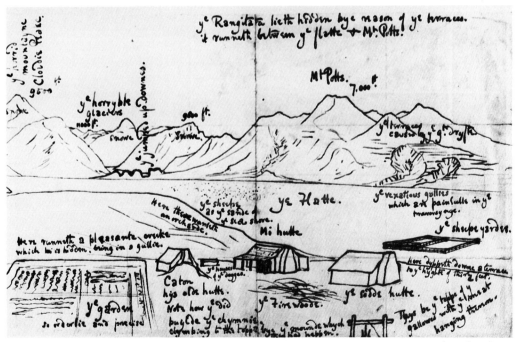

In this sketch of Mesopotamia, quite typical of early southern sheep stations, Samuel Butler shows that the precision of his thought and his reporting could be softened by the humour of his captions. (*Canterbury Museum, Christchurch*)

flax, fern and cabbage trees. They burned off the vegetation in a fire which was huge and destructive even by the standards of the day, and later explorers had an easier time as a consequence. The explorers hoped to discover a pass to the coast, but although near the Haast Pass they did not find it.

Hector, in turn, went to Wanaka and up the Matukituki to inspect the country, intending to approach it from seaward. While he was there he tried for a pass by land and followed the Matukituki to its source, crossing the saddle down into the Waipara. Hector's Col commemorates the famous explorer but it was not the route Otago needed. As the *Otago Witness* said, "This saddle, from which the Pacific is plainly visible, lies considerably above the winter snowline, and on account of the steep gradient is impracticable." Hector's party reached the Arawata but had to turn back within a few kilometres of Jackson's Bay. There was no link there with Melbourne. Giving up attempts by land from the east Hector went by ship to the west coast and up Milford Sound, only to be again thwarted. He could not find his way across the range towards Wakatipu. Leaving the ship at Martin's Bay, he set off inland to Lake McKerrow, up the Hollyford, then down the Greenstone to Lake Wakitipu and Queenstown. This was a Maori trail, more or less abandoned.

This major trip had added to the map in some ways but only showed there was no practical pass that far south, although there were other attempts to find one. The words "map" and "practical pass" indicate the purposes of such European exploration. In 1862 Charles Cameron explored the Dart River and followed the Routeburn to the watershed of its northern branch in search of a feasible pass across the divide. A reward of £1000 had been offered by Otago but he was not granted it for this work. But the dreamed-of pass, the Haast, was probably found in January 1863 by Cameron, and by coincidence just a few days later properly explored by Haast himself.

Whitcombe Pass, painted in 1866 by Julius von Haast. The pass was actually discovered by Samuel Butler and John Baker, but Henry Whitcombe explored it properly to the sea, only to lose his life crossing a coastal river. *(Alexander Turnbull Library, Wellington)*

In early 1863 Alphonse Barrington and two companions crossed the wild unknown country between the Hollyford and the Haast. The expedition confirmed that foolishness was as likely to bring fame as either sense or forethought. The Barrington party left Queenstown, followed the Pike River to Lake Plenty, went over a saddle to the headwaters of the Gorge river and reached the Cascade by the end of April. They found some gold but piercing mountain frosts heralded approaching winter and they had few supplies. Presumably after thought about the matter, they headed directly for Queenstown, straight across snowfields 2154 metres above sea level. In spite of walking over dangerous glaciers and travelling foodless for days, everyone arrived safely. It was a miracle granted to few. Barrington's party was said to have found much gold but people excited by their reports failed to discover significant amounts. By this time Otago goldfields were yielding precedence to the new fields of the West Coast; from now on most gold would be won within the sound of Tasman's "roaring surf."

Thomson stayed in Otago for some time after his exploration, and the gold boom, before becoming first Surveyor-General of New Zealand. Undoubtedly his greatest memorial is the survey system of Otago province which he had done as he had hoped to, achieving cheapness, rapidity and accuracy. His system, to a large extent, had been developed in India for accurately yet inexpensively surveying large territories. Surveyor Thomson, like so many Englishmen in India, and like America's god of surveying, George Washington, had gone inland ahead of the workers, exploiters and developers, to lay out large and pristine territories.

Thomson's legacy to Otago and to New Zealand is both real and intangible. Bridges which he designed and built are still in service in the modern automobile age. In his memoirs, J. H. Baker, a former chief surveyor of Southland and a fine explorer, praised Thomson's sense of design, which Baker's biographer found best exemplified in Invercargill. "To Mr. J. T. Thomson, who was the Chief Surveyor of Otago, belongs the credit of having planned the town and given it the wide streets and open spaces that are its characteristic. There is perhaps, no other town in New Zealand that has such a feeling of spaciousness and having been definitely and symmetrically planned."

Much Thomson left is less discernible but no less valuable. Many names Thomson bequeathed Otago evoke similar landscapes and similar people. Tweed Streets grace Invercargill and Oamaru, enshrining the surveyor's memory of the little river which divided England from Scotland. There is a St Bathan's, and a Mount St Cuthbert, named after the shepherd boy and saint-to-be who became Bishop of – and at – the Lindisfarne within sight of Thomson's birthplace. There is also a Twizel, named after Twizel Bridge, a key site in the Battle of Flodden, where the English slaughtered the Scots army of James IV. Northumberland breeding must have overcome Scottish blood at least that once. But Thomson did not use only his own Scottish and North of England names. He took great trouble to use Maori names too – and correctly.

CHAPTER TEN

# *Resources to Develop*

Settlers required the same knowledge of food sources and fertile land as the Maori had needed too. But in addition they had to have fuel for engines, metals for use and sale, timber for building, ways to move sheep inland from ships and yet-to-be-found overland trails to move stock from one province to another. They needed good harbours from which to export their produce and take in their European cloth, machines and luxuries. Their modern economy was one based on distant exchange. So while there was some overlap between the needs of different groups their key motivations were not the same. Stealing slaves or saving souls is quite different from the production of a modern world's goods for a modern world's rewards.

Many who looked for these things were those who wished to use them. But by the mid-19th century trained European immigrants were playing an important part. Their expertise was less navigation than knowledge of the resources sought; in this they were more like the missionaries than the sailors. They had first to find their way around and maintain themselves, and then to assess and chart such resources as they discovered. Julius, later Sir Julius, Haast had most of the qualities of a superb land explorer. Perhaps as important were his abilities in getting his work recognised and used; his reporting was impeccable and often eloquent, standing out not essentially as better but as different, as coming from one outside the British middle and county classes. Born in 1822 in Bonn, the present capital of Germany, and a talented worldly German of his time, in many ways he was like Albert, Prince Consort, whom he had saved from drowning in the Rhine. They were both very musical, a talent which stood Haast in good stead as a stranger in a new land.

Haast excelled in geology and mineralogy at the famous university at Bonn, and travelled in Russia, Austria and Italy to learn mountaineering and vulcanology. Although such a well-grounded geologist his topographical skill proved even more important in New Zealand; he produced outstanding geological maps of Canterbury and Westland which rank beside his great map of the Southern Alps. But in some ways his upbringing as a merchant's son, appreciative of effort, efficiency and organisation, taught him more about leading expeditions than did his formal studies or travel. New Zealand commemorated him with the Haast River and Haast Pass; Haast in turn commemorated teachers and associates when naming mountains.

Haast originally came to New Zealand to examine for a firm of English shipowners the prospects of large-scale German emigration to New Zealand. It might also have been that his liberal opinions made the Germany of the 1850s unsympathetic. It was a time of great emigration from Germany, especially to the northern American states; the Northern Army in the American Civil War of the 1860s benefited greatly from the many well-trained young Germans available. Haast did not arrive happily in New Zealand for he had so much to lose in the old world. He compared himself to a ship; "like it I flew proudly

252

through the world; now I stand lonely and broken, and like the desolate wreck, I still exist and weep." He did not often understate emotion.

Haast's arrival in New Zealand coincided with that of the Austrian frigate *Novara*, calling on her famed scientific cruise around the world. When visiting her, Haast met Ferdinand Hochstetter, who became a lifelong friend and one who so impressed New Zealand that there is a lake and an ice-fall named after him. An outstanding geologist of the Austrian Empire although still very young, Hochstetter influenced Haast and was able to control his buoyant nature. According to close friends, Haast was always "a boy in heart." But youthful spirit did not mean lack of thoroughness, effort or courage to outface difficulty and danger until his aims were achieved.

At this time Haast first really encountered the New Zealand bush, which he would come to know all too well. His description of his early impressions is lyrical. "The beauty of the forest made the greatest impression on everyone. The elegant Areca palm, Nikau, with its wealth of blossom and fruit beneath its crown of leaves, the different kinds of decorative tree-ferns with their scalloped leaves, the majestic Kauri, king of the New Zealand woods, the Rata, that tree murderer, which first embraces the giant of the woods as a tender creeper, gradually clasps its support with ever stronger growing arms, until it has slain it with its strangle-hold, and then, itself developing into a strong tree, takes its victim's place. Around them grew creepers and lianas, of every kind,

This 1850s picture shows what is described as typical New Zealand bush and scrub. *(Alexander Turnbull Library, Wellington)*

combining and interweaving on every side ….” And yet this passage is not overstated, as anyone who tramps virgin New Zealand bush in a well-watered area can verify: it is beautiful but challenging. The difficult "bush" made New Zealand exploration, in forested parts at least, much more arduous than in North America. And though well subtropical, New Zealand bush is more like African or Brazilian rain forest than anything in Europe.

Exploring 19th-century New Zealand was especially interesting because of peculiar, indeed unique, geological formations. New Zealand is different because it gathers close together features found rarely anywhere else, and there widely separated. The best example was the type of glaciation, just becoming understood in the 1850s.

In Auckland Haast gradually found his way into exploration, helped immensely by his personal qualities. He worked for the Provincial Government evaluating such resources as coal and pasturelands, and always seeking good transportation routes. With Hochstetter he examined geological formations near Auckland, especially extinct volcanic cones. And, according to his own words, he was "invited by the New Zealand government, at the express desire of

## N E W   Z E A L A N D   B U S H

New Zealand's forests are notoriously difficult to travel in. The Maori, with good reason, constantly expressed relief at any return to the open fernlands. Maori cut and burned the forest for their own reasons, exactly as Europeans did, and do, later. In a new land resources seem limitless. "It is evident that the forest has at some former period covered a greater extent of the land in the neighbourhood of Taupo than it now does; it does not appear to have been destroyed by volcanic eruptions, but by the fires kindled by the natives in order to clear the ground for the purpose of cultivation." Dieffenbach warned about the dangers inherent in destroying good soil laid down by vegetable decay on top of what was really an infertile clay. Fires often, and rather easily, destroyed the fertile lighter soil on top.

As well as wishing to clear land for cultivation, men faced with such an overpowering – in the truest sense – vegetable force, might respond with subconscious enmity; some burned to ease their travelling. Julius Haast's description of an Auckland forest tells us of beauty, but the claustrophobic pressure comes through clearly. "Everywhere, wherever there is any open space in the trees, parasites have established themselves, and these in combination with the creepers so cover the tree that often you cannot see its own foliage until you look up to its very crest. In between the trees the ground is covered with ferns of every size and shape, which delight the eye by their dainty forms and fresh green. The recumbent tree trunks are overgrown with mosses and lichens in varied forms or offer a fruitful seed-bed for the parasites. Everywhere luxuriates free and undisturbed the exuberant green plant world …."

Thomas Brunner, in the north-western part of the South Island, emphasised the constraints, which so swiftly pass from the purely physical to the psychological, of "an enormous and dense forest, too thick in places to see our way, from the quantity of supplejack, briar, ekiakia, with deep moss, rotten timber, and pools of water covering the surface of the ground, and no means of judging how far it might still be

Hochstetter, [to accompany] him on all his journeys in New Zealand, helping him whenever I could to the best of my ability."

Haast learned quickly that only bodily strength and health could cope with New Zealand wilderness in the 1850s and 60s. Bad tracks through genuinely primeval forests, through swamps and icy mountain rivers, all supplies carried, meant that even hiring porters did little to relieve the strain. Tea, pork and potatoes were the diet. Even so Haast's travels around Auckland were comparatively more luxurious than he realised. In Canterbury later he did not meet missionaries, or have Maori porters, and he came to accept spoiled potatoes and rancid pork.

In 1860 Haast moved to Nelson, where he began to build his fame. He took to Nelson, for he found Germans there. At once Haast felt more comfortable, and literally so: "instead of the uncomfortable English bar from behind which the host hands out to the guests the drinks they desire, that they swallow hastily, standing, we had a cheerful typical German guest-room before us. All round were tables and benches, at which guests were sitting; clouds of blue smoke from pipes and cigars filled the air ... and we thought we had found

found to extend." Further south the forest seemed to the surveyor Goldie to vary less, both in intrinsic detail and in its coverage of the land. "The bush, or properly forest, through the interior generally consisted of birch wood heavy timbered, and in one respect, not at all difficult to travel through, having little or no underwood; while in another respect it is quite the opposite, step after step, we sank to our knees in fogg [moss] and what, with rotten branches or huge fallen trees, our travelling was both tedious and toilsome .... A great extent of bush, mile after mile, hill and vale appear robed in the dark green foliage of the birch."

And in the south-western part of the South Island there could be the same frustration, and exhaustion too, that missionaries or land buyers suffered in the north. One southern surveyor, needing a vantage point, found it difficult to gain. "I will ask you to follow me while I go up it in fancy again. For the first hundred yards or so we had to creep on our hands and knees, if not serpent-like on our bellies ... through among thick growing, high overtopping scrub .... Then again we would be weltering amongst thick scrub and within grasp of that plague to man in all New Zealand bush – 'Maori lawyers'. Maori lawyers are a sort of briar which shoot from its parent stem numerous runners for a considerable distance round it, each runner being armed by a thousand hooks or 'hold-him-fast,' which show no quarter to clothes or skin ...."

Such climbs, in both islands, usually opened views which almost compensated the climber, whatever his original purpose. In south-west Otago, in its original state, one climber thought the battle with forest and scrub and even "bush lawyer" was well worth having won. "I can assure you that the scenery here though wild in its grandeur was beyond anything that I have ever seen for its beauty. For the last six or eight miles at the head of the stream, each side was clothed with the deep green waving birch tree, the forest extending, more or less in depth, up the mountain side, while here and there were to be seen splendid waterfalls teeming their waters rainbow-like over some rocks .... I have often read and heard tell of the Alpine scenery, and I could almost say that the scenery in some parts in the wilds of Otago could compare with it." It can indeed; the "almost" was not needed.

ourselves in Germany at the Antipodes." Haast was not there to drink with other Germans, but to make geological assessments of Nelson's resources. New Zealand's geology he found different from Europe's and studied it with a scientist's eye. Above all, in this distant colony Haast somehow kept up with world trends in scientific thought; as a result some of his reports are masterpieces.

In 1860 Haast explored the western district of Nelson Province, from Nelson to the mouth of the Grey, a good example of his expeditions. The Superintendent of Nelson Province set out a wide-ranging aim; "to extend as far as lay in their power the geological investigation commenced by Dr. Hochstetter ...." Haast was not only to find routes but to draw maps. On this expedition he went over much ground already covered by Brunner, Heaphy and others. But he did so with an expert's eye cocked for opportunities for the province to exploit. The party consisted of Haast and a surveyor, Major James Burnett, with three non-professional Europeans and two Maori. Two packhorses helped carry provisions, and more supplies were to be cached along rivers on the way. Haast carefully organised the expedition, packing flour, peas, bacon, ham, salt beef, tea, coffee, sugar, curry, chocolate, brandy, sherry, port and some tobacco, including cigars.

The supplying sounds luxurious but in the event was not enough, and it might well have been wiser to provide more plainly and live more "off the country", as surveyors did in Westland a quarter century later. Both Charles Douglas and Arthur Harper, explorer-surveyors, emphasised then that work-party planning depended on finding birds to eat. If they did not find birds then they went hungry: "It is no joke to be compelled to divide six good meals consisting of flour and rice into rations to extend over ten days, and at the same time do a considerable amount of heavy work."

Tales of wild poultry make it sound appetising enough, when prepared properly, to be civilised eating. Not all explorers and mountaineers were so particular, and some seemed to seek efficiency at any cost. One such was W.S. Green, an excellent mountaineer from Ireland, whom some photographs of New Zealand mountains fired with the ambition to be "first" in a way no longer possible in Europe. "Mount Cook was a splendid peak, and his conquest well worth the trouble of the long journey." Green achieved his ambition, if regarded reasonably, but at the cost of giving up Harper's well-cooked weka: "Roasting was very good where there was food to spare, but in our case it would be sheer and unwarrantable waste, so everything went into the pot to boil, and by eating the flesh and drinking the broth we secured all the nutriment .... It was no doubt a good plan under the circumstances, and I believe "souping it" as my men called it, stood well to us during our weeks of hard work."

Green mentioned the effect of pukeko soup on the "internal economy", a reminder that early travellers ran risks of dysentery or diarrhoea from strange foods or rough preparation, and were without modern medical supplies. Nor was there a way to let anyone know about serious illness, much less hope of skilled help or swift evacuation. One could pray, hope, or both, and use what medication one carried or try bush herbs and potions. Such remedies worked. Explorers were generally fit hardy men or they would not have been there; most of them died at home with whitened hair.

Another watercolour by Charles Heaphy, called "Nelson, November 1841", shows the founding vessels of that colony at anchor. *(Alexander Turnbull Library, Wellington)*

Eating regularly, whether souping or roasting, was only a means to success in exploring. Haast's work was not discovery, which all too often meant merely being first and learning little; it was exploration, more important and certainly better reported. The end was information. Haast's party took mining tools such as picks, spades, shovels and chisels, with a little grindstone to keep them sharp, and pannikins, billys and geological hammers as well as candles, powder, shot and percussion caps. The only instruments were a prismatic compass, a pocket sextant, two aneroids, four thermometers, and an apparatus to find altitude by boiling water. The equipment worked well enough for Haast to do his job as he wished.

Brunner's expedition twelve years earlier had been different. Although he was an experienced explorer, having made several successful expeditions with Charles Heaphy and various Maori, Brunner himself described his own venture modestly. Much too modestly, for he became an Assistant Surveyor under Frederick Tuckett, a capable man of some note later in Otago. By as early as 1846 Brunner was known as a "very zealous explorer." In his understated way, which somewhat mars the journal of a remarkable accomplishment, Brunner described his outfit. "Starting as I did on a purely amateur trip, single-handed, and having everything to carry myself, I could take no instruments, save a single compass and a sextant, which were soon spoiled by the wet ... unacquainted with geology, I am unable to give any description of the country. I only went to assure myself of the description of country ...." On this extraordinary journey, probably the greatest in New Zealand exploration, Brunner was the only European. He felt this a deprivation and when it was over complained that for "a period of nearly five hundred and fifty days ... during which time I have never heard a word of English, save the broken jargon of Ekehu and the echo of my own voice .... There have been many wet days when I have not spoken a word all day." This might have suited Charles Douglas, a later explorer and by choice a loner. Certainly it would not have pleased the sociable Haast. Wakefield, Dieffenbach and Williams, besides making shorter journeys in relatively well populated areas, had coped by learning to speak Maori well.

Haast was a cultivated man and one would like to know what reading he carried to lighten work, responsibility and the tedium of camping in the rain. His fields of interest were disparate, his energy immense. Every evening he almost certainly would "write up his journal, dry and change the papers which held his plants, make his note of their habitat, sort out and pack his geological specimens, and prepare his bird skins." We know about Arthur Harper, who thought a change was good for you. "By way of amusement I had 'Cook's Voyages', 'Milton's Poems', and 'Pliny's Letters' in pocket editions, also two

## BIRDS  AS  FOOD

Maori ate birds of many kinds in many ways, fresh and preserved. The chief survival of their avian diet is the muttonbird of Southland. European consumption of New Zealand birds probably began with Cook's first voyage, especially with the extraordinarily omnivorous Joseph Banks. When the French came they ate birds too for at first rats were the only alternative fresh flesh food. On Marion's expedition Crozet noted that "in exchange for nails" the Maori "furnished us with fish, quail, wood-pigeons, and wild duck." The introduction of pigs relieved the pressure on birds, but unfortunately in coincidence with the introduction of European rats which greatly increased the toll.

Whaling men from European and American ships shot wild pigeons, for example, in great quantities for a change of diet. Charles Heaphy wrote that the "wood-pigeon is in New Zealand very large ... and the flesh is excellent. I have not unfrequently killed a dozen of them from one tree, so little alarm do they show at the report of a gun." Not unnaturally they almost became extinct, but strict protection has restored their numbers.

Many kinds of birds helped feed exploring parties, and the possibilities of catching birds were important in planning. "To give some idea of the help that we derive from birds", Arthur Harper wrote, "I may safely say that stores which would usually last for ten days comfortably would only give perhaps three days of good meals in the event of finding no birds." Harper, who worked with Charles Douglas in the mountains of Canterbury and Otago some twenty or so years later than Haast did, thought that of birds available in the bush the weka, or Maori hen, the best. Brunner said they were "easily captured by any one who can imitate their cry; for, when they hear their cry, they will answer and approach, and then are very easily caught by a small flax snare tied to a short small stick....".

Weka were cooked in every way a bush camp provided, but Harper's method sounded most appetising. "The best mode of roasting a weka is to make an opening at the back of his neck and clean him, then get a stone, about an inch in diameter, and, having made it red-hot, put it inside the bird, and, passing a stick through his body, stand him in front of the fire to roast. When the bird is cooked – in about half an hour – we plant the stick in the ground and proceed to carve slices off as it stands up in packs of cards. The latter I found most useful when alone, as I played 'Patience' or a game of Cribbage – right hand against left – by way of a change. It is curious how one generally has a tendency to cheat in favour of the left hand!" This was – no doubt unwittingly – New Zealand political comment.

Perhaps inspired by unmentioned leisure reading, Haast delighted in picturesque description. At Lake Rotoiti "deep blue waters reflected the high rocky mountain chains on its eastern and southern shores ... the lake swarmed with birds, giving life to this magnificent scene .... Towards evening the weather cleared, a magnificent rainbow threw its arch across the lake, and the setting sun gilded with deep hues the snow which streaked the serrated peaks of the surrounding mountain chains." Haast was not a selfish outdoorsman, but willing to find resources, whether coal or scenery, and suggest uses. Arthur Harper, a few years later than Haast, admired the beauty of New Zealand too, but unlike many mountain lovers, such as Douglas, was happy that ordinary folk should

front of us." The weka's taste was not its only advantage. Besides being "perhaps the most nourishing" it provided "a large amount of oil when in good condition – over a quarter of a pint can be obtained from a fat bird, which, though not very palatable, is sustaining, and can be baked with flour to advantage." Weka oil was also a successful softener for leather boots. The oil had other virtues too. Samuel Butler, a New Zealand explorer and runholder who went home to England to write *Erewhon* about New Zealand and much else about humanity, lauded weka oil as "sovereign for wounds and for hair." Brunner used it to dress severe injuries received from falling on sharp granite rocks.

Weka were not the only useful bird in the bush. Dieffenbach claimed of North Island kaka that "their flesh is tender and well-flavoured ...." Harper agreed about the kaka but also thought the "kakapo, and kea of the parrot tribe, the wood pidgeon, blue, grey, and paradise ducks are all excellent for eating, and if one is hard pushed for food, the smaller birds, such as the crow, tui, paraquet, and saddle-backs, are all acceptable." In another place Harper, perhaps with a recent meal in mind, strongly qualified the "excellent" for at least the adult paradise duck: "The Paradise duck is too much like a tough goose, in my opinion, but the 'flappers', or young ones, are very good indeed when roasted." This sounds ruthless, but Harper did not spare even the unique among the species. "The kiwi is passable when one is hungry, though personally I do not like him, but being more nutritious than savoury, it is not to be despised." Eating some birds brought its own penalty. For the Irish mountaineer Green, a pukeko proved "but poor eating, there being but little flesh on his carcase, and the fat adhered so tenaciously to our pot that, had we wished to do so, we were unable to forget our friend of the gay plumage for many days." Brunner thought memorable birds all too common, for "birds, eaten by themselves, much disorder the stomach."

A bird-based Maori food industry which still flourishes is muttonbirding, preserving the flesh of the chick of the sooty shearwater. The chicks are taken from their nest burrows on islands immediately south of the South Island. According to an 1840s witness, "the muttonbird at this stage of life is a lump of fat, into which, when it is plucked and cold, the fingers sink, forming deep indentations ... curing them is to split open and slightly salt them, after which they are hung up in capacious chimneys and well smoked, dripping oil the while ...." This nourishing food keeps well; liking it is a matter of custom and taste.

share it. "This is one of the finest gorges I know, within easy reach of tourists ... the mountains rise abruptly to the height of 3,000 or 4,000 feet. The contrast of dark-green bush and the almost precipitous hillsides, with the grey rock walls of the gorge, rising 100 ft. sheer, and overhanging, out of the river, which comes boiling and roaring down over immense boulders, is very grand; while in the distance, between the bushclad hills, can be seen the glaciers of Drummond's Peak ...."

Others too, by Harper's time, were willing to advocate the commercial exploitation of wild beauty. As William McHutcheson wrote in 1882: "If a Mount Morgan or Bishchoff [Australian goldfields] were suddenly discovered in New Zealand, how the colony would throb with excitement, and what pleasurable anticipation would be indulged in of the wealth to be won from its golden ore! .... But behold! a greater than Mt. Morgan is here. Sooner or later the heaviest 'leads' dwindle to a thread, and the richest 'wash' runs out; but Fiordland is an everlasting possession its scenic attractions *a perpetual and ever increasing* mine of wealth to the colony. Fifty years hence, and the very name of Mount Morgan may be forgotten; while the lakes and rivers, the peaks and valleys of Fiordland will fully then be coming known and appreciated. What the 'tourist traffic' really means financially only those who have watched its ceaseless ebb and flow in some favorite world's resort can realise." Switzerland, Niagara Falls and Scotland demonstrate "what a purely tourist traffic may become." And they do it, "mark you, *in perpetuity.*"

Before tourism there had to be routes and then roads, and before them the basic work. On this trip Haast began to reduce into order various systems of mountains. His magnificent mountaineering won him views which allowed, even forced, such systemisation. "Towards the east rose chain above chain of wild and rugged mountain peaks .... Towards the west rose high rocky mountain-chains, only broken through where the Buller pierces them on its course towards the sea; on the south our view was shut in by the rocky spurs of a huge mountain." To an explorer-surveyor-cartographer these were not just beautiful mountains, but maps, systems, angles, distances, camps, trails, trig points, triangulation, requiring names for hills and ranges, creeks, rivers, falls and lakes. There were decades of challenge ahead.

After this view from Mount Robert, obstacles to travel seemed even more plentiful and difficult. Dense scrub of manuka and matagouri faced them everywhere, plucking at their clothes, scratching their flesh. But after leaving Lake Rotoiti Haast's party met two men, come to guide them to a camp on the Howard River. On the way Haast first saw the Spencer Mountains and named the highest peak Mount Franklin in honour of the recently lost Arctic explorer Sir John Franklin. When they reached Lake Rotoroa they found B, H, and F cut on a tree, definitely traces of the expedition of Brunner, Heaphy and Fox along the Buller. Moving on, they named mountains for a great geologist, Murchison, and for Owen, the creative and perceptive palaeontologist who, from a solitary thigh bone, had been able to reconstruct the great moa in his imagination.

Travelling was rough. Often they were foodless for many hours at a time because supplies, even of wild birds, were running short. The Maori wished to turn back, claiming this country might have wild men and enormous lizards. The party actually ran out of provisions and existed only on woodhens and eels.

A beautiful view of Nelson province's Lake Brunner as a modern fisherman would see it. *(P.R. May Collection, University of Canterbury Library, Christchurch)*

Eels were usually available and very fine eating too, particularly silver ones as compared to the black. Explorers also ate kiwi, however repulsive eating the national emblem seems today. Harper, like most of the hungry men, found kiwi "passable when one is hungry …." Harper knew much about the bush from the Maori, from Charles Douglas and from experience. Perhaps harder – or hungrier – men than Haast, they seemed more omnivorous. Harper ate "several edible plants … not very nourishing, nor can I honestly say very nice …." Various ferns, young supplejack vines, wild parsley, and fern roots too: Captain Cook would have smiled at Harper.

There were more problems than hunger on Haast's expedition. Mackay had branched off to fulfil a task of his own and became ill. He had run a spine of a Spaniard, a speargrass, into his knee, the wound forming a huge ball of matter; the knee swelled "as thick as his thigh." Cutting it with a razor gave him a little relief, but worry strained everyone. Here too Harper had bush answers. For cuts, presumably even from razors, miro pine gum was "the finest healing ointment for an open wound that I have ever used …." Harper had seen the Maori chew pepper tree leaves to poultice wounds, which had quickly healed. Others assured him that "the crop of a kakapo, when freshly killed, makes a capital poultice if applied to a sore, drawing out all poisonous matter quickly

261

and effectually ...." Kakapo crops were not easily obtained. For less dramatic but no less important complaints Harper knew effective plants too, one laxative and another costive. With or without Harper's bush remedies, Mackay survived. At the coast, reached with great suffering after a self-administered operation to drain the swelling, he met a former medical student who had learned enough to give some effective assistance.

Haast's supplies were running low and he worried that the Maori might simply give up, sit down, and die of depression and starvation, a risk against which he had been warned. Death from depression certainly happened, as a North Island explorer had found in the same years. "A stout young Maori of twenty years from Tolaga Bay, on the East Coast ... had attached himself to Colenso. Hearing that Koroneho was ill and likely to die, he became greatly depressed and was inconsolable and quickly sank into a low state. Despite Dr. Ford's declaration that there was nothing physically wrong with him, his condition gradually became worse, and, refusing to be removed from his place of vigil, he died within a few hours." However mysterious it might seem, Haast was right to worry about such things.

Brunner thought the Maori "bear hunger badly. They get irritable in temper, and lazy. I had much trouble with all but my own native Ekehu, the rest continually asking in what way I could compensate them for their sufferings ...

## PERSONALISED PESTS

Anglo-Saxon nationalism played a part in the naming of the various pests which plagued explorers and surveyors. The two worst pests in the South Island were called "Wild Irishman" (*Discaria toumatou*) and "Spaniard" (*Aciphylla colersoi*). There are other species of Spaniard too, called the Horrid (*A. horrida*) and the Fierce (*A. ferox*). There is something fitting in the names, for certainly the plants' namesakes had been historical thorns in many an Englishman's flesh. Like most weeds the plants flourished, the curses of their victims seeming only to spur their growth.

Samuel Butler, Canterbury runholder and English novelist, described the Wild Irishman as "a thorny tree growing with ungainly unmanageable boughs sometimes as large as our own hawthorn trees – generally about the size of a gooseberry bush. He does not appear to me to have a single redeeming feature being neither pleasant to the eye nor good for food. He is highly inflammable when dry, and a single match judiciously applied will burn acres and acres of him." The national names exercised some sort of subconscious influence, for those describing the pests seemed always to personalise, just as Butler had. His Mesopotamia run and the Mackenzie country were really overgrown with Wild Irishmen and Spaniards. Both pests grew in groves and were very big, some Wild Irishmen up to 5.5 metres high. Sheepmen claimed those big ones grew so thickly that if you managed to cut a square clear of them the trees left would form a proper holding pen for sheep.

Personalising presented some problems. A girl came out to marry a man who worked at Mount Peel. But she was met at Lyttelton by a station bullock wagon. While in Lyttelton a comic warned her that her prospective husband lived among Spaniards and Wild Irishmen "who drew blood from someone each day." The frightened girl took off her engagement ring and refused to be delivered to such a lawless constantly lamenting their coming into the bush." Dieffenbach sympathised with them on this point: "The natives in general are much too civilised and sociable, and know their own interests too well, to live in a gloomy and inhospitable forest." Colenso too had found that Maori did not like the bush, but whether they simply resented the difficulties there, or whether an ancestral revulsion or other cultural inhibition operated, no one seemed to know. Probably it was a matter of individual preference. Most of us reared very much as Harper was have not the slightest desire to climb through Harper's Saddle, even for pay.

Brunner, exploring earlier in the same area as Haast, did not have the happy experience with the Maori which Wakefield had in the North Island. The Maori insisted on taking their wives, with unfortunate consequences when the women quarrelled. On one occasion the wives fought physically and when the husbands joined in Brunner found it hard to restore the peace. From then on he gave way, even if he thought a different route better. The porters bluntly pointed out his dependence on them: "I am afraid to quarrel with the natives, for I am told to look out for myself if I choose, and they will do the same."

The Maori were not causing any trouble for Haast, but the party was worried. At last one of the party, Mackay, recognised some mountains and soon afterwards found a trail he knew from his exploration of 1857. They could now

---

community; it required all her would-be husband's power of persuasion to get her to marry him and live on Mount Peel.

Butler thought the Irishman "a nuisance, but Spaniard is simply detestable – he is sometimes called spear grass. He grows about the size of a molehill – all over the back country everywhere as thick as molehills in a very molehilly field at home. His blossom is attached to a high spike bristling with spears pointed every way and very acute – each leaf is pointed with a strong spear, and so firm is this leaf that if you come within its reach no amount of clothing about the legs will prevent you from feeling the effects of his displeasure. I have had my legs marked all over – red spots – from them. Horses hate him – and no wonder – in the back country when travelling without a track it is impossible to keep your horse from yawing about this way and that to dodge them, if the horse gets stuck up by three or four of them growing close together he will jump them or do anything rather than walk through them .... The whole plant burns with great brilliancy giving a peculiarly bright light and lasting for a long time ... a spaniard laid on the fire would throw an illumination on the subject which no amount of sticks would do." An early theory argued that Spaniard spines were to guard the plants from moa, but others consider that the spines developed as a response to drought. Whatever the reason this weed crossed the border from nuisance to actual danger for both men and horses.

Some Spaniards had virtue, if you took trouble to seek it. Edward Shortland, a very early European traveller through South Canterbury, gathered details from the Maori about the various plants. They apparently used the Spaniard more or less commercially. He described "how the taramea, the needle-pointed Spaniard of the pioneers, was held over a fire until it exuded a highly prized oil which the natives used as a perfume and sent to tribes in the North Island either as barter or as a present from one chief to another." The roots of another species were eaten in time of hunger, but had to be pulled up by rope to avoid the spines.

follow a blazed route. From the beginning Haast had carefully studied the terrain to carry out his assigned duty, as well as doing things which ordinary European exploration did not comprise. At sea it was relatively easy to take specialists along, as Cook had done, even if they were often a nuisance. It was not easy on land and so no one could specialise. "The scientist had not only to be a geologist and an explorer, but a porter, a scout, a surveyor, a botanist, a zoologist, an artist, a cook, a leader of men possessed of a Mark Tapley disposition, heartening his men however depressed his own spirits."

Fortunately a tireless worker, Haast was half a dozen specialists rolled into one. He combined these attributes with an iron will; in this he is reminiscent of Banks. It took such determination to climb mountains – along with immense physical exertion – and then to fill swags with botanical specimens, rocks and minerals, even on the way uphill in case they should see no more. On land, exploring scientists could never relax; an outcrop of rock might be important, a new plant must be examined, birds and animals must be studied as the chance offered. And every ridge top meant another sketch. Before small cameras made photography physically easy, sketching was part of every geologist's, explorer's or officer's training. And if an explorer did come to a plain, rare enough in New Zealand, he had to estimate its area, check its fertility, gauge its suitability for

After the mid-point of the 19th century photography began to show us more precisely what the living conditions of explorers and mountaineers could be. Even the glare of the open fire on the film does not disguise the uncomfortable simplicity of this bivouac. *(University of Canterbury Library, Christchurch)*

settlement. When these things were auspicious he must look for routes for roadbuilding.

Some explorers may have preferred such pressures in the field to what awaited in camp. They were approaching West Coast weather with its rain and when the sun shone they had to dry their plants, and often their papers too, before they could write up their diaries or sort and store specimens. In a small party, when all else was done they had to make a fire and cook whatever there was to eat. Haast knew all this well enough. Just as the great explorers Cook and d'Urville had to be competent sailors and commanders of men, so these early explorers of New Zealand's land mass had to be men of all tasks as well as officers of every responsibility.

Land explorers in New Zealand appreciated the absence of poisonous snakes or ferocious land animals. But water was a constant insidious enemy; dangerous rivers and torrential rain provided soakings and danger at crossings. In pre-antibiotic days pneumonia was very threatening but Haast fortunately was immensely strong in physique and health. Yet the rivers often formed primitive paths. And everyone knew that to walk down a river meant eventually coming to another river or the coast. In spite of this reassuring quality, both Haast and Burnett found river pathways frustrating. "Suppose you are walking down a riverbed, crossing and recrossing the stream as it winds ... to a place where it is too deep or rapid to cross ... in all probability there is a perpendicular precipice, or at all events the steep spur of a mountain over which you must scramble, sometimes to the height of a 1,000 feet ...." And then "Perhaps after toiling and spending your strength for hours, you find yourself on the riverbed again, perhaps a quarter of a mile from where you started."

River and coastal bluffs could be dangerously difficult. Brunner found these precipices frightening: "it tries one's nerves to be dangling on a flax rope 100 feet above a granite rock, with the load on the feet and no hold for the hands ... we had at least 100 feet perpendicular to descend ...." That was dangerous work for men not mountaineers, and worthy of Brunner's Oxford understatement. "Tries one's nerves" indeed! Further south the country was even rougher. After condemning one river, Harper said that Douglas spoke "of the Turnbull River further south – which he explored – as having 16 miles of gorges out of a total length of 18 miles. A small flat of half a mile on such a river would make the whole difference to the exploration ...." Harper once worked his way up a river, carrying all his provisions, which descended 740 metres through two gorges in only somewhat over five kilometres. Crossing rivers was dangerous as well as arduous. Shortage of provisions at one point forced Haast to send some men back. But they had come to a great river, the Buller, rising swiftly because of heavy rain. This meant that only those who could swim could be retained; non-swimmers faced the equally daunting trail home.

In pressing forward or countermarching home, walking through fern was often so difficult that in desperation they would set fire to it. They had little choice. The strong and reflexible stalks, often nearly two metres high, entangle a traveller as effectively as supplejack does in the bush. After burning the fern, loaded men could walk more easily but suffered from pervasive and choking dust, which the pollen season also provided. Further south such problems plagued them at least as badly, perhaps worse west of the divide. In much of his work Arthur Harper found the "undergrowth in the bush is as a rule so bad, that progress is very slow ... carrying anything it is almost impossible to make any way at all. It is therefore a saving of time to take a billhook and 'blaze', or cut a narrow track, before attempting to carry any load through the undergrowth." He once confronted impenetrable mountain scrub one to three metres in height, whose "denseness can hardly be appreciated by those who have not experienced it. I have seen it thick enough to walk and crawl on the top of ...." He found the only stuff impervious to the branches' pointed ends was "Gabardine", made by Burberry and Son in Basingstoke, England.

Travelling along the Buller was slow and difficult but Haast found some compensations. Like most Europeans he was favourably impressed by the songs of New Zealand birds; and not only by the songs, for there was much amusement and interest in kaka and kea, birds which did not sing. By this time they needed cheering up, for food was short. New Zealand had no dangerous

Heaphy sketched Thomas Brunner ascending a cliff near the West Coast and carefully guarding those essentials of bush travel, his dog and his gun. (*Alexander Turnbull Library, Wellington*)

animals but was also nearly free of edible mammals. And naturally, many birds are hard to catch. In March Burnett wrote that "our allowance for the last two or three weeks is 1 1/2 pints of oatmeal porridge morning and evening, sometimes with a little bacon boiled in it, and 1/2 lb. bread a day. Bread uses so much flour that we are determined to have no more, so we mix the oatmeal and flour together for the porridge …. Unfortunately our sugar and bacon are done and most of our salt. Fortunately we have plenty pepper."

A condiment like pepper is much more important in such context than it might seem. The food had little variety and spices were as important to explorers as they had been to Europeans in the Middle Ages. Dull food lessens appetite, even with unremitting physical labour, and explorers needed the energy which appetite finds. Brunner was well aware of this; he had found it out on his first exploration. So on his second: "when I left Nelson, Mr Heaphy smiled at my stock of pepper, from its quantity and bulk; but, were he here, he would find it a great relish to his sowthistle &c …. I would recommend anyone to take a good quantity who would be bound to the bush."

Pepper is no substitute for food with calories, and by now even the tough Haast was weak. Nonetheless he, Burnett and a Maori set out to ascend Mount Mueller, another Haast-bestowed name. Haast did not oppose using Maori names, but found difficulty doing so in the southern mountains. He explained that "with the exception of Kaimatau, at the head of the Waimakiriri, which is probably Mount Davie, Ao-rangi (Mount Cook) and Unuroa (the Arrowsmith Range), the Maori appeared to have no names for the principal peaks in the central chain, which is astonishing, considering that they have named almost every creek and every lake …."

Charles Heaphy, artist, explorer, colonist and soldier, seen here wearing his Victoria Cross.
*(Alexander Turnbull Library, Wellington)*

Harper would not have agreed with Haast about Mount Cook. His Maori friends told him that they did not name mountain peaks which were in ranges. Naturally a single peak, such as Taranaki, was named or took the name of its district. The Maori certainly named the great peaks of the North Island – indeed given their relative prominence it would have been hard not to – but Aorangi for Mount Cook is not certain. They told Harper, definitely and emphatically, that the word meant any large white fluffy cloud, and not the mountain. Brunner did not agree, for he was told by Maori that the highest peak in the range of mountains he could see was called Tuhaurahi (which could be a corruption of Aoraki, as in Te Aoraki), and was the highest in the land. Presumably this was Mount Cook, and if so it had a name. A fine modern writer, Barry Brailsford, gives the Maori name for Mount Algidus (Otumapuhi), a Maori name for a range of peaks (Ruahikihiki), and a Maori name for Cabot Ridge (Tauatamateraki). It is certain names were applied to some dominant southern natural features, but whether the significance had to be physical importance or the connection of an individual human with the feature, is less clear.

The Maori seemed to have their reservations about mountains, as indeed Europeans had until relatively recently. Colenso, in the North Island, found them extremely reluctant to go into mountain country. Wakefield found them opposed to people climbing mountains, because the local paramount chief usually linked their tapu with his. Dieffenbach found the Maori uneasy about helping him ascend Mount Egmont. "The natives could not understand what induced me to ascend Mount Egmont; they tried much to dissuade me from the attempt, by saying that the mountain was 'tapu', that there were ngarara (crocodiles) on it …." Yet, Dieffenbach said, Maori helped him with porters and supplies, even though to them "the mountains are peopled with mysterious and mishappen animals; the black points, which he sees from afar in the dazzling snow, are fierce and monstrous birds; a supernatural spirit breathes on him in the evening breeze, or is heard in the rolling of a loose stone." Harper, forty years later, spoke of "all the superstitions concerning the ranges that Maori have …." Yet those with Dieffenbach stuck to their agreement until quite near the top, and then they stopped only because they were suffering from the cold. There seemed a touch of ambivalence in North Island Maori attitudes; awe, reverence and fear usually overcame curiousity. The explorers and mountaineers of the West Coast found much the same Maori feeling there.

What the Maori thought of or named mountains were the least of the Haast party's worries as they faced Mount Mueller. They had only a pannikin of biscuit dough and one roasted weka. Probably to their relief, cloud and rain prevented their ascent. Back at camp Haast had a good look at provisions. They could last ten more days, if everyone were reduced to one small pot of boiled flour twice a day, added to whatever they could catch. Hungry but not lost, they were following Mackay's tracks. But by the end of the first week in March they left country the Maori knew. Again the Maori feared, or claimed to, that enormous lizards roamed the strange country.

Rain not reptiles hindered them. Reduced to a single meal a day, Haast's party found even undug fern root rotted by the rain. In spite of hunger-induced weakness, by heroic efforts in crossing a large pass and going through more mountains they finally reached the river Grey. Haast once pointed out that the source of the Grey was well known to Maori. He was always very interested in Maori geographic information and used what he learned effectively. Tarapuhi and his brother Tainui, from Kaiapoi, drew a map in the sand for him, with deep furrows for rivers and little mounds as mountains, showing the best way to the east coast. As Haast found it completely correct it gave him confidence in Maori assistance.

The Maori knew much of the information Europeans sought, but needed it for different reasons. A quick way to the West Coast for a Maori war party might not be sufficient or suitable for droving sheep. Large-scale agriculture or commerce had greater requirements than had minor trades or raids, so every route had to be assessed for these demands. Apart from this, Europeans placed information, once accurately measured, on paper for whoever needed it.

Towards the end of their West Coast journey Haast's party very nearly starved. Occasionally they caught an eel or a weka but that did not go very far. Haast was worried, and rationed food closely and carefully. "It was high time that we should have some prospect of speedily obtaining better rations ... though eleven days previously I had calculated that our provisions would then last but ten days, I had so arranged that we still had sufficient left for eight scanty meals." An exhausted Maori, Dicky, gave up: "I can go no further. No food in my belly." Haast had been forewarned and he inspired Dicky to carry on. Everyone who travelled with Haast described how cheerful and determined he appeared in adversity, how eager and willing to accept his share of every burden. Of Haast and food Burnett said that, "you cannot induce him to take the least particle more than his share; nay, though requiring it so much himself, he insists on contributing to the sick. He is a fine fellow. These are times to try a man's mettle."

The party saw wild dog tracks and would certainly have eaten a dog with delight. They did not see or catch one. Even men interested in birds and science gave way to real hunger in the New Zealand bush, so barren of food compared to the forests of North America or Europe. On one occasion Harper's dog caught a white kiwi. His party knew rarity gave it value, but "hunger for meat overcame scientific ardour, so we made it into stew! The skin is the most nutritious part of a kiwi, therefore we could not afford to keep it for stuffing." Poor quality, not scarcity, also plagued explorers. On Haast's trip, fern root, plentiful but often rotten, contributed little to appetite or sustenance. Near the journey's end one of the now ravenous party managed, after much trouble, to catch a very small eel. They roasted the meagre carcass upon a stick, and scraped their flour bags for what few grains stuck to them. Eel and flour paste made them all, especially Haast, used to hearty German living, realise the incongruity of it all. "Our situation would have afforded to a Schalken a fine opportunity for a splendid picture; our five figures with their thin faces and torn and patched clothes, standing round the blazing fire, gazing anxiously at our poor supper ...."

Finally they met a Maori from their reprovisioning party and then, Burnett said, "half a mile further down we came to the canoe and camp .... What a glorious sight – bags of flour, biscuit, sugar, and last but not least, salt! After our Maori salutations were over we each got a biscuit, a bottle of wine was broached .... It is truly astonishing to see the change in Beckman. He is quite another man

.... As for myself ... I felt 'James was himself again,' a weight taken from my heart, and a most comfortable weight was put in my stomach ...." As Brunner put it, "such is bush life, full of feasts and fasts."

Recovering astonishingly quickly, the little group reached the West Coast at a Maori pa, where they were given a strident Maori welcome. Haast's poetic comment on the gregarious turmoil is implicitly critical: "Instead of the soft murmur of the rivulet, the roaring of larger streams, the rush of the wind through the tops of the high evergreen trees, and the merry song and the variegated notes of the fearless birds ... we heard nothing but Maori songs and Maori noise from morning till night; insufficient, however (and this was our only consolation) to drown the majestic roaring of the surf as it flowed over the pebbly and sandy shores." This successful journey was an important achievement, albeit arduous. Starvation amid strenuous exertion had made the last days of it, Burnett said, "for one or two of the party ... a run for life." Haast learned lessons from that. But they had done what they were meant to do and science and geography in New Zealand were much augmented. The provincial government was grateful.

Over the succeeding years Haast's search for coal, his investigation and report on the Lyttelton tunnel for Canterbury, his exploration of the Canterbury rivers and his finding of moa bones, all added to his reputation as a scientific explorer. In 1862 he went exploring again, his life so busy in so many ways that perhaps getting off by himself, no matter the hardship, was the only way to relax.

Haast was sent to assess the likelihood of gold along the southern boundary line of Canterbury at the nearest points to the Otago goldfields. He also intended to go to the West Coast by way of Lake Wanaka, having heard from Maori of a pass there. A war party, some of Te Rauparaha's men from the north end of the South Island under the former Taranaki chief Te Puoho, had crossed to the West Coast in 1836, moved south along the coast, and gone inland. They raided Southland and took Tuturau, but a retaliatory taua or war party under Tuhawaiki and Taiaroa, who was visiting from Otago, regained the village and captured the northern raiders, except Te Puoho who was killed, and Ngawhakawa, who escaped. He made his way alone back the 1500 kilometres through the Haast Pass (Tiori-patea) and up the West Coast to Golden Bay, a daunting trip in 1836 and no less so in 1863. There was a pass; the expedition had used one.

Difficulties plagued Haast's expedition from the start. Extremely heavy falls of winter snow had filled the rivers and lakes of the area. And the snow had caused not only high waters but a series of colossal avalanches. Haast encountered one of them: "the sound accompanying it was like the firing of many guns of heavy calibre, or loud peals of thunder ... followed by rattling sounds ... resembling the platoon firing of an army. The first crash was produced by the main fall of the avalanche; the latter by smaller masses of snow and rocks being brought down in its trail." Haast found no goldfields in Canterbury but came across very active gold diggers in western Otago. He was happy about the minerals in spite of the mess, and he loved the country, Lake Wanaka reminding him of Lake Lucerne. However dear, European memories gave way to New Zealand action. In January 1863 Haast's group rode westward around Wanaka as far as the station of Stuart Kinross and Company, and from there took a boat to the end of the

A view of Haast Pass by Haast himself. The pass had been known and used by the Maori; now Haast himself had travelled it from the lakes to the sea, survived and told the tale to the world. *(Alexander Turnbull Library, Wellington)*

lake where they found a number of sawyers making timber products for the splendid market of the Clutha goldfields.

Haast consulted an aged Maori who knew the route to the coast. Because of the appearance of the mountains he was doubtful of the beginning of that route and picked another. So Haast and four men, two of them former sailors, started on foot carrying heavy packs of four weeks' provisions, tents and instruments. They led a horse packing eighty-eight kilograms of flour. Canterbury was less frugal than Westland or else Haast was extraordinarily valued. A few years later Arthur Harper was very critical of his provincial government for being so penurious as to send only two men out exploring. "It would have made our work considerably quicker and less trying had we been given a man who could carry a good load of provisions, for two or three days, from habitation, and then be sent back .... The authorities, however, did not consider it necessary, not having any idea of what rough work it really was; in fact, on one occasion when mention was made of the necessity of carrying heavy loads, someone asked, 'Why do not you employ a spring dray or pack-horse?' Imagine a spring dray over 50 foot boulders or along a narrow arête! It was often difficult to get the dog over the country."

Haast did not think they were well off. But in spite of shortsighted economy and the difficulties it caused, he loved exploration, especially when in truly new country. "Birds which never before have seen a human being, look inquisitively and without fear at the intruder in their domain. Though alone, you do not feel lonely .... Sometimes I was awakened from my happy dream, and brought back to stern reality when my load shifted to one side and the straps cut too deeply into my shoulders." After only a day's journey Haast sent the horse back at a steep rocky gorge, which meant carrying the provisions through in two loads each, except for Haast, who had only one. While the men brought their second loads he climbed 120 metres and believed he saw a pass in the distance. Upon proceeding through difficult country, water flow direction indicated, after a relatively small distance, that they had found the pass. Labouring on reasonably contentedly, soon the explorers were beyond doubting that following the Haast River would take them to the west coast; they gave three hearty cheers, followed by a "nobbler." By this time they deserved a treat, for they had travelled about eighty-eight kilometres through very difficult country.

To find the conditions and length of the way onward they climbed a majestic mountain which they named Mount Brewster, and used it as a site for a central topographical station. The mountain provided plenty of geological samples, but also new life in a seemingly barren environment. When the party had climbed about a hundred metres, "the true kings of the New Zealand Alps, the great, green, Alpine parrots ... made their appearance. Soaring above us, they soon approached, and, alighting close to us on the ground with a look of self-confidence, they examined the unknown strangers .... At other spots, carpets of flowers of indescribable beauty were spread .... All fatigue was now forgotten, and our hearts beat more freely in the lighter mountain air ...." Encountering kea turned out to be a curse, not blessing. Haast worked furiously on the mountain, both writing and collecting. But "true to its parrot's nature, one ... had begun to study botany, and in its attempt to open the paper [parcel of plants] had taken it from its secure place, and dragging it to the brink of the precipice, had sent it rolling down some thousands of feet. After vain attempts to find my precious treasures, addressing myself in Colonial language to the perpetrators of the evil deed, I reluctantly started to return." Provoking enough in a peaceful city, in those circumstances the loss must have been almost unbearable. Colonial language was forgivable.

As commonly happens in that area of New Zealand there was intermittent heavy rain and, between the downpours, rain of some measure almost continuously. By this time food was getting short, no new experience for Haast. A big man, he knew people doubted his tales of hardship: "looking at my well-fed body, I do not look like a man who has been starved; yet very often, half a pannikin of lilipi with a woodhen's leg in it was a great delicacy for me, and thinking of ... an Irish stew with onions, made my mouth water." Occasionally the bush and mountain men mention something special, but distance from civilisation lowered their standards and it does not sound particularly exciting, at least not in a positive way. Haast's point was well made.

Haast named rivers after Burke and Wills, the ill-fated Australian explorers, and another after Landsborough, one of the talented men who searched for them. In comparison with the first two, Haast was equally intrepid but also balanced. According to companions, he "never for a single moment lost his good temper, his courage or his perseverance." For he had troubles too. Not only was food getting scarce but he fell heavily when stepping on a treacherous piece of moss, and cut his leg badly. This was serious. Accidents were dreaded, for by definition exploring takes you far from competent medical help, from basics such as proper nursing and food. A few years later, on similar work,

Arthur Harper twisted his ankle badly, a relatively minor accident. But he was alone, multiplying the risk and often the accident. He managed to get back to camp, feed himself and cut enough firewood for the time he could be campbound. It took two days rest before he could move about at all freely. But as he said, "an accident like this, though slight, would be quite enough to lead to fatal results if it occurred far away from camp, because no anxiety would be felt by those in the low country for a week or two at least. Generally, indeed, two to three months might pass before a search party would be organized, as we often do not know how long we are going to be away." Larger parties such as Haast's avoided that particular consequence.

Even so, convalescence palled quickly in Haast's straitened circumstances. The main food was boiled flour, occasionally with some bird meat or a small piece of bacon put into it, "to give some taste to our 'billsticker's paste', as a prosaic member of our party called it. He did not understand the poetry of bush life." Seeking a little variety in provisions enthralled explorers, on land or sea. Their circumstances make our freeze-dried and powdered food seem gourmet fare by comparison. In the high mountain country Arthur Harper sometimes welcomed rain, notoriously unpleasant at height, because this gave time to properly prepare good big meals. Naturally the dishes were somewhat *cordon vert*. One of Harper's menus was: Piki-piki soup, sardines à la Karangarua, boiled kiwi with fern, roast weka, flapjack and jam, and one dried fig for dessert. He was

The Maori Saddle, here sketched by Charles Douglas, was an alternative route between Lake Wanaka and Westland, thought to be somewhat faster than Haast Pass. *(Alexander Turnbull Library, Wellington)*

273

proud of sardines à la Karangarua. "Cut a thin strip of bacon, roll the sardine in it, fry for a few minutes, and – as the cookery books say – 'serve hot' on toast." As it had at sea, canned food greatly helped provisioning, but there were risks in it too. Primitive transport battered cans, and whether fruit, meat or fish, leaks caused spoilage. A tin of sardines poisoned Charles Douglas seriously, the cause made certain when a test tin killed the camp cat.

During this forced convalescence from his accident Haast concluded that the "Norwesters" in the Canterbury Plains were winds resulting from the height of mountains in the west of the province. Lying ill west of the mountains he deduced from constant heavy rain beating on his frail shelter that most moisture that west winds picked up from thousands of miles of sea fell on the western slopes of the mountains. The warm dry "Norwester" on the east side matched the classic chinook of Alberta or foehn wind of Italy.

Difficulties seemed to multiply near the end of this successful pass expedition, mainly because of rain. Rivers flooded, nonetheless they had to camp near the streams; there was nowhere else. It could be unpleasant, as Haast recorded: "as the water from the river rose higher and higher it extinguished the fire and we were in the dark. Cold and wet to the skin, we huddled close together under the little bit of overhanging rock ...." They made the best of it: "one of my companions, a jolly sailor ... enlivened the night with his yarns. Sometimes we were with him in Chinese waters chased by a pirate, or at the Guano Islands ... or in Canada on the Lorenzo River loading timber ... like Bayard, without fear, but, unlike him, not always without reproach. After a time

A photograph of Sir Julius von Haast in his maturity. This vigorous traveller, able scientist, perceptive artist, and contro- versial writer made major contributions to 19th-century New Zealand's knowledge of itself – and to the world's knowledge of New Zealand. *(University of Canterbury Library, Christchurch)*

274

he became silent ... the howling of the wind, and above all, the thundering and deafening roar of the swollen river made the night dismal and dreary."

Every explorer had one unforgettable camp and Brunner's was the night when "the thatch we had barely kept our kits dry, and we had to brave the rain

---

## THE HAAST PASS CONTROVERSY

Worldwide honours did not save Haast from the windy buffeting of any tall poppy in New Zealand. There was controversy with Charles Cameron about who actually discovered the pass. The discussion at a chance meeting between three men of Haast's party and Cameron near the head of the Makarora River, continued in a series of letters in the press between one of Haast's men, Holmes, and Cameron in 1863. The controversy will never be satisfactorily settled because it involves individual definition of exploration and discovery.

Cameron, an officer in the Land Wars, and a competent explorer before that, had definitely gone into the area of the Pass, mere days before Haast. Probably he did not go through to the coast, as he claimed, for he quite incorrectly described it. But in 1881 a powder flask with a name on it was found west of the mountains. The finder, T.N. Brodrick, a competent explorer and surveyor, said that "on a peak to the west of Haast's Pass and considerably above the line of perpetual snow in a cairn of stones which were frozen together, I found a powder flask with the inscription deeply scratched into it on both sides 'Charles Cameron, Jany. 1863.' The place was wild enough when I was there and Charles Cameron, whoever he was and whatever his object, must have been an adventurous man to have visited it 18 years ago. I wrote his name and the date, 1863, and my own and the date, 1881, on a stone and left them there, but I brought away the tin for a curiosity. Cameron was the first man who explored this country, and I suppose no one had been up this hill since. I shall call it Mt. Cameron."

But the fine surveyor John H. Baker had "arrived at the top of the pass, afterwards called the Haast Pass" much earlier, as his diary of 1861 shows. Baker did not claim the discovery, perhaps because he, as a surveyor, knew that the real work was testing a pass by actually going through it right to the other end, thus verifying its practicability. If Cameron has a good claim as discoverer then so does Baker, who had actually explored the general area two years before Cameron entered it. There can be no doubt about that and perhaps it should be Baker's Pass.

Cameron had found the pass, almost certainly without knowing about Baker, a few days before Haast crossed through. As Brodrick said "whoever put [the flask] there could not have failed to see the Pass as he could not have ascended from any other direction. It was a very unfrequented place ...." Probably Charles Douglas, not at all unused to exploration's hardship, put the essence of the matter best. "Cameron like allmost all prospectors left no record of his journey except traditions of public house blowing. So to Dr. Haast who did leave an account of his journay & roughly laid off the country, all credit must be due." However he also suggested Haast be more generous in acknowledging information he gained from others. But his point about making information available is emphasising the whole purpose of real exploration; publicity is the key to credit but is also the only way to complete the task. Haast had explored the pass properly, travelled along it to the coast and back again. It is not unfittingly named. In any case the Maori knew the pass; Haast had learned of a pass from them.

until morning ... on a cliff in a black birch forest. The rain poured down, loosening the stones of which the hill was formed, which came rolling by us ... and the wind tore up the trees on all sides, causing a simultaneous shudder among all the party when we heard their crash." In a rainy mountainous country, floods, slips and sheer exposure endangered travellers. Roaring rivers were bad enough; the storms were worse. The sailor with Haast said that he had never seen anything like them on the world's oceans.

Things were not always bad, the scenery magnificent even if the going were rough. Haast's group passed many large rivers and finally found themselves on an open flat, an oasis in the wilderness of forest. He smiled to find this "the best hunting ground that I met with in all my New Zealand travels, literally alive with woodhens, and many kakapo to fill our larder .... Now the services of our faithful dog were fully appreciated. Before this, he was often in everyone's way." Food was not the only success; after crossing a large tributary of the Haast, which they named the Thomas, they saw the sea. Although it took two days to battle through the last ten kilometres of swamps and supplejacks, on 20 February they stood in the surf and gave three hearty cheers. They could find no Maori anywhere near, a disappointment, for they needed a change of food and of company too. Afterwards they learned no one had lived there for many years.

Regaining their large provision depot at the pass's summit took about ten days. A celebratory meal, hearty and happy, cheered them all, for it consisted "of doughboys, at discretion, with sugar and brandy sauce ... two teetotallers in the party ... thoroughly enjoyed the brandy sauce." Six weeks of most arduous travelling returned them to Thompson's station on Lake Wanaka. The men rested. Haast wrote his massive and eloquent report to the committee, dated 3 March, the day they reached Thompson's station, and published in Christchurch less than a month later. Given the exhaustion of the explorers and the travelling conditions, this brief interval exemplifies Haast's sense of duty and powers of recuperation.

In spite of all that was learned, in spite of the contributions to geology and botany, critics complained that Haast had not found a goldfield. By this time his reputation could survive attack. He was a scientist well enough known to correspond with Charles Darwin, who was grateful to him for interesting examples of New Zealand plant and wildlife adaptations to changes consequent to European immigration. There was controversy with Charles Cameron about who actually discovered the Pass. Cameron went into the area of the Pass, mere days before Haast, but almost certainly did not go through to the coast. The fine surveyor Baker also had a claim which he never asserted. But Haast had explored Tiori-patea thoroughly and revealed it to the world.

Haast Pass had, and perhaps still has, quite different travellers too, as the surveyor Brodrick wrote in 1881: "About 20 miles from the lake is the Haast Pass, the largest gap in the Southern Alps, about 1,700 ft above sea level and covered with dense bush through which is a horse track to the west coast. This strip of bush connecting the great forest of the coast with the bush in the Makarora Valley has made a pathway for the wingless coastal birds which are plentiful in the valley. The kakapo and kiwi, except here, are strangers to Canterbury ...." It was a true pass, a way through the mountains for those who knew. After Haast the world knew of it, perhaps even knew more because of disputes about priority.

Haast lived to be highly honoured in Europe, New Zealand, and particularly in Canterbury to whose progress he had so manifestly contributed. As a 19th-century man, and especially a scientist, by today's measurements his contribution was almost absurdly broad. Yet, as with his friend Darwin, this did not lessen the depth his mind could penetrate. Above all, he had loved his work as he loved life, deeply, wholeheartedly, joyously. His elegy, given in the three circumstances he would have wished – by a close friend, in a university convocation, and in Christchurch – reminded everyone of the secret of his vitality. "Who could meet him without feeling how young the world is; without taking into the blood a new draught of youth from his buoyant nature? ... his large-hearted energy cheered those who had to work with him in life." Those who worked closely with him not only gained from his qualities but contributed their own in such measure as a hard new land decreed.

# CHAPTER ELEVEN

# High Challenge

South-western New Zealand is hard and lonely country, and some of the mountains are giants, even as the world sees them. In spite of the frenzy of gold fever, inland exploration came last to the south-west. Its mountains were left unclimbed until nearly, and in some cases into, this century. Missionaries, land buyers, surveyors and naturalists in the relatively well-populated North Island had it much easier, even a generation earlier. For Dieffenbach on his most famous excursion, climbing Mount Egmont, his Maori guide would sometimes fetch dried fish or some oil, sometimes even a handful of leeks, from a hidden store in the forest. "There was no want of provisions; and pigeons, potatoes, leeks, taro, cabbage, turnips … were all at our command." Such a loner as Charles Douglas, the most famous south-western explorer, might have rejected so much luxury.

North Island peaks at first were climbed by those whose danger came less from the mountains than from the people around them. These beautiful cones, with little competition in the immediate vicinity, draw the eye. They challenged Europeans from the beginning. In 1834 the missionary A. N. Brown arrived at the headwaters of the Waipa River, having travelled through country unoccupied because of Hongi's wars. From the top of Kakepuku he saw, far to the south-east, Mounts Tongariro and Ruapehu, the latter resembling "a brilliant bank of fleecy clouds cradled in the rays of the setting sun." On Henry Williams's great walk from Wellington to Tauranga he camped at the foot of Mount Ruapehu, "the volcano Tongariro … before us, the summit covered with snow, a splendid sight." But Williams was on his wearing journey overland from Wellington to Tauranga, and he felt no inclination to climb either.

In 1840 Dieffenbach, of the New Zealand Company, "scrutinized the sides and lofty summit of Mount Egmont, which, once thrown up by the mysterious fires of the deep, was now apparently in a state of repose, to discover whether there was any possibility of ascending it, an undertaking which had never yet been achieved." It was a challenge. By good fortune, Dieffenbach found that the conquests of Te Rauparaha had so unsettled the local tribes that there was no chief with both power and a tapu interest in the mountain. As no one could forbid him to go he was able to get Maori assistance. "An old Tohunga, or priest, was therefore persuaded to show me the way as far as he knew it, and with him and an American man of colour, I started on the 3rd of December." The "man of color" was a cook, and Dieffenbach was perhaps making more thorough staffing arrangements than was commonly done. If so they did not work out, for this attempt was abandoned before it really started. But shortly Dieffenbach's "party was joined by Mr. Heberley, a European, who had come with us from Te-Awa-iti, where he had lived for several years as a whaler …." He was willing to make the climb.

As far as the Maori were concerned climbing the mountain was foolhardy: "the savage views such scenes with superstitious dread." On their way up they encountered the snowline, which ought to have been "about 1500 feet below the summit." Dieffenbach calculated that "Kirwan's formula" would have given 1635 feet [500 metres] below the summit as the lowest height, so there was reasonable agreement. New Zealand's permanent mountain snowline is 900 metres lower than in the European Alps. Dieffenbach then found the Maori "would not go any farther, not only on account of their superstitious fears, but because, from the intensity of the cold, their uncovered feet had already suffered severely." Dieffenbach and Heberley left them and went on, having to cut steps in the snow to reach the top. "We at length reached the summit, and found that it consisted of a field of snow about a square mile in extent." Dieffenbach then boiled water, calculating from the boiling temperature that the top of the mountain was about 8839ft. This compares with 2518 metres or 8393 feet, generally accepted as the height today. They were not the first creatures on the top. "On the summit of the mountain I found the entire skeleton of a rat, carried there, no doubt, by a hawk."

Somewhat later Dieffenbach found that the head chief of the Taupo tribes had laid a solemn tapu on Mount Tongariro. "This 'tapu' was imposed in consequence of a European traveller of the name of Bidwill having gone to the top without permission, which had caused great vexation, as the mountain is held in traditional veneration, and is much dreaded by the natives, being, as they tell you, the 'backbone of their Tapuna,' or great ancestor, and having a white head, like their present chieftain." Even Governor Sir George Grey could not get permission to climb the mountain.

Bidwill, as indicated, pressed on without permission and reached the top of the mountain. "As I progressed towards the cone, which now seemed quite close, I arrived at another stream of lava, so fresh that there was not the slightest appearance of even a lichen, on it, and it looked as if it had been ejected but yesterday. It was black, and very hard and compact, just like all the lava I have seen in this country .... I had no idea of the meaning of a 'sea of rocks' until I crossed them; the edges of the stony billows were so sharp, that it was very difficult to pass among them without cutting one's clothes into shreds. I at last arrived at the cone." Bidwill found that "the rocks on the top were covered with a whitish deposit from the stream of lava, and there was plenty of sulphur in all directions, but the specimens were not handsome, being mixed with earth. I did not stay at the top so long as I could have wished because I heard a strange noise coming out of the crater, which I thought betokened another eruption .... As I did not wish to see an eruption near enough to be either boiled or steamed to death, I made the best of my way down." At one point he wondered for a moment why he was there: "Had it not been for the idea of standing where no man ever stood before, I should certainly have given up the undertaking."

After the climb Bidwill saw the great chief Te Heu Heu, who was furious because the European had broken the tapu. He calmed down after receiving some tobacco and merely asked that Bidwill not tell anyone else about it. But the area was so remarkable that there was no hope of it being left in peace, tapu or no. Ruapehu was climbed in 1879, by a G. Beetham, on his second attempt. On the first try his party wisely rode horses as far as they could climb with them, a considerable distance. And there is another less direct and later connection with horses. Zane Grey, whose writing about cowboys and their horses helped create the American West of legend, came to New Zealand and admired everything from the fishing and the people to the scenery. The central North Island, he thought, "was on a sublime scale. League on league of rolling prairie-like land, almost gold in color, bare except for a green clump of forest here and there that accentuated the barrenness, swept up to the three noble peaks. All three were volcanoes. Tongariro smoked from several craters; Ngauruhoe sent aloft a grand column of steam and smoke; and Ruapehu lay asleep and cold, dead and extinct, or not yet responsive to the bursting fire and lava beneath. This was the scene by which I chose to remember New Zealand."

Surveyors and explorers climbed mountains for the outlook or for the vantage point for taking survey sights. Some men climbed them because they were on their line of march. In 1845 Colenso climbed the Ruahines while on one of his mission journeys: "we had not much farther to go ere we should reach the summit; and then to descend to the native villages on the western side …." But his expedient purpose did not prevent his appreciating what he had gained incidentally. "The view from the top from the eastern and northern sides was very extensive – extending from Cape Kidnappers to Table Cape, and thence to Mt Tongariro and further. The whole of Hawke's Bay with all the interior plains appeared like an immense panorama spread beneath us – but much too distant low and flat, and too dull in its colours – of rusty fern, and dingy Raupo, and pale cutting-grasses, and dry withered plains, with a lead-coloured misty-looking sea in the distance."

A few mountains men climbed simply "because they were there", even in those practical days, as with Bidwill's Tongariro or Dieffenbach's Mount Egmont. E.J. Eyre, the Lieutenant-Governor of New Munster, which included the South Island, climbed Mount Tapuaenuku, the highest peak of the Kaikouras. He was with Hamilton, who sensibly would not go above the snowline without mountain gear and equipment; nor did he have the instruments for a proper survey sight. Eyre and four Maori reached within a few minutes of the summit when they were forced back by failing light. The snow became very dangerous and one of the Maori slid down a slope, crashing from ledge to ledge to his death. Eyre himself was only saved by his iron-shod climbing pole.

Captain Stokes and Hamilton climbed Mount Grey and it was the view from there which convinced Stokes that the Canterbury Plains were "watered by a multitude of streams …." Hamilton intended to find, with Maori guides, the best of their various routes to the West Coast, and after he climbed Mount Grey again he determined to add detail to maps prepared by Brunner. Hamilton, who spoke Maori, suggested that they be asked to describe routes across the great southern ranges. This idea worked well, for the Reverend J.W. Stack learned at Kaiapoi of a pass up the Rakaia River, which was not Whitcombe's Pass. The party sent out to explore it met on the way a party from the coast who had just come through the pass (Browning's). Maori information was usually valuable, and they were generous in giving it.

Prospectors explored much of the western mountain country in their own way but few reports came of where they had been. But as the explorer and

# EELS

When the early explorers were working the chief problem was food, not labour, although the two are always intimately connected. Eels could be caught and were very fine eating, particularly the silver ones as opposed to the black. Harper's close friend and associate, the bushman and explorer Charles Douglas, praised the favoured species as "the long elegant formed light coloured Silver Eeel; a fish that eats like Salmon and is only found in large clear running streams never in Lakes or bogs, or Lagoons. Prejudiced people have come down to the Cascade who shuddered at the very thought of eating such water serpents, but in a week or two they went back full of Eel & gratitude, confessed they had discovered a new pleasure, and left the place with regret ...."

Brunner too learned much about eels in his exploration. There were plenty in the rivers, and he said the Maori preserved a surplus by taking out all the bones, cooking and putting them in a rimu bag, pouring in fat and tying the bag tightly, using whale oil for the preservation just as they did with birds. Both birds and eels were thought good. Drying eels to preserve them was another painstaking process. They had to be "skinned, the head cut off, and opened down the belly, the bone carefully taken out, and the flesh exposed to the smoke to dry, they would last some months, and this is, in my opinion, the best way to eat them." Brunner preferred his eels, of which he had to eat a great many, to be slowly and carefully prepared. In his opinion if a dried eel was "too dry, soaking it in water for a few hours, and then basting it over a slow fire, makes a very good dish." If this seems somewhat optimistic, the reports of New Zealand eels really were most positive. Nonetheless a few bush travellers either ate birds or went hungry.

Whether the traveller liked eel or merely was hungry enough to eat what was going, there could be some trouble getting them. "There is a particular tapu existing amongst the natives relative to the eel. You must wash your hands before going to catch them, and also on returning, and the bait must be prepared some distance from the house. There must be a distinct fire for cooking the eels, for which you must have a special tinder-box; your hands and mouth must be washed both before and after partaking of them, and should it be necessary to drink from the same stream from which the eels are caught, you must have two vessels of water, the one to drink from the other to dip from the stream." On one occasion Maori insisted that Brunner walk a kilometre for water even though a stream, presumably harbouring eels, ran within a few metres of their camp.

Brunner found the Maori obdurate in their determination to get eels, and misinterpreted the "hunting-dependant's" demand for a heavy supply when it was possible. "I believe if we had provisions spoiling for want of eating, and had loads under which we could scarcely stagger, nothing would induce Ekehu to pass a weka, or remain at the fire if there was the chance at an eel in the river, so great is his natural love of destruction. Last night I pressed on him to forbear fishing, but no – he must be off, and return with twenty eels."

The Maori dried eels to preserve them as well as bagging them in boiling fat. It was successful looting of the enemy's supply of dried eels which kept Te Puoho's expedition in shape to complete the raid on Otago Maori in 1836. Each tribe had its productive eeling spots, and they were key points in the economy. Such a place as Tuturau, with an eeling river, a birded forest, and good land for such crops as the area permitted was a natural location for a chief's village.

mountaineer Charles Edward Douglas said, there was evidence of their work in holes and in tailing piles. Compared with working in Auckland or Taranaki, Douglas was in the greatest wilderness of New Zealand, but that was not all. Surveying was becoming mountaineering; provisioning was becoming a matter of carrying tins; life was becoming, if not softer, at least more bearable. Douglas was not quite sure that he liked it all.

An explorer who could rival Brunner in his achievements in the field, Douglas was both more literate and more artistic. And, as Mr Explorer Douglas, he became a character in New Zealand life. So did Julius Haast; but they were not at all alike. Compared with him – indeed with Wakefield too – Douglas was a semi-recluse, happiest in the bush, and coming out only for supplies or news or an occasional booze-up. Both Haast and Douglas were necessary in New Zealand exploration. Each was a cultured European, although Douglas spent much of his life fighting what he saw as constraints. In contrast Haast passed his life winning recognition in the world which is acknowledged in New Zealand, that of the practical and the plain. He owed his success to his energy and ability and the thoroughness of his German education. In Haast there was no repudiation of the European culture which had created him, nor perhaps more important, any trace of the lonely man.

Like Haast, Charles Douglas was born and reared in urban culture; one of his brothers was a fine artist, knighted for his achievements and President of the Royal Academy of Scotland. Charles, scorning the conventional and convenient, left Scotland for somewhere new, presumably unconfined and unconventional. Belying his solid Scottish background, he became the typical English remittance man. Later Douglas regretted choosing New Zealand because it was not big enough to give full scope to his roaming. But what New Zealand lacked in distance fore and aft it made up in metres skyward. It was the lofty highlands,

On his trip south from Taupo to Wellington George Angas painted Tongariro and Ruapehu as seen across the volcanic pumice country of the area. *(Hocken Library, Dunedin)*

282

Two chiefs from Taupo, on the left, and two from Auckland, on the right. Old Te Heu Heu, on the left, was far-famed. "His hair is silvery white and his people compare it to the snowy head of the sacred Tongariro; there being no object of equal sanctity to permit of its being mentioned in connection with the head of this chief." *(Hocken Library, Dunedin)*

An abandoned Maori village at Lake Taupo in the area controlled by the prestigious Te Heu Heu, who was so angered by Bidwill's climbing of the tapu Mount Tongariro. *(Hocken Library, Dunedin)*

not the culture nor opportunities, much less a public service or public servants, that Douglas came to love. And although this eccentric Scot is even more famous for exploration than for climbing, his name is mingled with the mountains on our maps.

Douglas had attended the Royal High School in Edinburgh, where he was thoroughly trained in Classics, English and Arithmetic. It was a school for writers; Sir Walter Scott and James Boswell were among the more famous graduates. Douglas wrote much but also had a way with technical matters. So did others of the school: Alexander Graham Bell, inventor of the telephone; Lord Dalhousie, administrator of the Indian Empire; Captain Cargill of Otago, leader of immigrants and founder of a colony; and Sir James Hector, geologist in New Zealand, botanist in Canada, and successful explorer in both. Douglas would use harsh words about Hector later in their lives. All in all, school was an interesting beginning. His sound education was not evident in his spelling but in perceptive observation and thorough reporting. In wild lands, where challenge is on nature's terms, he won respect for accomplishment and affection for his person.

Douglas left Scotland at the age of twenty-two, perhaps yearning for novelty and adventure. Nothing in his writing hints of longing for the old land, and he never went back. After a brief stay in Dunedin he became a cadet on a sheep farm, quickly tiring of that to join the gold rushes. He learned much about the hill and mountain country of north-west Otago but that did not satisfy him. For beyond he could see the higher country of Westland, a harsh wilderness of mountains, rivers and gorges. It seemed good to him, magically softened as it was by rata blossom and countless kinds of fern. More important to Douglas, it was lightened by the songs of countless birds not yet decimated by man and his animals.

Westland was still almost unknown when Douglas came. Brunner had been there in 1847 and his discoveries were published in the Nelson press. But he had found nothing "important": no goldfield, no easy route, no safe and capacious harbour, nothing but good coal and that in deep seams. In 1857 Leonard Harper, a driving young man of twenty, travelled with Maori guides across Harper Pass, the first mountain crossing by a European. He saw some gold along the Taramakau River and this spurred exploration. Harper's son Arthur, skilled surveyor, photographer, explorer and mountaineer, a close friend and fellow-explorer of Douglas, recorded much of Douglas's work and personality.

Westland was almost empty. A few isolated and scanty settlements of Maori refugees, fearing raids from across the mountains to the east, provided shelter for other Maori who came seeking greenstone. The first Maori to cross the ranges was said to have been a woman, Raureka, although some say she was mad and others that it is all a romantic story. On her way back to Canterbury she crossed Brownings Pass (the pass about which Stack was told), thus finding a direct route to Westland, improving the roundabout greenstone trade. The Maori knew and used the passes. As we have seen, they also told Pakeha about the Haast and Lindis Passes. Europeans travelled the routes, confirmed their usefulness for more extensive transport, and mapped them, a completion of

Charles Douglas, Arthur Harper and Betsy resting amidst the Southern Alps. Throughout the mountain area Betsy was famous as a bird hunter. *(University of Canterbury Library, Christchurch)*

discovery and exploration. The world now knew the way to the passes, and what modern transport could be used.

The country needed opening up. Many played their parts in this. Samuel Butler, the author of *Erewhon*, found Whitcombe Pass when seeking new sheep country beyond the Rakaia Valley. A. J. Barrington, prospector and explorer, went through North Otago and South Westland in the mid-1860s and suffered greatly from the severe winter climate, made so by the elevation. Barrington narrowly survived several times and had to be treated for frostbite. Many others found gold strikes or locations for cattle stations, and some may have found much but did not get back to report it. Others got back but did not bother to tell what, if anything, they had discovered. Still others, like Thomson and Baker, explored as they surveyed, in some ways just as Cook, d'Urville and many of the exploring captains had surveyed as they explored.

Douglas was still in the goldfields of Otago in 1865, when South Westland boomed with gold seekers. Two years after his 1863 pass exploration, Haast returned for a geological survey of Westland. Prospectors, mainly from Otago, poured onto the coast by the thousands. They explored – or more accurately tramped over – much of the country without marking down tracks or positions. And, like whalers and sealers, prospectors meant to protect their discoveries by purposefully repressing geographical information. Douglas sardonically reported that "the results of the explorations were a lonely grave here & there a few wasted lives, and a few ozs of Gold which cost £10 per oz. to get." Arthur Harper was doubtful about the value of any miner's information; they never brought "out any information concerning the topography or appearance of the country .... In fact it is often quite impossible to find out how far they have been up a valley; sometimes the distance they say they went would land them, in reality, some miles out on to the Mackenzie plains."

Exploration done by prospectors almost always perished without trace – unless they found gold. In that case, a rare one, mining traces still show, if ordinary travellers ever get near them at all. A stricken landscape, gouged and sieved and sluiced, a litter of broken spades and old water pipes, and crumbling walls of stone huts, tell us that here a miner-explorer found pay dirt. Look carefully; this was not always wreckage, but tools and tenements of tough men, and single-minded ones too. And on their work Dunedin and southern New Zealand built flourishing provinces. The miners paid, for of the many who came precious few prospered.

Douglas admiringly described miners as "bands of men who in the hunt after Gold feared neither death nor the Devil. They didn't in those days sit down & whine to Government for Tracks, they didn't wait for Subsidised Ferrys or Charity Steamers, but they boldly penetrated Forest & Mountain, crossed rivers & scrambled round Bluffs, reckless of tomorrow, so long as today furnished them with a roast Maorie Hen or a Billy of Mussels & a pannican of Skilly." Douglas may well have used oral tradition left by prospectors, but he still had work to do following the rivers they had seen, marking down and measuring mountains, noting everything in his field books for his maps. The surveyor's hard work and careful observation provides the valuable information. Wandering through the hills, even with a golden reason, is not exploration.

Fortunately for posterity Douglas was a keen observer of not only Nature but also the nature of man; he was a humorist. Probably only his keen awareness of his own weaknesses saved him from cynicism. Parodying Shakespeare, Douglas described the three stages of "an ordinary digging township in Westland ... first the calico, sardine tin, and broken bottle era. Second the weather board and sheet iron period. Third the borough. Some never get beyond the first, a few reach the second, and still fewer the third." But in spite of townships lacking most characteristics of small town cosiness, out in the bush it was even wilder. Often the bush men existed without the bottles and tins. Men "clothed in rough moleskins, open-necked shirts, wide-brimmed hats, stout boots, and burdened with swags comprising a roll of blankets, short axe, pick and tin dish ... would thrive on birds ... Eels ... fresh water crabs ... Frost fish and flounders ...." When Douglas arrived the Coast was poor and tough, but there were foods aplenty.

Something had gone wrong. Brunner had foreseen a permanent and prosperous settlement at the mouth of the Grey: "could it but be connected with a harbour it would make a fine field for colonization, there being much good land fit for arable purposes, and some good grazing districts in well-sheltered positions; also some very fine timber for sawing, quite accessible, as well as a quantity of fine Kauri for spars – at least what I believe to be such. The shingle bed of this river in many places abounds with coal .... In it is also found the stone used by the natives for rubbing down their poenamo [greenstone]; it is something like a Newcastle stone, though rather closer in the grain, and has a fine cutting quality." This was all too optimistic. Greymouth came into being, but unlike other West Coast towns of its era, has not given up struggling to win the prominence Brunner foresaw.

Greymouth could not replace Edinburgh for Douglas, nor did he wish it to. He was somewhat at a loss in such an empty environment at first. He took odd jobs. In 1868 Douglas accompanied and assisted the Canterbury Provincial geologist, Julius Haast, already a figure in the scientific world. Douglas impressed Haast by his Classical knowledge and in turn he grasped the chance to learn some geology from Haast. Unfortunately Douglas thought, as did some others, that Haast was not generous with people who preceded him. Douglas believed Cameron the first white man over the Haast Pass, and perhaps Haast ought to have given Cameron more credit, for there was enough and to spare. Yet there was something odd about Douglas, a recluse, being so particular about

These climbers on the Tasman Glacier in the early years of mountaineering in New Zealand, the one on the left the famous climber and author G.E. Mannering, display an intrepid attitude modified by careful selection of clothes and equipment. *(Guy Mannering Collection, Christchurch)*

recognition. Douglas's streak of jealousy, for such it undoubtedly was, showed again in his relationship with Hector. Douglas himself was not unhonoured by his people; he was given the Gill Memorial Prize by the Royal Geographical Society and certainly he is now recognised as a fine mountaineer, surveyor, artist and humorously descriptive writer.

By 1874 Douglas had been left some money in Scotland and, having received it, spent it by farming cattle in Westland. After a short time his ranching partner drowned and the restless Douglas decided to give it up. As far as is known he never had a mining right; he was rather sceptical about finding gold and about the effects of doing so. But on the coast Douglas had met Gerhard Mueller, who in 1866 had been appointed District Surveyor of South Westland. The two became close friends and remained so, with profound effects on Douglas's career. Mueller influenced Douglas greatly, for his productive period started soon after they met. Douglas claimed in 1903 that he had been exploring for thirty-five years, and "for the last fifteen years I have been at it regularly. Before that I was generally about half my time only." Full or half, that is a long time in the Westland mountains.

As he had with Mueller, Douglas made a lifelong friend of G. J. Roberts, a fine surveyor who, like Chief Surveyor Thomson, had learned his profession in the Indian Survey. In Westland Roberts was to oversee setting up a system of triangulation, to be cheaper than the standard survey. All the provinces lacked funds. Roberts had the perception to see that Douglas could play an important part in development and from then on, clear of his cattle, he was a surveyor and explorer. In 1877 Douglas selected and prepared sites for triangulation and

A view from Whitcombe Pass looking north, as seen by Charles Douglas, remarkable explorer and mountaineer as well as a competent artist noted for his accuracy of portrayal. (*Alexander Turnbull Library, Wellington*)

explored the country at the head of the Parenga, some of this work a forerunner of his careful exploration later. Triangulation is difficult work, to be preferred to straight surveying only by comparison.

Roberts himself had done enough of rough work in his early days that as supervisor he recognised Douglas's difficulties, in work or in existing. Living conditions could be primitive. On one occasion, the surveyors working together, Mueller, Douglas and two helpers, caught three eels weighing a total of thirty-one kilograms. One of them, Douglas remembered, "was splendid eating – we took the backbone out, salted him, rolled him up for a night to let the salt get properly through the meat and then hung him over the smoke for two days and so he lasted us for a week ...." Smoked eel was good food and a welcome change, as usually they had only salted or tinned meat, but by this time New

## BIRDSONG

New Zealand birds, although there were not many species, became as famous for song as have Australian birds for beauty. Tasman said nothing of birdsong; presumably he was anchored too far from shore. But Cook and Banks and others with them said a great deal. Probably this was at least partly based on the reaction to the claustrophobic sounds of the ship as it answered to winds and waves. Banks's comment about the bellbirds at Queen Charlotte Sound is often quoted: "I was awaked by the singing of the Birds ashore ... who seem'd to strain their throats with emulation, perhaps their voices were certainly the most melodious wild musick I have ever heard, almost imitating small Bells, but with the most tuneable Silver sound imaginable ...."

Queen Charlotte Sound became famous for its birdsong. Simonov, there with the Russians in 1820, was "struck by the most delightful blending of the sounds of birdsong and a wide, babbling stream flowing into the sea .... We had long been deprived of such a pleasure, nor do I recall having heard such a harmonious choir of songbirds anywhere in the remaining five parts of the earth." Almost a century after Banks the appreciative Haast was moved to use the Englishman's metaphor: "at early dawn we were awakened by numerous feathered songsters with their harmonious notes, the morning concert of the korimako or bell bird resembling a peal of well tuned chimes ...."

Mr Explorer Douglas was not so uncritical of birdsong, in spite of his often expressed love for birds: "the Kiwi made night hedious with its piercing shreik, the Blue Duck crossed over to whistle a welcome. The Caw Caw swore & the Kea skirled ...." No bells there indeed. Like Banks he thought the early morning bellbirds sounded "like the tinkling of hundreds of well tuned silver bells." But he was perceptive and frank enough to point out that "as a solo, their ding dong is monotonus ... by hundreds ... the effect is magnificent."

Douglas's particular bane was the "swearing" of the kaka, and on one occasion he gave his reasons in full. He complained that "the Serenader Caw-Caw" had no "particular time fixed when to begin, or when to stop. It all depends on the state of his lungs & perhaps the temper of the community. Perched on the top of a high bushey pine he livens – as he imagines – the still hours of the night by whistling his national melodies with the power of a locomotive, & with all the confidence of the Amateur Cornet player who feels himself safe from bricks & shot guns." As a critic, perceptive or no, Douglas pulled no punches.

Zealand had developed to the point where eating eel for a week was hardship. Living standards were changing.

Work was changing too, becoming harder and more dangerous as the easier tasks were completed and the more difficult begun. By this time surveying was getting so far from easy country that it was becoming mountaineering, and surveyors needed ice axes. At first Douglas used a billhook or a slasher on the ice, until proper alpine axes arrived. In 1885 Douglas and Chief Surveyor Mueller explored the Arawata River and traced its tributary, the Waipara River, to the Bonar Glacier, which drains the west slopes of Mount Aspiring. They climbed Mount Ionia using axes for cutting steps and a rope, an important event in New Zealand's alpine history, but which they thought not too difficult. Although Mueller believed no one would ever climb the neighbouring Mount Eros, in 1935 a party which flew in to the Arawata flats reached its summit. Climbing Ionia had given Douglas a choice of high trig points: " about a thousand feet up ought to be a good place to fix a Cairn take bearing & Join on to Mt Aspiring Hiperia Point T &c." The survey was slowly and laboriously linking up.

Most men at Douglas's age would have avoided the new high-level work; Douglas seemed to welcome greater challenges. In 1886 he was said to be "about 5' 10" and slight to the point of skinny-ness – Eyes steely grey and hair

RIVER CROSSINGS

Drowning was called the New Zealand disease for many years, and the name would not be completely inappropriate today. Most deaths occurred in crossing rivers although, as with Tuhawaiki, the Otago chief, the coastal sea took its toll too. New Zealand is surrounded by rough and stormy seas and laced with active rivers, and so naturally there was all sorts of advice, varying somewhat in quality, for newcomers to adopt or ignore.

In all countries unpredictable rivers are dangerous but particularly so in New Zealand because the danger extends from the headwaters in the mountains right down to the coast; one can be swept away quickly by a sudden torrent when the mountains look to be a long way away. High country rains roar so swiftly down the short rivers to the east coast that deluges in the upper catchment produce very sudden and dangerous rises in level downriver. In some of the wider rivers, travellers can be caught literally in midstream, with the water rising so swiftly that they are swept away. Even now there is barely time for radio warnings, and posted signs warn campers and caravanners against the level and invitingly dry riverbeds, for it is a treacherous attraction. Flash floods make them extremely dangerous. This threat, this apparent animosity, was responded to. A modern runholder's wife lamented that, "The river rules my life", and from Charles Heaphy we learn that sometimes early Maori, once safely across, vented "vehement abuse of the river and all its tributaries."

There were drownings upriver too. In the mountains one did not often have horses to which to cling, as in the open country. Individuals used long poles, which would assist flotation, and be useful to catch a rock or the shore to prevent being swept away. They also gave a sense of security. Baker and a companion, each with a pole, once had trouble in one dangerous river crossing; they both hung onto their poles even though "swimming frantically." But Baker pointed out that in "such swiftly

An early sketch of travellers crossing a swollen river. The pole was meant to ensure that any individual swept off his feet would have the support of the others while regaining his foothold. *(Alexander Turnbull Library, Wellington)*

running water one is more or less carried on the surface. I don't think that the idea of being drowned crossed either his mind or mine." Heaphy's party did what he and other Europeans had learned from the Maori. The established technique for a party was for all to cross at once, with everyone holding onto one long, strong pole. This procedure intended that any individual loss of footing would be compensated for by the grasp on the communal pole. The strength of all was to hold individuals against the current. This did not always work. On one of Baker's trips "after one man had been washed off the pole and carried down the river some distance before we could pull him out, we decided to make a canoe."

If there were many supplies to shift, parties would build Maori flax rafts (mokihi) or even dugout canoes. Baker tells of three men making such a canoe in a day. Douglas thought the mokihi "rather an elaborate contrivance to make and requires teaching," but as for wooden canoes, "two men ought to be able to make a dug out that will carry three or four men and their swaggs, accross or down any river in Westland, and out to sea for that matter in a couple of days or even less." Out to sea could be relevant in quite another way, and in the opposite direction. To cross the Waitaki River, widely considered the most treacherous in New Zealand, so many travellers built flax rafts of the local rushes that in the months of heavy travel the coast north of the river's mouth was strewn with abandoned rafts swept there by river and ocean currents.

Douglas claimed that a traveller's swag, usually covered with some waterproof material, was sufficient to float him across most streams, at least if he knew what he was doing: "the Art in safe Fording is to always select a place with the current running into a back." And he went on to say that anything waterproof would do. One of his friends, carrying a "Tin pump", arrived at the Waiho in full flood. Unfazed, "he stuffed his Coat in one end of the Pump & his shirt & Trousers into the other, tied some flax guys round to keep all tight … and whoop the Pump held athwart the stream, shot him accross at once his head & shoulders weren't even Wet." A dry head, much less anything else, was a notable and unusual triumph. New Zealand rivers are still not to be taken lightly, jet boats or no.

always worn very long (down to the shoulders) and ever unkempt. He steadfastly refused to permit anyone to cut it." His choice of literature, his way of living, his love of solitude: all marked him as different. No matter – or a matter of pride – away he went, with Topsy as companion and bird supplier, taking only "a batwing tent one blanket sewn into a bag, tea, oatmeal, a copy of Homer and a Greek Testament." He lived off the country to a greater extent than most explorers did. Dependence on birds, and somewhat less on the dog which caught them, was worrying: "I must eat plenty of birds, and spare the Flour as I don't know what is ahead of me yet." Most food was carried in its simplest form: "Bread & Jam is very good no doubt but not the thing for swagging …."

His schooling had influenced him markedly. Douglas "often mentioned his college – to which he was very attached, but never his people." He was always very much a loner, at least in his working days. "Even the quiet camp of the gang of 6 men irritated him and he would never stick it more than about three days with the gang. When at the main camp he never shared a tent." So reticent was Douglas that when he set off on a trip his friends always worried until he came back; they never knew when he was due. The only way of estimating was to find out at the store how much tobacco he had taken. They could reckon the

A coach photographed on the main highway north of the West Coast's Wanganui River in the 1890s. Explorers in the 19th century worked and suffered to provide routes for railways, coaching roads and telegraphs. *(Peter Lucas Collection, University of Canterbury Library, Christchurch)*

probable date of return from that, for as a nicotine addict he suffered classic withdrawal symptoms when without tobacco for too long.

Douglas had some of his family's artistic ability and he sketched as he explored, his ability to read land making his sketches accurate. He was modest about his sketching; he felt neither artistic nor talented, and probably also well in the shadow of his brother of the Scottish Royal Academy. But when discussing his technical failings he invariably pointed out that at least he knew more than his critics, of whom he had many. He thought his keenest critics the kea, who with interest and intense concentration watched him sketch and then criticised directly from a bird's eye. "Talking of sketching, I once met a couple of most unflattering Critics, & in the most peculiar place. I was sitting sketching with my back against a rock, as is usual, when finished I held it at arms length to admire my handiwork, when in that mountain Solitude I was startled by a Yell of derision. Looking up, there were two Kea peeping over my shoulder with their head cocked to one side, as I have seen featherless bipeds do in a picture gallery. I held out the Sketch for them to admire. One came hopping along with his top knot up & one eye closed to examine it. He looked first out of one eye, then the other, gave his mate a dig in the ribs & gave vent to a Yell of derision. No. two came trotted along sideways, then struck an attitude, shaded his eyes with his claw if I recollect aright, although I am not quite sure, then he sniggered, & gave a Yell that brought Kea round in dozen. What they thought exactly I don't know ...."

Artist or not Douglas was quite efficient. In 1888 he was hired permanently, from then on exploring continuously as a fully equipped surveyor, skilled with instruments, able to cope with rivers and gorges, bush and mountains, glaciers and snowfields. He was an excellent climber, having learned most of his mountaineering skills from Arthur Harper, who had learned his in Switzerland. By this time amateur climbing, for men spurred on by challenge, the hope of fame rather than the satisfaction of a job completely done, had reached the alps of New Zealand.

But exploring had to be done, whatever the temptations of white peaks and slopes, and the slogging work and hard conditions wore heavily on Douglas. Quite often the born loner pulled his canoe – which he called the *Surveyor-General* for his own reasons – along a handy river by ropes, finding that he could move a heavy load very efficiently by himself that way. He started his exploration of the Waiatoto River valley with a canoe-load of "two Batwing Tents & two flys – can be pitched as a 6 x 5 tent or halved making two Camps to stage Tucker. A bill hook, half axe & Pick, Field books Compass Drawings & writing material, A Pea Rifle and Betsey Jane to catch Birds, and about 100 lbs of assorted Tucker." This canoe was a working craft, whereas others were sometimes roughhewn and temporary. For example, Baker and his men made one quickly for a specific river crossing. "After one man had been washed off the pole and carried down the river some distance before we could pull him out, we decided to make a canoe. In a wooded country like the Makarora Valley it did not take long to find a suitable dead tree and in a single day we hollowed it out and shaped it sufficiently for our purpose. We then lashed a large bundle of dead Koradis (flax sticks) to each side to give it more stability, fixed a rough frame over it projecting about a foot beyond each side to hold the thole-pins,

## INTRODUCED ANIMALS

Arthur Harper and Charles Douglas, exploring the south-western South Island, thought that introduced animals such as weasels and cats were exterminating the birds. Harper, for one, did not think that even the fiercest of weka would survive the new and seemingly irresistible onslaught from introduced animals. "Most of the native birds of the country are gradually disappearing .... This is largely due to cats and weasels. The digger is very fond of his cat, and nearly always carries one with him; but in the past, when new 'rushes' were frequent ... if the cat was not at hand it was left behind, and naturally became wild. These have increased and multiplied enormously, and I have seen their tracks for miles up unexplored valleys .... It is, therefore, only a question of time before our most interesting birds – those that cannot fly – become extinct."

Members of all introduced animals became feral. In New Zealand they had no competition from the truly wild, such as the wolves, bears or various sizes of wild cats in North America. Dieffenbach visited Maori in the North Island who had "great quantities of pigs, which have run wild, but are easily caught by dogs. The common domestic fowl has also emancipated itself; but the cats, which, on becoming wild, have assumed the streaky grey colour of the original animal while in a state of nature, form a great obstacle to the propagation of any new kind of birds, and also tend to the destruction of the indigenous species." Pigs were not always so easy to handle as Dieffenbach implies. Early travellers in Otago worried about any bush "infested with wild pigs, that made it unsafe to wander alone."

Charles Douglas's views on wild life are always interesting, and he took a dim view of ferret damage to bird life: "the Ferrets have not got among the Birds on this River evidently, as Kakapo are squealling about in hundreds." Rabbits had only an indirect effect on other wildlife, destroying them by damaging their habitat. As early as 1844 rabbits were well established near Tautuku Bay in Southland, so almost certainly near another whaling station, Jacob's River, as well.

and we had a boat capable of carrying three men and our instruments and tools." Often such homely craft could be found near a river crossing for the use of any who needed it. If on the wrong side the best swimmer could go across for it.

On one trip Douglas passed places which had been homesteaded for cattle farms. A former cattleman himself – but briefly – he thought cattlemen's failures probably caused by distance from markets. It was typical of Douglas to discuss this in his notes, for his writing ranges far beyond minerals and surveying. His information about wild life is always interesting: "Kakapos ... in hundreds. Will have to tie up the Dog if I don't want the Camp full of Corpses in the morning. But what is up with the Blue Ducks. When up here before they were in hundreds, now I have seen only one & he travelled as if Old Nick was after him."

Douglas's long-time friend and fellow surveyor Arthur Harper fully shared, and often discussed, Douglas's interest in birds. Harper thought that weka were not only appetising and easy to catch but "as good a camp companion as one could wish for, with his tameness, impudence, and almost human power of expression ... he is only approached by the kea (or mountain parrot) as a

Both ferrets and rabbits had been introduced much later than had rats, which landed from the first ships, and were probably a greater menace to bird life than any other introduced animal. In the South Island Heaphy, even in his day, thought the kakapo "nearly or quite extinct", and thought introduced rats the likely culprits. Rats were not big enough to take on the adult kakapo and were not the only animal which could and would eat eggs and young. So will cats. But the rats would certainly have done much damage.

Rats were an accidental introduction, although the Maori wanted them in order to increase the size of New Zealand rats, which they ate. Interbreeding did not occur and the native animals were killed out quickly although some survive to this day on offshore islands. One missionary told Dieffenbach "that there are some native rats still to be found in the district." Unfortunately he "could not obtain one to determine the species." Dieffenbach's theory (based on thinking "pero" the Maori name for rat, rather than kiore) was that they must have originated from a Spanish ship, for "pero" is rat in Spanish. There are certainly theories that ships from Spain may have sailed or drifted to New Zealand. If one did, for example, in the early 16th century, rats might just possibly have come with it. It seems highly speculative, to say the least. But the Maori rat is the Polynesian rat and almost certainly came on the canoes. Rat teeth marks on bones in early middens suggest scavenging, and there are rat bones in all ages of midden, some there since long before the possibility of a ship from anywhere in Europe.

Ships' rats came, without doubt, on every ship after Tasman, and many would have deserted for the soft life on a Pacific island. Tasman did not approach close enough to shore for any rat to land, except possibly individuals driven mad by mal-de-mer, and if so we have no record of reproduction. Rats certainly deserted later ships, often deliberately driven out of the ship by the captain "smoking ship" to suffocate vermin and save supplies. In early seafaring days sailors thought rats tasty and the Maori liked them too. There is no sign that the new species interbred with New Zealand rats. The newcomers killed out the native rats and bred in swarms, severely threatening birdlife. They had brought little in return.

source of amusement and interest." He said the weka walks with a "very genteel step, and bobs his short tail up spasmodically; his whole action suggesting the exaggerated motions of a teacher of deportment, if such a person exists outside novels." Douglas and Harper were extremely upset by the threat to their beloved birds from newly introduced animals. But when in dire straits himself Douglas was practical even about birds. "Being pushed with hunger, I ate the pair [of rare mountain kiwi] … under the circumstances I would have eaten the last of the Dodos." It seems facile to condemn men of his time for carelessness about conservation of mountain wildlife without walking some kilometres in their shoes, or perhaps starving a week in their camp.

When exploring Douglas sought and surveyed practical routes for hoped-for commercial and tourist traffic. He was somewhat cynical about those who wanted good trails to walk on while they enjoyed what he and others had suffered to find. But he did not shirk his duty in any way; he knew the world was changing. The ways for road or rail were scarce. A typical report is one by E. H. Wilmot in 1897 on proposed routes from Lake Manapouri to the western sounds, routes which modern machinery has finally made reality. "We had to cross the Mackenzie Pass, and a further and closer inspection of it quite confirmed my opinion as to its utter impracticability for a through road. From our camp to the saddle there is a rise of 700 feet, and the longest route a road could be graded down would give a grade of 1 in 6 of an average grade, and this to be cut in hard rock ... indeed we shall probably have considerable difficulty in getting a track for swagging."

In virgin areas Douglas – and probably later men such as Wilmot – watched for gold and other resources. Douglas reported types of rock encountered and whether any intrusive rocks or traces of metal indicated its presence. "From Wotney all the way up to Fingalls head, the range is nearly perpendicular a hard solid Gneiss, & on the other side towards the Ino it is the same rock, but the range is not so steep except near Palmers Creek. On the beach opposite the camp, which is composed of very small Gravel, the Laminated Schist predominate which shows that the line of brake is not far off."

Douglas also estimated the make-up of rocks upstream by drifted material in the river. "The drift in this river shows a variety of rock that have come down, Schists, Chloride & otherwise, Quartz of great variety but nothing in it but Iron Pyrites, some Muscovite Jasparoid Slates, & a few others .... I must keep an eye on the various creeks going up & try & find the In Situ of some of those rocks." One of Douglas's labour-saving methods was to go in and back by the same route, picking up the rocks he had marked going in because, he said, "I can't carry rocks going up, the Swag is heavy enough already, and planting specimens in bags the Labels are bound to get wet."

On one productive trip he seemed sentimentally introspective. "I often ask myself in amazement what impulse drives me into the Wilds. Had I remained at home in the Old Country, I might now have been the respectable Father of a family, passing the same Lampost – on the road to office – the exact same minute day after day .... A tooth in a Wheel of a Mercantile machine a perambulating Ink bottle, Ledger & blooting pad .... But such a life was not for me ... the desire to then settle must have been omitted in my moral character, as here I am after thirty years wandering, crouched under a few yards of Calico, with the rain pouring & the Wind & Thunder roaring among the mountains a homeless, friendless Vagabond, with a past that looks dreary & a future still more so, still I can't regret having followed such a life ...."

Yet he had his daily complaints as most surveyors did at the time. Douglas criticised the penury of the Survey Department. The provinces were without lavish resources and surveying had to be done as cheaply as possible. "Through the Supernatural meanness of the Survey & Mines Depart[t], I am without an Aneroid, so I must guess the heights as I go along. At the round Pool, say 30 feet above Sea Level, through the half Gorge the River rises 100 feet, & up to this Camp say 70, making the height here 200 feet above Sea level." It sounds a rather rough measure.

As Tasman and Cook had found, travel by sea along the west coast of the South Island is dangerous. And travelling along the beach was just as dangerous. The Tasman swells, which awed Cook and Tasman, sometimes forced travellers to run literally for life. Brunner described the difficulties and risks: "in walking therefore along the coast between these points, you have frequently to clamber over a rocky promontory jutting out into the sea, or ... the granite fragments which have been detached by the action of the water; and having toiled among

Mount Cook as seen from the Tasman River. *(Canterbury Museum, Christchurch)*

the broken rocks … you again come to … another precipice to try the goodness of your footing and your nerves." In spite of recognising the danger, Brunner nonetheless "slipped, or was rather washed from a rock, by the sea, which crushed my foot between the rocks, and severely strained my right ancle." The next day he "crawled to Parika, where I bound up my leg, and repeatedly bathed it in cold water … and dressed the other scratches with Weka oil."

Westland has more danger to offer than the surf or promontories of its coast. Its mountains have claimed many lives and are claiming more. But to mountaineers the risk is as much the challenge as the effort or the technical problems. Towards the end of the century people began to come to New Zealand to climb mountains for the sake of climbing them. They were forced to set up expeditions in much the way that Westland explorers and surveyors were doing; they encountered much the same problems and settled for most of the same solutions. By this time New Zealand mountains were attracting attention in Europe which, having forgotten Hannibal's problems in the Alps and looking for other dangerous recreation than war, was running short of unclimbed peaks. The Southern Alps were mighty mountains in a beautiful land, one neither too risky to visit nor too soft to provide challenge and the meed of success.

In the distant British Isles in the early 1880s, W. S. Green, a fine alpinist, felt "the craving to get to mountain ranges hitherto unexplored, to glaciers as yet untrodden by human foot." New Zealand was distant and its greatest mountains reputed beautiful and virgin. Green sent for pictures and examined shipping schedules while he waited. "In many ways these photographs were unsatisfactory, but they showed me enough to convince me that Mount Cook was a splendid peak, and his conquest well worth the trouble of the long journey." And so a man, motiveless except for knowing the peak's summit was "there", set up an expedition dedicated to standing on it.

Green planned thoroughly and spent freely, and was proud of his effort to prepare properly. No detail escaped examination. The party took sleeping bags made of felt, "a material better suited for this purpose than flannel, and particularly light when dry." He also had an opossum rug and felt special pride in a "particularly handy camping canteen planned for three persons" to hold the productions of "a little spirit-lamp and saucepan cuisine for mountain expeditions." Green apparently did not know that newly arrived Britishers in the colonies were supposed to uphold a reputation, hard-won over many years, of incompetence at daily colonial tasks. He set his hand to everything and made himself climbing fit.

Shooting birds, of course, was something men of Green's class usually did well. "A pair of fine Paradise ducks rose and came wheeling round towards me. I missed them the first shot, or I rather think I fired when they were yet too far off, a mistake I often make here, owing to the difficulty of judging distance correctly, when in close proximity to the lofty mountains ...." No doubt this missed shot upset Green for he learned a different – and rewarding – tactic for blue ducks, who "were stupid birds, and to save our cartridges we often pelted them with stones till they came close enough together for two or more to be tumbled in the one shot." It sounds suspiciously like shooting them sitting, perhaps permissible when hungry enough.

Green's skills were broad enough to lend variety to the diet. "Mixing soda and tartaric acid with the flour, I worked it with water into a great lump of dough which we divided into tidy loaves, and when the boulder [set in the fire for the purpose] was nearly red hot we placed the loaves on it, building a little wall round each loaf, and laying a flat stone on the top; then piling up the fire over the whole erection, we left them to bake for forty-five minutes, which from experience we found was the correct time for turning out loaves baked in the centre, well risen, and with a nice thin jacket of brown crust."

The party, however well fed, could not escape all colonial hazards. "The large blowflies, like overgrown blue-bottles" laid their eggs in any cloth left lying around, "blankets being their special weakness ...." Fortunately an old colonial told them that the blowflies never laid eggs in anything hanging at any distance from the ground. Colenso had suffered from something similar a half-century earlier in the Ruahines. A kind of "large blue-bottle fly" burrowed into their clothes and blankets in thousands until these "were literally filled with its eggs ... we left the tent etc and retreated ...." But Green's party had additional insects to worry about, for under "the larger stones within our tent ... we discovered living beneath them the most hideous creature ... of a greenish hue, and immense legs like a grasshopper, it was more like a gigantic flea than anything else I can think of. Its body was about the size of my thumb ...." Green feared they would come out and bother them in the night. He was almost certainly right. Douglas had experience with whatever teased or stung or trespassed on your sleep in Westland, and he feared wetas, which Green's "hideous creature" almost certainly was. In the case of Open Bay Island wetas, Douglas claimed, at night you could "feel the playfull creatures running races, and dancing hornpipes all over you ...."

Such off-putting company in the tent encouraged climbing. Green's party made several attempts and suffered various dangers, many difficulties, and much wear and tear. On one occasion, "our knuckles were all barked, the skin was

W.S. Green centre, his Swiss friend Emil Boss on the right, and the guide Kaufman on the left pose near the time of their semi-successful climbing of Mount Cook. As they reached the top but not the actual summit they narrowly missed the triumph of primacy. *(Guy Mannering Collection, Christchurch)*

quite worn off the tips of our fingers from clutching the sharp rocks, and as for our clothes, all I need say is that those portions most exposed to friction during our descent were entirely removed." Such reconnaissance and several failures indicated "that the route to the plateau was quite practicable by the Mount Tasman spur." Partial triumphs spurred them on as they climbed, in progression over or around or in retreat from some obstacle, only to advance again: "As we rose above the glacier and looked down the crags at the blue grottoes in the great ice cascade, we made the rocks ring with the true Alpine [yodel], to which the echoes responded as though they knew the sound full well."

The solitude must have longed for sound, for it was solitude indeed. "The only bird we met with was an absurd-looking little tailless wren ...." The tiny party pressed on, determined and hopeful, seeing omens of success where others would have seen only nature. "Other fleecy masses had sailed aloft to the summits of the higher range, and we tried to think that our virgin peak was putting on her bridal veil." Mount Cook required, and still does, determination far beyond the ordinary. Given that, success may follow. "We bore away to the left to avoid the highest part of the bergschrund above us, and surmounting the cornice without any difficulty, at 6 P.M. stepped onto the top-most crest of Ao-Rangi." The problem of whether that crest really was topmost was to linger. To

Mount Cook was finally climbed by Graham, Fyfe and Clarke, but by a different route from that used by Green. The successful climbers rested in the forest after their long tramp down. On the left Jack Clarke, only 19 years old; in the centre George Graham; on the right Tom Fyfe, young but like Graham an experienced and able climber. *(Guy Mannering Collection, Christchurch)*

300

Green, with approaching night threatening the safety of his men, the exact whereabouts of the summit "seemed a mere matter of detail." Besides, "we were all agreed that we were fairly on the summit of the peak ...." They descended, sensibly and safely, leaving the purists to say what they would. And indeed they have. In his account Green was unrepentant if defensive. "It may be said that I have claimed the ascent of Mount Cook, without having set foot on the actual summit. Be it so – I shall willingly relinquish any such claims to the man who passes the point where we turned." Green willing or not, there have been other claimants. The overseas climber made the valid point that he had found the practical way to the top. He had explored, found and publicised. If he failed, at worst it was Tasman's failure repeated; each found the way to a place on which he never set foot. Tasman is remembered and Green should be too.

In 1894 Tom Fyfe, George Graham and Jack Clarke finally got to the very top of Mount Cook. On one earlier attempt to climb the mountain Fyfe and Graham, like Green, had to turn back just short of the actual summit. But now they had made it, and it was exciting. They were literally, given their latitude and

The fine climber and photographer, G.E. Mannering, here portrays Miss du Faur as she indeed was: a fit, energetic, ambitious woman and superb mountaineer. *(Guy Mannering Collection, Christchurch)*

longitude, on top of the world. "I am afraid that the reckless way in which we romped over those last rocks was very foolhardy, but one would indeed need to be phlegmatic not to get a little excited on such an occasion." To be more than a little excited would surely have been forgiven. But they proceeded sensibly. "The slope of the final ice-cap was easy and only required about 100 steps, which were quickly cut, and at 1.30 on Christmas Day we exultantly stepped on to the highest pinnacle of the monarch of the Southern Alps." One beautiful element of their extensive view, Mount Tasman, was climbed the very next year, in 1895.

In 1910 an Australian, Freda du Faur, became the first woman to climb Mount Cook. "It was only 8.40 a.m., and we had beaten any previous record by two hours, and I a mere woman!" The mountain was an Everest of its day and the natural reaction of male or female seemed always to blend disbelief with elation and triumph. "I felt bewildered, and could not realize that the goal I had dreamed of and striven for for years was beneath my feet. I turned to them with a flash and asked if it were 'really, truly the summit of Mt Cook', whereat they laughed very much and bade me look. Truly we were on the top of the world, our little island world. Nothing impeded the eye – east, west, north, and south the country unrolled itself at our feet; range after range stretched away to the foothills in the north-east." Mountains enough for the most avid of climbers. At the summit of a great mountain successful climbers knew where they were, but in one sense only; for the rest they were lost or transported or transcended. It was a common experience of most uncommon individuals.

In 1909 Major Bernard Head, of the Alpine Club of London, had climbed Mount Aspiring, with two New Zealanders, Jack Clarke and Alex Graham, of whom Clarke had been in the first party to climb Mount Cook. Aspiring was a difficult climb, as indeed it looks to be: "for the last few hundred feet of steep icy ridge it was necessary to cut every step with the ice-axes" and "the final part of the ridge was found to be very sharp ...."

Besides the great peaks there are other mountains, and in many aspects of New Zealand life these are far more important than Mount Cook has ever been. These are the mountains which can be climbed and used, and the Marthas, the plain and useful, have a place in history with the beautiful and impressive. In a scene repeated in dozens of places and decades of springs in the South Island, anyone who volunteered to help the shepherd, "went on with him, following the sheep up over the top." In this particular case there was "some stiff climbing and it was nearly four before we reached the top. There are beautiful springs of water all over the mountain, the water is most delicious, cool and fresh and if all water was like that I might possibly become a teetotaller! .... The view from the top was grand, right down below us was the station and stretching beyond were the Canterbury Plains, between forty and fifty miles wide, and beyond them, the sea right out to the horizon." For while mountains, or at least their smaller relatives, are always in sight in New Zealand, almost as omnipresent is the sea.

Mountains are part of New Zealand life to a degree matched only in the Switzerlands, Nepals and Perus of the world. It is fitting that they were the last land areas to be explored and that even yet the seeking and finding is not finished. For what makes the highlander different is not only the highland air

The brothers Alex (left) and Peter Graham, of the highly regarded mountaineering family, accompanied Miss du Faur when she became the first woman to climb Mount Cook. *(Guy Mannering Collection, Christchurch)*

and beauty and solitude, but an unexplained, unnamed ambience which penetrates the soul and is never quite eroded. Charles Douglas claimed to know "many secrets of nature & glimmerings of truths unknown to others, which if they don't benefit me in this world, will in the next when it is to be hoped darkness will be light." Although few would realise it, and far fewer have said it, this was in some degree true for all explorers.

In our age of helicopter rescue, of parachute supply, of aircraft doing the initial carrying, of computers or satellite photography displaying more than a thousand sketch maps could, the energy, determination and enterprise of the early explorers may seem outdated. But such attributes will remain of value, and will be valued. Tasks and challenges change; virtues – courage, intelligence, integrity – do not. Today it takes courage to walk a city street at night. Perhaps the next great achievement of exploration will be to find the "true ways" between the islands, plains and mountains of the human psyche.

# Selected Bibliography

Anderson, A., *When all the moa-ovens grew cold*. Dunedin, Otago Heritage Books, 1983.

Anderson, A., *Te Puoho's Last Raid*. Dunedin, Otago Heritage Books, 1986.

Andrews, J.R.H., *The Southern Ark*. Auckland, Century Hutchinson, 1986.

Angus, J.H., *Aspiring Settlers*. Dunedin, John McIndoe, 1981.

Bagnall, A.G. and Petersen, G.C., *William Colenso*. Wellington, A.H. & A.W. Reed, 1948.

Baker, N., ed., *A Surveyor in New Zealand 1857-1896*. Auckland, Whitcombe & Tombs, 1932.

Barratt, G., *Bellingshausen, a visit to New Zealand: 1820*. Palmerston North, Dunmore Press, 1979.

Beaglehole, J.C. ed., *The Journals of Captain James Cook on his Voyages of Discovery*. 3 vols. Cambridge, University Press for the Hakluyt Society, 1955 - 1967.

Beaglehole, J.C., ed., *The Discovery of New Zealand*. 2nd ed. London, Oxford University Press, 1961.

Beaglehole, J.C., ed., *The Endeavour Journal of Joseph Banks 1768-1771*. 2 vols. Wellington, Angus & Robertson, 1962.

Beaglehole, J.C., ed., *The Life of Captain James Cook*. London, Adam & Charles Black, 1974.

Beattie, H., *Mackenzie of the Mackenzie Country*. Dunedin, Otago Daily Times and Witness Newspapers, 1946.

Beattie, H., *The Pioneers Explore Otago*. Dunedin, Otago Daily Times and Witness Newspapers, 1947.

Begg, A.C. and Begg N.C., *The World of John Boultbee*. Christchurch, Whitcoulls, 1979.

Bellwood, P.S., The Peopling of the Pacific, *Scientific American*, 243, 5, November 1980, pp. 174-85.

Best, E., *The Maori As He Was*. Wellington, Government Printer, 1924.

Best, E., *The Pa Maori*. Wellington, Government Printer, Dominion Museum Bulletin No. 6, 1927, 1975.

Best, E., *Polynesian Voyagers*. Wellington, Government Printer, Dominion Museum Monograph No. 5, 1975.

Best, E., *Maori Agriculture*. Wellington, Government Printer, 1976.

Best, E., *The Maori Canoe*. Wellington, Government Printer, Dominion Museum Bulletin No. 7, 1925, 1976.

Best, E., *The Forest Lore of the Maori*. Wellington, Government Printer, Dominion Museum Bulletin No. 14, 1942, 1977.

Best, E., *The Astronomical Knowledge of the Maori*. Wellington, Government Printer, Dominion Museum Monograph No. 3, 1978.

Bidwill J.C., *Rambles in New Zealand*. London, W.S. Orr & Co. & J, Fitze, 1841.

Brailsford, B., *Greenstone Trails*. Wellington, A.H. & A.W. Reed, 1984.

Brunner, T., *The Great Journey*. Christchurch, The Pegasus Press, 1952.

Buck, Sir Peter (Te Rangi Hiroa), *Vikings of the Sunrise*. Christchurch, Whitcombe & Tombs, 1954.

Butler, S., edited by A.A. Brassington and P.B. Maling, *A First Year in Canterbury Settlement*. Auckland, Blackwood & Janet Paul, 1964.

Colenso, W., *Excursion in the Northern Island of New Zealand, in the summer of 1841-2*. No. 1 in Travels and History. Launceston, Printed at the office of the Launceston Examiner, 1844.

Colenso, W., *The Authentic and Genuine History of the Signing of the Treaty of Waitangi*. Wellington, Government printer, 1890. (1971 Capper Press, Christchurch, facsimile.)

Condliffe, J.B., *Te Rangi Hiroa, The Life of Sir Peter Buck*. Christchurch, Whitcombe & Tombs, 1971.

Craig, E.W.G., *Man of the Mist*. Wellington, A.H. & A.W. Reed, 1964.

Cruise, R.A., *Journal of a Ten Months' Residence in New Zealand*. London, Longman, Hurst, Rees, Orme, Brown and Green, 1824. (1974 Capper Press, Christchurch, facsimile.)

Cumpston, J.S., *Shipping Arrivals & Departures, Sydney 1788 to 1825*. 2nd ed., Canberra, Roebuck Society, 1977.

Darwin, C., *Journal of Researches into the Geology & Natural History of the Various Countries visited during the Voyage of H.M.S. Beagle round the World*. London, J.M. Dent & Sons, 1906.

Davidson, J., *The Prehistory of New Zealand*. Auckland, Longman Paul, 1984.

Dieffenbach, E., *Travels in New Zealand*. 2 vols. London, J. Murray, 1843.

Druett, J., *Exotic Intruders*. Auckland, Heinemann, 1983.

Duff, R., *the moa-hunter period of maori culture*. Wellington, Government Printer, 1977.

Duncan, A.H., *The wakatipians or Early days in New Zealand*. Arrowtown, Lakes district Centennial Museum Inc., 1964 (first pub. 1888).

Dunmore, J., *French Explorers in the Pacific*. 2 vols. Oxford, Clarendon Press, 1965.

Elder, J.R., ed., *The Letters and Journals of Samuel Marsden 1765-1838*. Dunedin, Coulls Somerville Wilkie and A. H. Reed/Otago University Council, 1932.

Fox, A., *Prehistoric Maori Fortifications in the North Island of New Zealand*. Auckland, Longman Paul, 1976.

Gilkison, R., *Early Days in Central Otago*. 4th ed., Christchurch, Whitcoulls Publishers, 1978

Gillespie, O.A., *South Canterbury*. Timaru, The South Canterbury Centennial History Committee, 1958.

Golson, J. ed., *Polynesian Navigation*. 3rd ed., Wellington, A.H. and A.W. Reed, 1972.

Green, R.C., *A Review of the Prehistoric Sequence in the Auckland province*. Auckland, New Zealand Archaeological Association, 1963.

Green, W.S., *The High Alps of New Zealand*. London, Macmillan and Co., 1883.

Griffiths, G. and Goodall, M., *Maori Dunedin*. Dunedin, Otago Heritage Books, 1980.

Haast, H.F. von, *The Life and Times of Sir Julius von Haast*. Wellington, Haast, H.F. von, 1948.

Hall-Jones, J., *Mr Surveyor Thomson*. Wellington, A.H. & A.W. Reed, 1971.

Hall-Jones, J., *Fiordland Explored*. Wellington, A.H. & A.W. Reed, 1976.

Hall-Jones, J., *The South Explored*. Wellington, A.H. & A.W. Reed, 1979.

Harper, A.P., *Pioneer Work In The Alps Of New Zealand*. London, T. Fisher Unwin, 1896.

Heaphy, C., *Narrative of a Residence in Various Parts of New Zealand*. London, Smith, Elder and Co, 1842. (1972 Capper Press, Christchurch, facsimile.)

Hervé, R., trans. J. Dunmore, *Chance Discovery of Australia and New Zealand by Portugese and Spanish Navigators between 1521 and 1528*. New Zealand, The Dunmore Press, 1983.

Holcroft, M.H., *The Shaping of New Zealand*. Auckland, Paul Hamlyn, 1974.

Holmes, C. ed., *Captain Cook's Final Voyage*. Manuka, ACT., Brian Clouston, Caliban Books, 1982.

Houghton, P., *The First New Zealanders*. Auckland, Hodder & Stoughton, 1980.

Howells, W., *The Pacific Islanders*. Wellington, A.H. & A.W. Reed, 1973.

Jennings, J.D., ed., *The Prehistory of Polynesia*. Canberra, Australian National University Press, 1979.

Kelly, L.G., *Marion Dufresne at the Bay of Islands*. Wellington, A.H. & A.W. Reed, 1951.

Knox, R., ed., *A Thousand Mountains Shining*. Wellington, A.H. & A.W. Reed, 1984.

Leach, F.R., The Prehistory of the Southern Wairarapa, *Journal of the Royal Society of New Zealand,* 11, 1, 1981, pp.11-33.

Leach, H.M., A Hundred Years of Otago Archaeology: A Critical Review, *Records of the Otago Museum*. Anthropology Number 6, Dunedin, Otago Museum Trust Board, 1972.

Lewis, D., *We, the Navigators*. Wellington, A.H. & A.W. Reed, 1972.

Lewis, D., *From Maui to Cook*. Sydney, Doubleday, 1977.

Lewis, D., *The Voyaging Stars*. Sydney, Collins, 1978.

Lewis, D., and Forman W., *The Maori Heirs of Tane*. London, Orbis, 1982.

McClymont, W.G., *The Exploration of New Zealand*. 2nd ed., London, Oxford University Press, 1959.

McLintock, A.H., *The History of Otago*. Christchurch, Otago Centennial Historical Publications, 1949.

McNab, R., ed., *Historical Records of New Zealand*. 2 vols., Wellington, John Mackay Government Printer, 1908, 1914.

McNab, R., *The Old Whaling Days*. Auckland, Golden Press, 1975.

Maling, P.B., *Samuel Butler at Mesopotamia*. Wellington, Govt Printer/National Historic Places Trust, 1960.

Mead, A.D., *Richard Taylor, Missionary Tramper*. Wellington, A.H. & A.W. Reed, 1966.

Mead, S.M., ed., *Te Maori*. Auckland, Heinemann, 1984.

Mitchell, T.C., ed., *Captain Cook and the South Pacific*. The British Museum Yearbook 3. London, British Museum Publications, 1979.

Moorehead, A., *Darwin and the 'Beagle'*. London, Book Club Associates, 1973.

Morrell, W.P., ed., *Sir Joseph Banks in New Zealand*. Wellington, A.H. & A.W. Reed, 1958.

Morton, H., *The Wind Commands*. Dunedin, John McIndoe, 1976.

Morton, H., *The Whale's Wake*. Dunedin, University of Otago Press, 1982.

Mueller, G., edited by M.V. Mueller, *My Dear Bannie*. Christchurch, Pegasus Press, 1958.

Natusch, S., *Brother Wohlers*. Christchurch, Pegasus Press, 1969.

Natusch, S., *The Cruise of the 'Acheron'*. Christchurch, Whitcoulls, 1978.

Natusch, S., *Southward Ho!*. Invercargill, Craig Printing, 1985.

Nicholas, J.L., *Narrative of a Voyage to New Zealand Performed in the Years 1814 and 1815.* 2 vols. London, James Black and Son, 1817.

Parham, W.T., *Von Tempsky, Adventurer.* London, Hodder and Stoughton, 1969.

Pascoe, J., ed., *Mr. Explorer Douglas.* Wellington, A.H. & A.W. Reed, 1957.

Pascoe, J., *Great Days in New Zealand Exploration.* Auckland, Collins/Fontana Silver Fern, 1976.

Pearce, G.L., *The Story of the Maori People.* Auckland, Collins, 1968.

Porter, F., ed., *The Turanga Journals 1840-1850.* Wellington, Price Milburn for Victoria University Press, 1974.

Reed, A.H. and A.W., eds., *Captain Cook in New Zealand.* Wellington, A.H. & A.W. Reed, 1971.

Reed, A.W., *Treasury of Maori Exploration.* Wellington, A.H. & A.W. Reed, 1977.

Rogers, L.M., ed., *The Early Journals of Henry Williams 1826-1840.* Christchurch, Pegasus Press, 1961.

Rogers, L.M., *Te Wiremu.* Christchurch, Pegasus, 1973.

Ross, J.O'C., *This Stern Coast.* Wellington, A.H. & A.W. Reed, 1969.

Ross, J.O'C., *Capt. F.G. Moore, Mariner and Pioneer.* Wanganui, Wanganui Newspapers, 1982.

Roth, H.L., trans., *Crozet's Voyage to Tasmania, New Zealand, the Ladrone Islands, and the Philippines in the years 1771-1772.* London, Truslove & Shirley, 1891.

Salmond, A., *Hui.* Wellington, A.H. & A.W. Reed, 1975.

Savage, J., *Some Account of New Zealand.* London, 1807, Dunedin, Hocken Library Facsimile, 1966.

Sharp, C.A., *Ancient Voyagers in the Pacific.* Harmondsworth, Middlesex, Penguin Books, 1957.

Sharp, C.A., *Ancient Voyagers in Polynesia.* Auckland, Longman Paul, 1963

Sharp, C.A., *The Voyages of Abel Janszoon Tasman.* Oxford, Clarendon Press, 1968.

Sharp C.A., ed., *Duperrey's Visit to New Zealand in 1824.* Wellington, Alexander Turnbull Library, 1971.

Shortland, E., *The Southern Districts of New Zealand.* London, Longman, Brown, Green, & Longman, 1851. (1974 Capper Press, Christchurch, facsimile.)

Simmons, D.R., A New Zealand Myth: Kupe, Toi and the Fleet, *The New Zealand Journal of History,* 3, 1, April 1969, pp. 14-31.

Simmons, D.R., *The Great New Zealand Myth.* Wellington, A.H. & A.W. Reed, 1976.

Skinner, H.D., *Comparatively Speaking*. Dunedin, University of Otago Press, 1974.

Sorrenson, M.P.K., *Maori Origins and Migrations*. Auckland, Auckland University, 1979.

Trotter, M., and McCulloch, B., *Prehistoric Rock Art of New Zealand*. Wellington, A.H. & A.W. Reed, 1971.

Villiers, A., *Captain Cook, the Seamen's Seaman*. London, Hodder and Stoughton, 1969.

Wakefield, E.J., *Adventure in New Zealand*. Christchurch, Whitcombe and Tombs, 1908.

Woodhouse, A.E., *George Rhodes of the Levels and his Brothers*. Auckland, Whitcombe & Tombs, 1937.

Wright, O., ed. and trans., *New Zealand 1826-1827*, from the French of Dumont d'Urville. London, Olive Wright, 1950.

Wright, O., ed. and trans., *The Voyage of the 'Astrolabe' - 1840*. Wellington, A.H. and A.W. Reed, 1955.

Wright-St Clair, R.E., Diet of the Maoris of New Zealand, *Food, Ecology and Culture*, Robson, J.R.K., ed., New York, Gordon and Breach Science Publishers, 1980.

Wright-St Clair, R.E., *Thoroughly a Man of the World, A biography of Sir David Monro M.D.*. Christchurch, Whitcombe and Tombs, 1971.

# INDEX

310